EAST–WEST RELATIONS

East–West Relations

Volume 1:
A Systematic Survey

Daniel Frei
Dieter Ruloff
University of Zurich

with the collaboration of
Urs Luterbacher
Pierre Allan

Oelgeschlager, Gunn & Hain, Publishers, Inc.
Cambridge, Massachusetts

International Standard Book Number: 0-89946-136-0

Library of Congress Catalog Card Number: 81-22356

Printed in the U.S.A.

Library of Congress Cataloging in Publication Data

Frei, Daniel.
East-West relations.

Bibliography: p.
Contents: v. 1. A systematic survey—v. 2. Methodology and data.
1. World politics—1965–1975. 2. World politics—1975–1985. 3. Détente. I. Ruloff, Dieter. II. Title.
D849.F688 327'.0904 81-22356
ISBN 0-89946-136-0 (v. 1) AACR2
ISBN 0-89946-137-9 (v. 2)

Contents

	List of Graphs	ix
	List of Tables	xiii
	List of Abbreviations	xvii
	Note to the Reader	xix
	Acknowledgments	xxi
Chapter 1	**Introduction**	1
	1.1 The Purpose of This Study: Providing an Objective Record of East-West Relations	1
	1.1.1 The Main Task and Its Rationale	
	1.1.2 Credibility and Acceptability as Crucial Concerns	
	1.2 The Design of This Study	4
Chapter 2	**The Dimensionality of East-West Relations: A Content Analysis of CSCE Statements**	10
	2.1 Sources and Methods	10
	2.1.1 The Selection of Documentary Sources	
	2.1.2 The Coding Procedure	
	2.2 The Thirty-Five CSCE Governments and Their Emphasis on the Three "Baskets" from Helsinki to Madrid	12
	2.2.1 Introduction	
	2.2.2 The 1973 Helsinki Statements	
	2.2.3 The 1975 Helsinki Statements	
	2.2.4 The Belgrade Opening Statements	
	2.2.5 The Belgrade Closing Statements	
	2.2.6 The Madrid Opening Statements	
	2.2.7 From Helsinki to Madrid: The Shifting Emphasis on the CSCE "Baskets"	

2.3 The Major Issues of East-West Relations 23
2.3.1 Introduction
2.3.2 The 1973 Helsinki Statements
2.3.3 The 1975 Helsinki Statements
2.3.4 The Belgrade Opening Statements
2.3.5 The Belgrade Closing Statements
2.3.6 The Madrid Opening Statements
2.3.7 From Helsinki to Madrid: The Shifting Emphasis on CSCE Issues
2.4 The Crucial Dimensions in East-West Relations: A Factor Analysis 36
2.4.1 Introduction
2.4.2 The 1973 Helsinki Statements
2.4.3 The 1975 Helsinki Statements
2.4.4 The Belgrade Opening Statements
2.4.5 The Belgrade Closing Statements
2.4.6 The Madrid Opening Statements
2.4.7 From Helsinki to Madrid: Shifting Concerns for Ten Major Factors
2.5 "Camps" and Polarization in the CSCE: A Cluster Analysis 59
2.5.1 Introduction
2.5.2 The 1973 Helsinki Statements
2.5.3 The 1975 Helsinki Statements
2.5.4 The Belgrade Opening Statements
2.5.5 The Belgrade Closing Statements
2.5.6 The Madrid Opening Statements
2.5.7 Conclusions: Convergencies and Divergencies from Helsinki to Madrid

Chapter 3 What Really Happened in East-West Relations in Europe? The Structure and Dynamics of East-West Relations 69
3.1 Introduction: Criteria for Selecting Indicators 69
3.1.1 What Is to Be Measured? The Choice of Selected Dimensions
3.1.2 What Indicators Are to Be Picked? The Choice of Valid, Reliable, and Noncontroversial Indicators
3.2 Disarmament and Security 72
3.2.1 Introduction
3.2.2 Military Expenditures
3.2.3 American and Soviet Strategic Nuclear Forces
3.2.4 Eurostrategic Weapons
3.3 Peace and Conflict 102
3.3.1 The Evolution of East-West Relations, 1960–1980

3.3.2 Cooperation and Conflict: Clusters of Nations
3.3.3 Cooperation and Conflict among the Thirty-Five CSCE States in the United Nations General Assembly
3.3.4 Cooperation and Conflict in the Third World
3.4 Economic Cooperation 150
3.4.1 Introduction
3.4.2 The Evolution of East-West Trade, 1960-1980
3.4.3 Partners in Trade: Some Considerations Concerning the Structure of East-West Trade
3.4.4 The Transfer of Technology
3.5 Human Rights and Contacts 173
3.5.1 Introduction
3.5.2 Indices of Political Rights and Civil Liberties
3.5.3 Human Rights in the Perspective of Amnesty International
3.5.4 Political Rights and Economic Rights
3.5.5 East-West Tourism
3.5.6 Migration from East to West
3.5.7 Sovereignty and Independence

Chapter 4 A Comprehensive View of East-West Relations: Changing Perceptions and Changing Realities 203
4.1 Introduction: A Descriptive Analysis in the Perspective of Selected Groups of Countries 203
4.2 East-West Relations in NATO Perspective 205
4.3 East-West Relations in WTO Perspective 209
4.4 East-West Relations in N+N Perspective 209

Chapter 5 Reexamining Some Theoretical Assumptions about "Détente" 213
5.1 Major Theories of "Détente": A Brief Inventory 213
5.1.1 Introduction
5.1.2 Propositions Regarding International Requirements of Political "Détente"
5.1.3 Intrasystems Requirements of Political "Détente"
5.1.4 The Consequences and Inner Logic of "Détente"
5.2 Testing Some Theories 231
5.2.1 Introduction
5.2.2 Empirical Evidence Regarding International Requirements of "Détente"
5.2.3 Empirical Evidence Regarding Internal Requirements of political "Détente"
5.2.4 Empirical Evidence Regarding the Consequences and Inner Logic of "Détente"

Chapter 6 The Outlook: "Détente"—an Episode? 275
6.1 The Rise, Saturation, and Fall of East-West Cooperation 276
6.2 The Riddle of Incongruous Evolution 277
6.3 The Pains of Coordinating Asynchronous Processes 279
6.4 Thought versus Action in Intersystems Relations 281

Bibliography 285

About the Authors 299

List of Graphs

2.1	Distribution of Attention on Parts of the Final Act: A Frequency Block Chart	22
2.2	Distribution of Attention on Dimensions of East-West Relations: A Frequency Block Chart	47
2.3	Clustering of CSCE Countries According to Their Attention Profile in the 1973 Helsinki Statements	61
2.4	Clustering of CSCE Countries According to Their Attention Profile in the 1975 Helsinki Statements	63
2.5	Clustering of CSCE Countries According to Their Attention Profile in the Belgrade Opening Statements	64
2.6	Clustering of CSCE Countries According to Their Attention Profile in the Belgrade Closing Statements	66
2.7	Clustering of CSCE Countries According to Their Attention Profile in the Madrid Opening Statements	67
3.1	Military Expenditure of NATO, WTO, and the Two Major Powers	78
3.2	Military Expenditure of NATO Countries	79
3.3	Military Expenditure of WTO Countries	80
3.4	Rates of Change in Military Expenditure of the United States and the Soviet Union	82
3.5	Rates of Change of Military Expenditure of NATO Countries	83
3.6	Strategic Nuclear Forces of the US and the USSR, Bomber Forces	85
3.7	Strategic Nuclear Forces of the US and the USSR, Submarines	86

3.8 Strategic Nuclear Forces of the US and the USSR, ICBMs and SLBMs 87
3.9 Strategic Nuclear Forces of the US and the USSR, Warheads and Delivery Systems 88
3.10 Ratio of Warheads and Delivery Systems 89
3.11 Eurostrategic Forces of NATO and WTO (IRBMs and MRBMs) 96
3.12 Eurostrategic Forces of NATO and WTO (SLBMs) 97
3.13 Eurostrategic Forces of NATO and WTO (Bombers) 99
3.14 Eurostrategic Forces of NATO and WTO (Total Number of Systems) 100
3.15 Cooperative Interactions Between the United States and the Soviet Union 106
3.16 Conflictive Interactions Between the United States and the Soviet Union 107
3.17 Cooperative Interactions Between Great Britain and the Soviet Union 113
3.18 Conflictive Interactions Between Great Britain and the Soviet Union 114
3.19 Cooperative Interactions Between France and the Soviet Union 118
3.20 Conflictive Interactions Between France and the Soviet Union 119
3.21 Cooperative Interactions Between the FRG and the USSR 125
3.22 Conflictive Interactions Between the FRG and the USSR 126
3.23 Clusters of Countries in East-West Interactions, 1960-1964 129
3.24 Clusters of Countries in East-West Interactions, 1965-1969 130
3.25 Clusters of Countries in East-West Interactions, 1970-1974 131
3.26 Clusters of Countries in East-West Interactions, 1975-1979 132
3.27 Interblock Affinities in UN Voting 135
3.28 Intrablock Affinities in UN Voting Among NATO Countries (1) 137
3.29 Intrablock Affinities in UN Voting Among NATO Countries (2) 138
3.29 Intrablock Affinities in UN Voting Among NATO Countries (2) 138
3.30 Affinities in UN Voting Between the United States and Neutral/Nonaligned Countries 140
3.31 Affinities in UN Voting Between the Soviet Union and Neutral/Nonaligned Countries 141
3.32 Affinities in UN Voting of Neutral and Nonaligned Countries (1) 143
3.33 Affinities in UN Voting of Neutral and Nonaligned Countries (2) 144

3.34 Major-Power Interactions with Latin American Countries 146
3.35 Major-Power Interactions with Asian Countries (Excluding Vietnam) 147
3.36 Major-Power Interactions with African Countries 148
3.37 Major-Power Interactions with Middle Eastern Countries 149
3.38 Monthly Average Exports of EEC to CMEA and CMEA to EEC 152
3.39 Monthly Average Exports of Selected Western Countries to the Soviet Union 153
3.40 Monthly Average Exports of the Soviet Union to Selected Western Countries 155
3.41 Exports from Western Countries and the EEC to the CMEA and the Soviet Union as Percentage of Total EEC Exports and Total Exports of the Respective Western Countries 157
3.42 Exports from the CMEA and the Soviet Union to the EEC and Western Countries as Percentage of Total CMEA and Soviet Exports 158
3.43 Imports of the CMEA and the Soviet Union from the EEC and Selected Western Countries as Percentage of Total CMEA and Soviet Imports, Respectively 159
3.44 Imports of the EEC and Selected Western Countries from the CMEA and the Soviet Union as Percentage of Total EEC Imports and Total Imports of the Respective Country 161
3.45 Clusters of Countries, Based on Trade Figures for 1965 162
3.46 Clusters of Countries, Based on Trade Figures for 1970 163
3.47 Clusters of CSCE Countries, Based on Trade Figures for 1975 164
3.48 SITC-7 Exports from EC to CMEA and CMEA to EC 166
3.49 SITC-7 Exports from Selected Western Countries to the Soviet Union 167
3.50 SITC-7 Exports from the EC and Selected Western Countries as Percentage of Total Exports to the CMEA and the Soviet Union 168
3.51 SITC-3 Exports from EC to CMEA and from CMEA to EC 171
3.52 SITC-3 Exports of the Soviet Union to Selected Western Countries 172
3.53 Unemployment in NATO Countries and Neutral/Nonaligned Countries as Percentage of Total Labor Force 181
3.54 Unemployment in Selected Western Countries as Percentage of Total Labor Force 182
3.55 Number of Political Sanctions in WTO Countries (2) 183

3.56 Number of Political Sanctions in WTO Countries (1) 184
3.57 Visitors from Western Countries to the Soviet Union 186
3.58 Visitors from Socialist Countries to the FRG 187
3.59 Exchange of Visitors Between the GDR and the FRG 188
3.60 Migration from Eastern Europe to the FRG 191
3.61 Migration from the GDR to the FRG and from the USSR to Israel 192
3.62 Cooperative Interactions of NATO Countries with "Camps" as Percentage of Total Cooperative Interactions of NATO Countries 201
3.63 Cooperative Interactions of WTO Countries with "Camps" as Percentage of Total Cooperative Interactions of WTO Countries 202
4.1 East-West Relations in NATO Perspective 208
4.2 East-West Relations in WTO Perspective 210
4.3 East-West Relations in the Perspectives of Neutral and Nonaligned Countries 211
5.1 Relationship Between Major-Power Activities in Third World Regions and US and USSR Behavior 239
6.1 Reality and Expectation in East-West Relations 282

List of Tables

2.1	The 1973 Helsinki Statements: Percentage Distribution of Attention on Parts of the Final Act	14
2.2	The 1975 Helsinki Statements: Percentage Distribution of Attention on Parts of the Final Act	16
2.3	The Belgrade Opening Statements: Percentage Distribution of Attention on Parts of the Final Act	18
2.4	The Belgrade Closing Statements: Percentage Distribution of Attention on Parts of the Final Act	19
2.5	The Madrid Opening Statements: Percentage Distribution of Attention on Parts of the Final Act	21
2.6	The 1973 Helsinki Statements: Rank-Order by Frequency of Categories Quoted by Delegations for Selected Aggregated Groups of Countries	24-25
2.7	The 1975 Helsinki Statements: Rank-Order by Frequency of Categories Quoted by Delegations for Selected Aggregated Groups of Countries	28-29
2.8	The Belgrade Opening Statements: Rank-Order by Frequency of Categories Quoted by Delegations for Selected Aggregated Groups of Countries	30-31
2.9	The Belgrade Closing Statements: Rank-Order by Frequency of Categories Quoted by Delegations for Selected Aggregated Groups of Countries	32-33
2.10	The Madrid Opening Statements: Rank-Order by Frequency of Categories Quoted by Delegations for Selected Aggregated Groups of Countries	34-35

2.11	Selected Categories Entering the Commputations of the Factor Analysis and Shares of Attention in all CSCE Statements	38-39
2.12	Dimensions Represented in the Factor Structure of the 1973 Helsinki Statements	40
2.13	Dimensions Represented in the Factor Structure of the 1975 Helsinki Statements	41
2.14	Dimensions Represented in the Factor Structure of the Belgrade Opening Statements	42
2.15	Dimensions Represented in the Factor Structure of the 1978 Belgrade Closing Statements	43
2.16	Dimensions Represented in the Factor Structure of the Madrid Opening Statments	44
2.17	Dimensions Represented in the Factor Structure of All Five Sets of Statements	45
2.18	The 1973 Helsinki Statements: Distribution of Attention on the Ten Dimensions of East-West Relations	48-49
2.19	The 1975 Helsinki Statements: Distribution of Attention on the Ten Dimensions of East-West Relations	50-51
2.20	The Belgrade Statements: Distribution of Attention on the Ten Dimensions of East-West Relations	52-53
2.21	The Belgrade Statements: Distribution of Attention on the Ten Dimensions of East-West Relations	54-55
2.22	The Madrid Opening Statements: Distribution of Attention on the Ten Dimensions of East-West Relations	56-57
3.1	Operationalizations of Dimensions of East-West Relations	74-77
3.2	NATO/WTO Ratios in Military Expenditures	84
3.3	Intrablock Affinities in UN Voting Among WTO Countries	136
3.4	Growth Rate of GNP and Net Hard Currency Indebtedness	169
3.5	Political and Civil Rights in CSCE Countries	175
3.6	Dispersion of External Interactions as Percentage of Total Possible Interactions	195
3.7	Summary List of Countries, by Direction of Change in the Dispersion of Their External Relations, 1950-1978	196
3.8	Share of Interactions Exchanged Between NATO Countries and the USA, 1950-1978	198
3.9	Share of Interactions Exchanged Between WTO Countries and the USSR, 1950-1978	199
4.1	Weights for the Computation of Curves Representing the Evolution of East-West Relations as Perceived by Three Groups of Countries	206
5.1	Relationship Between US and USSR Behavior and Various Indicators of Military Strength	232

5.2 Relationship Between US and USSR Behavior and Military Ratios 233
5.3 Relationship Between US and USSR Behavior (Time-lagged) and Behavior of Selected West European Countries and the USSR 235
5.4 Relationship Between US and USSR Behavior (Time- lagged) and Behavior of Selected Countries in East and West Europe 236
5.5 Relationship Between Major-Power Activities in Africa and Bilateral Relations Between the USA and the USSR 241
5.6 Relationship Between Major-Power Activities in the Middle East and Bilateral Relations Between the USA and the USSR 242
5.7 Relationship Between Major-Power Activities in Asia and Bilateral Relations Between the USA and the USSR 243
5.8 Relationship Between Major-Power Activities in Latin American Countries and Bilateral Relations Between the USA and the USSR 244
5.9 A Summary of Significant Correlations Found for the Impact of Major-Power Relations with Third World Countries on US-USSR Relations 246
5.10 Time-lagged Relationships Between Soviet "Westpolitik" and Western Responses 248
5.11 Relationship Between Unemployment in the US and Three Selected Indicators for US Behavior Toward the USSR 249
5.12 Relationship Between Domestic Stability in the US and Three Selected Indicators for US Behavior with Regard to the USSR 250
5.13 Relationship Between Soviet Economic Growth and Soviet Behavior with Regard to the US 251
5.14 Relationship Between US–USSR Technology Transfers and US–USSR Relations 252
5.15 Relationship Between FRG–USSR Technology Transfers and FRG–USSR Relations 253
5.16 Coefficients of Correlation Between the Number of Persons Leaving East European Countries and Interactions Between the Country of Origin and the Country of Destination 254
5.17 Relationship Between the Number of Internal Sanctions Exerted by the Soviet Union and the Relaxation of Sanctions, and Major-Power Cooperation and Conflict 256
5.18 Relationship Between US–USSR Relations and WTO Member Interactions with NATO Countries 257
5.19 Relationship Between US–USSR Relations and Major-Power Activities in Latin America 259

5.20 Relationship Between US–USSR Relations and Major-Power Activities in Africa 260
5.21 Relationship Between US–USSR Relations and Major-Power Activities in the Middle East 261
5.22 Relationship Between US–USSR Relations and Major-Power Activities in Asia 262
5.23 A Summary of Significant Correlations Found for the Impact of US–USSR Relations on the Relations Between Major Powers and Third World Countries 263
5.24 Relationship Between US–USSR Relations and US and USSR Military Expenditure 265
5.25 Relationship Between US–USSR Relations and US–USSR Trade 268
5.26 Relationship Between FRG–USSR Relations and FRG–USSR Trade 271
5.27 Relationship Between the Ratio of USSR–US/US-USSR Trade and US-USSR Relations 272
5.28 Relationship Between Balance/Imbalance of East-West Relations in Various Fields and US–USSR Relations 272

List of Abbreviations

ABM	Anti-Ballistic Missile
ACDA	Arms Control and Disarmament Agency, Washington, D.C.
AI	Amnesty International
AUST	Austria
BIB	Bundesministerium für Innerdeutsche Bezichungen, Bonn
BJC	Bibliotheque Juive Contemporaire, Paris
BLGM	Belgium
BLGR	Bulgaria
CMEA	Council for Mutual Economic Assistance
CNDA	Canada
COCOM	Coordinating Committee for East–West Trade Policy
COPDAB	Azar's Conflict and Peace Data Bank
CSCE	Conference on Security and Cooperation in Europe
CYPR	Cyprus
CPRI	Canadian Peace Research Institute, Dundas, Ontario (see Newcombe and Wert 1979)
CPSU	Communist Party of the Soviet Union
CZCH	Czechoslovakia
DNMK	Denmark
EC	European Communities
EDC	European Defense Community
EEC	European Economic Community
FOBS	Forward Based Systems
FNLD	Finland
FRNC	France
FRG	Federal Republic of Germany
GDR	German Democratic Republic
GLCM	Ground-Launched Cruise Missile
GRCE	Greece
HNGR	Hungary
ICBM	Intercontinental Ballistic Missile
ICLD	Iceland

IRBM	Intermediate-Range Ballistic Missile
IRLD	Ireland
IISS	International Institute for Strategic Studies, London
INF	Intermediate-Range Nuclear Forces
ITLY	Italy
LICH	Liechtenstein
LRTNF	Long-Range TNF
LXBG	Luxembourg
MBFR	Mutual Balanced Force Reductions (Conference on MBFR in Vienna)
MFN	Most-Favored Nation
MIRV	Multiple Independently Targetable Re-entry Vehicle
MLTA	Malta
MNCO	Monaco
MRBM	Medium-Range Ballistic Missile
MRTNF	Medium-Range TNF
NATO	North Atlantic Treaty Organization
N + N	Neutral and Nonaligned Countries
NTHL	Netherlands
NRWY	Norway
OECD	Organization for Economic Cooperation and Development, Paris
PLND	Poland
PRTG	Portugal
RMNA	Romania
SALT	Strategic Arms Limitation Talks
SANM	San Marino
SITC	Standard International Trade Classification
SITC-3	Section 3 of the SITC: Hydrocarbons and Fuels
SITC-7	Section 7 of the SITC: Machinery and Transport Equipment
SIPRI	Stockholm International Peace Research Institute
SLBM	Submarine-Launched Ballistic Missile
SPAN	Spain
START	Strategic Arms Reduction Talks
SWDN	Sweden
SWTZ	Switzerland
TNF	Theatre Nuclear Forces
TRKY	Turkey
UK	United Kingdom of Great Britain and Northern Ireland
UN	United Nations
USA	United States of America
USSR	Union of the Socialist Soviet Republic
VATC	Vatican (Holy See)
WB	World Bank
WHB3	World Handbook of Political and Social Indicators (3rd edition); see Taylor (1981)
WTO	Warsaw Treaty Organization
WTOG	World Tourism Organization, Madrid
YGSL	Yugoslavia

Note to the Reader

For convenience, this study is divided into two volumes. The first volume offers a comprehensive survey of our findings, written in a form accessible to any interested reader irrespective of his acquaintance with modern social science approaches. We hope that the results presented in this volume have a practical meaning not only to the academic specialist but also to the diplomatic practitioner, to the policymaker, and to the commentators.

Volume 2 contains additional findings (mainly complete and detailed data sets and elaborate tables) as well as ample explanations of the methods and techniques used for producing the results. It also presents the results of a simulation analysis done by Professor Urs Luterbacher and Dr. Pierre Allan, providing some data-based and systematic projections of possible futures of East–West relations and insights concerning the results of various strategies. The second volume is written for readers who either wish to acquire additional and/or more specific information about the many aspects of East–West relations or want to gain insight into the rationale and the individual steps undertaken by us in our research.

D. F.
D. R.

Acknowledgments

We wish to express our gratitude to all those many people and institutions in both East and West who helped us meet the ambitious goal set by this study. Our debts in this regard are numerous. The Swiss National Science Foundation (Schweizerischer Nationalfonds zur Förderung der wissenschaftlichen Forschung) has provided, under grant number 1.584.–0.77, the material support that enabled us to gather the data. The Volkswagen Foundation (Volkswagen-Stiftung) gave a grant for an international East–West symposium on approaches to definitions and measurement of "détente," held in Zurich in November 1979, which served as a "testing ground" for a critical examination of the concept underlying this study. The results of that symposium can be found in Daniel Frei's *Definitions and Measurement of Détente: East and West Perspectives (Cambridge, Mass. 1981: Oelgeschlager, Gunn & Hain).* The first "test-run," however, was done in a panel chaired by Professor Longin Pastusiak (Warsaw, Poland) at the 1978 convention of the International Studies Association in Washington, D.C.

We are also happy to register our appreciation to all those colleagues and institutions who offered us their assistance in collecting data. In particular, we would like to mention Professor Charles L. Taylor (Virginia Polytechnic Institute and State University/Science Center Berlin), Professor Edward Azar (University of North Carolina at Chapel Hill), Dr. Ivan Tyulin and cand. V. B.

Lukov (Moscow State Institute of International Relations), Dr. André Daguet (Amnesty International, Switzerland), Dr. Hannah Newcombe (Canadian Peace Research Institute), the U.S. Arms Control and Disarmament Agency (Washington D.C.), the Bibliothèque Juive Contemporaine (Paris), the International Labour Office (Geneva), the International Institute for Strategic Studies (London), Mrs. Elisabeth Sköns (Stockholm International Peace Research Institute).

In addition, Daniel Frei was twice kindly offered an opportunity to take part, as an "associate member" of the Swiss delegation, in the CSCE negotiations in Belgrade and Madrid; he thus received a first-hand insight into the diplomatic reality reflected by the data of this study. He wishes to thank ambassadors Rudolf Bindschedler and Edouard Brunner for their helpful cooperation. Above all, however, we would like to thank all those who offered us valuable advice on a variety of aspects covered in this study. Among them are:

Dr. Pierre Allan (Graduate Institute of International Studies, Geneva, Switzerland)
Professor J. Berendt (Karl Marx University, Budapest, Hungary)
Dr. Lew Burnjaschew (International Institute for Peace, Vienna, Austria)
Dr. Evgeny Chossudovsky (UNO/UNITAR, Geneva, Switzerland)
Dr. Wolf-Dieter Eberwein (Science Center Berlin, Berlin, Federal Republic of Germany)
Professor Kjell Goldmann (University of Stockholm, Stockholm, Sweden)
Professor Charles F. Hermann (Ohio State University, Columbus, Ohio, USA)
Dr. Hanns-Dieter Jacobsen (Foundation of Science and Politics, Ebenhausen, Federal Republic of Germany)
Dr. David A. Jodice (Harvard University, Cambridge, Massachusetts, USA)
Dr. Peter Klein (Institute for International Politics and Economics, Berlin, German Democratic Republic)
Professor Peter Knirsch (Free University of Berlin, Berlin, Federal Republic of Germany)
Dr. Gernot Koehler (Canadian Peace Research Institute, Oakville, Canada)
Dr. Kari Möttölä (Finnish Institute of International Relations, Helsinki, Finland)
Dr. Hanspeter Neuhold (Austrian Institute of International Affairs, Laxenburg, Austria)
Professor Jurii Pankow (Institute of Public Science at the Central Committee of the CPSU, Moscow, USSR)
Dr. E. Raymond Platig (Office of External Research, Department of State, Washington, D.C., USA)
Dr. Hans-Jürg Renk (Riehen, Basel, Switzerland)

Norbert Ropers (German Society for Peace and Conflict Research, Bonn, Federal Republic of Germany)
Dr. Reimund Seidelmann (Justus Liebig University, Giessen, Federal Republic of Germany)
Dr. Margret Sieber (University of Zurich, Zurich, Switzerland)
Professor J. David Singer (University of Michigan, Ann Arbor, Michigan, USA)
Professor Raimo Väyrynen (University of Helsinki, Helsinki, Finland)
Professor Radovan Vukadinovic (University of Zagreb, Zagreb, Yugoslovia)
Professor Erich Weede (University of Cologne, Cologne, Federal Republic of Germany)

Of course, this alphabetical enumeration cannot pay justice to the many stimulating ideas offered, a considerable number of which induced us to rethink a number of key issues involved in this study. We sincerely hope that, based on the advice offered from all sides, the results of this study will be acceptable to all sides concerned irrespective of their political orientation.

We also gratefully acknowledge the assistance of Christian Catrina, Cathérine Däniker, Martin Knoepfel, Bernadette Koller, Walter Linsi, and Max-Peter Stüssi, who took over the tedious task of collecting the data and performing the content analyses.

Our acknowledgments would be entirely incomplete, however, without gratefully mentioning Aurelia Boermans-Flory, who with unparalleled skill and patience wrote and partly also several times rewrote the manuscript of this study.

Chapter 1

Introduction

1.1 THE PURPOSE OF THIS STUDY: PROVIDING AN OBJECTIVE RECORD OF EAST–WEST RELATIONS

1.1.1 The Main Task and Its Rationale

This study will examine, as systematically as possible, what has been called "détente." The type of East–West interaction that led to the Conference on Security and Cooperation in Europe (CSCE) can be expected to constitute a long-term interaction pattern among the thirty-five states that took part in the CSCE negotiations in Helsinki, Belgrade, and Madrid. The majority of current and future events taking place within the framework of East–West relations can be understood only if evaluated against the background of this long-term process. Yet, this process is not at all transparent, and it does not exhibit any momentum pointing in a specific direction. Thus it continues to be a matter of great concern not only to the decisionmaking elites of all countries in East and West but to the general public as well. The enormous amount of public attention paid to "détente" and the increasingly complex stock of political literature covering this subject from a variety of perspectives give ample proof of this fact.

However, when talking about the "progress" or "stagnation,"

the "crisis" or even the "end", or about the "irreversibility" and "reversibility," of the process of "détente," the situation and development trends are usually assessed by a rule-of-thumb interpretation, that is, by pure intuition. References, for example, to a "typical" statement of politician *X* or politician *Y* or to arbitrary events (meetings, contracts, protests, incidents, and so on) are used as more or less "significant" proofs for one's theory. Such methods by no means comply with modern standards of social-science theory and methodology and, in the long run, will prove unsatisfactory.

At this juncture social-science research, based on skills developed by the indicators movement, may be applied and make an important and useful contribution. The question is whether it might be possible to describe and evaluate the process of East–West relations in its complexity in a more systematic, valid, and reliable manner than has been the case until now. Judgments on "progress" and "regression" in the process of "détente" would thus become more objective. At the same time one could assess more accurately to what extent and where "détente" is subject to stagnation or regression in a given period. In other words, by developing indicators of East–West relations, it would become possible to monitor the East–West interaction process in Europe and elsewhere and provide useful information; such information is the most crucial requirement for deciding on future courses of action for making East–West relations more sober, more peaceful, more stable, and more cooperative. Given the present level of armaments, the governments and peoples of the East and West really cannot afford any misunderstandings, which would simply be too costly or even disastrous.

This assumption can be said to be the object of a minimum consensus operative in present East–West interactions. In this study, careful attention will have to be paid to observe the confines of this minimum consensus, that is, to base value judgments, if any, on the few perceptions and normative expectations that Eastern and Western governments share.

1.1.2 Credibility and Acceptability as Crucial Concerns

For a monitoring device to benefit all members of the East–West system, it must be designed so that it is acceptable to all members. This requirement has implications as to (1) the institution adopting such a task as well as to (2) the approach chosen to perform this task. Both are problems of credibility that have already been discussed in the context of other monitoring projects.

In view of the "legitimacy" of the institution in charge of a monitoring system, one may envision a private (i.e., nongovernmental) transnational organization, as Snyder, Hermann, and Lasswell suggest in *Global Monitoring System of Human Dignity*

(1976). In that publication, the authors propose a number of organizational checks and balances to reduce bias such as publicity, competition, and rotation of positions of responsibility. Other possible techniques are using criteria for the selection of individuals in key positions that demonstrate a reputation for objectivity; conducting research with rival hypotheses and multiple indicators; employing independent and cross-checking teams for the collection and analysis of data; and so on. An alternative way to achieve universal institutional credibility would be to choose all members from a team composed of people devoted to universal values. Such a procedure is preferred by the World Order Models team working on the *State of the Globe Report* (Mazrui 1977). Yet the chapter on "Détente and Competitive Imperialism" in that report raises slight doubts as to the universal acceptability of this approach.

In conclusion, it seems to be difficult to find any institutional arrangement guaranteeing *a priori* legitimacy and universal acceptability of a monitoring system designed for such a touchy matter as East–West relations. However, the authors of this study believe that the fact that this project is financed by and developed in a neutral country may at least not constitute a severe handicap —and they hope that it will provide a relative advantage over similar projects in countries belonging to one of the military alliances.

As to the second aspect of credibility, certain precautions are to be observed with regard to the procedural aspect of the project. The main concern here is to avoid both theoretical and normative "preemptions," which will be discussed in Section 1.2. The central aspect, in this context, is to avoid a premature use and projection of a specific definition of "détente." It is commonplace that "détente" is not defined the same everywhere, which means that the chosen theoretical framework will not necessarily meet unanimous consent everywhere.

The conclusion to be drawn from this observation is that any monitoring attempt seeking to attain universal recognition and acceptability must find a way to do justice to the plurality of definitions given by different actors. More precisely, it has to be based on the very perceptions of "détente" that differ and that cannot be substituted for by any single scholarly definition. For this reason, this study, as presented in this paper, has a "multitheoretical" foundation. It rests on the assumption that, in interaction processes such as the one between East and West, what really counts is what the actors involved *think* to be real. According to Thomas' theory, situations defined by men to be real tend to become finally real as a consequence. As there were and still are thirty-five states involved in the CSCE process, at least thirty-five definitions of "détente" are to be expected. In contrast to other studies describing the development of East-West relations such as the contribution by Nygren (1979), this study will not be based on any preliminary decision of which dimension should be looked at when trying to measure East-West interactions. The practical consequence of these assumptions and their implications for the design of a research strategy are outlined in Section 1.2.

A first and preliminary test of the pertinence of this assumption was made by contacting scholars from East European countries. In December 1977 a presentation of the project was given at the Institute of World Economy and International Relations (IMEMO) of the Soviet Academy of Sciences, and the proposal was generally met by consent. Similar presentations were made at the 1978 Annual Convention of the International Studies Association (Washington, D.C.) and at the World Congress of the International Political Science Association (Moscow, 1979). In 1979 the authors convened an international symposium in Zurich to discuss the subject matter further (cf. Frei 1981), and since then both authors had manyfold opportunities to present their project at various places, thus constantly collecting critical feedback.

1.2 THE DESIGN OF THIS STUDY

As we have pointed out, the basic idea of this study is to find indicators for the various dimensions constituting the process of East-West interaction; however, the dimensions to be operationalized* will be chosen on the basis of the perceptions of the actors involved. In the light of these assumptions, we have taken the following steps:

Step 1: Assessment of relevant actors; choice of a document category suitable for content analysis. Since the CSCE basically constitutes a diplomatic process, the relevant actors are primarily official state actors. Hence the definitions given by official spokesmen of the thirty-five governments are considered to be the most appropriate source for assessing different conceptions and meanings of "détente." For these reasons, it seems out of place to consider other actors, like opposition parties and other groups dissenting with official governmental positions, nor do the various scholarly definitions proposed in the literature matter in this perspective.

The documents used for identifying the thirty-five official conceptions of "détente" must be homogeneous and mutually comparable. One category of documents meeting these requirements is the series of statements at the occasion of the opening of the Helsinki Meeting of the CSCE by the heads of delegations (1973), by the heads of state and government at the time when the Helsinki Final Act was signed (July 31–August 2, 1975), the opening and closing statements offered by the heads of delegations to the Belgrade Meeting (1977/78) and the Madrid Meeting of the CSCE (1980/81).

*In social-science terminology, to *operationalize* means to find specific, observable indicators of the variable or dimension to be studied, usually defined in abstract terms.

All these statements are uniform in character; they have served the same purpose and were carefully drafted by the foreign-policy decisionmaking bureaucracies, most of them under close supervision of and authorization by the top decisionmakers. They aimed at giving a general assessment of the idea and reality of East–West relations as seen by the participating governments at a particular moment.

Step 2: Content analysis of CSCE statements. In order to determine the dimensions of East–West interactions that are considered to be relevant for East–West relations by the thirty-five governments concerned, as well as their order of importance, a systematic quantitative content analysis of the statements has to be made. Here, for the first time, problems concerning the political credibility and acceptability of this study arose because the selection of a set of categories to be used for a content analysis usually requires some decisions that have theoretical implications. Yet it is suggested that a solution can be found to solve this problem. It refers to the striking fact that during the CSCE negotiations, a kind of "semantic currency" was developed, a largely standardized list of terms universally applied by all participating delegations. This list of terms finally became the collection of themes that are enumerated in the different "baskets" of the Final Act. They supply a system of categories or a coding scheme suitable for a content analysis, and all statements made afterward, as a rule, refer to the text of the Final Act. The Final Act provides a list of several hundred themes. By condensing very specific themes into more general categories, they can be reduced to approximately 120 themes.

When using the CSCE Final Act categories to identify the dimensions perceived to be relevant, some methodological decisions again have to be made. How can the importance attributed by a speaker to the individual dimensions be determined? Obviously, the importance of a theme is expressed in two different ways: first, by the amount of attention devoted to the individual themes and, second, by qualitative emphasis explicitly characterizing some themes as more important than others.

As a result, the second step yields thirty-five lists of themes ranked and weighted by the order of importance attributed by each individual participating state, and for each set of statements (1973, 1975, 1977/78, 1980/81) the analysis refers to. Based on these data, the following additional analyses can be made:

a. Identifying the dynamics of the perceptions of East–West relations: Is there any change in the rank orders attributed by the individual governments from 1973 to 1975 and from 1977/78 to 1980/81?
b. Comparing the profiles of the perceptions of East–West relations: To what extent are the rank orders identified similarly or dissimilarly (paired comparison)? What is the degree of cohesion?

c. Aggregating the rank orders by groups of states (e.g., military alliances, regional subsystems)

The content analysis and the resulting additional analysis will be presented in Chapter 2.

Step 3: Search for suitable "hard" (or, as hard as possible) indicators for the dimensions identified by step 2. Step 3 and 2 constitutes the main task of this study. Here one has to expect a number of difficult validation problems, which again have to be seen in the context of political credibility and acceptability. Some dimensions may be operationalized quite easily since face validity can be expected. This holds true, for instance, for the theme "desirability of growth of trade," which can be operationalized by looking simply at East–West trade figures.

However, the task of finding indicators becomes much more arduous when themes like "cultural cooperation" or "respect of human rights" enter into consideration. From the CSCE negotiations, we know that the governments concerned do have quite precise ideas about how to define concepts like the ones mentioned —but these ideas unfortunately often diverge diametrically. "Cultural cooperation," for instance, may be measured by one side by noting the balance of the number of books translated from and/or into the language(s) of the other side or by the number of official delegations of artists sent to the other side, whereas others may prefer to look at the possibility for artists from different countries to a free exchange of ideas and to coproduction. In such cases, in order to save universal credibility, the only way out is to use two (or more) different indicators whereby the juxtaposition of the results may be revealing too. Viewed from one side (by using one indicator), East–West relations in a specific field may have progressed; viewed from the other side (by using another indicator), it may have taken a step backward. Hence it will be possible to trace exactly where and in what respect there is disagreement. This task will be done in Chapter 3, based on time-series data to be collected for the period from 1960 to 1980.

Step 4: Developing weighted indices according to the "mixture" of dimensions identified by step 2 combined with the indicator system constructed in step 3. According to the relative rank and weight attributed to the individual dimensions (as identified by Step 2), combined indices can be computed indicating the overall perceptions held by the individual governments (and/or aggregate groups of states) and indicating also the operational measures for such an overall perception. The results of the analysis combining perceptions and indicators will be presented in Chapter 4. As a result, "détente curves" describing the history and present state of East–West relations as perceived by aggregate groups of states will be produced.

Step 5: Reexamining some theoretical assumptions about "détente." The data collected in this project, although originally sought for the purely descriptive purpose of assessing the course and actual state of affairs in East–West relations, can also be utilized for a large variety of analytical purposes such as hypothesis testing. To mention just a few:

a. Comparing "deeds" and "words" by correlating the time-series data referring to the indices with general statements on the state of East–West relations made by spokesmen of participating governments; or by correlating such data with behavioral data collected in the context of events data projects. This type of analysis may provide insight into possible differences between "real" and "rationalized" perceptions (Kadushin 1968);
b. Using the indices as dependent variables and inquiring into the "causes" that explain variations within such data (e.g., systemic variables referring to the overall change in the global political system such as competition in the Third World and variables referring to the trends in domestic economies);
c. Using the indices as independent variables and finding out the consequences of the process of East–West relations (again with regard to international and domestic consequences)

A selection of major theoretical approaches to "détente" will be presented and examined empirically in Chapter 5.

Theories can be expected to have also some predictive potential. This potential is being explored by a computer simulation carried out, on the basis of the data gathered in this study and starting from different assumptions regarding the future evolution of some key parameters, by Professor Urs Luterbacher and Dr. Pierre Allan (Graduate Institute of International Studies, Geneva). A summary of their findings is presented in the second volume (Appendix A5).

Chapter 2

The Dimensionality of East-West Relations: A Content Analysis of CSCE Statements

2.1 SOURCES AND METHODS

In this chapter, we will identify dimensions of East-West relations that are perceived as relevant in the views held by the thirty-five governments participating in the Conference on Security and Cooperation in Europe (CSCE). The intention is to find out something about the subjective "reality" or "realities" of East-West relations. Yet it is also important for its own sake since the similarity and dissimilarity of perceptions as well as the rank-order of issues perceived and their dynamics can thus be observed, measured, and interpreted.

Two questions have to be answered, however, before engaging in such an analysis: (1) Which texts are to be taken as a source for finding out perceptions? (2) Which methods are to be used?

2.1.1 The Selection of Documentary Sources

As to the first question, it is important to base the analysis on a set of documents that are homogeneous and, that, in a mutually comparable way, provide official interpretations of East-West relations. For reasons outlined previously, the text chosen are the statements made at the CSCE meetings held in Helsinki (1973 and 1975), Belgrade (1977/78), and Madrid (1980/81). The focus is on opening statements and closing statements only since these statements give a carefully prepared general evaluation of the situation from a specific national angle and represent the official views of the governments concerned.

The method used to analyze the texts was *content analysis*, which is a systematic process of identifying the manifest meaning expressed in a text. The various types of content analysis and the choice made therefrom in the context of this project is being dealt with in Appendix A2. A question often asked about content analysis is to what extent official texts produced by government representatives really tell the truth. More precisely, it might be doubted whether the authors of such texts feel that it is opportune to reveal their real beliefs and preferences (cf. also Hart 1976, pp. 221 ff., and Mouritzen 1981). Yet these doubts do not invalidate the documents used for this analysis. The first author of this study participated in the Belgrade and Madrid CSCE meetings and paid particular attention to the way the delegations drafted their statements. In fact, it can be shown that the opening and closing statements, far from being an ad-hoc expression of feelings motivated mainly by tactical considerations, are the result of a most conscientious and precise drafting procedure within the delegations and, in almost all cases, also involving the foreign-ministry apparatus back home. There are good reasons therefore to assume that these texts constitute policy-statements of a highly representative and programmatic nature.

When using texts as indicators for perceptions, one might also doubt the validity of such texts because they may refer to specific situations within a negotiation process and thus reflect motives of a tactical nature that are hardly relevant for what is meant to be tapped when reading and content analyzing these texts. This may in fact be the case when looking at statements made in the context of specific discussions held in commission meetings and plenary meetings; such statements usually refer to statements made by previous speakers and therefore do not reflect a balanced overall expression of views held by the delegate's government. By restricting the content analysis to the statements made on the formal ceremonies of opening and closing meetings, however, this risk of making inappropriate conclusions can be avoided.

In sum, there is hardly any alternative set of documents that reflects the views of the thirty-five governments taking part in the CSCE with a higher degree of validity, comparability, and homogeneity.

2.1.2 The Coding Procedure

In order to guarantee a reliable and objective analysis of the text, it is necessary to develop a set of coding rules consisting mainly of a list of categories suitable for identifying the issues and themes mentioned in the statements. Such a list was prepared on the basis of the CSCE Final Act, thus using the items of the CSCE agenda as a kind of "semantic currency" representing a highly standardized and generally acceptable set of categories.

This list is neither fully exclusive nor exhaustive since the Final Act is not an academic paper but the result of diplomatic activities involving certain compromises. Thus the Final Act contains some overlapping categories, and some aspects of East–West relations mentioned in the Helsinki, Belgrade, and Madrid statements are not in the Final Act; these categories have been added to the basic list of categories. All together the list of codes comprises 120 categories (see Appendix A2).

The basic assumptions underlying this approach to content analysis are very simple:

1. A speaker is likely to focus on those issues in his statement that he assumes to be of importance and interest to his country.
2. Text entries of important categories are likely to occur significantly more often than those of less important categories.
3. Entries of important categories are likely to be qualified as "important."

The sequence of categories and issues treated in a statement seems to be of only minor relevance since it is subject to considerations of style and rhetoric.

The practical procedure applied in this study can be summarized as follows: As a first step, each statement is broken down into association sequences with an average length of 120 to 210 words. An *association sequence* is a set of sentences referring to one specific issue or theme. Intersections dividing one association sequence from the next are made where an obvious change in the major issue or theme of the current text takes place.

Second, each sentence of a statement is scrutinized for potentially relevant entries, that is, words or groups of words that are either relevant for East–West relations or important in the context of the statement under consideration. Each entry receives its appropriate code and an additional code for its verbal qualification, where 0 denotes no verbal qualification, 2 a modest, 3 a high, and 4 maximum verbal qualification.

Third, category codes and associated values for the verbal qualification are then transferred into machine-readable form. These raw data are then processed by a set of computer programs in order to produce appropriate datasets for further statistical analyses. Category scores for countries in each of the five sets of CSCE statements in the analysis are computed by counting the occurrence of categories in the statements and adding the respective values for the verbal qualification. Detailed information on the coding rules and the codebook used for the collection of data is provided in Appendix A2.

The material gathered by this procedure is extremely rich and vast. Therefore, only a small selection will be presented in the following analysis. The complete category score tables for countries and groups of countries in the CSCE are presented in Appendix A2.2

2.2 THE THIRTY-FIVE CSCE GOVERNMENTS AND THEIR EMPHASIS ON THE THREE "BASKETS" FROM HELSINKI TO MADRID

2.2.1 Introduction

The Final Act and thus the agenda of the CSCE meetings before and after the adoption of the Final Act cover a wide variety of issues. For practical purposes these issues were "bundled" into three "baskets" plus a special chapter on the Mediterranean. The three baskets are: (1) questions relating to security in Europe; (2) cooperation in the field of economics, of science, and technology and of the environment; and (3) cooperation in humanitarian and other fields.

In this section two questions will be asked: (1) What share of attention did the thirty-five states devote to each of the three "baskets"? (2) To what extent and in which direction was this distribution of attention subject to change between 1973 and 1980?

Based on the content analysis of the five sets of statements made by the delegates of the thirty-five states participating in the CSCE meetings, a series of tables will be presented in this section pointing at variations by country and variations in time that can be observed in the course of the evolution of East-West relations between 1973 and 1980. The data presented in the following tables are shares of attention in percent calculated for both individual countries participating in the CSCE meetings from Helsinki to Madrid and groups of countries. The data base for the computation of these tables is presented in Appendix A2.2. (Raw scores were computed for each of the 120 categories by counting the occurrence of categories and adding values for the verbal qualification).

In the following tables, mean values are given for each group of countries, that is, NATO, WTO, and N + N (neutral and nonaligned countries). Since percentages add up to 100 percent, these figures are group means of attention in percent for parts of the Final Act *and* actual shares of attention by groups when summing up scores for all respective group members. Figures for "means" therefore may be interpreted in both ways.

Furthermore, when analyzing the figures referring to parts of the Final Act, one has to bear in mind that the first "basket" comprises a considerable variety of issues since the Declaration on Principles Guiding Relations between Participating States is part of this "basket"; at least one of the principles listed in this "decalogue" refers to the theme that for the rest is elaborated in greater detail in the third "basket" (Principle VII: "Respect for human rights and fundamental freedoms, including the freedom of thought, conscience, religion or belief"). The first "basket" usually accounts for twice the percentage of attention devoted jointly to "baskets" 2 and 3; in other words, the approach by "baskets" does not yield a very refined picture of the emphasis expressed by the delegations. For this reason, an additional analysis presented in Section 2.4 will identify "factors" underlying the entire structure of categories.

2.2.2 The 1973 Helsinki Statements

In the statements presented at the 1973 Helsinki meeting of the CSCE—as in all subsequent meetings—the first "basket" was in a position to catch the main share of attention: 43 percent of all categories mentioned by all thirty-five speakers referred to this "basket." It is interesting to note that the group of neutral nonaligned countries seemed to be more attracted by the first "basket" than any other group. As far as the second "basket" is concerned, the highest percentage share of attention was scored by the WTO member countries. The emphasis put by these countries on the second "basket" remained preponderant during the entire period observed in this study. The third "basket" receives much more attention by the NATO countries (14 percent) than by the WTO countries (8 percent). This fact may suggest the conclusion that as early as 1973, the issue of cooperation in humanitarian and other fields began to emerge as a controversial topic, one that provoked major disagreement.

A more detailed picture is offered by Table 2.1 presenting the attention scores identified for the individual countries. The USA devoted 28 percent of her attention to the third "basket," as compared with the USSR (5 percent), while the second "basket" was given 6 percent of the US attention and 2 percent of the Soviet attention. Among the WTO countries, Bulgaria, the CSSR, and Hungary devote relatively much attention on the third "basket." The section on the Mediterranean received highest degree of attention by Malta, Monaco, and Turkey.

2.2.3 The 1975 Helsinki Statements

When in 1975 the heads of states and governments signed the Final Act and made their solemn statements, the overall distribution of attention they paid to the various "baskets" remained roughly the same as two years before. However, the emphasis put on the "baskets" by the different groups of countries now had somewhat shifted. Now it is the WTO countries that favor most the first "basket," whereas the corresponding share of attention given by the N + N countries has declined; the N + N countries, on the other hand, now express growing interest for the second "basket."

Table 2.1. The 1973 Helsinki Statements: Percentage Distribution of Attention on Parts of the Final Act

COUNTRY GROUP	COUNTRY	BASKET 1	BASKET 2	BASKET 3	SECTION ON THE MEDITERRANEAN	OTHER CATEGORIES
NATO						
	BLGM	31.91	12.06	18.44	0.0	37.59
	CNDA	38.67	10.67	16.00	0.0	34.67
	DNMK	48.75	7.50	23.75	0.0	20.00
	FRNC	41.25	11.25	5.00	0.0	42.50
	FRG	34.39	11.46	19.75	0.0	34.39
	GRCE	42.99	9.35	5.61	3.74	38.32
	ICLD	46.30	16.67	11.11	0.0	25.93
	ITLY	44.68	8.51	12.77	3.19	30.85
	LXBG	47.06	5.88	10.78	0.0	36.27
	NTHL	45.95	9.91	17.12	0.0	27.03
	NRWY	32.43	26.35	23.65	0.0	17.57
	PRTG	50.00	3.92	8.82	.98	36.27
	TRKY	39.01	20.57	3.55	11.35	25.53
	UK	43.28	10.45	10.45	0.0	35.82
	USA	40.68	5.93	27.97	0.0	25.42
MEAN		41.8233	11.3649	14.3169	1.2838	31.2110
WTO						
	BLGR	42.00	19.00	14.00	0.0	25.00
	CZCH	29.46	20.54	13.39	0.0	36.61
	GDR	48.23	4.26	2.13	0.0	45.39
	HNGR	32.32	22.22	5.05	1.01	39.39
	PLND	43.11	10.78	9.58	0.0	36.53
	RMNA	48.94	8.51	4.26	0.0	38.30
	USSR	43.78	2.30	4.61	0.0	49.31
MEAN		41.1204	12.5152	7.5736	.1443	38.6464
N+N						
	AUST	46.30	4.63	12.96	0.0	36.11
	CYPR	54.62	6.72	3.36	6.72	28.57
	FNLD	46.77	12.90	5.65	0.0	34.68
	IRLD	34.72	5.18	10.88	0.0	49.22
	LICH	57.69	7.69	7.69	0.0	26.92
	MLTA	52.31	7.69	6.15	15.38	18.46
	SANM	39.13	6.09	.87	0.0	53.91
	SWDN	41.45	11.18	9.21	0.0	38.16
	SWTZ	43.33	3.33	8.33	0.0	45.00
	YGSL	44.78	5.97	5.22	1.49	42.54
MEAN		46.1094	7.1396	7.0334	2.3600	37.3576
OTHER						
	MNCO	25.00	30.00	5.00	15.00	25.00
	SPAN	36.23	18.12	13.04	10.14	22.46
	VATC	50.49	.97	2.91	0.0	45.63
MEAN		37.2391	16.3623	6.9854	8.3816	31.0316
MEAN		42.5144	10.8161	10.2588	1.9718	34.4389

Disagreement about the third "basket" can be noticed in a similar way as in 1973, yet it is not as explicit now as it used to be at the 1973 Helsinki meeting and at a later stage again at the 1978 Belgrade meeting.

As far as the preferences expressed by individual countries are concerned, it deserves to be mentioned that some countries very markedly stress the importance of the third "basket"; among them are Iceland (41 percent), Denmark (32 percent), the Netherlands (21 percent), Hungary (20 percent), and Switzerland (21 percent). The second "basket" receives overproportionate attention by Iceland (25 percent) and Bulgaria (26 percent).

2.2.4 The 1977 Belgrade Opening Statements

By the time when, in 1977, the delegations of the thirty-five states convened again for the Belgrade meeting of the CSCE, the issues dealt with in the third "basket" had become a major bone of contention. The NATO countries devoted 16 percent of their attention to this "basket," yet their interest in the second "basket" had also increased considerably, i.e., doubled from 10 percent in 1975 to 20 percent in 1977. On the other hand, the delegations representing the WTO emphasized the first "basket," and so did the N + N delegations. The structure of preference expressed by the N + N delegations in fact closely resembles the one expressed by the WTO countries. Apart from the focus on the third "basket," there is also a significantly growing interest for the second "basket."

Looking at the distribution of scores for individual countries, a striking feature can be seen in the intensive care for the third "basket" exhibited by countries such as the USA (22 percent), Canada (24 percent), Iceland (20 percent), the Federal Republic of Germany (31 percent), Denmark (20 percent), and Belgium (28 percent). The delegations of these countries thus gave a signal for the controversial debate about human rights that characterized the Belgrade negotiations right from the beginning and finally led to a certain polarization among the thirty-five CSCE states.

2.2.5 The Belgrade Closing Statements

The discussions held in Belgrade seemed to have divisive impact on the structure of preference expressed by the various groups for the "baskets" of the Final Act. Compared with the situation presented by the opening statements, the statements made by the delegations from N + N countries underwent the most substantial change by the end of the Belgrade meeting. Now their distribution of attention almost completely coincided with the attitudes adopted by the NATO countries: 46 percent for the first "basket" (NATO, 49 percent); 19 percent for the second "basket" (NATO, 18 percent); and 15 percent for the third "basket" (NATO, 18 percent). On the other hand, the delegations of the WTO member countries quite

Table 2.2. The 1975 Helsinki Statements: Percentage Distribution of Attention on Parts of the Final Act

COUNTRY GROUP	COUNTRY	BASKET 1	BASKET 2	BASKET 3	SECTION ON THE MEDITERRANEAN	OTHER CATEGORIES
NATO						
	BLGM	58.52	6.67	8.89	1.48	24.44
	CNDA	34.78	15.94	4.35	0.0	44.93
	DNMK	35.38	12.31	32.31	0.0	20.00
	FRNC	38.46	2.56	15.38	0.0	43.59
	FRG	34.04	11.70	12.77	0.0	41.49
	GRCE	75.36	7.25	0.0	2.90	14.49
	ICLD	29.11	25.32	40.51	0.0	5.06
	ITLY	32.97	8.79	16.48	5.49	36.26
	LXBG	53.70	5.56	10.19	0.0	30.56
	NTHL	40.54	11.71	20.72	0.0	27.03
	NRWY	58.28	12.88	5.52	0.0	23.31
	PRTG	53.85	10.77	9.23	7.69	18.46
	TRKY	63.86	7.83	.60	9.64	18.07
	UK	31.48	4.32	9.88	0.0	54.32
	USA	31.85	7.64	9.55	0.0	50.96
MEAN		44.8126	10.0835	13.0917	1.8137	30.1984
WTO						
	BLGR	45.59	26.47	5.88	0.0	22.06
	CZCH	38.00	17.00	11.00	0.0	34.00
	GDR	55.88	7.35	4.41	0.0	32.35
	HNGR	37.63	12.90	20.43	0.0	29.03
	PLND	37.50	16.67	4.17	0.0	41.67
	RMNA	49.82	10.32	6.41	2.14	31.32
	USSR	46.97	13.64	7.58	0.0	31.82
MEAN		44.4852	14.9071	8.5532	.3050	31.7494
N+N						
	AUST	25.53	19.15	2.13	0.0	53.19
	CYPR	55.56	6.35	7.14	3.97	26.98
	FNLD	58.59	11.72	3.13	0.0	26.56
	IRLD	29.27	14.63	14.63	1.22	40.24
	LICH	21.74	13.04	17.39	0.0	47.83
	MLTA	28.77	10.96	6.85	28.77	24.66
	SANM	27.52	12.84	2.75	4.59	52.29
	SWDN	41.98	11.45	9.92	0.0	36.64
	SWTZ	50.49	10.68	21.36	0.0	17.48
	YGSL	56.22	9.73	2.70	0.0	31.35
MEAN		39.5665	12.0557	8.8008	3.8542	35.7227
OTHER						
	MNCO	10.53	42.11	5.26	2.63	39.47
	SPAN	59.49	6.96	13.29	5.06	15.19
	VATC	37.17	7.96	2.65	3.54	48.67
MEAN		35.7294	19.0106	7.0697	3.7449	34.4454
MEAN		42.4697	12.3769	10.4419	2.2605	32.4510

saliently tried to avoid the issues of cooperation in the humanitarian field, as listed in the third "basket," putting primary emphasis on the first "basket" (58 percent, that is, the highest percentage ever attributed to any single "basket"). In sum, the Belgrade negotiations had a polarizing impact on the structure of preferences held by the thirty-five CSCE member states. The process of polarization that took place in Belgrade is also conspicuously reflected by the sudden diminuition of the percentage figures referring to the attention devoted to "other categories." While in 1973 and 1975 still one-third of all discussions concerned the miscellaneous items collapsed into this general group of categories, the respective share now dropped to a mere 13 percent.

As the breakdown by individual countries (see Tables 2.3 and 2.4) demonstrates, this shift in emphasis cannot be attributed to the preferences expressed by the two major powers. It is rather an outcome of the strong emphasis put, by certain Western and nonaligned countries, on the third "basket"; these countries are Canada (32 percent); Norway (24 percent); Italy (19 percent); the Federal Republic of Germany (25 percent); France (21 percent); Denmark (34 percent); the Netherlands (53 percent); Luxemburg (23 percent); Sweden (17 percent); Finland (29 percent); Austria (18 percent); Liechtenstein (50 percent); and Spain (24 percent).

2.2.6 The Madrid Opening Statements

Generally speaking, the distribution of attention observed in the opening statements made at the Madrid meeting of the CSCE may be characterized as a kind of return to normalcy—if *normalcy* means the state of affairs existing prior to the Belgrade meeting, that is, during the Helsinki phase of the CSCE negotiations. The interest in "baskets" two and three that had sharply risen during the Belgrade meeting is now again confined to the proportion expressed previously. There is, however, a considerable decline of importance of the second "basket," which now reaches its lowest percentage share ever observed (8 percent). This neglect for—or maybe disappointment about—cooperation in the field of economics, of science and technology, and of the environment, as dealt with in the second "basket," is equally shared by both NATO and WTO countries (8 percent and 7 percent, respectively), and the N + N delegations seem to be even more sceptical about it (5 percent). At the same time the various allusions to the miscellaneous items summed up under the heading "other categories" become important again (31 percent).

The scores observed for individual countries are particularly interesting in the case of the two major powers. The United States expressed a clear preference for matters included in the first "basket" while the third "basket" received the lowest degree of attention by all NATO countries. The USSR, on the other hand, devoted still a considerable share of her attention to matters of the second

Table 2.3. The Belgrade Opening Statements: Percentage Distribution of Attention on Parts of the Final Act

COUNTRY GROUP	COUNTRY	BASKET 1	BASKET 2	BASKET 3	SECTION ON THE MEDITERRANEAN	OTHER CATEGORIES
NATO						
	BLGM	31.69	12.68	28.17	4.23	23.24
	CNDA	44.96	10.85	24.03	0.0	20.16
	DNMK	40.24	12.80	20.12	1.22	25.61
	FRNC	30.95	26.19	15.48	1.19	26.19
	FRG	25.56	12.78	31.11	2.22	28.33
	GRCE	57.41	24.07	12.96	3.70	1.85
	ICLD	36.00	24.00	20.00	0.0	20.00
	ITLY	42.86	19.05	7.94	4.76	25.40
	LXBG	42.14	14.29	12.86	2.86	27.86
	NTHL	50.49	11.65	16.99	1.94	18.93
	NRWY	44.70	29.92	10.98	0.0	14.39
	PRTG	34.55	22.36	4.47	4.47	34.15
	TRKY	28.66	36.59	3.66	1.22	29.88
	UK	24.51	25.49	6.86	0.0	43.14
	USA	40.59	10.89	21.78	0.0	26.73
MEAN		38.3539	19.5739	15.8277	1.8542	24.3903
WTO						
	BLGR	60.82	12.89	4.12	0.0	22.16
	CZCH	30.19	20.28	21.23	0.0	28.30
	GDR	40.28	8.80	16.20	0.0	34.72
	HNGR	39.51	28.81	10.70	0.0	20.99
	PLND	54.04	10.10	6.57	0.0	29.29
	RMNA	61.73	19.75	3.46	1.48	13.58
	USSR	31.93	21.85	12.61	0.0	33.61
MEAN		45.4998	17.4965	10.6973	.2116	26.0948
N+N						
	AUST	42.74	14.52	11.29	.81	30.65
	CYPR	46.79	9.17	8.26	9.17	26.61
	FNLD	54.24	23.31	3.81	0.0	18.64
	IRLD	44.85	27.84	8.76	0.0	18.56
	LICH	56.00	12.00	4.00	0.0	28.00
	MLTA	17.06	8.53	8.53	29.86	36.02
	SANM	73.50	2.56	3.42	0.0	20.51
	SWDN	55.40	12.95	6.47	0.0	25.18
	SWTZ	35.14	31.53	4.50	0.0	28.83
	YGSL	47.00	15.47	18.18	2.32	17.02
MEAN		47.2712	15.7880	7.7234	4.2160	25.0013
OTHER						
	MNCO	10.42	66.67	4.17	0.0	18.75
	SPAN	62.50	10.83	.83	1.67	24.17
	VATC	36.81	3.07	19.02	.61	40.49
MEAN		36.5755	26.8558	8.0061	.7601	27.8025
MEAN		42.1784	18.7009	11.8157	2.1067	25.1982

Table 2.4. The Belgrade Closing Statements: Percentage Distribution of Attention on Parts of the Final Act

COUNTRY GROUP	COUNTRY	BASKET 1	BASKET 2	BASKET 3	SECTION ON THE MEDITERRANEAN	OTHER CATEGORIES
NATO						
	BLGM	57.69	30.77	9.62	0.0	1.92
	CNDA	55.26	7.02	32.46	0.0	5.26
	DNMK	31.03	17.24	34.48	0.0	17.24
	FRNC	46.77	3.23	20.97	0.0	29.03
	FRG	34.78	19.57	25.00	0.0	20.65
	GRCE	66.67	27.78	0.0	5.56	0.0
	ICLD	62.50	25.00	0.0	0.0	12.50
	ITLY	45.45	16.88	19.48	10.39	7.79
	LXBG	56.41	7.69	23.08	0.0	12.82
	NTHL	47.06	0.0	52.94	0.0	0.0
	NRWY	55.17	13.79	24.14	0.0	6.90
	PRTG	32.14	53.57	3.57	3.57	7.14
	TRKY	36.36	21.82	3.64	14.55	23.64
	UK	58.72	9.17	11.93	0.0	20.18
	USA	51.94	13.95	12.40	0.0	21.71
MEAN		49.1980	17.8322	18.2464	2.2708	12.4526
WTO						
	BLGR	56.38	21.28	4.26	0.0	18.09
	CZCH	65.57	18.03	0.0	0.0	16.39
	GDR	59.51	17.79	6.75	0.0	15.95
	HNGR	52.14	23.93	10.26	0.0	13.68
	PLND	44.31	15.69	18.04	0.0	21.96
	RMNA	67.65	25.00	2.94	0.0	4.41
	USSR	58.01	14.36	6.08	2.21	19.34
MEAN		57.6535	19.4405	6.9026	.3157	15.6877
N+N						
	AUST	63.33	15.00	18.33	0.0	3.33
	CYPR	50.88	22.81	3.51	17.54	5.26
	FNLD	48.68	11.84	28.95	0.0	10.53
	IRLD	62.50	19.64	7.14	0.0	10.71
	LICH	0.0	50.00	50.00	0.0	0.0
	MLTA	21.74	8.70	0.0	52.17	17.39
	SANM	57.32	6.10	7.32	3.66	25.61
	SWDN	53.97	19.05	17.46	0.0	9.52
	SWTZ	54.76	19.05	11.90	0.0	14.29
	YGSL	46.84	16.46	6.33	6.33	24.05
MEAN		46.0016	18.8636	15.0944	7.9705	12.0698
OTHER						
	MNCO	27.27	63.64	9.09	0.0	0.0
	SPAN	42.35	15.29	23.53	1.18	17.65
	VATC	42.62	13.11	18.03	8.20	18.03
MEAN		37.4162	30.6817	16.8844	3.1244	11.8933
MEAN		48.9660	19.5499	14.9603	3.5814	12.9423

"basket." The section on the Mediterranean again scored highest in the cases of Malta and Monaco, and also the Italian delegation expressed some interest in this issue.

2.2.7 From Helsinki to Madrid: The Shifting Emphasis on the CSCE "Baskets"

A comparison of the tables summarizing the content of the Helsinki, Belgrade, and Madrid statements is somewhat difficult because of the high degree of complexity of the material and because of the fact that the first "basket" encompasses so many aspects as to offer an opportunity for appropriate interpretation of the orientation and interests underlying the preference for this "basket." To facilitate the evaluation of these trends, the percentage figures presented in Tables 2.1 to 2.5 are translated into Graph 2.1.

The emphasis attributed by the main groups of countries to the three "baskets" and to the section on the Mediterranean has both certain stable elements and unstable elements. There is stability in the overall attention paid to the first "basket"; the mean percentages vary from 42 percent (1977) to a maximum of 49 percent (in 1978). On the other hand, the concern expressed for "baskets" 2 and 3 is clearly subject to considerable change: Both "baskets" catch a modest share of attention at the beginning of the negotianegotiation process; yet the respective percentage figures are nearly doubled at the end of the Belgrade meeting in 1978, falling back, however, to the original level and less by 1980. The section on the Mediterranean constantly gets only marginal attention; as can be seen in the tables presenting attention scores by individual countries, the interest in problems of the Mediterranean, for obvious reasons, represents a special concern by some Mediterranean countries such as Malta, Italy, Turkey, and Cyprus.

This overall picture, however, becomes more vivid if one looks at change and stability in the perception expressed by the three main groups of countries. The interest in the first "basket" remains relatively stable in the case of NATO and of the N + N countries while the WTO countries intensify their emphasis on the first "basket" at the end of the Belgrade meeting. Quite in contrast to general assumptions held by many commentators of the European scene, a similar trend can be identified for the third "basket." NATO's interest in the third "basket" does not oscillate very much, and WTO's concern for these issues also seems to shift within well-defined limits; only the N + N nations for some time, in 1978, deviate somewhat from this general trend. A high degree of instability can be discerned only with regard to the second "basket"; all groups seem to have been sceptical about it at the beginning and highly attentive during the Belgrade meeting; yet in the Madrid opening statements, the share of attention devoted to issues of economic cooperation drops to a very modest level never observed before.

Table 2.5. The Madrid Opening Statements: Percentage Distribution of Attention on Parts of the Final Act

COUNTRY GROUP	COUNTRY	BASKET 1	BASKET 2	BASKET 3	SECTION ON THE MEDITERRANEAN	OTHER CATEGORIES
NATO						
	BLGM	35.48	7.53	30.11	6.45	20.43
	CNDA	59.33	6.00	12.00	0.0	22.67
	DNMK	45.35	8.14	24.42	0.0	22.09
	FRNC	49.18	6.56	19.67	0.0	24.59
	FRG	46.70	1.76	18.50	0.0	33.04
	GRCE	36.45	29.91	12.15	3.74	17.76
	ICLD	40.74	11.11	27.78	0.0	20.37
	ITLY	50.00	12.31	10.77	11.54	15.38
	LXBG	34.94	18.07	18.07	2.41	26.51
	NTHL	52.73	1.82	6.36	0.0	39.09
	NRWY	55.90	6.21	8.70	0.0	29.19
	PRTG	60.00	0.0	11.11	0.0	28.89
	TRKY	66.67	5.00	6.67	0.0	21.67
	UK	57.53	2.74	21.23	0.0	18.49
	USA	70.14	2.08	6.25	0.0	21.53
MEAN		50.7426	7.9491	15.5859	1.6092	24.1132
WTO						
	BLGR	41.05	5.26	14.74	1.05	37.89
	CZCH	54.26	9.57	0.0	0.0	36.17
	GDR	55.15	1.47	8.09	.74	34.56
	HNGR	51.83	6.10	11.59	.61	29.88
	PLND	52.78	3.47	5.56	0.0	38.19
	RMNA	55.44	7.48	9.18	.68	27.21
	USSR	37.04	15.56	8.15	3.70	35.56
MEAN		49.6487	6.9881	8.1854	.9688	34.2089
N+N						
	AUST	34.29	8.57	17.14	0.0	40.00
	CYPR	39.53	4.65	1.16	8.14	46.51
	FNLD	43.00	16.00	24.00	1.00	16.00
	IRLD	61.62	17.17	8.08	0.0	13.13
	LICH	38.10	0.0	4.76	0.0	57.14
	MLTA	23.29	0.0	0.0	26.03	50.68
	SANM	40.98	0.0	0.0	1.64	57.38
	SWDN	57.89	4.09	5.26	0.0	32.75
	SWTZ	55.33	0.0	12.67	0.0	32.00
	YGSL	54.14	1.91	1.27	3.82	38.85
MEAN		44.8171	5.2399	7.4352	4.0628	38.4450
OTHER						
	MNCO	16.67	50.00	0.0	16.67	16.67
	SPAN	53.09	3.61	3.09	5.15	35.05
	VATC	41.43	.71	20.00	0.0	37.86
MEAN		37.0627	18.1075	7.6976	7.2738	29.8584
MEAN		47.6583	7.8535	11.1009	2.6677	30.7196

Graph 2.1. Distribution of Attention on Parts of the Final Act: A Frequency Block Chart

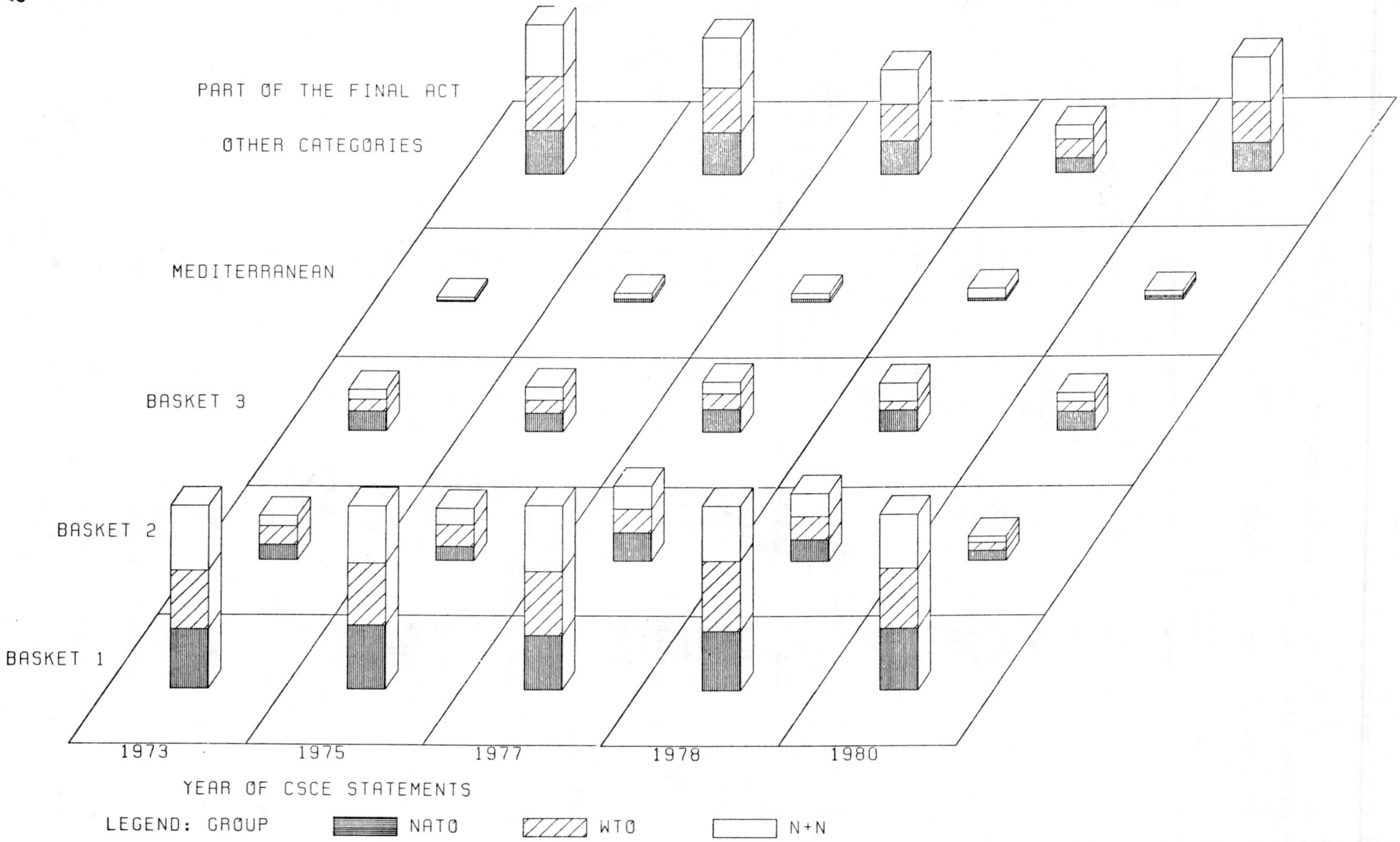
PART ØF THE FINAL ACT
ØTHER CATEGØRIES
MEDITERRANEAN
BASKET 3
BASKET 2
BASKET 1
1973
1975
1977
1978
1980
YEAR ØF CSCE STATEMENTS
LEGEND: GRØUP
NATØ
WTØ
N+N

As has already been noted, the share of attention devoted to the miscellaneous items summed up under the general heading of "other categories" may serve as an indicator for the degree of controversy about the substance matter listed in the "baskets"; the controversy seems to have been most intensive in 1978 when only a minor share of attention was caught by the other categories.

2.3 THE MAJOR ISSUES OF EAST–WEST RELATIONS

2.3.1 Introduction

More detailed information about the various concepts of East-West relations as expressed by the delegates of the thirty-five states participating in the Helsinki, Belgrade, and Madrid conferences can be obtained by looking at the relative rank-orders of individual categories.

By contrast to subsection 2.2, which referred to the lump sets arranged according to the three "baskets," a refined analysis looking at individual categories may offer an opportunity for making more detailed observations and drawing more differentiated conclusions. The following tables list the top 10 (out of 120) categories for each country or group of countries, and this is done for each of the five sets of statements.

2.3.2 The 1973 Helsinki Statements

Looking at all thirty-five statements made by the official delegations at the 1973 preparatory meeting held in Helsinki and identifying the ten issues referred to most frequently yield the rank-order of categories listed in Table 2.6. Cooperation among states is the most frequent category coded in the 1973 Helsinki statements, and this also holds true for the NATO and WTO groups. For the N + N countries, cooperation among countries is the second important category. References to the first "basket" of the Final Act (code 1) are also frequent, followed by concerns for peace (code 103) and conflict/confrontation (code 104). An often-mentioned category from the first "basket" refers to confidence-building measures, security, and disarmament. Cooperation in the field of economics, that is, general references to the second "basket" (code 19) is also frequent. Surprisingly, the topic of paramount importance in later sets of statements—respect for human rights and fundamental freedoms (code 9)—does not rank among the first ten categories in either group of countries. Only the delegates from NATO countries mention the issue of human contacts quite frequently, but even here it is given only rank 8.

Summarizing the results, one can conclude that in the 1973 Helsinki statements, not only those categories among the ten highest-ranking categories are very much the same. Also the rank-order

Table 2.6. The 1973 Helsinki Statements: Rank-Order by Frequency of Categories Quoted by Delegations for Selected Aggregated Groups of Countries

NATO COUNTRIES

RANK	CODE	CATEGORY	%	CUMULATIVE %
1.	11	COOPERATION AMONG STATES AS A PRINCIPLE OF INTERNATIONAL RELATIONS	8.31	8.31
2.	1	BASKET ONE: QUESTIONS RELATING TO SECURITY IN EUROPE	7.61	15.92
3.	14	DOCUMENT ON CONFIDENCE-BUILDING MEASURES AND CERTAIN ASPECTS OF SECURITY AND DISARMAMENT	6.98	22.89
4.	103	PEACE	5.20	28.09
5.	104	CONFLICT AND CONFRONTATION	4.25	32.34
6.	2	GENERAL REMARKS CONCERNING THE DECLARATION ON PRINCIPLES GUIDING RELATIONS	3.80	36.14
7.	19	BASKET TWO: COOPERATION IN THE FIELD OF ECONOMICS, SCIENCE, TECHNOLOGY, AND THE ENVIRONMENT	3.61	39.76
8.	59	GENERAL REMARKS CONCERNING HUMAN CONTACTS	3.42	43.18
9.	119	SPECIFIC INTERNATIONAL AGREEMENTS	3.11	46.29
10.	114	POLITICAL COOPERATION AND POLITICAL DISCUSSIONS	2.79	49.08

WTO COUNTRIES

RANK	CODE	CATEGORY	%	CUMULATIVE %
1.	11	COOPERATION AMONG STATES AS A PRINCIPLE OF INTERNATIONAL RELATIONS	11.43	11.43
2.	103	PEACE	11.23	22.66
3.	1	BASKET ONE: QUESTIONS RELATING TO SECURITY IN EUROPE	9.38	32.03
4.	14	DOCUMENT ON CONFIDENCE-BUILDING MEASURES AND CERTAIN ASPECTS OF SECURITY AND DISARMAMENT	4.39	36.43
5.	119	SPECIFIC INTERNATIONAL AGREEMENTS	4.39	40.82
6.	104	CONFLICT AND CONFRONTATION	4.30	45.12
7.	19	BASKET TWO: COOPERATION IN THE FIELD OF ECONOMICS, SCIENCE, TECHNOLOGY, AND THE ENVIRONMENT	4.20	49.32
8.	114	POLITICAL COOPERATION AND POLITICAL DISCUSSIONS	3.71	53.03
9.	108	IDEOLOGY AND IDEAS	3.61	56.64
10.	5	INVIOLABILITY OF FRONTIERS	3.13	59.77

NEUTRAL AND NON-ALIGNED COUNTRIES

RANK	CODE	CATEGORY	%	CUMULATIVE %
1.	1	BASKET ONE: QUESTIONS RELATING TO SECURITY IN EUROPE	9.95	9.95
2.	11	COOPERATION AMONG STATES AS A PRINCIPLE OF INTERNATIONAL RELATIONS	9.95	19.89
3.	103	PEACE	7.76	27.65
4.	104	CONFLICT AND CONFRONTATION	5.02	32.66
5.	2	GENERAL REMARKS CONCERNING THE DECLARATION ON PRINCIPLES GUIDING RELATIONS	4.20	36.86
6.	16	QUESTIONS RELATING TO DISARMAMENT	3.74	40.60
7.	19	BASKET TWO: COOPERATION IN THE FIELD OF ECONOMICS, SCIENCE, TECHNOLOGY, AND THE ENVIRONMENT	3.47	44.07
8.	14	DOCUMENT ON CONFIDENCE-BUILDING MEASURES AND CERTAIN ASPECTS OF SECURITY AND DISARMAMENT	3.38	47.45
9.	7	PEACEFUL SETTLEMENT OF DISPUTES	2.83	50.27
10.	99	UN AND UN SPECIAL ORGANISATIONS	2.74	53.01

ALL CSCE COUNTRIES

RANK	CODE	CATEGORY	%	CUMULATIVE %
1.	11	COOPERATION AMONG STATES AS A PRINCIPLE OF INTERNATIONAL RELATIONS	9.68	9.68
2.	1	BASKET ONE: QUESTIONS RELATING TO SECURITY IN EUROPE	9.10	18.77
3.	103	PEACE	7.88	26.65
4.	14	DOCUMENT ON CONFIDENCE-BUILDING MEASURES AND CERTAIN ASPECTS OF SECURITY AND DISARMAMENT	5.10	31.76
5.	104	CONFLICT AND CONFRONTATION	4.42	36.18
6.	19	BASKET TWO: COOPERATION IN THE FIELD OF ECONOMICS, SCIENCE, TECHNOLOGY, AND THE ENVIRONMENT	3.66	39.84
7.	2	GENERAL REMARKS CONCERNING THE DECLARATION ON PRINCIPLES GUIDING RELATIONS	3.41	43.25
8.	119	SPECIFIC INTERNATIONAL AGREEMENTS	3.13	46.39
9.	108	IDEOLOGY AND IDEAS	2.75	49.14
10.	16	QUESTIONS RELATING TO DISARMAMENT	2.60	51.74

between groups does not differ considerably. The CSCE negotiations were initiated in a mood of general understanding and good will. Controversial issues were by and large excluded from the panel.

2.3.3 The 1975 Helsinki Statements

Two years later, in 1975, the general notion of "peace," not surprisingly, becomes the most favored category to be found in the thirty-five statements made by heads of state or government. The second and third rank also refer to very general categories: "security" and "cooperation." In retrospect, it is interesting to note that the category "human rights" ranks last among the top ten categories; for the NATO countries, "human rights" has rank 8 and rank 10 for the N + N group, while for the WTO group this issue ranks not among the ten most important themes. Still, in comparison with the beginning of the conference in 1973, "human rights" increases somewhat in importance since the inclusion of respective paragraphs into the Final Act among the ten principles guiding relations had been a difficult and controversial task. The comparison between groups again reveals some common elements. The similarities are obvious not only as far as the selection of categories is concerned; the rank-ordering also shows some common aspects beyond the bounds of traditional "camps." In all groups, "security" is the first or second category. "Cooperation" is found in all groups with rank 3 or 4. The other categories shared by all groups are: principles guiding relations, peace, conflict/confrontation, general references to "basket" 1 and to "basket" 2. Disarmament is also found in each of the groups. The picture of a relatively broad communality of views is confirmed in the following sections of this study. Maybe the existence of such a high number of values shared in common, as expressed by the similarity of profiles of those rank-orders, constitutes the very base that made possible the CSCE process.

2.3.4 The Belgrade Opening Statements

The overall view presented in Table 2.8 offers a picture quite distinct from the one offered by the two preceding Helsinki meetings. Now "disarmament" ranks high, and the issue of "human rights," which in 1975 was found at the bottom, emerges as the issues ranking second in importance to the thirty-five CSCE delegations. For the rest again a preference for relatively general categories such as "cooperation among states" and general references to the three "baskets" is paramount.

Table 2.8 displays the rank-order of categories for each group of countries. Again all groups seem to prefer basically the same categories among the top ten categories, but the rank-order observed differs considerably. One general characteristic is that all groups except the WTO group show human rights in one of the higher ranks. Another general characteristic is the importance of both "disarmament" and "economic cooperation" ("basket" 2) in the rank-order for all groups.

2.3.5 The Belgrade Closing Statements

The rank-order of categories mentioned by all thirty-five delegations shows a paramount importance of the human-rights issue, followed by the categories "disarmament" and "basket" 2 in general. The bottom categories in this rank-order of the top ten categories refers to "principles guiding relations."

As in the Helsinki and Belgrade opening statements, there are, however, differences among groups. The NATO countries are primarily concerned with human rights. In the WTO group, questions relating to disarmament and security rank highest. For the N + N group, general references to "basket" 2 are given priority. Again, as in the case of the Helsinki and Belgrade opening statements, all nations share in common a relatively large proportion of the top ten categories.

Thus the rank-order of the most-favored individual categories by groups of nations seems to offer an appropriate description of the situation of the CSCE process at the end of the Belgrade meeting, with the NATO and EC countries stressing human rights, while the WTO countries focus on disarmament and security with the N + N delegations trying to save the situation by putting emphasis on cooperation in general and economic cooperation in particular.

2.3.6 The Madrid Opening Statements

In the 1980 Madrid opening statements, the issue of "human rights" ranks still second in importance (highest ranking in the NATO group and fourth in the N + N group). However, "cooperation among states" (code 11) now becomes the most important theme (rank 2 in the NATO group, rank 1 in the WTO group, but only rank 7 in the N + N group). Obviously, the common determination to continue the CSCE process beyond all difficulties and controversies becomes manifest in the statements of the heads of delegations. While NATO countries and WTO countries apparently preferred very general appeals to maintain the momentum of the CSCE process, the neutral and nonaligned nations stressed some of their principal concerns, among them disarmament, security, and confidence-building measures.

2.3.7 From Helsinki to Madrid: The Shifting Emphasis on CSCE Issues

Two major changes have occurred as far as the comparison of the rank-order of the ten top-ranking categories from the Helsinki and Belgrade opening statements and final statements are concerned:

Table 2.7. The 1975 Helsinki Statements: Rank-Order by Frequency of Categories Quoted by Delegations for Selected Aggregated Groups of Countries

NATO COUNTRIES

RANK	CODE	CATEGORY	%	CUMULATIVE %
1.	17	QUESTIONS RELATING TO SECURITY	7.37	7.37
2.	2	GENERAL REMARKS CONCERNING THE DECLARATION ON PRINCIPLES GUIDING RELATIONS	6.80	14.18
3.	11	COOPERATION AMONG STATES AS A PRINCIPLE OF INTERNATIONAL RELATIONS	6.36	20.53
4.	1	BASKET ONE: QUESTIONS RELATING TO SECURITY IN EUROPE	5.47	26.00
5.	103	PEACE	5.40	31.40
6.	19	BASKET TWO: COOPERATION IN THE FIELD OF ECONOMICS, SCIENCE, TECHNOLOGY, AND THE ENVIRONMENT	5.15	36.55
7.	16	QUESTIONS RELATING TO DISARMAMENT	4.96	41.51
8.	9	RESPECT FOR HUMAN RIGHTS AND FUNDAMENTAL FREEDOMS	4.13	45.65
9.	104	CONFLICT AND CONFRONTATION	4.01	49.65
10.	98	INTERNATIONAL ORGANISATIONS OTHER THAN UN	3.37	53.02

WTO COUNTRIES

RANK	CODE	CATEGORY	%	CUMULATIVE %
1.	103	PEACE	13.47	13.47
2.	17	QUESTIONS RELATING TO SECURITY	8.42	21.89
3.	19	BASKET TWO: COOPERATION IN THE FIELD GF ECONOMICS, SCIENCE, TECHNOLOGY, AND THE ENVIRONMENT	8.42	30.31
4.	11	COOPERATION AMONG STATES AS A PRINCIPLE OF INTERNATIONAL RELATIONS	8.03	38.34
5.	1	BASKET ONE: QUESTIONS RELATING TO SECURITY IN EUROPE	7.25	45.60
6.	16	QUESTIONS RELATING TO DISARMAMENT	5.96	51.55
7.	104	CONFLICT AND CONFRONTATION	5.96	57.51
8.	2	GENERAL REMARKS CONCERNING THE DECLARATION ON PRINCIPLES GUIDING RELATIONS	4.92	62.44
9.	3	SOVEREIGN EQUALITY, RESPECT FOR THE RIGHTS INHERENT IN SOVEREIGNTY	3.89	66.32
10.	20	GENERAL REMARKS CONCERNING COMMERCIAL EXCHANGES	2.59	68.91

NEUTRAL AND NON-ALIGNED COUNTRIES

RANK	CODE	CATEGORY	%	CUMULATIVE %
1.	103	PEACE	8.84	8.84
2.	19	BASKET TWO: COOPERATION IN THE FIELD OF ECONOMICS, SCIENCE, TECHNOLOGY, AND THE ENVIRONMENT	7.65	16.48
3.	11	COOPERATION AMONG STATES AS A PRINCIPLE OF INTERNATIONAL RELATIONS	7.55	24.03
4.	17	QUESTIONS RELATING TO SECURITY	7.25	31.28
5.	1	BASKET ONE: QUESTIONS RELATING TO SECURITY IN EUROPE	6.95	38.23
6.	2	GENERAL REMARKS CONCERNING THE DECLARATION ON PRINCIPLES GUIDING RELATIONS	6.06	44.29
7.	104	CONFLICT AND CONFRONTATION	5.86	50.15
8.	3	SOVEREIGN EQUALITY, RESPECT FOR THE RIGHTS INHERENT IN SOVEREIGNTY	4.57	54.72
9.	16	QUESTIONS RELATING TO DISARMAMENT	2.98	57.70
10.	9	RESPECT FOR HUMAN RIGHTS AND FUNDAMENTAL FREEDOMS	2.48	60.18

ALL CSCE COUNTRIES

RANK	CODE	CATEGORY	%	CUMULATIVE %
1.	103	PEACE	8.77	8.77
2.	17	QUESTIONS RELATING TO SECURITY	7.59	16.36
3.	11	COOPERATION AMONG STATES AS A PRINCIPLE OF INTERNATIONAL RELATIONS	6.97	23.33
4.	19	BASKET TWO: COOPERATION IN THE FIELD OF ECONOMICS, SCIENCE, TECHNOLOGY, AND THE ENVIRONMENT	6.53	29.86
5.	1	BASKET ONE: QUESTIONS RELATING TO SECURITY IN EUROPE	6.36	36.22
6.	2	GENERAL REMARKS CONCERNING THE DECLARATION ON PRINCIPLES GUIDING RELATIONS	6.01	42.23
7.	104	CONFLICT AND CONFRONTATION	4.86	47.09
8.	16	QUESTIONS RELATING TO DISARMAMENT	4.51	51.60
9.	3	SOVEREIGN EQUALITY, RESPECT FOR THE RIGHTS INHERENT IN SOVEREIGNTY	3.25	54.85
10.	9	RESPECT FOR HUMAN RIGHTS AND FUNDAMENTAL FREEDOMS	2.73	57.58

Table 2.8. The Belgrade Opening Statements: Rank-Order by Frequency of Categories Quoted by Delegations for Selected Aggregated Groups of Countries

NATO COUNTRIES

RANK	CODE	CATEGORY	%	CUMULATIVE %
1.	9	RESPECT FOR HUMAN RIGHTS AND FUNDAMENTAL FREEDOMS	9.79	9.79
2.	11	COOPERATION AMONG STATES AS A PRINCIPLE OF INTERNATIONAL RELATIONS	6.32	16.11
3.	19	BASKET TWO: COOPERATION IN THE FIELD OF ECONOMICS, SCIENCE, TECHNOLOGY, AND THE ENVIRONMENT	6.28	22.39
4.	16	QUESTIONS RELATING TO DISARMAMENT	4.48	26.87
5.	17	QUESTIONS RELATING TO SECURITY	4.21	31.08
6.	2	GENERAL REMARKS CONCERNING THE DECLARATION ON PRINCIPLES GUIDING RELATIONS	4.17	35.25
7.	99	UN AND UN SPECIAL ORGANISATIONS	3.86	39.11
8.	1	BASKET ONE: QUESTIONS RELATING TO SECURITY IN EUROPE	3.51	42.63
9.	59	GENERAL REMARKS CONCERNING HUMAN CONTACTS	3.34	45.96
10.	14	DOCUMENT ON CONFIDENCE-BUILDING MEASURES AND CERTAIN ASPECTS OF SECURITY AND DISARMAMENT	2.81	48.77

WTO COUNTRIES

RANK	CODE	CATEGORY	%	CUMULATIVE %
1.	16	QUESTIONS RELATING TO DISARMAMENT	9.61	9.61
2.	17	QUESTIONS RELATING TO SECURITY	7.44	17.06
3.	1	BASKET ONE: QUESTIONS RELATING TO SECURITY IN EUROPE	6.57	23.62
4.	11	COOPERATION AMONG STATES AS A PRINCIPLE OF INTERNATIONAL RELATIONS	6.27	29.89
5.	19	BASKET TWO: COOPERATION IN THE FIELD OF ECONOMICS, SCIENCE, TECHNOLOGY, AND THE ENVIRONMENT	6.27	36.17
6.	103	PEACE	5.51	41.68
7.	119	SPECIFIC INTERNATIONAL AGREEMENTS	5.16	46.83
8.	97	INTERNATIONAL CONFERENCES	5.10	51.93
9.	2	GENERAL REMARKS CONCERNING THE DECLARATION ON PRINCIPLES GUIDING RELATIONS	4.69	56.62
10.	26	INDUSTRIAL COOPERATION AND PROJECTS OF COMMON INTEREST	2.99	59.61

NEUTRAL AND NON-ALIGNED COUNTRIES

RANK	CODE	CATEGORY	%	CUMULATIVE %
1.	16	QUESTIONS RELATING TO DISARMAMENT	9.30	9.30
2.	11	COOPERATION AMONG STATES AS A PRINCIPLE OF INTERNATIONAL RELATIONS	6.89	16.18
3.	19	BASKET TWO: COOPERATION IN THE FIELD OF ECONOMICS, SCIENCE, TECHNOLOGY, AND THE ENVIRONMENT	6.30	22.48
4.	9	RESPECT FOR HUMAN RIGHTS AND FUNDAMENTAL FREEDOMS	5.76	28.23
5.	17	QUESTIONS RELATING TO SECURITY	5.02	33.25
6.	1	BASKET ONE: QUESTIONS RELATING TO SECURITY IN EUROPE	3.94	37.19
7.	3	SOVEREIGN EQUALITY, RESPECT FOR THE RIGHTS INHERENT IN SOVEREIGNTY	3.59	40.78
8.	2	GENERAL REMARKS CONCERNING THE DECLARATION ON PRINCIPLES GUIDING RELATIONS	3.10	43.88
9.	99	UN AND UN SPECIAL ORGANISATIONS	2.90	46.78
10.	97	INTERNATIONAL CONFERENCES	2.71	49.48

ALL CSCE COUNTRIES

RANK	CODE	CATEGORY	%	CUMULATIVE %
1.	16	QUESTIONS RELATING TO DISARMAMENT	7.50	7.50
2.	9	RESPECT FOR HUMAN RIGHTS AND FUNDAMENTAL FREEDOMS	6.52	14.02
3.	11	COOPERATION AMONG STATES AS A PRINCIPLE OF INTERNATIONAL RELATIONS	6.40	20.42
4.	19	BASKET TWO: COOPERATION IN THE FIELD OF ECONOMICS, SCIENCE, TECHNOLOGY, AND THE ENVIRONMENT	6.10	26.51
5.	17	QUESTIONS RELATING TO SECURITY	5.39	31.90
6.	1	BASKET ONE: QUESTIONS RELATING TO SECURITY IN EUROPE	4.54	36.44
7.	2	GENERAL REMARKS CONCERNING THE DECLARATION ON PRINCIPLES GUIDING RELATIONS	3.81	40.25
8.	103	PEACE	3.17	43.42
9.	119	SPECIFIC INTERNATIONAL AGREEMENTS	3.09	46.50
10.	97	INTERNATIONAL CONFERENCES	2.90	49.40

Table 2.9. The Belgrade Closing Statements: Rank-Order by Frequency of Categories Quoted by Delegations for Selected Aggregated Groups of Countries

NATO COUNTRIES

RANK	CODE	CATEGORY	%	CUMULATIVE %
1.	9	RESPECT FOR HUMAN RIGHTS AND FUNDAMENTAL FREEDOMS	18.23	18.23
2.	16	QUESTIONS RELATING TO DISARMAMENT	7.86	26.09
3.	19	BASKET TWO: COOPERATION IN THE FIELD OF ECONOMICS, SCIENCE, TECHNOLOGY, AND THE ENVIRONMENT	6.33	32.42
4.	11	COOPERATION AMONG STATES AS A PRINCIPLE OF INTERNATIONAL RELATIONS	6.00	38.43
5.	58	BASKET THREE: COOPERATION IN HUMANITARIAN AND OTHER FIELDS	5.24	43.67
6.	59	GENERAL REMARKS CONCERNING HUMAN CONTACTS	4.26	47.93
7.	17	QUESTIONS RELATING TO SECURITY	3.28	51.20
8.	1	BASKET ONE: QUESTIONS RELATING TO SECURITY IN EUROPE	2.95	54.15
9.	2	GENERAL REMARKS CONCERNING THE DECLARATION ON PRINCIPLES GUIDING RELATIONS	2.84	56.99
10.	70	IMPROVEMENT OF THE CIRCULATION, ACCESS TO, AND EXCHANGE OF INFORMATION	2.84	59.83

WTO COUNTRIES

RANK	CODE	CATEGORY	%	CUMULATIVE %
1.	16	QUESTIONS RELATING TO DISARMAMENT	16.29	16.29
2.	17	QUESTIONS RELATING TO SECURITY	10.33	26.62
3.	19	BASKET TWO: COOPERATION IN THE FIELD OF ECONOMICS, SCIENCE, TECHNOLOGY, AND THE ENVIRONMENT	7.77	34.40
4.	11	COOPERATION AMONG STATES AS A PRINCIPLE OF INTERNATIONAL RELATIONS	6.50	40.89
5.	1	BASKET ONE: QUESTIONS RELATING TO SECURITY IN EUROPE	6.07	46.96
6.	103	PEACE	6.07	53.04
7.	9	RESPECT FOR HUMAN RIGHTS AND FUNDAMENTAL FREEDOMS	5.43	58.47
8.	14	DOCUMENT ON CONFIDENCE-BUILDING MEASURES AND CERTAIN ASPECTS OF SECURITY AND DISARMAMENT	3.41	61.87
9.	2	GENERAL REMARKS CONCERNING THE DECLARATION ON PRINCIPLES GUIDING RELATIONS	2.98	64.86
10.	97	INTERNATIONAL CONFERENCES	2.98	67.84

NEUTRAL AND NON-ALIGNED COUNTRIES

RANK	CODE	CATEGORY	%	CUMULATIVE %
1.	9	RESPECT FOR HUMAN RIGHTS AND FUNDAMENTAL FREEDOMS	11.72	11.72
2.	19	BASKET TWO: COOPERATION IN THE FIELD OF ECONOMICS, SCIENCE, TECHNOLOGY, AND THE ENVIRONMENT	10.44	22.16
3.	11	COOPERATION AMONG STATES AS A PRINCIPLE OF INTERNATIONAL RELATIONS	8.97	31.14
4.	16	QUESTIONS RELATING TO DISARMAMENT	6.23	37.36
5.	14	DOCUMENT ON CONFIDENCE-BUILDING MEASURES AND CERTAIN ASPECTS OF SECURITY AND DISARMAMENT	6.04	43.41
6.	17	QUESTIONS RELATING TO SECURITY	5.68	49.08
7.	1	BASKET ONE: QUESTIONS RELATING TO SECURITY IN EUROPE	5.31	54.40
8.	58	BASKET THREE: COOPERATION IN HUMANITARIAN AND OTHER FIELDS	5.13	59.52
9.	2	GENERAL REMARKS CONCERNING THE DECLARATION ON PRINCIPLES GUIDING RELATIONS	4.58	64.10
10.	103	PEACE	3.48	67.58

ALL CSCE COUNTRIES

RANK	CODE	CATEGORY	%	CUMULATIVE %
1.	9	RESPECT FOR HUMAN RIGHTS AND FUNDAMENTAL FREEDOMS	11.69	11.69
2.	16	QUESTIONS RELATING TO DISARMAMENT	10.59	22.28
3.	19	BASKET TWO: COOPERATION IN THE FIELD OF ECONOMICS, SCIENCE, TECHNOLOGY, AND THE ENVIRONMENT	7.86	30.14
4.	11	COOPERATION AMONG STATES AS A PRINCIPLE OF INTERNATIONAL RELATIONS	6.88	37.02
5.	17	QUESTIONS RELATING TO SECURITY	6.41	43.43
6.	1	BASKET ONE: QUESTIONS RELATING TO SECURITY IN EUROPE	4.65	48.08
7.	103	PEACE	3.87	51.95
8.	14	DOCUMENT ON CONFIDENCE-BUILDING MEASURES AND CERTAIN ASPECTS OF SECURITY AND DISARMAMENT	3.67	55.63
9.	58	BASKET THREE: COOPERATION IN HUMANITARIAN AND OTHER FIELDS	3.60	59.23
10.	2	GENERAL REMARKS CONCERNING THE DECLARATION ON PRINCIPLES GUIDING RELATIONS	3.17	62.39

Table 2.10. The Madrid Opening Statements: Rank-Order by Frequency of Categories Quoted by Delegations for Selected Aggregated Groups of Countries

NATO COUNTRIES

RANK	CODE	CATEGORY	%	CUMULATIVE %
1.	9	RESPECT FOR HUMAN RIGHTS AND FUNDAMENTAL FREEDOMS	11.43	11.43
2.	11	COOPERATION AMONG STATES AS A PRINCIPLE OF INTERNATIONAL RELATIONS	6.90	18.34
3.	14	DOCUMENT ON CONFIDENCE-BUILDING MEASURES AND CERTAIN ASPECTS OF SECURITY AND DISARMAMENT	6.34	24.67
4.	16	QUESTIONS RELATING TO DISARMAMENT	5.09	29.77
5.	17	QUESTIONS RELATING TO SECURITY	4.70	34.47
6.	114	POLITICAL COOPERATION AND POLITICAL DISCUSSIONS	3.45	37.92
7.	59	GENERAL REMARKS CONCERNING HUMAN CONTACTS	3.34	41.26
8.	103	PEACE	3.17	44.43
9.	104	CONFLICT AND CONFRONTATION	3.17	47.59
10.	2	GENERAL REMARKS CONCERNING THE DECLARATION ON PRINCIPLES GUIDING RELATIONS	2.89	50.48

WTO COUNTRIES

RANK	CODE	CATEGORY	%	CUMULATIVE %
1.	11	COOPERATION AMONG STATES AS A PRINCIPLE OF INTERNATIONAL RELATIONS	10.52	10.52
2.	14	DOCUMENT ON CONFIDENCE-BUILDING MEASURES AND CERTAIN ASPECTS OF SECURITY AND DISARMAMENT	9.91	20.43
3.	103	PEACE	8.78	29.22
4.	16	QUESTIONS RELATING TO DISARMAMENT	6.87	36.09
5.	97	INTERNATIONAL CONFERENCES	5.48	41.57
6.	1	BASKET ONE: QUESTIONS RELATING TO SECURITY IN EUROPE	4.87	46.43
7.	17	QUESTIONS RELATING TO SECURITY	4.87	51.30
8.	104	CONFLICT AND CONFRONTATION	4.87	56.17
9.	114	POLITICAL COOPERATION AND POLITICAL DISCUSSIONS	4.26	60.43
10.	119	SPECIFIC INTERNATIONAL AGREEMENTS	3.65	64.09

NEUTRAL AND NON-ALIGNED COUNTRIES

RANK	CODE	CATEGORY	%	CUMULATIVE %
1.	16	QUESTIONS RELATING TO DISARMAMENT	9.10	9.10
2.	14	DOCUMENT ON CONFIDENCE-BUILDING MEASURES AND CERTAIN ASPECTS OF SECURITY AND DISARMAMENT	5.97	15.07
3.	17	QUESTIONS RELATING TO SECURITY	5.79	20.86
4.	9	RESPECT FOR HUMAN RIGHTS AND FUNDAMENTAL FREEDOMS	5.61	26.47
5.	103	PEACE	5.61	32.08
6.	104	CONFLICT AND CONFRONTATION	5.61	37.68
7.	11	COOPERATION AMONG STATES AS A PRINCIPLE OF INTERNATIONAL RELATIONS	4.96	42.65
8.	97	INTERNATIONAL CONFERENCES	4.69	47.33
9.	114	POLITICAL COOPERATION AND POLITICAL DISCUSSIONS	3.77	51.10
10.	2	GENERAL REMARKS CONCERNING THE DECLARATION ON PRINCIPLES GUIDING RELATIONS	3.31	54.41

ALL CSCE COUNTRIES

RANK	CODE	CATEGORY	%	CUMULATIVE %
1.	11	COOPERATION AMONG STATES AS A PRINCIPLE OF INTERNATIONAL RELATIONS	7.63	7.63
2.	9	RESPECT FOR HUMAN RIGHTS AND FUNDAMENTAL FREEDOMS	7.24	14.88
3.	14	DOCUMENT ON CONFIDENCE-BUILDING MEASURES AND CERTAIN ASPECTS OF SECURITY AND DISARMAMENT	7.24	22.12
4.	16	QUESTIONS RELATING TO DISARMAMENT	6.39	28.51
5.	103	PEACE	5.59	34.10
6.	17	QUESTIONS RELATING TO SECURITY	5.13	39.24
7.	104	CONFLICT AND CONFRONTATION	4.42	43.66
8.	97	INTERNATIONAL CONFERENCES	3.90	47.56
9.	114	POLITICAL COOPERATION AND POLITICAL DISCUSSIONS	3.71	51.27
10.	1	BASKET ONE: QUESTIONS RELATING TO SECURITY IN EUROPE	2.93	54.21

(1) the importance of the human-rights issue has increased; and (2) the relative homogeneity of the rank-orders for all groups has disappeared.

The interpretation of these findings is difficult, however, for two reasons. First, the aggregation for groups of countries according to the scheme of "camps" and geographical location is not fully justified, as is suggested by the sequence of the ten highest-ranking categories for the individual countries presented in Appendix A2.3. Second, the rank-order of individual categories can be justified as meaningful only if these categories are mutually exclusive and uncorrelated and if the categories themselves belong to the same level of aggregation. This is obviously not the case.

Nevertheless, one might interpret the findings regarding the comparison of rank-orders as an evidence of increasing difficulties in the CSCE process. But still the question has to be asked whether it might be possible to find a basis for aggregation of categories that does not follow the scheme of "baskets" of the Final Act since "baskets" are not sufficiently homogeneous to allow such an aggregation. A solution to this problem is proposed in the following chapter by means of a factor analysis.

2.4 THE CRUCIAL DIMENSIONS IN EAST-WEST RELATIONS: A FACTOR ANALYSIS

2.4.1 Introduction

In the two preceding sections of Chapter 2, the perceptions expressed by the thirty-five delegations to the CSCE meetings held in Helsinki in 1973 and 1975, Belgrade in 1977/78, and Madrid in 1980/81 were analyzed in terms of "baskets" (Section 2.2) and by looking at the rank-order of the most preferred categories (Section 2.3). These two approaches somehow constitute two extremes, the first offering a general view only, the second pointing at individual categories only. The official "baskets," although offering the advantage of an "authorized" grouping together of issues, to some extent also lack coherence and clarity; for example, issues concerning the field of human rights can be found in the principles guiding relations, as part of the first "basket" as well as the third "basket."

In this section, another mode of aggregation will be suggested by using a factor-analytical research technique. Factor analysis is a common technique of aggregation in content analysis (see, for example, the work of Iker and his collaborators). Especially in the case of this study, with a set of categories that are mutually not exclusive but overlap considerably, aggregation by factor analysis solves some of the problems envisaged in the previous analysis of simple category scores. The objective is descriptive rather than theoretical. Factor analysis is a statistical procedure that helps to identify latent structures in data; it looks for underlying similarities and thus yields arrangements of categories that, due to the statistical nature of the distribution of frequencies observed, belong together.

Each set of statements will be factor analyzed separately, based on the forty most frequent categories representing a share of 78.9 percent of the sum total of categories mentioned in all sets of statements. The results summarized in the following tables present a sequence of ten factors for each of the five sets, indicating also the fraction of variance "loaded" by the individual categories on the factor concerned. The forty categories that entered the factor-analytical computation are listed in Table 2.11.

After having thus determined the factors underlying each set of statements, an additional step will be made in order to find out the relative importance of the ten factors for the individual countries and groups of countries. This task will be done by calculating factor scores for each country. (For more detailed information regarding this application of factor analytical techniques, see Appendix A2.4)

2.4.2 The 1973 Helsinki Statements

When the thirty-five delegations in 1973 made their statements on the overall perspectives of cooperation and security in Europe, they were referring to "cooperation" in very general terms, and they did not spend much time on specifying the types of cooperation they would prefer. This finding clearly emerges from the results of the factor analysis presented in Table 2.12. As this table shows, 49 percent of the attention was devoted to the general factor cooperation and conflict. The structure of East–West cooperation was not yet apparent to the delegates except for a general interest in cooperation and in diminishing the intensity of conflict existing between East and West. The issues that in the subsequent phases of CSCE became so important (such as human contacts, human rights, and economic cooperation) were mentioned, but the percentage of attention they caught is clearly inferior to the paramount general concern for cooperation and conflict. Among the more specific factors only disarmament, confidence-building, and security had some importance.

2.4.3 The 1975 Helsinki Statements

By 1975 the structure of factors underlying the statements made by the heads of state or government had become more elaborate. Although, as in 1973, the general factor cooperation and conflict attracts the largest share of attention (36 percent), other issues of East–West relations now emerge with increasing strength. The principles guiding relations are very much emphasized, as is the general desire for strengthening security. Human contacts and

Table 2.11. Selected Categories Entering the Computations of the Factor Analysis and Shares of Attention (in Percentages) in all CSCE Statements

No.	Category	% Attention
1	Basket One: Questions Relating to Security in Europe	5.0
2	Principles Guiding Relations	3.5
3	Sovereign Equality, Respect for the Rights Inherent in Sovereignty	1.7
4	Refrain from the Threat of Use of Force	1.0
5	Inviolability of Frontiers	0.5
7	Peaceful Settlement of Disputes	0.9
8	Non-intervention in Internal Affairs	0.9
9	Respect for Human Rights and Fundamental Freedoms	5.2
11	Cooperation among States	7.0
14	Confidence-building Measures	3.6
15	Prior Notification of Military Maneuvers	0.7
16	Questions Relating to Disarmament	5.8
17	Questions Relating to Security	4.9
19	Cooperation in the Field of Economics, Science, Technology, Environment	4.8
20	Commercial Exchanges	1.4
26	Industrial Cooperation	0.9
46	Development of Transport	0.4
48	Economic and Social Aspects of Migrant Labor	0.4
51	Questions Concerning the Mediterranean	1.0
58	Cooperation in Humanitarian Fields	1.7
59	Human Contacts	1.7

Table 2.11. *(continued)*

No.	Category	% Attention
69	Questions Relating to Information	0.9
70	Exchange of Information	0.9
74	Cooperation and Exchange in the Field of Culture	1.0
94	Dangers of Nuclear Proliferation	0.3
95	Energy Problems	0.5
97	International Conferences	2.4
98	International Organizations Other than UN	1.2
99	UN and UN Special Organizations	1.5
103	Peace	5.3
104	Conflict and Confrontation	3.1
108	Ideological Confrontation	1.3
109	Freedom	0.6
111	Welfare and Prosperity	0.6
112	Responsibility of Participating States	0.9
114	Political Cooperation and Political Discussions	1.3
115	Religious Freedom	0.4
117	Questions Relating to Developing Countries	0.7
119	Specific Agreements and Treaties	2.1
120	Stability, Strategic and Political Balance	0.9
Total		78.9

Table 2.12. Dimensions Represented in the Factor Structure of the 1973 Helsinki Statements

No.	Dimension Name	Loaded by Categories No.	Mean % of Attention
1	Cooperation and Conflict	1, 2, 3, 11, 14, 17, 19, 51, 98, 99, 103, 104, 108, 109, 111, 112, 114, 117, 119, 120	49
2	Sovereignty	1, 2, 3, 4, 5, 7, 8, 9, 99, 103, 115	8
3	Human Contacts	11, 14, 58, 59, 69, 70, 74, 108	7
4	Transport and Energy Problems	19, 46, 95, 117	2
5	Political Cooperation and Conferences	1, 11, 14, 16, 17, 94, 97, 103, 104, 108, 114, 119	8
6	Disarmament and Confidence-building Measures, Security	1, 14, 15, 16, 17, 104, 119, 120	13
7	Human Rights	2, 7, 8, 9, 17, 58, 108, 109, 115	1
8	Economic Cooperation	19, 20, 108, 111, 112, 117	5
9	United Nations	1, 2, 5, 9, 11, 99, 119	6
10	Special Aspects of Economic Cooperation	11, 19, 26, 46, 48	1

other more specific factors, however, still get minor shares of attention. (When comparing the 1975 statements with the 1973 and other sets of statements it should be noted that the factors are not completely identical in each set, as each set was factor analyzed individually. For an overall comparative analysis of the shifts in emphasis expressed between 1973 and 1980, see Section 2.4.7, which offers an analysis based on a factor structure underlying the aggregated totality of all statements.)

Table 2.13. Dimensions Represented in the Factor Structure of the 1975 Helsinki Statements

No.	Dimension Name	Loaded by Categories No.	Mean % of Attention
1	Principles Guiding Relations	1, 2, 3, 4, 5, 6, 8, 9, 11, 17, 46, 99, 103, 104	19
2	Human Contacts	9, 11, 19, 20, 58, 59, 69, 70, 74, 108	7
3	Cooperation and Conflict	1, 11, 17, 19, 20, 98, 103, 104, 108, 117	36
4	Security	1, 2, 3, 11, 17, 19, 98, 103, 104, 108, 117	17
5	Industrial Cooperation	5, 8, 19, 20, 26, 46	0
6	Disarmament	7, 15, 16, 17, 97, 104, 119	6
7	Welfare and Prosperity	3, 9, 58, 103, 108, 109, 111, 117, 120	2
8	International Global Problems	1, 17, 19, 20, 94, 97, 99, 103, 104, 111, 112, 117, 119, 120	9
9	Confidence-building Measures	14, 15, 16, 17, 20, 97	2
10	Ideological Confrontation and Exchange of Ideas	9, 26, 46, 70, 108, 109	2

2.4.4 The Belgrade Opening Statements

Three years later, at the opening of the Belgrade meeting of the CSCE in 1977, the shift from a vague support for cooperation in general toward more specific concerns has become more articulate. At the same time the various concerns are beginning to cluster around a number of main focal issues, particularly economic coop-

Table 2.14. Dimensions Represented in the Factor Structure of the Belgrade Opening Statements

No.	Dimension Name	Loaded by Categories No.	Mean % of Attention
1	Economic Cooperation	1, 2, 3, 11, 17, 19, 58, 103, 104, 108, 111, 112, 119, 120	23
2	Commercial and Industrial Cooperation	19, 20, 26, 97, 99, 117	6
3	Security	1, 11, 17, 19, 103	16
4	Human Contacts and Information Exchange	9, 11, 58, 59, 69, 70, 74	9
5	Disarmament and Confidence-building Measures	1, 3, 11, 14, 15, 16, 17, 19, 97, 103, 104, 112, 114, 119, 120	23
6	Energy Problems and Transportation	46, 95	1
7	Peaceful Settlement of Disputes	1, 2, 3, 4, 5, 7, 8	2
8	Inviolability of Frontiers	3, 4, 5, 8, 119	3
9	International Organizations	11, 19, 20, 26, 48, 51, 97, 98, 99, 117, 119	7
10	Human Rights	2, 3, 9, 58, 103, 104, 108, 109, 111, 112, 115	10

eration (23 percent), disarmament and confidence-building measures (23 percent), and security (16 percent). The human-rights issue (10 percent) is also gaining increased importance; together with the related concern for human contacts and exchange of information (9 percent), it accounts for 19 percent of the overall distribution of attention.

2.4.5 The Belgrade Closing Statements

As the Belgrade meeting of the CSCE was considerably determined by heated arguments about the human-rights issues and other controversial issues, it is not surprising to see (Table 2.15) that the

Table 2.15. Dimensions Represented in the Factor Structure of the Belgrade Closing Statements

No.	Dimension Name	Loaded by Categories No.	Mean % of Attention
1	Security	1, 11, 14, 16, 17, 19, 74, 103	16
2	Commercial and Industrial Cooperation	20, 26, 74, 97, 99	5
3	Transport and Energy Problems	46, 95, 97	3
4	Cooperation, General	1, 2, 11, 17, 19, 103	22
5	Human Rights and Human Contacts	2, 9, 26, 58, 59, 69, 70, 74, 103	27
6	Disarmament	2, 9, 14, 16, 17, 58, 97, 104, 108, 114, 117	22
7	Freedom	9, 109, 119	0
8	Sovereignty	2, 3, 4, 7, 8, 9, 103, 104, 120	3
9	Strategic Problems	3, 14, 15, 16, 97, 120	1
10	Inviolability of Frontiers	2, 5, 9, 115	1

delegations in their closing statements gave emphasis to the respective factors. Accounting for a share of 27 percent paramount attention was paid to the issue of human rights and human contacts. Yet, with regard to the relative importance, it is nearly matched by the issues of cooperation in general (22 percent), disarmament (22 percent), and security (16 percent). The interest in commercial and industrial cooperation now drops to a mere 5 percent.

2.4.6 The Madrid Opening Statements

By 1980, when the delegations of the thirty-five CSCE member countries met again in Madrid, the situation had changed again (Table 2.16). Now it is no longer the human-rights issue that is catching the main share of attention; the respective percentage

Table 2.16. Dimensions Represented in the Factor Structure of the Madrid Opening Statements

No.	Dimension Name	Loaded by Categories No.	Mean % of Attention
1	Disarmament	1, 7, 11, 14, 16, 17, 94, 97, 99, 103, 104, 114, 119, 120	28
2	Sovereignty	2, 3, 4, 5, 7, 8, 99, 103, 104	10
3	Human Contacts	9, 19, 58, 59, 69, 70, 74, 108	8
4	Cooperation and Conflict	1, 2, 3, 11, 17, 51, 103, 104, 108, 112, 114, 117, 119, 120	24
5	Commercial and Industrial Cooperation	20, 26, 46, 95	0
6	Economic Cooperation	11, 19, 20, 46, 48, 69, 74, 95, 117, 119	7
7	Human Rights and Freedom	2, 9, 58, 103, 108, 109, 115	13
8	Peace, Welfare, Prosperity	1, 11, 17, 19, 74, 98, 103, 111, 119	8
9	Peaceful Settlement of Disputes	3, 4, 7, 114	1
10	Security Problems	14, 15, 17, 94, 103, 120	0

figure is 13 percent; if added to the 8 percent of attention devoted to human contacts, the overall share for this concern accounts for 21 percent, which is still below the 28 percent attributed to disarmament and the 24 percent attributed to cooperation and conflict in general.

2.4.7 From Helsinki to Madrid: Shifting Concerns for Ten Major Factors

In this subsection, the factor analysis will be carried further by identifying the ten major factors underlying the totality of the

Table 2.17. Dimensions Represented in the Factor Structure of All Five Sets of Statements

No.	Dimension Name	Loaded by Categories No.	Mean % of Attention
1	Human Contacts and Free Flow of Information	9, 11, 58, 59, 70, 74, 108	9
2	Sovereignty and Territorial Integrity	1, 2, 3, 4, 5, 6, 8, 9, 11, 17, 99, 103, 104	11
3	Disarmament and Confidence-building Measures	1, 11, 14, 15, 16, 17, 94, 97, 103, 104	19
4	Commercial and Industrial Cooperation	19, 20, 26, 99, 117	3
5	Cooperation, General	1, 11, 17, 19, 103, 104, 108	15
6	Security	1, 11, 15, 17, 19, 103	12
7	Transportation and Energy	46, 95	1
8	Peace, Conflict, and Ideological Confrontation	1, 2, 3, 11, 17, 19, 103, 104, 109, 111, 112, 114, 117, 119, 120	17
9	International Organizations	1, 2, 3, 19, 20, 26, 51, 97, 98, 99, 119	5
10	Human Rights and Religious Freedom	2, 9, 58, 108, 109, 111, 115	8

statements held at the various CSCE meetings between 1973 and 1980. Looking at the factor structure emerging on these broadened data base yields a more balanced picture of the concerns expressed, by the official spokesmen of the thirty-five CSCE nations, during the whole era of negotiations. Three factors seem to be of overriding importance: disarmament and confidence-building measures (19 percent), peace, conflict, and ideological confrontation (17 percent), and cooperation in general (15 percent). They also seem to constitute what might be called the general "spirit of détente"—a grave concern about the never-ending arms race and a very general, sometimes rather vague and fuzzy desire for more cooperation and peaceful resolution of conflicts. This general thrust is also confirmed by the share of attention devoted to factors such as the concern for security (12 percent) and for sovereignty and territorial integrity (11 percent). It must be noted, however, that the two factors human contacts and free flow of information (9 percent) and human rights and religious freedom (8 percent), if taken together, also account for a sum of 17 percent; the importance of this controversial issue obviously had a decisive impact on the possibilities to achieve tangible progress in the sense of the "spirit of détente" as reflected by the three main factors. Finally, and somehow surprisingly, issues of commercial and industrial cooperation (3 percent) and cooperation in the field of transportation and energy (1 percent) came out to be of clearly inferior importance in the overall context of the seven years of East–West negotiations. In the following tables (Tables 2.18–2.22) the attention distribution on the ten dimensions identified in this step of the analysis is presented, broken down by statements and groups of countries. Of course, this general picture must be modified considerably when looking at the preferences expressed by the individual countries. Some countries seem to specialize in expressing their concern for human-rights issues; chief among them are the Holy See, the USA, the Netherlands, the United Kingdom, Iceland, and Norway. On the other hand, the concern for disarmament and confidence-building measures is gravest in the countries such as Sweden (which seems to promote the cause of disarmament as an expression of a kind of national mission), the German Democratic Republic, Norway, the USSR, Czechoslovakia, Denmark, Poland, and Romania, in other words, Nordic countries and WTO member countries.

A further elaboration of this tendency toward specialization on certain issues is presented in a frequency block chart (Graph 2.2) which offers a survey of the percentage distribution of attention scores for five master factors by group of countries. For the convenience of the reader, the percentage figures for related factors are collapsed into master dimensions according to the following formula:

Transformation of the Ten Factors into Five Master Dimensions

Master Dimension	*Original Factor Number*	*Percent Share of Attention*
Disarmament and security	3 + 6	31
Peace and conflict	8 + 9	22
Economic cooperation	4 + 5 + 7	19
Human rights and contacts	1 + 10	17
Sovereignty and independence	2	11

Graph 2.2. Distribution of Attention on Dimensions of East–West Relations: A Frequency Block Chart

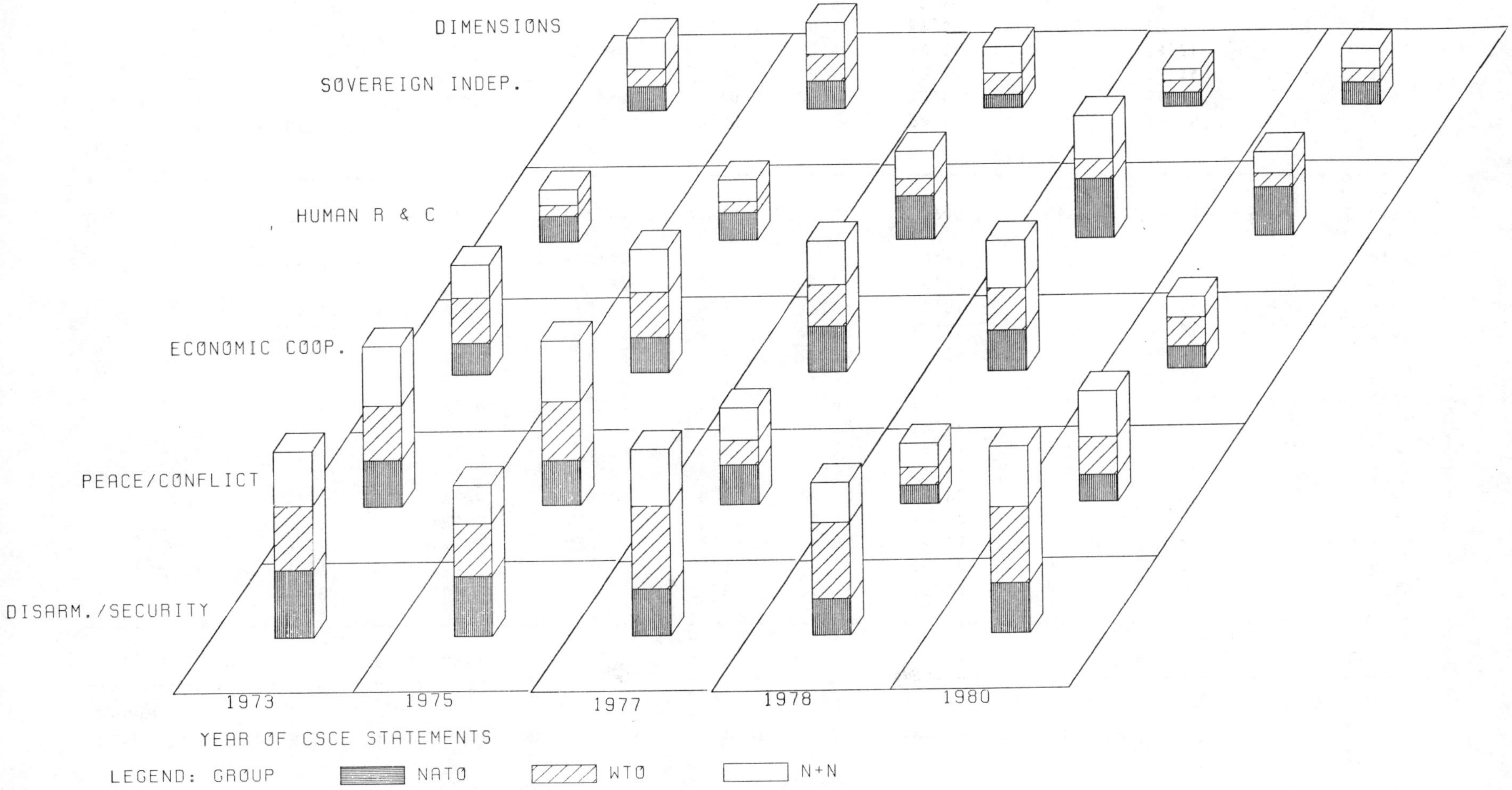
DIMENSIONS
SØVEREIGN INDEP.
HUMAN R & C
ECONØMIC COOP.
PEACE/CØNFLICT
DISARM./SECURITY
1973
1975
1977
1978
1980
YEAR ØF CSCE STATEMENTS
LEGEND: GRØUP
NATØ
WTØ
N+N

Table 2.18. The 1973 Helsinki Statements: Distribution of Attention on the Ten Dimensions of East–West Relations

	COUNTRY	HUMAN CONTACT	SOVEREIGNTY	DISARMAMENT	ECONOMIC COOP.	COOP. GENERAL	SECURITY	TRANSPORT ENERGY	PEACE CONFLICT	INTERN. ORGANIS.	HUMAN RIGHTS
1 NATO											
	BLGM	13.86	10.89	20.79	.99	20.79	5.94	0.0	19.80	1.98	4.95
	CNDA	15.00	11.67	21.67	0.0	16.67	15.00	0.0	20.00	0.0	0.0
	DNMK	21.62	14.86	24.32	2.70	14.86	6.76	0.0	9.46	1.35	4.05
	FRNC	2.99	10.45	17.91	2.99	10.45	19.40	0.0	28.36	2.99	4.48
	FRG	12.71	11.86	18.64	0.0	24.58	5.93	.85	21.19	2.54	1.69
	GRCE	6.45	10.75	11.83	0.0	19.35	12.90	3.23	31.18	4.30	0.0
	ICLD	11.11	2.22	33.33	0.0	15.56	13.33	0.0	20.00	2.22	2.22
	ITLY	9.72	9.72	22.22	0.0	15.28	18.06	0.0	15.28	5.56	4.17
	LXBG	9.68	13.98	22.58	0.0	11.83	15.05	0.0	19.35	4.30	3.23
	NTHL	6.41	16.67	23.08	1.28	6.41	15.38	1.28	17.95	7.69	3.85
	NRWY	8.33	8.33	26.19	4.76	19.05	14.29	0.0	16.67	0.0	2.38
	PRTG	9.18	13.27	16.33	0.0	16.33	17.35	0.0	25.51	2.04	0.0
	TRKY	.94	18.87	13.21	0.0	17.92	13.21	2.83	22.64	10.38	0.0
	UK	11.67	1.67	31.67	5.00	6.67	18.33	0.0	21.67	3.33	0.0
	USA	18.95	17.89	22.11	0.0	3.16	8.42	0.0	22.11	2.11	5.26
MEAN		10.5751	11.5403	21.7250	1.1815	14.5931	13.2905	.5457	20.7440	3.3859	2.4188
WTO											
	BLGR	13.92	8.86	12.66	2.53	20.25	20.25	0.0	20.25	1.27	0.0
	CZCH	6.02	6.02	9.64	1.20	28.92	12.05	4.82	31.33	0.0	0.0
	GDR	2.48	15.70	23.14	0.0	16.53	12.40	.83	23.14	5.79	0.0
	HNGR	4.71	1.18	22.35	9.41	25.88	10.59	0.0	24.71	1.18	0.0
	PLND	8.63	8.63	21.58	0.0	20.14	19.42	.72	17.27	2.88	.72
	RMNA	3.82	12.74	22.93	0.0	15.92	12.10	1.27	29.30	1.91	0.0
	USSR	4.02	12.56	20.10	.50	12.56	12.56	0.0	35.68	1.01	1.01
MEAN		6.2297	9.3855	18.9148	1.9501	20.0300	14.1965	1.0913	25.9527	2.0030	.2463

N+N											
	AUST	5.56	10.00	14.44	0.0	13.33	15.56	1.11	25.56	5.56	8.89
	CYPR	.94	25.47	15.09	0.0	16.04	13.21	0.0	16.98	12.26	0.0
	FNLD	6.00	10.00	14.00	0.0	21.00	18.00	1.00	28.00	2.00	0.0
	IRLD	5.77	10.90	17.95	0.0	12.82	11.54	0.0	30.13	9.62	1.28
	LICH	8.33	20.83	8.33	0.0	25.00	12.50	0.0	20.83	0.0	4.17
	MLTA	3.28	8.20	13.11	0.0	22.95	22.95	0.0	14.75	14.75	0.0
	SANM	1.11	22.22	5.56	0.0	11.11	4.44	0.0	42.22	0.0	13.33
	SWDN	8.59	9.38	23.44	0.0	19.53	8.59	4.69	20.31	5.47	0.0
	SWTZ	7.32	26.83	12.20	0.0	9.76	17.07	0.0	26.83	0.0	0.0
	YGSL	3.51	13.16	8.77	0.0	15.79	25.44	0.0	22.81	6.14	4.39
MEAN		5.0411	15.6984	13.2896	0.0	16.7330	14.9302	.6799	24.8423	5.5798	3.2057
OTHER											
	MNCO	0.0	0.0	15.38	0.0	7.69	30.77	0.0	15.38	30.77	0.0
	SPAN	9.52	3.81	9.52	2.86	20.95	20.00	.95	20.00	12.38	0.0
	VATC	2.15	15.05	9.68	0.0	10.75	20.43	0.0	38.71	0.0	3.23
MEAN		3.8914	6.2878	11.5286	.9524	13.1325	23.7331	.3175	24.6981	14.3834	1.0753
MEAN		7.5520	11.8472	17.8789	.9780	16.1667	14.8353	.6736	23.2956	4.6788	2.0940

Table 2.19. The 1975 Helsinki Statements: Distribution of Attention on the Ten Dimensions of East–West Relations

	COUNTRY	HUMAN CONTACT	SOVEREIGNTY	DISARMAMENT	ECONOMIC COOP.	COOP. GENERAL	SECURITY	TRANSPORT ENERGY	PEACE CONFLICT	INTERN. ORGANIS.	HUMAN RIGHTS
2 NATO											
	BLGM	6.45	16.13	22.58	.81	14.52	24.19	0.0	8.06	4.03	3.23
	CNDA	1.56	4.69	21.88	10.94	10.94	20.31	0.0	26.56	1.56	1.56
	DNMK	27.87	1.64	19.67	4.92	14.75	22.95	0.0	3.28	4.92	0.0
	FRNC	12.12	3.03	3.03	0.0	9.09	33.33	0.0	30.30	9.09	0.0
	FRG	5.13	12.82	37.18	10.26	8.97	3.85	0.0	21.79	0.0	0.0
	GRCE	0.0	56.92	7.69	3.08	9.23	7.69	0.0	9.23	6.15	0.0
	ICLD	37.50	8.93	10.71	10.71	12.50	14.29	0.0	0.0	5.36	0.0
	ITLY	13.58	11.11	0.0	3.70	12.35	9.88	0.0	11.11	27.16	11.11
	LXBG	7.29	18.75	9.38	0.0	11.46	19.79	0.0	17.71	5.21	10.42
	NTHL	9.89	8.79	15.38	4.40	23.08	8.79	0.0	19.78	4.40	5.49
	NRWY	3.29	3.95	19.08	0.0	25.00	20.39	0.0	13.16	3.29	11.84
	PRTG	3.77	18.87	5.66	1.89	26.42	18.87	0.0	16.98	5.66	1.89
	TRKY	.69	28.97	2.76	4.83	13.10	17.93	0.0	16.55	3.45	11.72
	UK	3.79	10.61	37.12	4.55	3.79	6.06	0.0	16.67	16.67	.76
	USA	2.27	12.12	23.48	2.27	4.55	6.06	.76	35.61	0.0	12.88
MEAN		9.0138	14.4879	15.7072	4.1561	13.3158	15.6259	.0505	16.4532	6.4629	4.7267
WTO											
	BLGR	3.64	5.45	10.91	3.64	30.91	23.64	0.0	18.18	3.64	0.0
	CZCH	3.61	13.25	4.82	7.23	19.28	18.07	0.0	32.53	1.20	0.0
	GDR	1.64	18.03	8.20	3.28	6.56	32.79	0.0	24.59	4.92	0.0
	HNGR	15.00	17.50	12.50	8.75	8.75	12.50	0.0	21.25	3.75	0.0
	PLND	3.57	16.67	2.38	1.19	27.38	8.33	0.0	36.90	3.57	0.0
	RMNA	2.87	15.16	11.48	.41	20.08	18.85	0.0	24.59	2.87	3.69
	USSR	4.92	14.75	11.48	3.28	18.03	16.39	0.0	31.15	0.0	0.0
MEAN		5.0355	14.4036	8.8224	3.9676	18.7127	18.6535	0.0	27.0278	2.8499	.5269

N+N											
	AUST	2.56	7.69	7.69	2.56	41.03	0.0	0.0	33.33	5.13	0.0
	CYPR	3.00	34.00	4.00	3.00	6.00	24.00	0.0	15.00	8.00	3.00
	FNLD	3.20	16.80	2.40	.80	24.00	28.00	0.0	15.20	9.60	0.0
	IRLD	14.47	9.21	3.95	0.0	26.32	3.95	0.0	15.79	19.74	6.58
	LICH	12.50	18.75	0.0	0.0	25.00	6.25	0.0	37.50	0.0	0.0
	MLTA	5.66	1.89	15.09	9.43	9.43	18.87	0.0	20.75	16.98	1.89
	SANM	1.15	6.90	2.30	0.0	22.99	2.30	0.0	41.38	2.30	20.69
	SWDN	5.93	7.63	14.41	3.39	16.10	20.34	0.0	26.27	4.24	1.69
	SWTZ	18.68	30.77	3.30	6.59	6.59	13.19	0.0	10.99	2.20	7.69
	YGSL	0.0	23.46	9.88	3.09	16.67	19.75	0.0	25.31	.62	1.23
MEAN		6.7161	15.7089	6.3013	2.8868	19.4126	13.6643	0.0	24.1526	6.8797	4.2777
OTHER											
	MNCO	5.56	0.0	0.0	0.0	0.0	22.22	0.0	72.22	0.0	0.0
	SPAN	3.36	26.89	20.17	1.68	13.45	22.69	0.0	5.04	6.72	0.0
	VATC	1.00	7.00	2.00	0.0	17.00	14.00	0.0	43.00	3.00	13.00
MEAN		3.3056	11.2969	7.3894	.5602	10.1485	19.6371	0.0	40.0881	3.2409	4.3333
Σ MEAN		7.0724	14.5464	10.9299	3.4475	15.8656	16.0148	.0216	22.7938	5.5832	3.7247

Table 2.20. The Belgrade Opening Statements: Distribution of Attention on the Ten Dimensions of East-West Relations

	COUNTRY	HUMAN CONTACT	SOVEREIGNTY	DISARMAMENT	ECONOMIC COOP.	COOP. GENERAL	SECURITY	TRANSPORT ENERGY	PEACE CONFLICT	INTERN. ORGANIS.	HUMAN RIGHTS
3 NATO											
	BLGM	22.95	5.74	13.93	3.28	11.48	10.66	0.0	4.10	22.13	5.74
	CNDA	14.81	6.48	22.22	7.41	8.33	12.96	0.0	14.81	0.0	12.96
	DNMK	16.55	15.83	17.99	5.76	5.76	0.0	0.0	9.35	12.23	16.55
	FRNC	12.70	6.35	3.17	11.11	19.05	9.52	0.0	23.81	1.59	12.70
	FRG	20.14	5.04	22.30	5.76	9.35	4.32	1.44	15.11	6.47	10.07
	GRCE	11.76	7.84	19.61	7.84	29.41	23.53	0.0	0.0	0.0	0.0
	ICLD	17.19	15.63	6.25	15.63	7.81	6.25	0.0	7.81	12.50	10.94
	ITLY	6.03	6.03	6.03	3.45	30.17	19.83	0.0	18.97	6.03	3.45
	LXBG	8.80	6.40	20.80	7.20	11.20	6.40	0.0	10.40	17.60	11.20
	NTHL	18.82	12.90	15.05	2.15	18.82	7.53	0.0	8.06	5.91	10.75
	NRWY	9.35	1.40	21.50	16.82	11.21	10.28	0.0	5.14	1.40	22.90
	PRTG	5.08	3.95	12.43	0.0	22.60	15.25	0.0	11.86	19.77	9.04
	TRKY	2.82	6.34	14.79	7.75	21.13	8.45	13.38	17.61	7.75	0.0
	UK	7.14	1.19	16.67	10.71	17.86	4.76	7.14	11.90	19.05	3.57
	USA	6.67	2.67	19.33	.67	12.00	7.33	0.0	14.67	4.00	32.67
MEAN		12.0544	6.9193	15.4719	7.0350	15.7451	9.8049	1.4641	11.5738	9.0961	10.8354
WTO											
	BLGR	4.26	11.17	31.38	1.06	20.21	14.89	1.06	14.36	.53	1.06
	CZCH	11.70	2.34	51.46	11.11	7.02	7.02	0.0	4.68	4.68	0.0
	GDR	13.64	16.16	41.92	1.52	13.13	6.06	0.0	6.57	1.01	0.0
	HNGR	2.72	8.70	21.20	14.13	15.22	16.85	0.0	16.30	1.09	3.80
	PLND	6.18	16.85	11.24	3.37	10.67	24.72	0.0	14.61	1.69	10.67
	RMNA	3.27	12.53	25.61	7.63	15.80	25.07	0.0	7.08	3.00	0.0
	USSR	5.32	11.70	21.28	5.32	17.55	10.64	9.57	13.30	3.72	1.60
MEAN		6.7248	11.3510	29.1551	6.3057	14.2300	15.0350	1.5198	10.9856	2.2448	2.4483

N+N											
	AUST	11.21	6.90	27.59	1.72	10.34	10.34	12.07	13.79	2.59	3.45
	CYPR	5.43	20.65	10.87	2.17	11.96	19.57	0.0	13.04	13.04	3.26
	FNLD	3.77	10.85	11.32	4.72	33.96	20.28	0.0	8.96	3.77	2.36
	IRLD	10.56	8.70	33.54	8.07	12.42	3.11	0.0	8.07	3.11	12.42
	LICH	4.35	8.70	0.0	0.0	39.13	8.70	0.0	21.74	0.0	17.39
	MLTA	4.96	3.55	22.70	1.42	9.93	5.67	0.0	14.89	34.04	2.84
	SANM	2.08	44.79	8.33	0.0	5.21	14.58	0.0	5.21	0.0	19.79
	SWDN	5.58	5.58	32.27	3.98	16.73	9.56	0.0	9.96	1.59	14.74
	SWTZ	3.77	17.61	10.69	9.43	20.75	7.55	0.0	19.50	2.52	8.18
	YGSL	9.44	9.44	32.69	7.02	12.11	10.65	1.69	5.33	5.08	6.54
MEAN		6.1164	13.6758	18.9996	3.8548	17.2548	11.0014	1.3764	12.0498	6.5745	9.0964
OTHER											
	MNCO	11.76	0.0	5.88	0.0	23.53	11.76	0.0	47.06	0.0	0.0
	SPAN	.98	6.86	15.69	1.96	9.80	24.51	0.0	8.82	1.96	29.41
	VATC	10.87	6.52	10.14	0.0	7.25	4.35	0.0	12.32	1.45	47.10
MEAN		7.8716	4.4615	10.5712	.6536	13.5266	13.5408	0.0	22.7337	1.1367	25.5044
MEAN		8.9334	9.5254	18.7964	5.4335	15.6832	11.5130	1.3247	12.5487	6.3232	9.9185

Table 2.21. The Belgrade Closing Statements: Distribution of Attention on the Ten Dimensions of East–West Relations

	COUNTRY	HUMAN CONTACT	SOVEREIGNTY	DISARMAMENT	ECONOMIC COOP.	COOP. GENERAL	SECURITY	TRANSPORT ENERGY	PEACE CONFLICT	INTERN. ORGANIS.	HUMAN RIGHTS
4 NATO											
	BLGM	9.62	11.54	15.38	26.92	7.69	3.85	0.0	0.0	1.92	23.08
	CNDA	28.97	.93	15.89	1.87	11.21	13.08	0.0	4.67	0.0	23.36
	DNMK	31.88	4.35	23.19	5.80	2.90	2.90	0.0	0.0	21.74	7.25
	FRNC	20.97	0.0	17.74	0.0	4.84	17.74	0.0	27.42	1.61	9.68
	FRG	18.75	8.75	3.75	10.00	20.00	3.75	0.0	17.50	3.75	13.75
	GRCE	0.0	22.22	0.0	0.0	55.56	11.11	0.0	0.0	5.56	5.56
	ICLD	0.0	0.0	25.00	0.0	50.00	0.0	0.0	12.50	0.0	12.50
	ITLY	13.43	2.99	8.96	2.99	23.88	7.46	0.0	0.0	19.40	20.90
	LXBG	21.62	8.11	43.24	2.70	5.41	0.0	0.0	0.0	2.70	16.22
	NTHL	52.94	11.76	0.0	0.0	0.0	0.0	0.0	0.0	0.0	35.29
	NRWY	25.00	17.86	14.29	0.0	17.86	7.14	0.0	0.0	3.57	14.29
	PRTG	5.88	5.88	5.88	11.76	35.29	23.53	0.0	5.88	5.88	0.0
	TRKY	4.55	18.18	15.91	0.0	40.91	0.0	0.0	18.18	0.0	2.27
	UK	8.16	7.14	19.39	2.04	8.16	4.08	0.0	15.31	1.02	34.69
	USA	6.60	4.72	13.21	6.60	6.60	7.55	0.0	3.77	0.0	50.94
MEAN		16.5586	8.2955	14.7882	4.7124	19.3542	6.8130	0.0	7.0157	4.4774	17.9848
WTO											
	BLGR	4.40	2.20	36.26	2.20	28.57	8.79	4.40	5.49	1.10	6.59
	CZCH	0.0	12.28	19.30	10.53	3.51	17.54	0.0	8.77	7.02	21.05
	GDR	4.93	9.15	27.46	4.23	4.23	26.76	7.04	9.15	0.0	7.04
	HNGR	6.19	18.56	15.46	2.06	22.68	16.49	4.12	6.19	2.06	6.19
	PLND	10.55	4.59	24.31	2.75	20.18	14.68	.92	14.22	4.13	3.67
	RMNA	3.03	1.52	30.30	9.09	27.27	24.24	0.0	4.55	0.0	0.0
	USSR	4.55	3.25	32.47	0.0	10.39	22.08	9.09	12.34	0.0	5.84
MEAN		4.8053	7.3627	26.5104	4.4078	16.6903	18.6557	3.6528	8.6729	2.0438	7.1982

N+N											
	AUST	19.30	8.77	8.77	0.0	21.05	24.56	1.75	1.75	0.0	14.04
	CYPR	2.00	16.00	12.00	0.0	40.00	4.00	2.00	0.0	18.00	6.00
	FNLD	28.77	0.0	36.99	5.48	13.70	8.22	0.0	2.74	4.11	0.0
	IRLD	4.00	14.00	4.00	0.0	24.00	8.00	0.0	4.00	8.00	34.00
	LICH	50.00	0.0	0.0	0.0	50.00	0.0	0.0	0.0	0.0	0.0
	MLTA	0.0	0.0	0.0	0.0	30.77	15.38	0.0	30.77	15.38	7.69
	SANM	7.79	9.09	20.78	0.0	12.99	12.99	0.0	12.99	2.60	20.78
	SWDN	8.16	14.29	20.41	0.0	28.57	8.16	0.0	0.0	2.04	18.37
	SWTZ	12.50	7.50	5.00	10.00	10.00	15.00	0.0	15.00	0.0	25.00
	YGSL	4.55	7.58	19.70	6.06	24.24	18.18	0.0	13.64	6.06	0.0
MEAN		13.7066	7.7224	12.7643	2.1540	25.5321	11.4497	.3754	8.0887	5.6193	12.5874
OTHER											
	MNCO	14.29	0.0	0.0	28.57	28.57	28.57	0.0	0.0	0.0	0.0
	SPAN	18.67	1.33	28.00	0.0	21.33	8.00	0.0	9.33	1.33	12.00
	VATC	5.26	15.79	15.79	0.0	15.79	10.53	0.0	2.63	2.63	31.58
MEAN		12.7385	5.7076	14.5965	9.5238	21.8981	15.6992	0.0	3.9883	1.3216	14.5263
MEAN		13.0657	7.7234	16.5380	4.3329	20.8046	11.2680	.8378	7.3942	4.0464	13.9889

Table 2.22. The Madrid Opening Statements: Distribution of Attention on the Ten Dimensions of East–West Relations

	COUNTRY	HUMAN CONTACT	SOVEREIGNTY	DISARMAMENT	ECONOMIC COOP.	COOP. GENERAL	SECURITY	TRANSPORT ENERGY	PEACE CONFLICT	INTERN. ORGANIS.	HUMAN RIGHTS
5 NATO											
	BLGM	28.99	10.14	14.49	0.0	10.14	4.35	0.0	14.49	5.80	11.59
	CNDA	8.00	16.80	20.80	.80	11.20	4.00	0.0	20.80	0.0	17.60
	DNMK	23.08	6.41	30.77	0.0	10.26	7.69	1.28	10.26	0.0	10.26
	FRNC	11.76	17.65	9.80	1.96	9.80	17.65	0.0	19.61	0.0	11.76
	FRG	11.68	6.09	19.29	0.0	19.29	7.61	0.0	27.92	0.0	8.12
	GRCE	10.26	15.38	17.95	5.13	16.67	10.26	6.41	12.82	2.56	2.56
	ICLD	30.95	9.52	28.57	2.38	14.29	2.38	0.0	7.14	0.0	4.76
	ITLY	5.00	13.00	18.00	0.0	22.00	14.00	0.0	10.00	10.00	8.00
	LXBG	17.19	7.81	31.25	3.13	4.69	9.38	0.0	12.50	3.13	10.94
	NTHL	6.86	7.84	12.75	0.0	6.86	9.80	0.0	19.61	0.0	36.27
	NRWY	2.10	13.29	46.85	0.0	8.39	5.59	0.0	13.99	0.0	9.79
	PRTG	6.45	32.26	3.23	0.0	6.45	9.68	0.0	9.68	0.0	32.26
	TRKY	7.02	10.53	36.84	0.0	17.54	8.77	0.0	15.79	0.0	3.51
	UK	21.95	12.20	8.94	0.0	8.13	10.57	0.0	11.38	0.0	26.83
	USA	5.22	9.70	16.42	0.0	7.46	11.19	0.0	6.72	0.0	43.28
MEAN		13.1002	12.5750	21.0635	.8930	11.5451	8.8616	.5128	14.1799	1.4324	15.8363
WTO											
	BLGR	10.59	8.24	29.41	0.0	17.65	8.24	0.0	22.35	1.18	2.35
	CZCH	0.0	7.95	22.73	0.0	19.32	17.05	0.0	30.68	0.0	2.27
	GDR	7.26	8.87	32.26	0.0	12.90	15.32	0.0	21.77	.81	.81
	HNGR	4.32	5.04	33.81	0.0	18.71	15.11	.72	16.55	.72	5.04
	PLND	4.62	7.69	40.00	0.0	16.92	11.54	0.0	19.23	0.0	0.0
	RMNA	7.36	10.85	28.29	1.55	17.83	12.02	1.55	16.67	.39	3.49
	USSR	3.77	7.55	45.28	0.0	7.55	3.77	2.83	26.42	0.0	2.83
MEAN		5.4166	8.0270	33.1125	.2215	15.8390	11.8627	.7286	21.9526	.4414	2.3981

N+N											
	AUST	11.25	3.75	26.25	0.0	11.25	8.75	0.0	28.75	0.0	10.00
	CYPR	1.52	13.64	18.18	0.0	19.70	9.09	0.0	24.24	6.06	7.58
	FNLD	14.29	10.00	41.43	0.0	10.00	10.00	0.0	5.71	1.43	7.14
	IRLD	9.41	10.59	31.76	8.24	9.41	7.06	0.0	12.94	0.0	10.59
	LICH	6.25	12.50	31.25	0.0	18.75	6.25	0.0	18.75	0.0	6.25
	MLTA	0.0	0.0	12.73	0.0	7.27	16.36	0.0	47.27	16.36	0.0
	SANM	0.0	21.74	4.35	0.0	17.39	4.35	0.0	41.30	2.17	8.70
	SWDN	1.94	4.52	49.68	0.0	5.16	14.84	0.0	10.32	0.0	13.55
	SWTZ	8.93	26.79	26.79	0.0	1.79	16.96	0.0	16.07	0.0	2.68
	YGSL	1.50	17.29	15.79	0.0	9.77	9.02	0.0	30.08	4.51	12.03
MEAN		5.5080	12.0809	25.8203	.8235	11.0494	10.2687	0.0	23.5444	3.0538	7.8510
OTHER											
	MNCO	0.0	0.0	14.29	0.0	14.29	14.29	0.0	14.29	28.57	14.29
	SPAN	1.72	8.05	23.56	.57	16.67	12.64	0.0	24.71	2.87	9.20
	VATC	6.12	11.22	12.24	0.0	11.22	4.08	0.0	21.43	0.0	33.67
MEAN		2.6155	6.4235	16.6979	.1916	14.0590	10.3370	0.0	20.1423	10.4817	19.0515
MEAN		8.4956	10.9970	24.4582	.6787	12.4777	9.9903	.3655	18.9211	2.4731	11.1427

The picture offered by the frequency block chart is highly instructive. Obviously, NATO's preference structure for the five master dimensions is less stable than in the case of the WTO. The human-rights and contacts dimension suddenly gets much more attention after 1977 than before. This does not imply, however, that this shift in emphasis is done at the expense of any peculiar other dimension; rather all other dimensions receive slightly less attention while the attention for human rights grows. In 1980 the trends point at a certain "normalization"; the distribution of attention becomes more balanced again, and the issue of disarmament and security now catches even slightly more attention than the human-rights issue. Human rights, which constitute the paramount concern of delegations representing NATO countries, now are matched by security considerations as at the beginning of the negotiation period, in 1973, when priority was given to disarmament and security.

On the other hand, the WTO countries slightly responded to the human-rights "campaign," which took place in 1977/78; afterward, the human-rights issue in WTO perspective fell back to the low status it had previously. The WTO priority during the whole period is clearly focused on disarmament and security; as a matter of fact, the curve indicating the share of attention devoted to this issue reached a level (a share of 45 percent of the overall attention in 1978/80) never matched by any other issue or by any other group of countries. The high emphasis put on peace and conflict in general from 1973 to 1975 is now being focused on the concern for disarmament, but it ranks second again in 1980. Compared with the distribution of attention by NATO countries, human rights and contacts, in the WTO preference structure, constantly is only half as (or even less) important than in the NATO perspective. But the WTO countries' concern for disarmament and security increases as the NATO countries are concentrating on the issue of human rights and contacts. There is also a noticeable drop of interest in economic cooperation.

The N + N countries, in their distribution of attention paid to the cause of human rights and human contacts, to a certain extent follow the NATO pattern, however, without giving this issue the same emphasis in absolute percentage (26 percent at the peak in 1978 as compared with 35 percent in the case of NATO). Their primary concern is on disarmament and security, as in the case of the WTO countries, and their preference for this issue is conspicuously growing at the end of the period observed (36 percent in 1980). A striking feature is the N + N countries' interest in the issue of economic cooperation; yet this suddenly looses strength in 1980. Summing up the observations made on the basis of the factor structure underlying the statements presented between 1973 and 1980, the conclusion seems to be legitimate that despite some marked differences existing between the three groups of countries of NATO, WTO, and the N + N group, there is nevertheless a considerable degree of agreement about the relative importance of the five main factors. The preference structures indicated in Graph 2.2 certainly do not coincide, but they are not so dissimilar in shape as to exclude any dialogue and mutual understanding between the various groups. The agenda of the CSCE having been prepared in the early seventies and the field of debate having been defined by the Final Act in 1975, the framework of East–West relations is clearly established. As can be seen from the relatively calm evolution of the shares of attention devoted to the main factors, this framework has acquired a remarkable degree of stability.

2.5 "CAMPS" AND POLARIZATION IN THE CSCE: A CLUSTER ANALYSIS

2.5.1 Introduction

Thirty-five governments were represented in Helsinki, Belgrade and Madrid, and they offered thirty-five different views on what they consider to be important in the large field of problems and issues constituting East–West relations. It may be assumed that certain governments express positions that are close to positions expressed by certain other governments. In other words, one may expect that the thirty-five concepts of East–West relations will group or cluster together according to specific patterns. Some elements of this grouping together are, of course, preconditioned by institutional bonds; in all CSCE meetings, there were formal and informal groups that had a more or less official character (NATO, WTO, N + N, and so on). Yet one might ask whether there are other, less obvious similarities and dissimilarities among certain countries.

This chapter is attempting to detect groups or clusters of countries on the basis of what their representatives in Helsinki, Belgrade, and Madrid *said* rather than on the basis of established institutional bonds. More precisely, two questions are to be answered: (1) To what extent do clusters of countries emerge in the process of East–West relations? (2) To what extent do these clusters resemble the traditional structure of "camps"?

The methods used to identify similarities and dissimilarities among nations on the basis of the views expressed in statements made by their CSCE delegations is a statistical technique called *cluster analysis*. In a first step, measures of proximity between countries have to be computed. This is done by calculating correlation coefficients between countries using the ten dimensions of East–West relations representing the attention profile of countries observed in the five sets of statements as "cases" (see Appendix A2.5 for further comments on the technique of cluster analysis and for the matrices of correlation coefficients for pairs of countries). Cluster analyses based on correlation proceed stepwise, extracting groups by comparing each nation's proximity to all other nations. The nations that are closest to each other constitute the nucleus of the first cluster. Other nations then form separate clusters if they are not added to one of the existing groups, until all nations are merged into one cluster comprising all previously separated groups. Two different algorithms for clustering are employed: the connectedness method and the diameter method. Both have advantages and disadvantages (see Appendix A2.5). The analytical solutions for both methods are visualized in a combined dendrogram in the subsequent graphs. These dendrograms are produced on the line printer of a computer and very easy to read. Countries close in distance that are merged together in a cluster are "linked" by bars of X, whereby the length of the bars indicates the degree of proximity. Clusters of countries, consequently, correspond to clusters of X on the printer dendrograms. The reader will find each dendrogram exactly thirty-four characters wide since thirty-four steps in the program are required to merge thirty-five countries into clusters: In each of the thirty-four steps, either a new cluster is formed, or a country or a group of countries is merged into an existing cluster.

Dendrograms are a convenient way for visualizing the structure of proximity matrices. In the case of thirty-five countries, such a matrix contains 595 single correlation coefficients (see Appendix A2.5). Cluster analysis is rigid in the sense that multiple-group membership or overlapping of groups is neglected. Still, it is a formidable technique for reducing the complexity of matrices. When interpreting the findings, it should be kept in mind that the dendrogram represents mere structural properties inherent to the data; the explanation of these structural characteristics, however, is something different.

2.5.2 The 1973 Helsinki Statements

The differences in the preference structure among the thirty-five nations participating in the CSCE as expressed in the 1973 Helsinki statements, with respect to the ten dimensions of East–West relations, are not enormous. Consequently, most of the correlations between countries are also comparatively high. The clustering of countries provided in the dendrogram of Graph 2.3 is based on the remaining differences. It is a striking fact that in the 1973 Helsinki statements clusters along the lines of "camps" do not emerge, with the exception of a small group of WTO countries. Apparently, very similar views were expressed by the USSR, Romania, and the GDR: Less than 5 percent of the total attention was devoted to questions concerning human contacts; that is still well below the WTO mean of 6.2 percent, whereas sovereignty attracted between 13 and 16 percent of this small group's attention, now well above the WTO mean of 9.4 percent. The proximity of Belgium and the Federal Republic of Germany is mainly the result of both countries'

Graph 2.3. Clustering of CSCE Countries According to Their Attention Profile in the 1973 Helsinki Statements

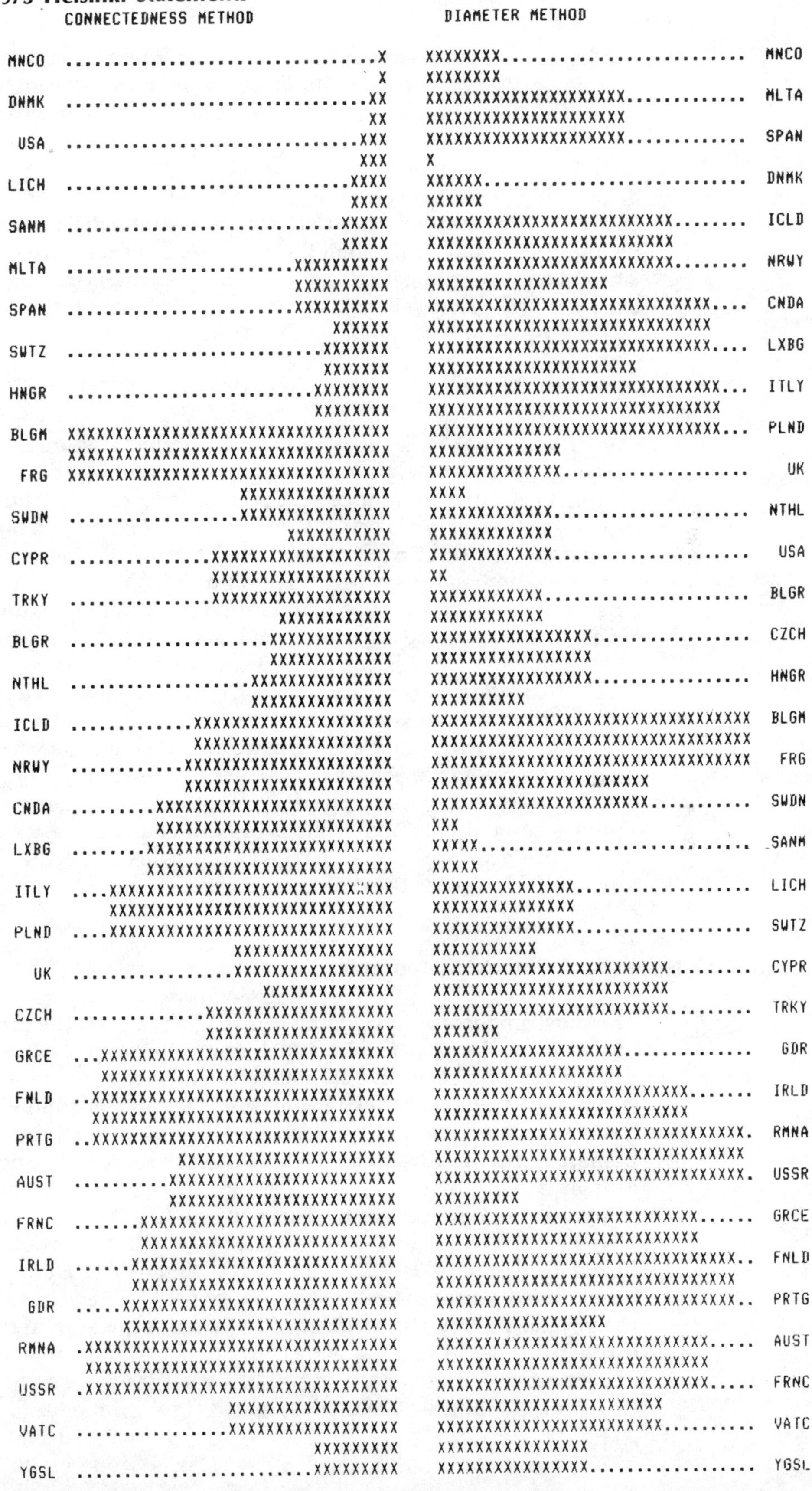
CONNECTEDNESS METHOD
MNCO
DNMK
USA
LICH
SANM
MLTA
SPAN
SWTZ
HNGR
BLGM
FRG
SWDN
CYPR
TRKY
BLGR
NTHL
ICLD
NRWY
CNDA
LXBG
ITLY
PLND
UK
CZCH
GRCE
FNLD
PRTG
AUST
FRNC
IRLD
GDR
RMNA
USSR
VATC
YGSL
DIAMETER METHOD
MNCO
MLTA
SPAN
DNMK
ICLD
NRWY
CNDA
LXBG
ITLY
PLND
UK
NTHL
USA
BLGR
CZCH
HNGR
BLGM
FRG
SWDN
SANM
LICH
SWTZ
CYPR
TRKY
GDR
IRLD
RMNA
USSR
GRCE
FNLD
PRTG
AUST
FRNC
VATC
YGSL

emphasis on cooperation as a principle of international relations. Belgium's 21 percent and the West German 25 percent are well above the NATO mean of 15 percent. Although clusters along the border lines of the alliances do not emerge, a surprising fact may be that still no pairs of closely related countries from each alliance do develop. One exception is Poland and Italy which share in common very similar attention profiles, although both countries do not deviate markedly from the means of their respective "camp." This illustrates the general conclusion that the attention profiles expressed in the Helsinki statements of 1973 would not suffice to discriminate among alliances and groups.

2.5.3 The 1975 Helsinki Statements

The change that took place in the 1975 Helsinki statements compared to the 1973 Helsinki statements is not dramatic. Distances between countries computed on the basis of a comparison of their attention profiles are very low in general. Clusters corresponding to "camps" in the CSCE (NATO, WTO, neutral, and nonaligned countries) do hardly emerge. Only a group of WTO countries comprising the USSR, Czechoslovakia, and Romania appears to crystallize, with two neutral-nonaligned countries (Sweden and Yugoslavia) in close neighborhood. By contrast to 1973, there are some East–West pairs of countries. Both Bulgaria and the Netherlands have high proportions of attention on cooperation (dimension 5) in common. Norway joins this group due to emphasis on security similar to Bulgaria. Another pair with a relatively high spatial proximity is France and the GDR. Again, the focus on security appears to be a common element of both countries' attention profile. There are three pairs of NATO countries emerging from the analysis. However, they do not merge into a compact NATO cluster.

2.5.4 The Belgrade Opening Statements

The most important development in 1977 has been the increasing attention on human rights and human contacts (Section 2.4.4). The effects with respect to the clustering of countries are somewhat surprising. Contrary to what one might expect, a solid cluster of NATO countries cannot be detected. On the average, the issues of human rights and human contacts attract 12 percent and 11 percent of attention in the NATO group of countries, respectively, compared to 7 percent and 2 percent in the WTO group. These obvious differences, however, are still, by statistical criteria, insufficient to discriminate between NATO and WTO. Human rights and human contacts are only two out of ten dimensions. Surprisingly, also the relative neglect of both human rights and human contacts by the WTO countries would not suffice as a common denominator for the clustering. What emerges is a cluster of neutral and nonaligned countries including Finland and Cyprus,

Graph 2.4. Clustering of CSCE Countries According to Their Attention Profile in the 1975 Helsinki Statements

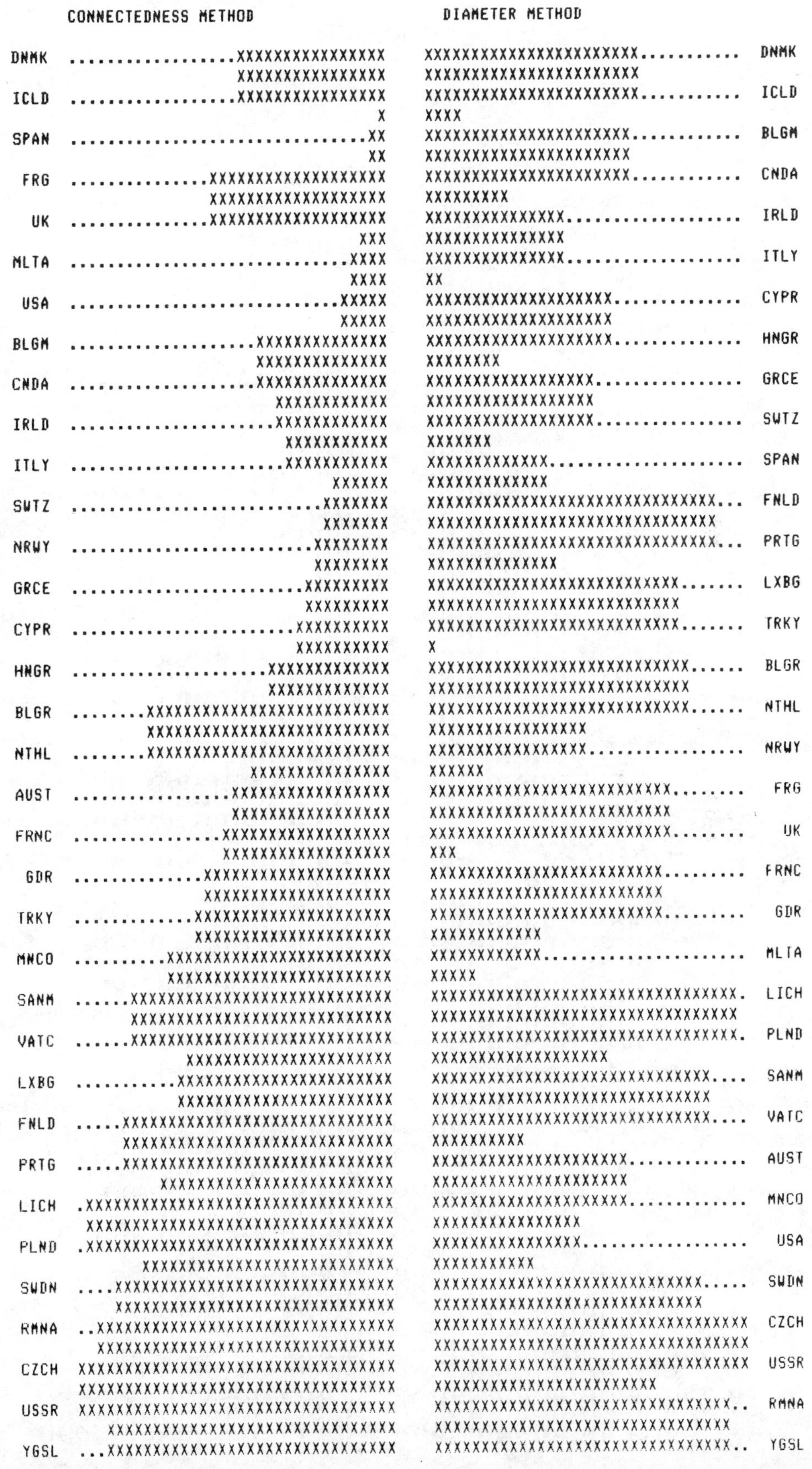
CONNECTEDNESS METHOD
DIAMETER METHOD
DNMK
ICLD
SPAN
FRG
UK
MLTA
USA
BLGM
CNDA
IRLD
ITLY
SWTZ
NRWY
GRCE
CYPR
HNGR
BLGR
NTHL
AUST
FRNC
GDR
TRKY
MNCO
SANM
VATC
LXBG
FNLD
PRTG
LICH
PLND
SWDN
RMNA
CZCH
USSR
YGSL
DNMK
ICLD
BLGM
CNDA
IRLD
ITLY
CYPR
HNGR
GRCE
SWTZ
SPAN
FNLD
PRTG
LXBG
TRKY
BLGR
NTHL
NRWY
FRG
UK
FRNC
GDR
MLTA
LICH
PLND
SANM
VATC
AUST
MNCO
USA
SWDN
CZCH
USSR
RMNA
YGSL

Graph 2.5. Clustering of CSCE Countries According to Their Attention Profile in the Belgrade Opening Statements

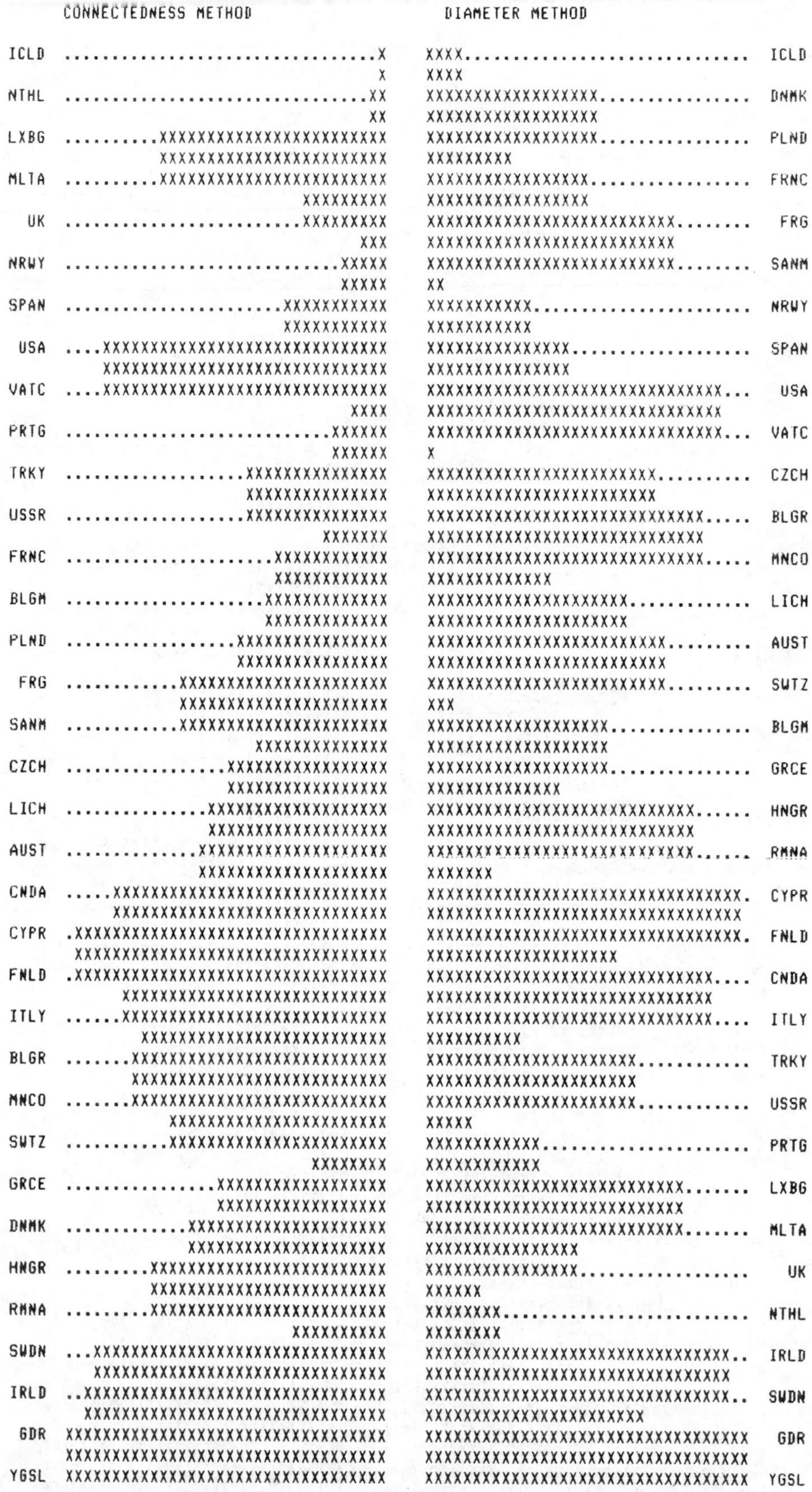
CONNECTEDNESS METHOD
DIAMETER METHOD
ICLD
NTHL
LXBG
MLTA
UK
NRWY
SPAN
USA
VATC
PRTG
TRKY
USSR
FRNC
BLGM
PLND
FRG
SANM
CZCH
LICH
AUST
CNDA
CYPR
FNLD
ITLY
BLGR
MNCO
SWTZ
GRCE
DNMK
HNGR
RMNA
SWDN
IRLD
GDR
YGSL
ICLD
DNMK
PLND
FRNC
FRG
SANM
NRWY
SPAN
USA
VATC
CZCH
BLGR
MNCO
LICH
AUST
SWTZ
BLGM
GRCE
HNGR
RMNA
CYPR
FNLD
CNDA
ITLY
TRKY
USSR
PRTG
LXBG
MLTA
UK
NTHL
IRLD
SWDN
GDR
YGSL

joined then by Switzerland and Austria together with the NATO countries Canada and Italy, and the WTO country Bulgaria. The common element is a relatively low share of attention on the issues of human rights and human contacts but relatively high attention on disarmament and security. Also sovereignty is stressed by the respective countries. The emphasis on disarmament, however, is not as massive as in the case of most WTO countries (Czechoslovakia, 51 percent; GDR, 42 percent.

2.5.5 The Belgrade Closing Statements

Divergencies on the issue of human rights and human contacts create two opposing clusters in 1978: those favoring the issue and those stressing rather disarmament as the focal problem of the CSCE. As might be expected, these two groups, however, do not correspond perfectly to the "camps." Neutral and nonaligned countries are distributed on both groups or remain outside the clusters, whereas the group led by Poland, Romania, and Yugoslavia comprises not only the Soviet Union but Canada and Spain as well. In contrast, the cluster of supporters of the human-rights theme does not include any WTO country. Interestingly, most of the WTO countries (the GDR, Hungary, Bulgaria, and Czechoslovakia) are not in the opposing cluster led by Poland. Still, the low attention on human rights and human contacts would not suffice for the creation of a cluster, whereas maximum attention on both issues is the main characteristic of the cluster led by the United States and Great Britain.

2.5.6 The Madrid Opening Statements

In the Madrid statements of 1980, the structure of the dendrogram changed again. Now there are three clusters to be distinguished: A first cluster of countries with Poland, Turkey, Romania, and the Soviet Union emphasizes disarmament. Poland devotes 40 percent of its total attention to disarmament, the USSR 45 percent, Turkey 37 percent, and Romania 28 percent. Sweden and Norway join this cluster at a lower level of proximity. A second group of countries are those that favor human rights and human contacts, as in Belgrade 1978, among them the Holy See, the Netherlands, Denmark, the United States, and Finland. It does not include any members of the WTO. A third cluster contains countries with a more even distribution of attention on the ten dimensions, among them Spain, Italy, and Ireland. In close proximity also WTO countries can be found, namely, the GDR and Czechoslovakia.

Graph 2.6. Clustering of CSCE Countries According to Their Attention Profile in the Belgrade Closing Statements

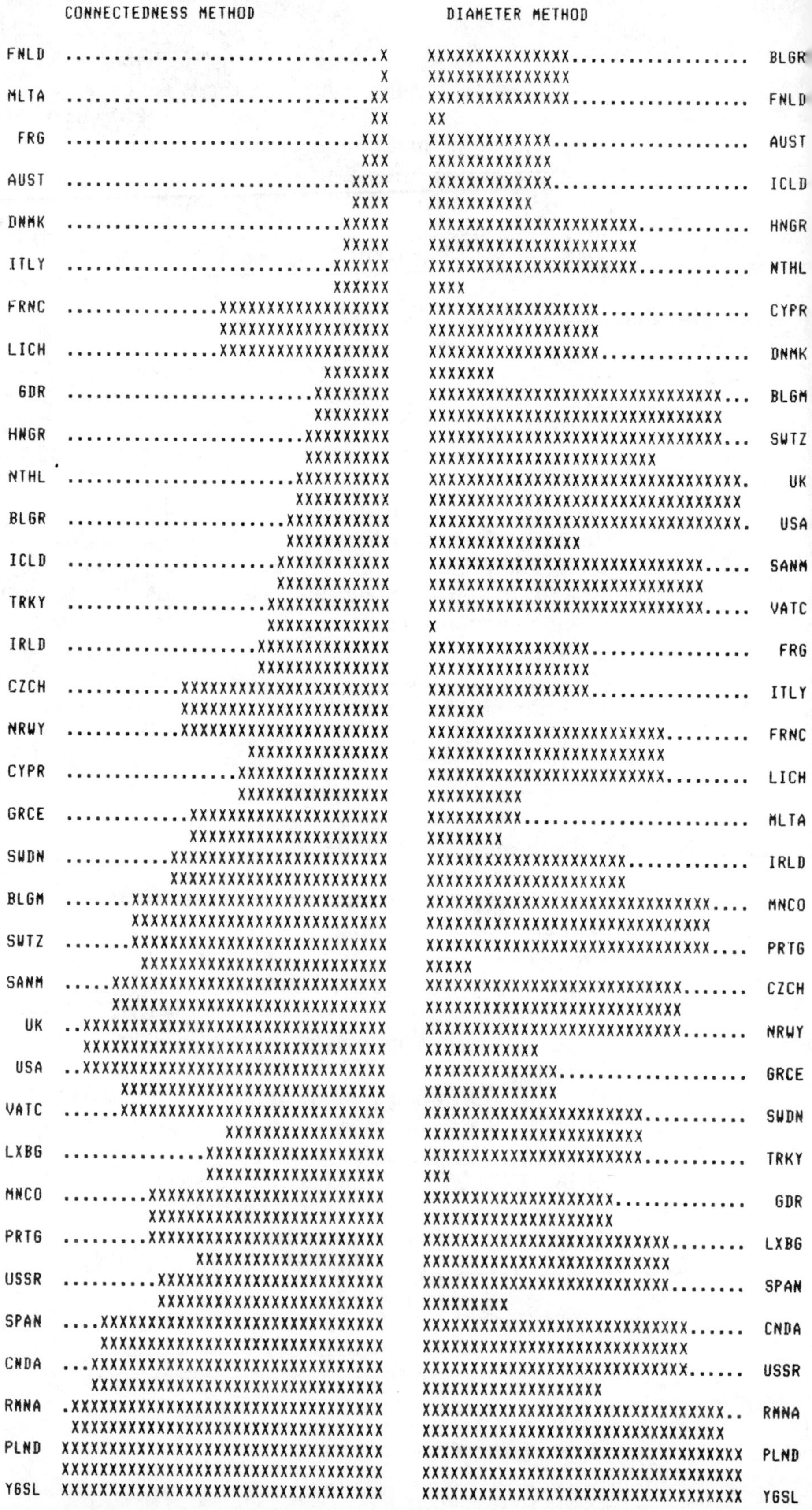
CONNECTEDNESS METHOD
DIAMETER METHOD
FNLD
MLTA
FRG
AUST
DNMK
ITLY
FRNC
LICH
GDR
HNGR
NTHL
BLGR
ICLD
TRKY
IRLD
CZCH
NRWY
CYPR
GRCE
SWDN
BLGM
SWTZ
SANM
UK
USA
VATC
LXBG
MNCO
PRTG
USSR
SPAN
CNDA
RMNA
PLND
YGSL
BLGR
FNLD
AUST
ICLD
HNGR
NTHL
CYPR
DNMK
BLGM
SWTZ
UK
USA
SANM
VATC
FRG
ITLY
FRNC
LICH
MLTA
IRLD
MNCO
PRTG
CZCH
NRWY
GRCE
SWDN
TRKY
GDR
LXBG
SPAN
CNDA
USSR
RMNA
PLND
YGSL

Graph 2.7. Clustering of CSCE Countries According to Their Attention Profile in the Madrid Opening Statements

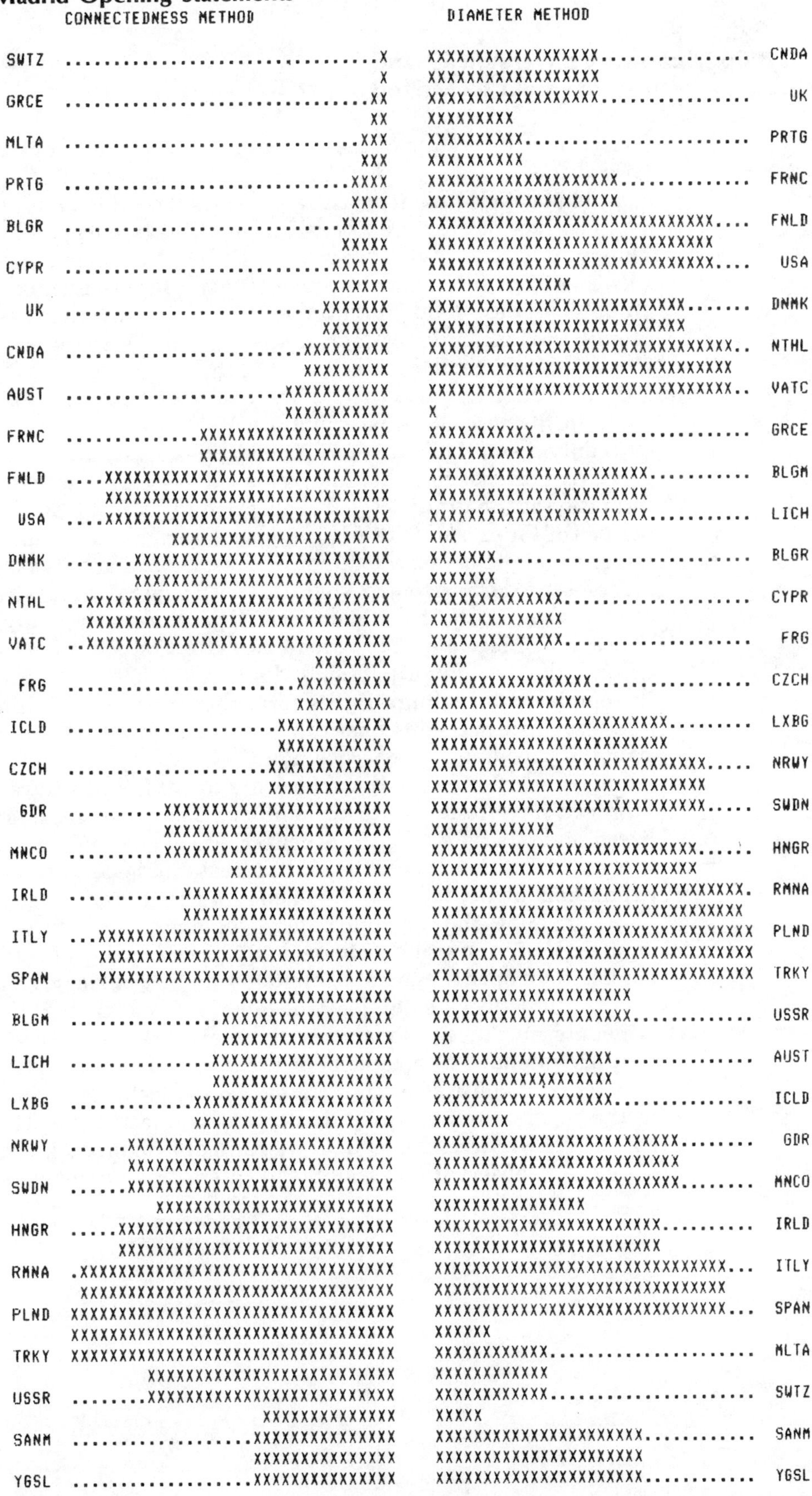
CONNECTEDNESS METHOD
DIAMETER METHOD
SWTZ
GRCE
MLTA
PRTG
BLGR
CYPR
UK
CNDA
AUST
FRNC
FNLD
USA
DNMK
NTHL
VATC
FRG
ICLD
CZCH
GDR
MNCO
IRLD
ITLY
SPAN
BLGM
LICH
LXBG
NRWY
SWDN
HNGR
RMNA
PLND
TRKY
USSR
SANM
YGSL
CNDA
UK
PRTG
FRNC
FNLD
USA
DNMK
NTHL
VATC
GRCE
BLGM
LICH
BLGR
CYPR
FRG
CZCH
LXBG
NRWY
SWDN
HNGR
RMNA
PLND
TRKY
USSR
AUST
ICLD
GDR
MNCO
IRLD
ITLY
SPAN
MLTA
SWTZ
SANM
YGSL

2.5.7 Conclusions: Convergencies and Divergencies from Helsinki to Madrid

Comparing the results of the preceding analysis, a clear tendency toward the emergence of clusters can be observed. This development is paralleled by decreasing correlation coefficients computed as a measure of proximity between countries (see Appendix A2.5). This may lead to several conclusions: First, an increasing difference among countries, irrespective of their alliance membership or group loyalties, tends to evolve, and these divergencies grow rapidly from Helsinki to Madrid. Second, a tendency toward cluster formation can be observed; however, the clusters do not resemble the traditional "camps." Therefore, *polarization* is perhaps not an apt term to describe this evolution. While in Helsinki 1973 and 1975 only a small cluster of WTO countries crystallizes, the divergence over the issue of human rights led to a more profiled cluster formation in Belgrade 1977. Yet surprisingly, this cluster consists neither of those countries favoring human rights and human contacts, as might be expected, nor of those opposing these issues; it is represented by a group of countries with a more even distribution of attention on the ten dimensions. This "mediating" group disappears in Belgrade 1978, where two clusters of nations emerge around the two favorite issues discussed: Those countries with the emphasis on human rights form the first cluster, while those stressing disarmament constitute the second group. In Madrid, the group of "mediators" emerges again.

Any conclusions regarding the evolution of East-West relations, however, have to take into account that the preceding analysis is based on texts reflecting the official views of governments. Again, a word of caution has to be added: Texts indicate only *manifest* expression of attitudes and policies. Furthermore, it should be borne in mind that in multilateral diplomatic negotiations, the similarity of views and policies is not necessarily reflected by a similarity of openly expressed opinions; on the contrary, it can also result in a deliberate "division of labor" among cooperating governments and delegations whereby one speaker expresses views that are intended to complement the views expressed by another speaker. It is quite clear that the statistical techniques as applied in this section do not grasp this type of connectedness. However, as was shown here, the method was still able to produce a number of relevant observations leading to interesting conclusions.

Chapter 3

What Really Happened in East–West Relations in Europe? The Structure and Dynamics of East–West Relations

3.1 INTRODUCTION: CRITERIA FOR SELECTING INDICATORS

3.1.1 What Is to Be Measured? The Choice of Selected Dimensions

Chapter 3 will go one step further toward measuring East–West relations by looking for indicators suitable for reflecting what is being meant by the various dimensions of East–West relations. Therefore, for each dimension identified previously by the content analysis and factor analysis, one or more indicators have to be chosen serving as criteria for observing and, if possible, measuring the development of East–West relations grasped on these dimensions. In addition, for each indicator, time-series data are collected that allow for a relatively accurate reporting of trends and developments in East–West relations. The authors hope that the data collected in this study will facilitate any further discussion about "détente" by providing a more systematic, valid, and reliable base for the assessment of what has been achieved in the field of East–West relations.

As shown in Chapter 2, "détente" is a very complex and fuzzy concept exhibiting many dimensions and comprising many fields. So there is no single and clear-cut definition of *détente*, nor can there be any single indicator representing the whole of "détente."

The Final Act signed in Helsinki on 1 August 1975 lists more than a hundred issues that are all important for détente, ranging from sovereign equality of all nations to the promotion of the study of foreign languages and from prior notification of military maneuvers to reunification of families.

Depending on its political perspective, each of the thirty-five governments involved in the CSCE negotiations perceives some items to be more relevant than others. The content analysis of official texts authored by the thirty-five governments offered a refined and accurate picture of what is being considered as relevant and important by each of the participating countries. The content analysis thus provided thirty-five different definitions of East–West relations, all definitions representing different distributions of shares of attention devoted to the various issues of the Final Act.

Ideally, it would be desirable to offer one indicator for each of the issues or problems perceived to be relevant for East–West relations, yet for obvious reasons, such a comprehensive collection of indicators is going far beyond anything feasible. Therefore a selection has to be made among the large number of possible indicators and, first of all, a selection has to be made among the various issues.

The latter task was performed by applying the method of factor analysis which, as a result, yielded ten factors or underlying dimensions. A further aggregation of these factors lead to five master dimensions indicating the five main areas of concern expressed by the thirty-five CSCE governments with reference to East–West relations: (1) disarmament and security, (2) peace and conflict, (3) economic cooperation, (4) human rights and contacts, and (5) sovereignty and independence.

3.1.2 What Indicators Are to Be Picked? The Choice of Valid, Reliable, and Noncontroversial Indicators

Suggesting an indicator means to suggest something that can be observed representing something that is being meant. Most of the dimensions mentioned in the Helsinki Final Act, by their very nature, refer to abstract theoretical concepts that can neither be observed nor measured. They therefore need a kind of translation from the theoretical level onto the level of observable, real phenomena—and that is actually what an indicator is supposed to do.

The nature and purpose of indicator construction imply four additional criteria that have to be observed if the system of indicators is to be able to fulfill its task: (1) validity, (2) reliability, (3) availability of data, and (4) absence of political implications leading to controversy.

The first two criteria do not require any explanation; they are familiar to all social sciences. *Validity* refers to the degree of correspondence between concept and indicator, that is, it refers to the question, To what extent does the indicator reflect and "indicate" what it is supposed to reflect? *Reliability* refers to the stability, consistency, and accuracy of the measurement procedure and the resulting data, that is, reliability is given if an indicator always yields the same results observed if in reality the values are identical.

The third criterion has to be taken into consideration also for obvious reasons. If an indicator does not lead to data, it has no practical significance. For instance, a valid and reliable indicator for the concept "mutual confidence" would be an attitude measure based on a set of interview questions asked in a comparative survey comprising representative samples in all thirty-five CSCE countries; yet, as it is out of the question to gather data by using comparative survey research methods on a broad all-European scale, it makes no sense to include the respective indicator.

As to the fourth criterion, indicators may be subject to controversy especially when it comes to observing and measuring politically sensitive concepts such as human rights. In order to avoid implicit decisions in favor or against certain definitions of concepts, alternative sets of indicators may be applied reflecting the differing interpretations of the same concept as perceived from different political perspectives.

Considering these four criteria, the indicators of the dimensions chosen for reflecting the reality of East–West relations will be selected according to the following order of priority:

Top priority is given to indicators that, by their very nature, have the property of face validity and hence are not controversial. Only a very few indicators belong to this class, for example, export and import figures indicating economic cooperation.

Second priority is given to indicators that can be inferred directly or indirectly from the individual categories that were summed up to constitute aggregate aspects of "détente." Some of these categories can lead to indicators that may be considered to be beyond controversy. Others offer some useful hints for the construction of indicators. In the field of human contacts, for example, references to categories "regular meetings on the basis of family ties" and "reunification of families" (mentioned in the third "basket" of the Final Act) may suggest indicators based on statistical material on Jewish emigration from the Soviet Union to Israel and travel between the Federal Republic of Germany and the German Democratic Republic, respectively.

Third priority is given to indicators where the cues observed in the documents point at different directions. If a concept is defined in mutually exclusive terms by authors in the West and authors in the East, at least two different indicators have to be used. In the context of human rights, for example, also unemployment figures are included to take into account the view put forward by the East that the right to work constitutes one of the essentials of human civilization.

Fourth and last priority is given to concepts for which an indicator can be found only on the basis of scholarly discussions in the specialized literature or simply has to be developed, on an ad hoc basis, by the authors of this study. An example is the measurement of the state of political rights and civil liberties by means of an index developed by Gastil (1978).

Table 3.1 presents the indicators selected on the basis of the criteria just mentioned. These indicators lead to two categories of data: (1) time-series data on specific issues such as emigration from the Soviet Union and other East European countries or time-series data on relations between selected dyads of nations; (2) complete matrices representing the structure of relationship among the complete set of all thirty-five nations participating in the CSCE negotiations in a certain year. Since these matrices contain a huge amount of data, namely, $35 \times 35 - 35 = 1{,}190$ single pieces of information in the case of the complete matrix, they are presented for selected years only. The indicators and their rationale will be discussed in the sections that follow.

3.2 DISARMAMENT AND SECURITY

3.2.1 Introduction

Security is one of the terms universally favored by international negotiators but extremely hard to define. Nevertheless, when referring to CSCE negotiations, it may be appropriate to conceptualize security primarily in military terms. As a matter of fact security, in the European context, is mainly discussed in the perspective of military expenditure and arms procurement. In this section, the evolution of East–West relations will thus be examined with regard to the record of military spending and the ratios of funds allocated to military purposes on the one hand and the development of the military balance on both the global and the regional level calculated on the basis of weapons systems deployed on the other hand. The first approach, so to speak, refers to the "input" aspect of the problem, that is, to the resources consumed for military purposes, whereas the second approach is envisaging the effect or "output" of this allocation of resources in terms of military hardware acquired.

3.2.2 Military Expenditure

The comparative measurement of defense expenditures has a long tradition, and the problems involved are well known. First, the general comparability of defense expenditures is to some extent doubtful since different accounting systems and different price levels are to be taken into consideration. As a matter of fact, the levels of wages for military personnel differ from one nation to the other and sometimes they do so quite considerably. Furthermore, differences in the structure of armies have also to be taken into account. Any evaluation of military hardware depends largely on the strategic conception the armed forces are supposed to serve. Furthermore, official figures of defense budgets published by governments tend to differ considerably as to the budgetary components they include or exclude, (for example, military research and development, construction and maintenance expenditures for military facilities, the operational costs of military training establishments, the costs of stockpiling strategic defense materials (Leitenberg 1979, p. 264)).

An additional difficulty arises from the fact that realistic exchange rates do not necessarily correspond to the official exchange rates, at least in the case of the centrally planned economies. There are three annually published sources on national military expenditures that allow for a comparison of the efforts made in this respect, each source representing, however, a different philosophy as to the definition of defense expenditures and exchange rates applied: *Military Balance*, published by the International Institute for Strategic Studies (since 1959/60); *SIPRI Yearbook*, published by the Stockholm International Peace Research Institute (since 1968/69); and *World Military Expenditures and Arms Trade*, published by the US Arms Control and Disarmament Agency (issues for 1963–75, 1965–75, 1966–1975). The *United Nations Statistical Yearbook* and *Yearbook of National Accounts Statistics* publishes among other budgetary figures also data for defense expenditures, provided they are submitted by the respective governments, but these figures refer to budget data, and not to actual expenditures; furthermore they are in local currency and vary according to local definitions.

The following three graphs (3.1 to 3.3) present time series of defense expenditures communicated by SIPRI and, partly, published in the 1981 *Yearbook*. In addition, the rates of change of defense expenditures of the two major powers computed on the base of the previous data are presented in graphs 3.4 and 3.5.

While the trend indicates a steady annual growth of military expenditures during twenty years in the case of the WTO countries, the NATO figures seem to fluctuate as a result of political decisions in the course of the sixties and seventies. The defense expenditures of the USA, corrected for changes in prices, fell after the end of the Vietnam war to a level close to the one reached in the early sixties. Similar reductions can be noted in the evolution of British, West German, and French defense expenditures.

In comparison to the high pace characterizing the arms race in the sixties, the early seventies were in fact a period of a decreasing Western defense expenditures, which were stabilized, however, at a rather high level; as far as the WTO countries are concerned, the early seventies were characterized by a slower increase of defense

Table 3.1. Operationalizations of Dimensions of East-West Relations

Dimension	Indicators	Data Sources
Disarmament and Security	Military expenditure of NATO, WTO, and neutral/nonaligned countries (1960-1980)	SIPRI
	Rates of change of military expenditure in NATO, WTO, and neutral/nonaligned countries (1961-1980)	computed
	Strategic bombers, USA and USSR (1960-1980)	SIPRI, IISS
	ICBMS, USA and USSR (1960-1980)	SIPRI, IISS
	SLBMs, USA and USSR (1960-1980)	SIPRI, IISS
	Strategic submarines (1960-1980)	SIPRI, IISS
	Strategic nuclear warheads on delivery systems, USA and USSR (1960-1980)	SIPRI, IISS
	Strategic nuclear delivery systems, USA and USSR (1960-1980)	computed
	Ratio of strategic nuclear delivery systems, USA/USSR (1960-1980)	computed
	Ratio of strategic nuclear warheads on delivery systems, USA/USSR (1960-1980)	computed
	Eurostrategic bombers, NATO and WTO (1960-1980)	IISS, ACDA
	Eurostrategic IRBM and MRBM, NATO and WTO (1960-1980)	IISS, ACDA

Table 3.1. *(cont.)*

Dimension	Indicators	Data Sources
Disarmament and Security (cont.)	Eurostrategic SLBM, NATO and WTO (1960-1980)	IISS, ACDA
	Eurostrategic systems, NATO and WTO (1960-1980)	computed
Peace and Conflict	Cooperative interactions between selected dyads (1960-1978)	COPDAB
	Conflictive interactions between selected dyads (1960-1978)	COPDAB
	Interaction matrix, cooperation and conflict (1960, 1965, 1970, 1975)	COPDAB
	Affinities in UN voting for selected dyads (1960-1977)	CPRI
	Cooperative interactions: USA, USSR with Latin American countries (1960-1978)	COPDAB
	Cooperative interactions: USA, USSR with African countries (1960-1978)	COPDAB
	Cooperative interactions: USA, USSR with Middle Eastern countries (1960-1978)	COPDAB
	Cooperative interactions: USA, USSR with Asian countries (1960-1978)	COPDAB
	Conflictive interactions: USA, USSR with Latin American countries (1960-1978)	COPDAB
	Conflictive interactions: USA, USSR with African countries (1960-1978)	COPDAB

Table 3.1. *(cont.)*

Dimension	Indicators	Data Sources
Peace and Conflict (cont.)	Conflictive interactions: USA, USSR with Middle Eastern countries (1960-1978)	COPDAB
	Conflictive interactions: USA, USSR with Asian countries (1960-1978)	COPDAB
Economic Cooperation	Monthly average trade between selected countries (1960-1979)	OECD
	Total imports and exports for selected countries (1960-1979)	OECD
	Imports and exports as % of total imports and exports for selected pairs of countries (1960-1979)	computed
	Trade in SITC-7 items for selected pairs of countries (1960-1979)	OECD
	Trade in SITC-3 items for selected pairs of countries (1960-1979)	OECD
	Imports and exports of SITC-3 and SITC-7 items as % of total imports/exports for selected pairs of countries	computed
	Trade matrix for CSCE countries (1965, 1970, 1975)	OECD
Human Rights	Index values for political rights and civil rights for all CSCE countries (1973-1979)	WHB3

Table 3.1. *(cont.)*

Dimension	Indicators	Data Sources
Human Rights and Contacts (cont.)	Numbers of political sanctions in WTO countries (1960-1978)	WHB3
	Unemployment as % of total labor force for selected Western and neutral/nonaligned countries (1960-1979)	OECD
	Tourism between selected countries (1960-1977)	WTOG
	Emigration from East to West (1960-1979)	BJC, BIB
Sovereignty and Independence	Dispersion of external interactions as % of total possible interactions (6 periods 1950-1978)	COPDAB
	Share of interactions exchanged with block leaders of NATO and WTO by block members (6 periods 1950-1978)	COPDAB
	Intersystemic and intrasystemic cooperative interactions for NATO, WTO, and neutral/nonaligned countries (1960-1978)	COPDAB

Graph 3.1. Military Expenditure of NATO, WTO, and the Two Major Powers (in millions of US dollars, at 1978 prices and exchange rates)

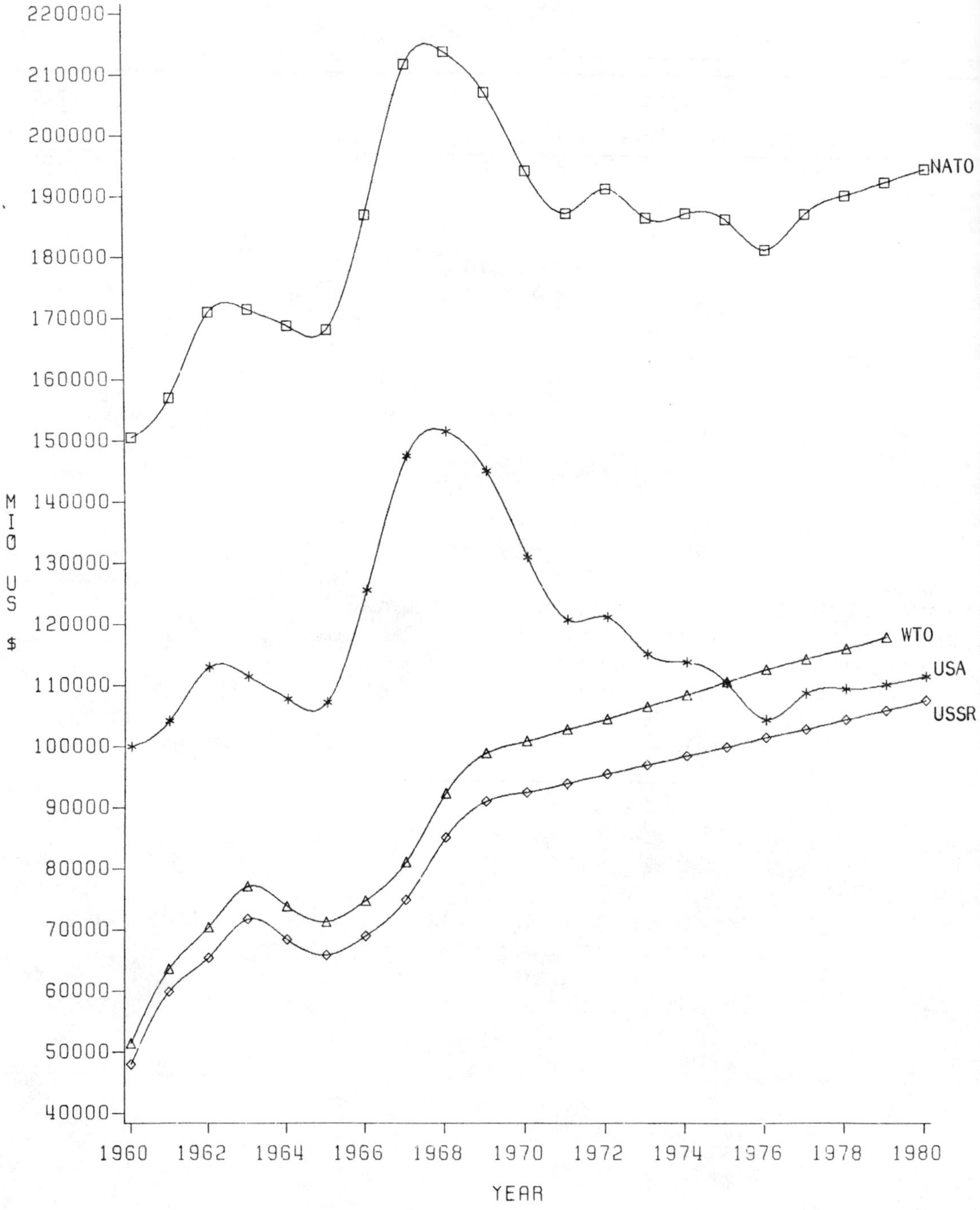
220000
210000
200000
190000
180000
170000
160000
150000
140000
130000
120000
110000
100000
90000
80000
70000
60000
50000
40000
MIO US $
NATO
WTO
USA
USSR
1960
1962
1964
1966
1968
1970
1972
1974
1976
1978
1980
YEAR

Graph 3.2. Military Expenditure of NATO Countries (in millions of US dollars, at 1978 prices and exchange rates)

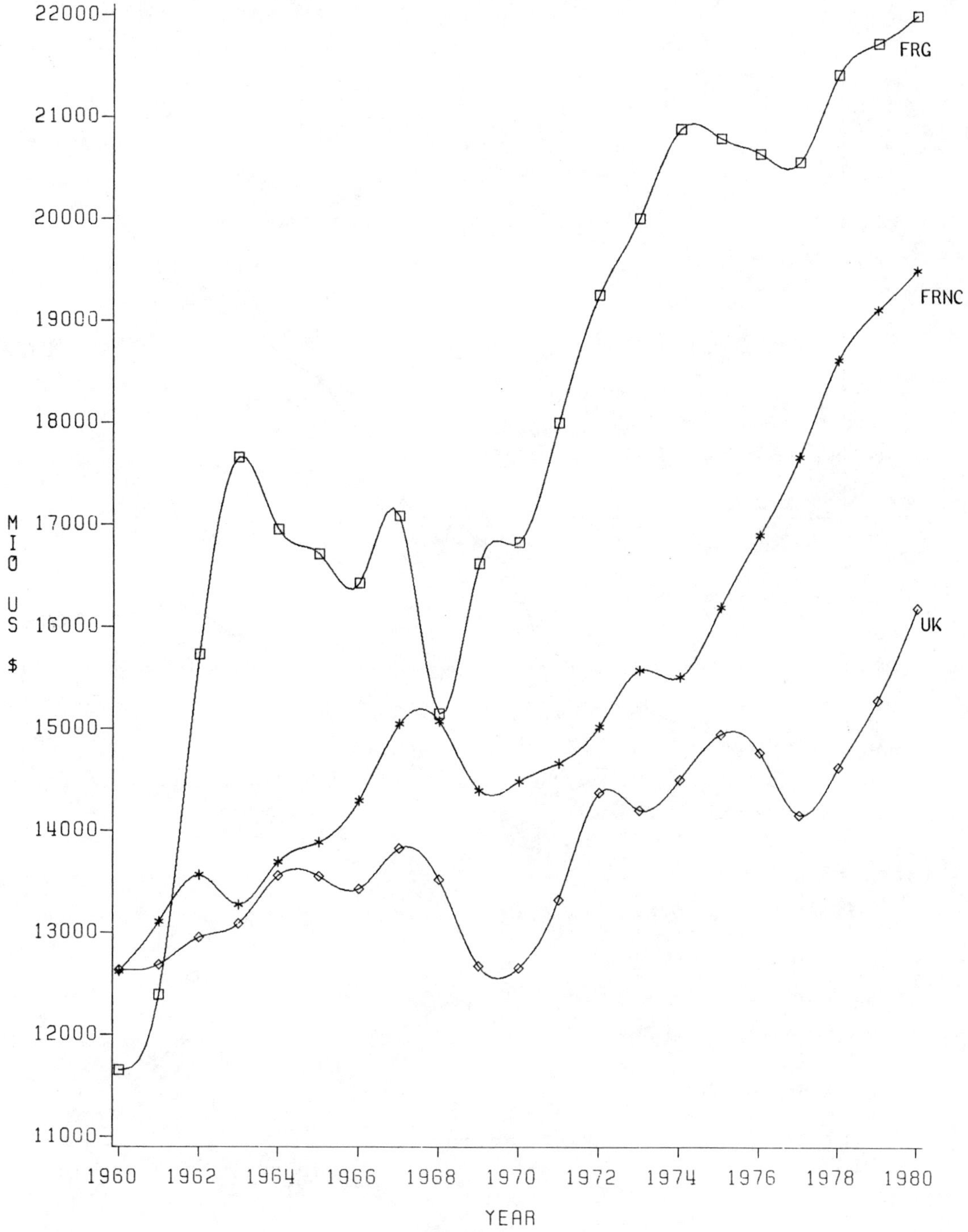
22000
21000
20000
19000
18000
17000
16000
15000
14000
13000
12000
11000
MIO US $
FRG
FRNC
UK
1960
1962
1964
1966
1968
1970
1972
1974
1976
1978
1980
YEAR

Graph 3.3. Military Expenditure of WTO Countries (in millions of US dollars, at 1978 prices and exchange rates)

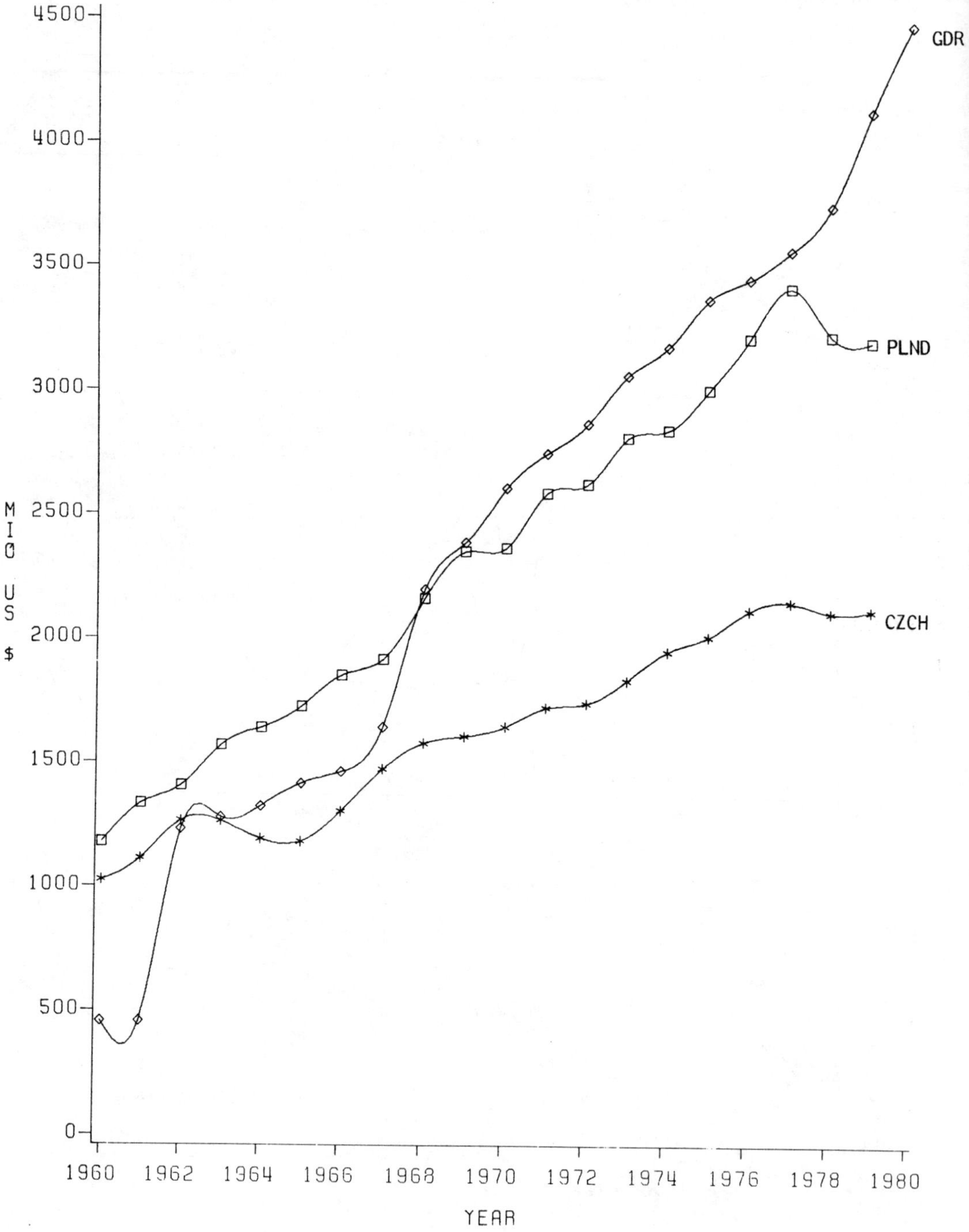
4500
4000
3500
3000
2500
2000
1500
1000
500
0
MIO US $
GDR
PLND
CZCH
1960
1962
1964
1966
1968
1970
1972
1974
1976
1978
1980
YEAR

expenditure although there was no reduction. Using the pace of the arms race as an indicator of insecurity and increasing tensions as assumed implicitly or explicitly by many scholars of the arms race, the early seventies can in fact be said to have been, to some extent, a period of growing security and tension reduction. Whether this is due to the evolution of the mutual understanding between the Soviet Union and the United States as well as to the CSCE negotiations and to the progress of German "Ostpolitik" is difficult to tell. One should not forget, however, that the end of the Vietnam war, the economic difficulties experienced as a consequence of the military engagement in Southeast Asia, and the preoccupation with internal problems in the United States may also have had a considerable impact on US and Western defense-spending behavior. As a result of the oil-price increase and associated economic difficulties, the defense burden became a pressing problem for most European NATO states in the middle of the seventies.

There is a clear trend reversal in Western military spending taking place in 1975, maybe as a consequence of the fact that WTO and Soviet defense expenditure never decreased correspondingly. Alarmed by a continuing build-up of conventional and INF-forces by the WTO countries and mainly the Soviet Union, the heads of state and heads of governments of the NATO countries in 1977 initiated the Long Term Defense Program. There have been ample controversies within the NATO alliance as well as in the press and among academic commentators in all NATO countries about whether the growth rates agreed upon were actually met or not. The figures suggest indeed a notable increase in defense spending after 1977 in most NATO countries as a consequence.

The changes and shifts referred to can be grasped more easily when looking simply at the annual growth rates (graphs 3.4 and 3.5). From the early sixties until about 1970, the initiative to change clearly originated on the American side of the major-power dyad, and the Soviet Union constantly responded with a time lag of one or two years—first with a marked decrease of military spending after 1961, followed, from 1965, by a sudden increase, which again turned into a reduction of the growth rates after 1967. Yet after 1970 the evolution of the growth rates differs considerably: The American growth rates fluctuate at rates below 0, whereas the Soviet growth rate remains constant at a level above 0. This uneven relationship continues to last for five years until, in 1976, the American government decides to "catch up" by reintroducing a growth rate above 0. Apart from the use of this type of historical explanation, these time-series data on defense expenditures and growth rates of defense expenditure may not seem very meaningful. They become more conclusive, however, when analyzing them in view of the power ratio they reflect. The ratios computed in Table 3.2 indicate a thorough change in the balance of military spending.

There is a clear decline of the ratio of NATO/WTO defense

Graph 3.4. Rates of Change in Military Expenditure of the United States and the Soviet Union (fixed 1978 prices and exchange rates)

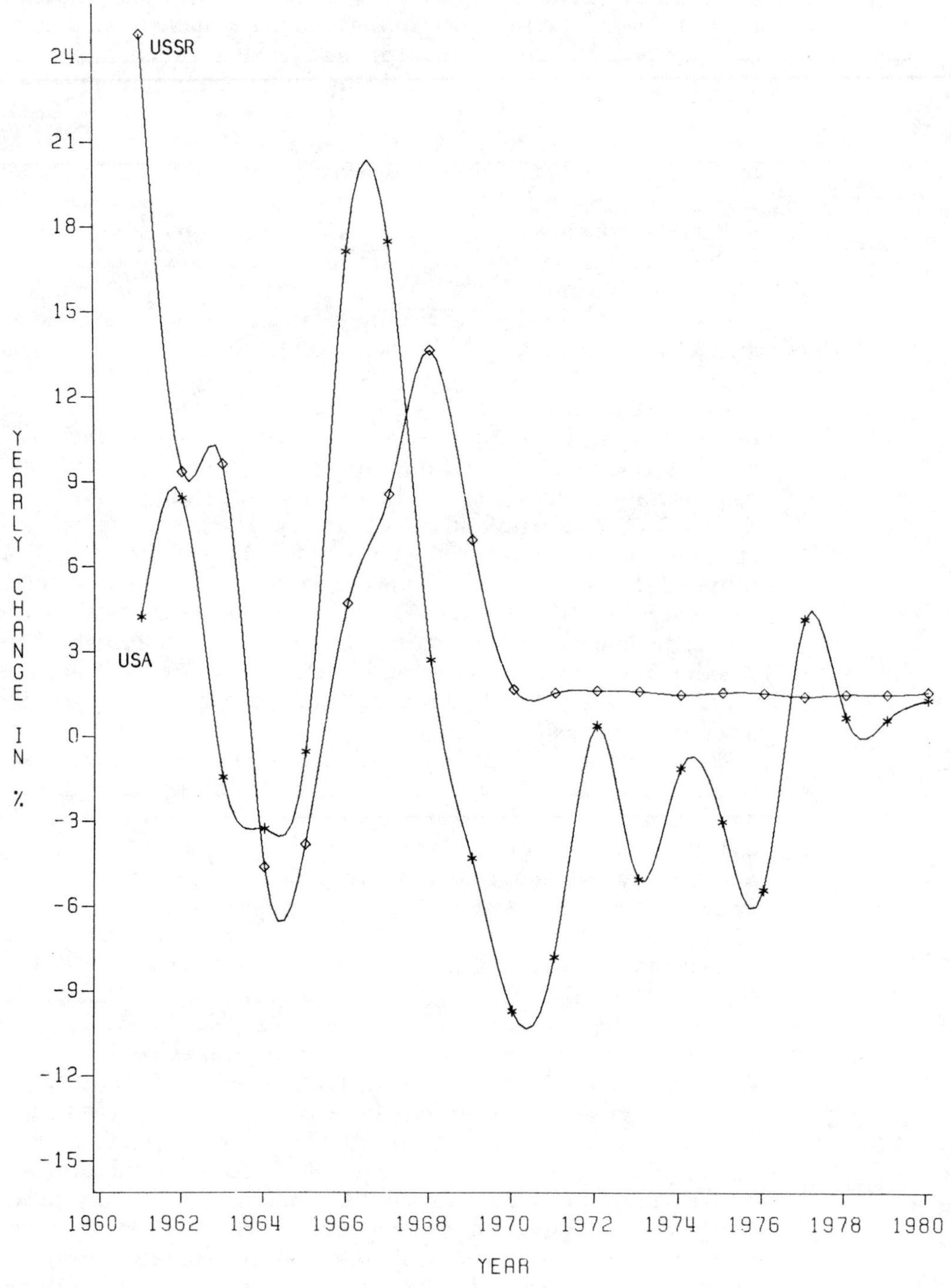
USSR
USA
24
21
18
15
12
9
6
3
0
-3
-6
-9
-12
-15
YEARLY CHANGE IN %
1960
1962
1964
1966
1968
1970
1972
1974
1976
1978
1980
YEAR

Graph 3.5. Rates of Change of Military Expenditure of NATO Countries (fixed 1978 prices and exchange rates)

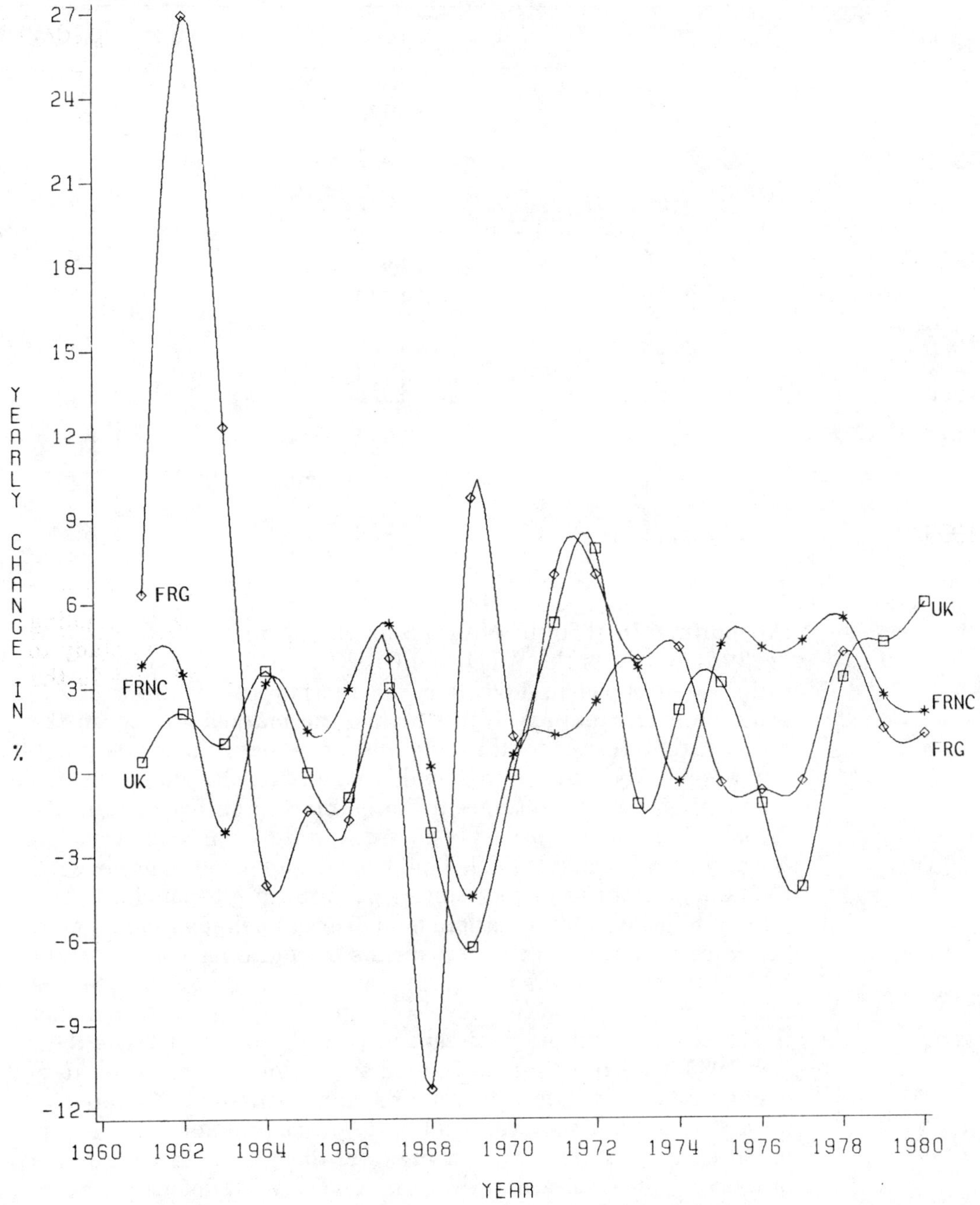
27
24
21
18
15
12
9
6
3
0
-3
-6
-9
-12
YEARLY CHANGE IN %
FRG
FRNC
UK
UK
FRNC
FRG
1960
1962
1964
1966
1968
1970
1972
1974
1976
1978
1980
YEAR

Table 3.2. NATO/WTO Ratios in Military Expenditures

year	ratio NATO/WTO	year	ratio NATO/WTO
1960	2.93	1970	1.92
1961	2.45	1971	1.82
1962	2.43	1972	1.83
1963	2.22	1973	1.75
1964	2.29	1974	1.73
1965	2.36	1975	1.68
1966	2.50	1976	1.61
1967	2.61	1977	1.64
1968	2.31	1978	1.64
1969	2.09	1979	1.63

expenditure: In 1960 the NATO countries spent nearly three times (2.93) as much as the WTO countries; by 1979 the corresponding ratio has dropped to 1.63. It is not the purpose of this study to evaluate such findings. Nevertheless, the marked change in the power ratio reflected by these figures (or, to put it in the terminology applied by authors in socialist countries, the change in the "correlation of forces") appears to be more than accidental. Obviously, it indicates a deeply rooted, highly significant trend in East-West relations. It is also not easy to say whether or not such fundamental shifts in the relative potential are beneficial to stability and peace. Many authors tend to assume that a roughly even "balance of power" is the best means to guarantee peace (Wright 1942); yet other authors propose that parity (Garnham 1976) breeds insecurity and thus may lead to war, and they therefore contradict the classical assumption. Recent empirical research (Weede 1981; Ash 1980) confirms that states with approximate parity do tend to engage relatively often in war and that therefore a "balance of power" is not the panacea leading to peace and stability as supposed by the classical balance-of-power theories. If these findings are correct, the decline in the ratio of NATO/WTO defense expenditure that took place in the context of "détente" would ultimately not contribute to broaden the basis for security in Europe. Yet at this point such interpretations must be left to speculation. A more refined analysis of the preconditions and consequences of shifts in the power ratios will be offered in Chapter 5.

Graph 3.6. Strategic Nuclear Forces of the US and the USSR, Bomber Forces

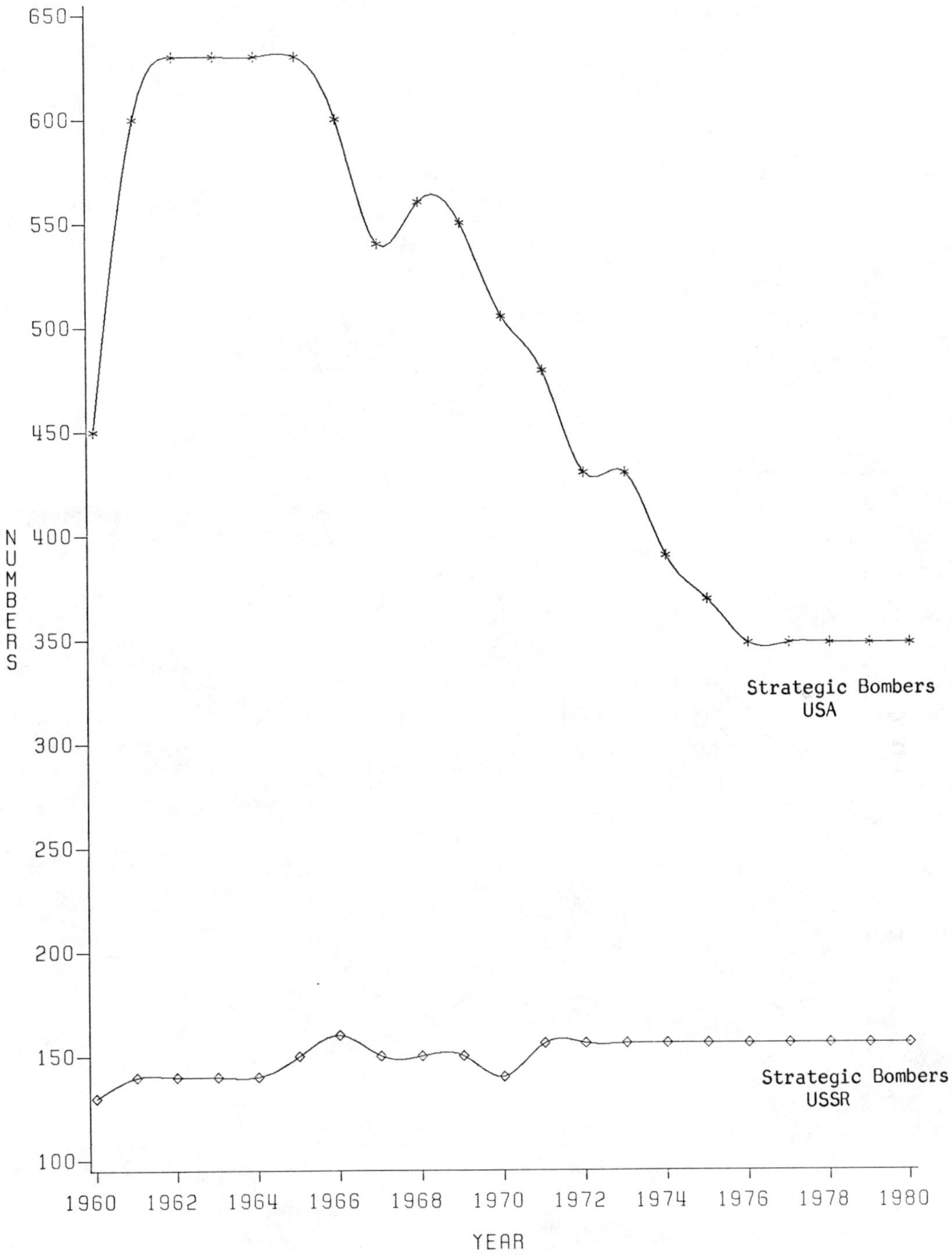
650
600
550
500
450
400
350
300
250
200
150
100
NUMBERS
1960
1962
1964
1966
1968
1970
1972
1974
1976
1978
1980
YEAR
Strategic Bombers
USA
Strategic Bombers
USSR

Graph 3.7. Strategic Nuclear Forces of the US and the USSR, Submarines

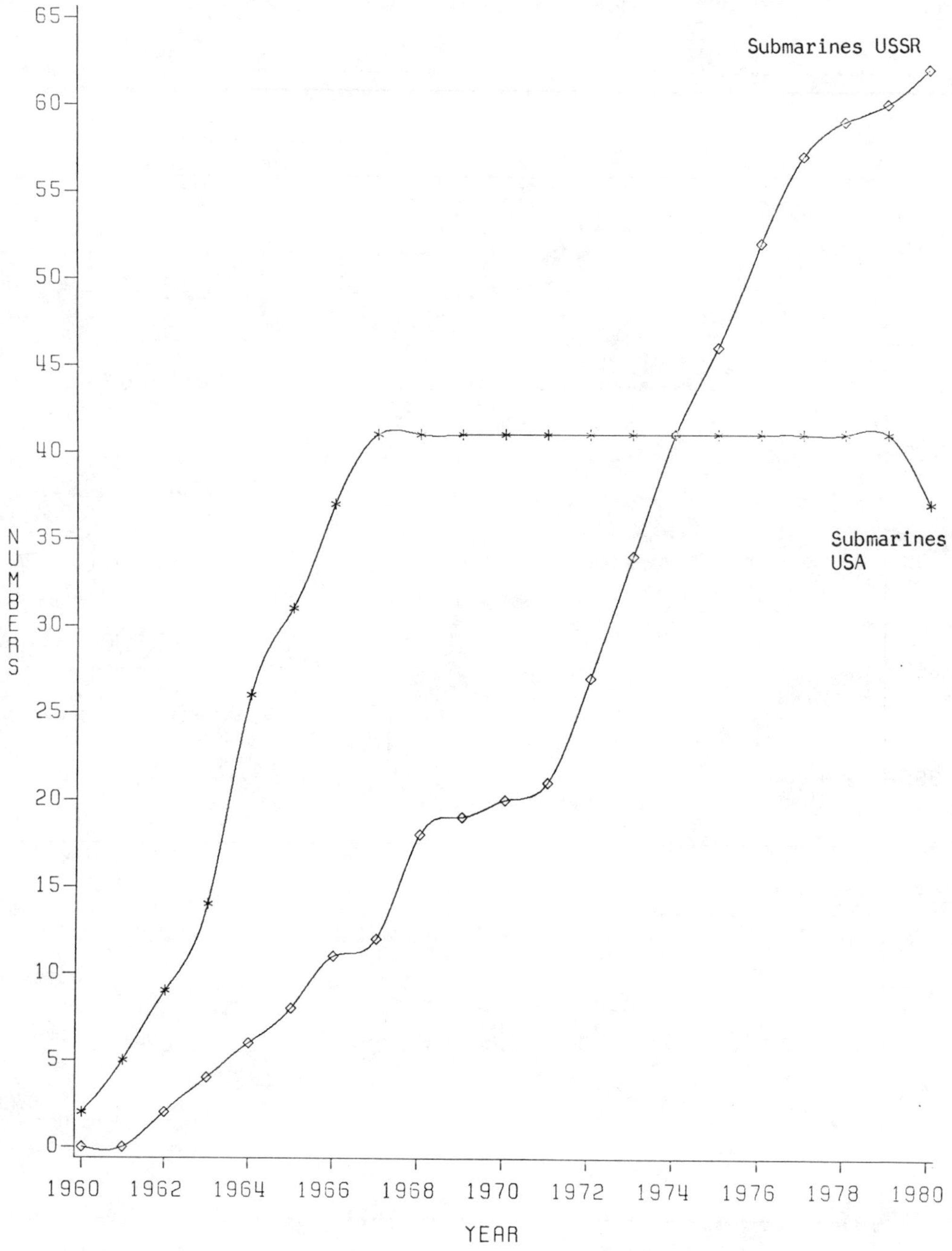
Submarines USSR
Submarines
USA
NUMBERS
0
5
10
15
20
25
30
35
40
45
50
55
60
65
1960
1962
1964
1966
1968
1970
1972
1974
1976
1978
1980
YEAR

Graph 3.8. Strategic Nuclear Forces of the US and the USSR, ICBMs and SLBMs

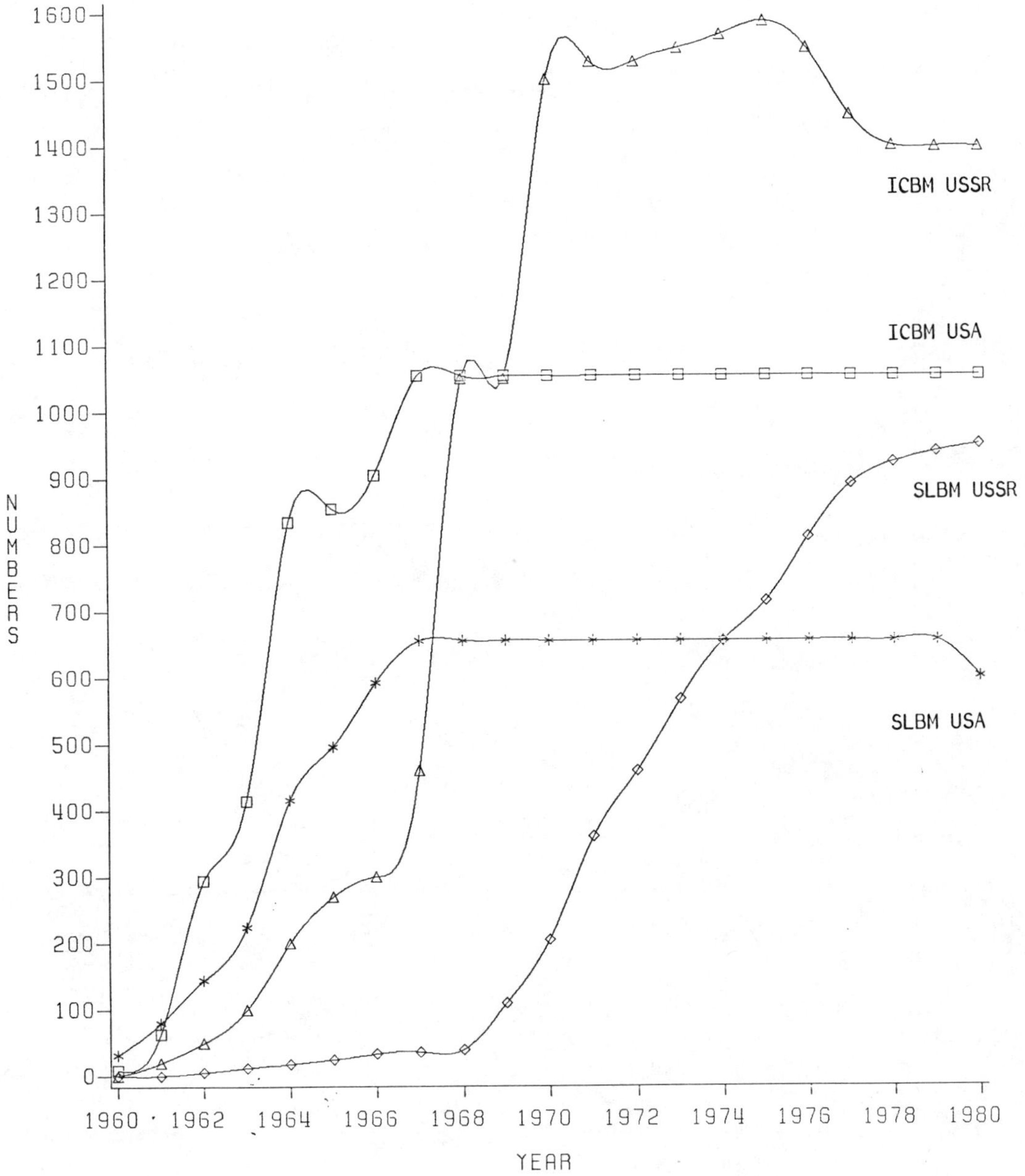
1600
1500
1400
1300
1200
1100
1000
900
800
700
600
500
400
300
200
100
0
NUMBERS
1960
1962
1964
1966
1968
1970
1972
1974
1976
1978
1980
YEAR
ICBM USSR
ICBM USA
SLBM USSR
SLBM USA

Graph 3.9. Strategic Nuclear Forces of the US and the USSR, Warheads and Delivery Systems

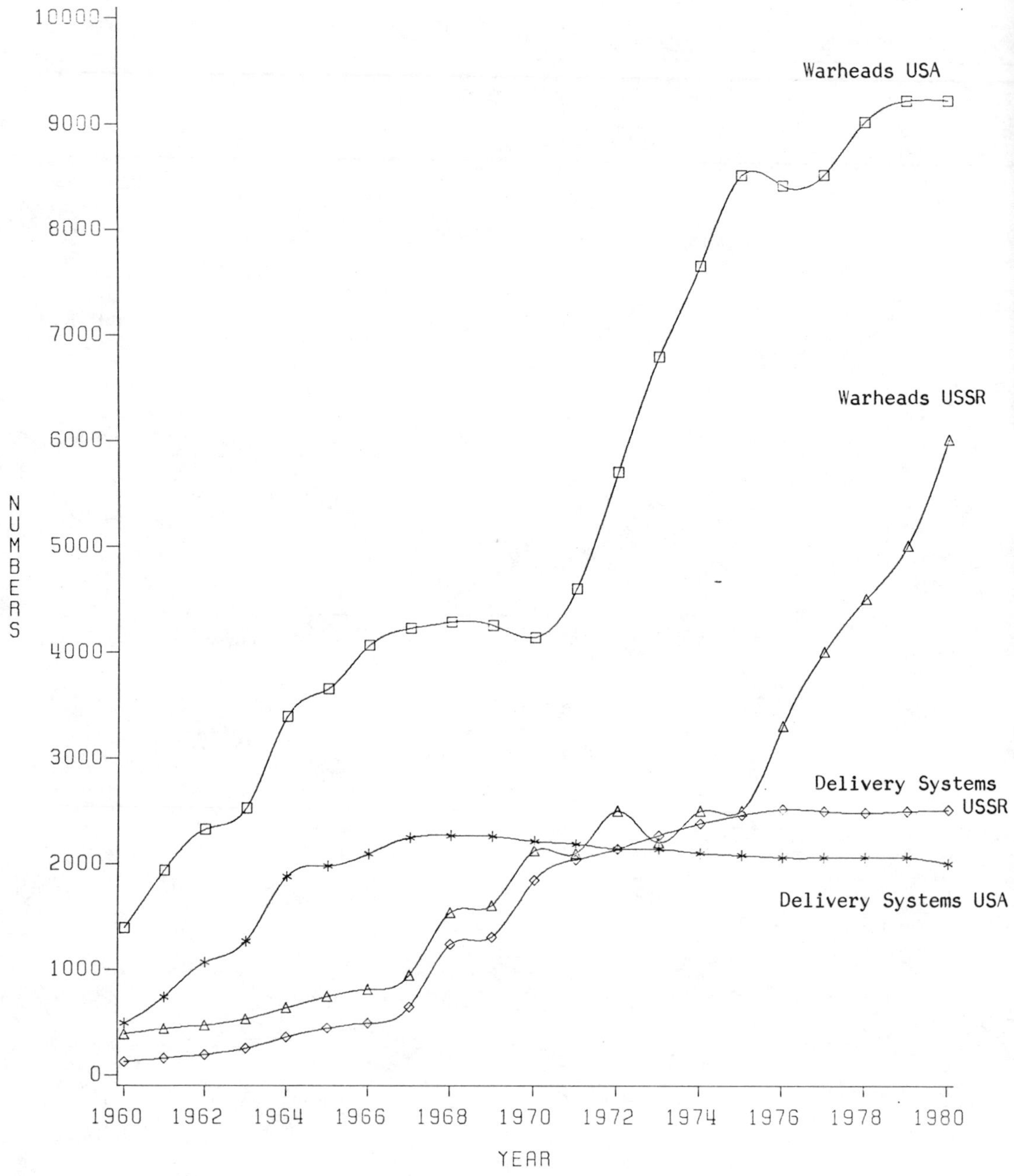
Warheads USA
Warheads USSR
Delivery Systems USSR
Delivery Systems USA
NUMBERS
10000
9000
8000
7000
6000
5000
4000
3000
2000
1000
0
1960
1962
1964
1966
1968
1970
1972
1974
1976
1978
1980
YEAR

Graph 3.10. Ratio of Warheads and Delivery Systems (US/USSR)

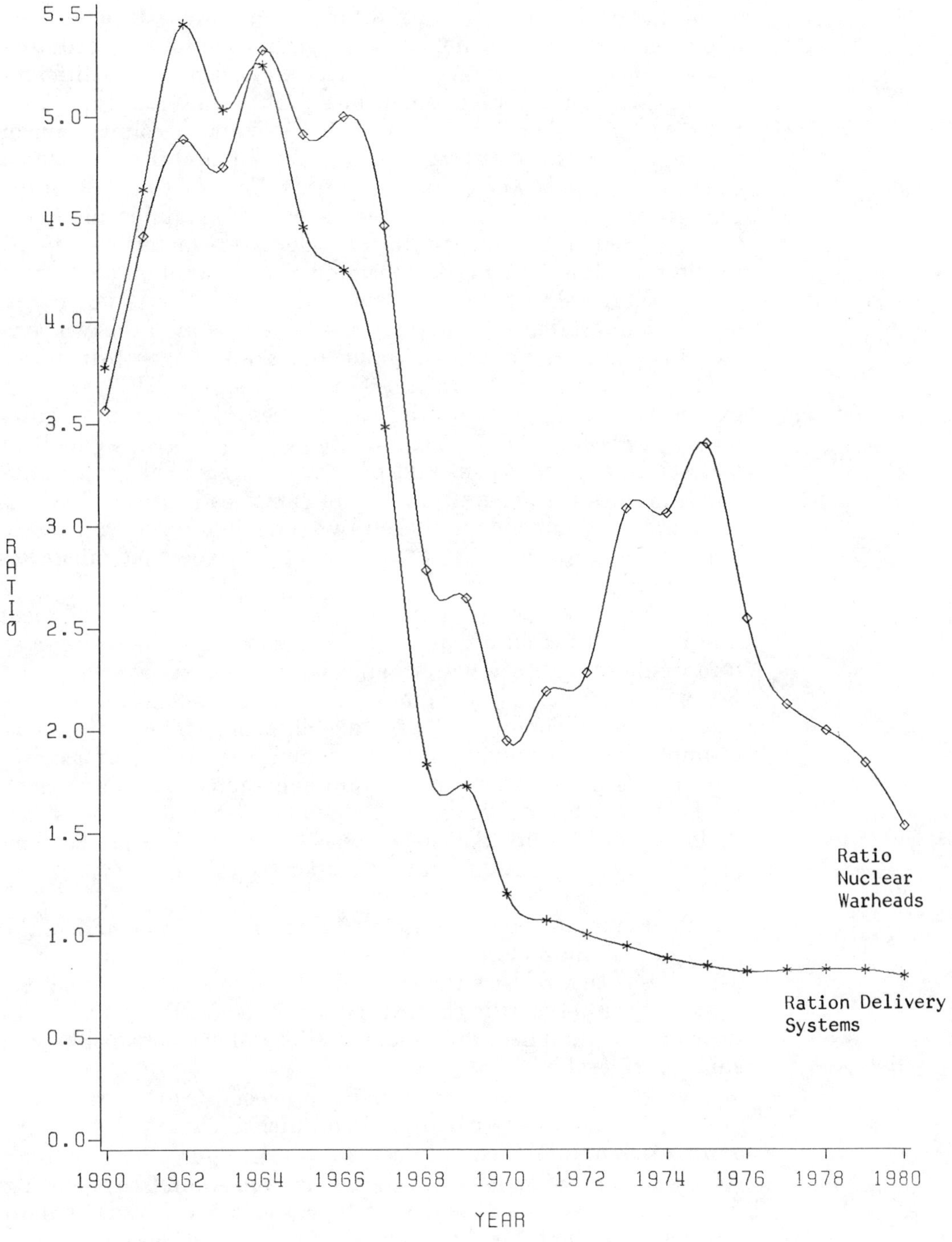
5.5
5.0
4.5
4.0
3.5
3.0
2.5
2.0
1.5
1.0
0.5
0.0
RATIO
1960 1962 1964 1966 1968 1970 1972 1974 1976 1978 1980
YEAR
Ratio Nuclear Warheads
Ration Delivery Systems

3.2.3 American and Soviet Strategic Nuclear Forces

The comparative analysis of military strength is a difficult task, and even more so in the field of strategic nuclear forces. According to Lawrence and Sherwin (1978), there are basically five different approaches to the measurement of quantity and quality of weapons systems. The first approach is based on a comparison of production costs, the inference being that capabilities are related directly to the costs of weapons systems. Yet exact figures on the production costs of weapons systems, even if available, are likely to differ from one country to the other due to the factors mentioned in the preceding section. Furthermore, the assumption of a stable linear relationship between costs and capabilities is not necessarily appropriate. With increasing sophistication of the weapons systems, the marginal costs of production are also likely to increase.

The second approach, practiced by SIPRI and the IISS, relies on expert judgment of technical capabilities by assigning utility values to specific technical capabilities such as speed, payload, or technological innovation, and production costs. The major difficulty, besides the general problem of expert estimates as such, is of course how to combine these raw scores into an overall index: additive, multiplicative, or different. Again, expert judgment has to be used.

The third approach relies on mere counts of types of equipment and the construction of balance sheets, sometimes including also information on certain performance parameters. As a devaluation factor, the date of introduction of a weapons system can be used.

As a fourth approach, these raw data may be combined, for example, by multiplying inventory numbers with performance parameters, thus ending up with an aggregated capability index for specific types of weapons. Individual series of weapons and performance characteristics of these weapons can also be combined by means of multivariate-reduction techniques such as factor analysis.

A fifth approach uses inventory figures on and indicators of the performance characteristics of weapons in order to evaluate their usefulness with respect to certain tactical or strategic tasks assigned within a specific context. However, depending on the strategic scenario implied, the assumed utility of weapons is likely to shift considerably.

In conclusion, it seems hard to find an accurate and perfect way of comparing military capabilities. Rather, different purposes require different approaches. In contrast to the figures for an overall strategic index computed by Luterbacher and Allan (see Appendix A5) for the Soviet and the US strategic weaponry, inventory data are presented here for the following categories of weapons: strategic bombers; strategic submarines; submarine-launched ballistic missiles (SLBMs); intercontinental ballistic missiles (ICBMs); and the total number of strategic nuclear delivery vehicles. These categories are discussed in the Strategic Arms Limitation Talks (SALT) and usually serve as a starting point for the definition of ceilings for weapons systems. Another important indicator, although so far not yet employed for the definition of weapons ceilings, is the number of nuclear warheads that can be delivered by all systems together. The strategic index of Luterbacher and Allan relies heavily on these figures.

The following graphs clearly indicate that the SALT agreements of 26 May 1972 and 18 June 1979 had an important impact on the quantitative and qualitative development of strategic nuclear weapons. SALT comprised an agreement on the limitation of offensive strategic weapons and a treaty on the limitation of ABM systems. The ceilings negotiated for the United States and the Soviet Union, respectively, were: for ICBMs, 1,054/1,618; for SLBMs, 710/950; for strategic nuclear submarines, 44/62. In Article 1 of the agreement, both countries declared not to start construction of additional fixed land-based intercontinental ballistic missiles launchers beyond those currently in service. In Article 2, the conversion of land-based launchers for light ICBMs or older ICBMs deployed prior to 1964 into land-based launchers of heavy ICBMs was banned. The exact ceilings were defined in a protocol added to the interim agreement. SALT I, apart from the ABM treaty, consisted only of executive agreements and protocols that did not require ratification, thus avoiding the difficulties that the Carter administration had to face with SALT II.

The SALT II treaty was supposed to remain valid until 31 December 1985; a protocol to the treaty covering issues not ready for a long-term resolution, namely the problem of mobile ICBMs, was assumed to be valid until 31 December 1981. The quantitative ceilings negotiated were the following, for the United States and the Soviet Union, respectively: 850 ICBMs with multiple and independently targetable reentry vehicles (MIRVs); 1,200 of the same including MIRVed SLBMs; 1,320 of the same including cruise missile bombers; 2,250 of the same including single-target ICBMs and SLBMs as well as bombers without cruise missiles. By contrast to SALT I allowing the Soviet Union a numerical superiority in order to compensate for the American lead with respect to technology, SALT II defines equal ceilings for both parties to the treaty.

In fact, the actual development of the inventory of strategic nuclear weapons as illustrated by Graphs 3.6–3.8 shows a clear adjustment to the ceilings negotiated in SALT I. The strategic bomber force of the United States, after its build-up in the fifties and early sixties, experienced a steady decline until being stabilized at a level of 348 in 1976. With the development of ICBMs and SLBMs and increasing precision of these weapons, strategic bombers tended to become obsolete; furthermore, the advance of air-defense systems made strategic bombers increasingly vulnerable. The number of Soviet strategic bombers remained at a level of around 150 during the whole period, probably for much the same reasons. Therefore, SALT I did not contain any provisions as to the number of strategic bombers since figures were decreasing anyway. Yet the development of cruise missiles changed the situation by assigning a new task to American bombers as cruise-missile carriers.

Within the limitations agreed upon in SALT I, the Soviet Union was entitled to build up a fleet of strategic nuclear submarines; by 1980 the number of Soviet strategic submarines had reached 62, while the United States maintained a level of 41 units since 1967. Accordingly, also the number of Soviet SLBMs grew while the level of American SLBMs remained at 656 since 1967. Also the number of American ICBMs was stabilized at the ceiling reached in the late sixties (1,054). The Soviet expansion of ICBM reached its climax in 1975 with 1,587, still within the ceiling negotiated at SALT I. This number was reduced to around 1,400 missiles by 1978 in order to meet the overall delivery systems' ceiling of SALT II discussed since the Vladiwostok meeting on 24 November 1974. The overall ceiling was initially 2,400 with a subsequent reduction to 2,250 planned for the end of 1981. In order to comply with these ceilings, the Soviet Union would have to dismantle some 250 strategic missile systems, while the United States could increase its strategic nuclear forces by the same number of systems.

With respect to the number of warheads (Graphs 3.9 and 3.10), the United States still has an approximate advantage vis-à-vis the Soviet Union. Still the period of a virtual monopoly of the United States in the field of strategic nuclear weapons of the early sixties has definitively passed. All evidence suggests that SALT, even if the treaty of 1979 would have been ratified, never "limited" or curbed the arms race in the field of strategic nuclear weapons; it was "controlled" only in the very vague meaning of the word. As President Carter pointed out in his address before a joint session of the Congress on 18 June 1979, "SALT II does not end the arms competition, but it does make that competition safer and more predictable, with clear rules and verifiable limits where otherwise there would be no rules and there would be no limits." Also, renaming "SALT" to "START" is not more than a mere verbal concession.

The motive that led the two major powers to sign the SALT agreement of 1972 and the treaty of 1979 were mixed on both sides. For the Soviet Union, SALT implied international recognition of her status as a major power by the other major power, thereby satisfying some of the Soviet security needs. Furthermore, SALT I saved the Soviet Union from a competition in the field of ABM where they were lagging behind the United States for several years (SIPRI 1980, p. 88). Finally, the prospect of limiting the defense burden was surely an important incentive to depart upon the SALT negotiations. Also the United States pursued mixed goals in the SALT negotiations. It was certainly one of the crucial aspects of the Nixon administration's design of security policy to share responsibilities with the Soviet Union. Also, the massive build-up of Soviet missiles at the end of the sixties was alarming. Kissinger noted that in 1970, "the Soviets were in a position to add numbers [of ICBMs] immediately and we [the United States] were not." And: "We needed a freeze not only for arms control but for strategic reasons.... We froze a disparity in order to gain time to reverse the situation...." In fact, this objective was successfully achieved as the numbers of strategic nuclear warheads on delivery systems indicate (Kissinger, quoted in SIPRI 1980, p. 88). The SALT process regulated the arms competition in a certain way thus making force planning more predictable and transparent. On the other hand, as noted before, SALT did not halt or curb the arms race despite establishing equal numerical ceilings for weapons systems. SALT also was not capable of encouraging a shift to less threatening and more survivable systems [cf. *Arms Control Today* vol 9, no. 7 (July/August 1979); SIPRI 1980, p. 87]. To some extent, the negotiations of armament ceilings worked indeed at cross-purposes because ceilings were established at a considerable level beyond existing numbers of systems.

Most important, the SALT process did not retard the competitive momentum of the arms race but rather shifted it to new areas of competition: First, the limitation imposed on certain categories of weapons stimulated the improvement of these weapons, thereby replacing the quantitative arms race by a qualitative arms race. Innovations included considerable improvements in precision, destruction power, mobility, and easy and fast retargeting. The most important qualitative improvement certainly is the expansion of the number of warheads each system is capable of delivering. This may upgrade the survivability of the system, but it may also constitute a threat to the existing systems of the opponent jeopardizing his second-strike capability. Second, the arms competition spilled over into the field of INF in Europe.

In sum, a reexamination of the history of the strategic arms race as just outlined suggests the conclusion that this arms race and also efforts to control it evolved out of its own momentum and largely decoupled from the rest of East–West relations. And increasingly, the strategic arms race seems to be driven by its own momentum. This can be seen even when glancing simply at the shape of the curves presented in this section and comparing it with curves referring to other dimensions of East–West interactions; these curves evolve in a way different from other curves and seem to be unconnected with efforts aimed at promoting "détente" in other fields. However, proposing that the arms race is mainly determined by its own inherent logic is one thing, and it is quite another to draw the corollary conclusion that the arms race in turn does not affect the rest of "détente." Quite the opposite may be true. The interrelation between the arms race and other aspects of East–West relations will be analyzed in Chapter 5.

Yet again there is one element in the arms race of the two major powers that despite these reservations may have something to do with the process of "détente." As in the preceding section, the ratios calculated for the US/USSR "balance" are quite revealing. As can be seen in Graph 3.10, the US/USSR ratio of strategic delivery systems declined constantly. The ratio concerning the number of warheads rapidly dropped already in the sixties, improved again for the US in the first half of the seventies but continued its rapid decline since 1975. Again some doubts have to be expressed as to whether such a fundamental restructuring of the global power relations in the long run is conducive to international security and peace.

As has already been pointed out, the strategic arms race eventually tended to blur the distinction between the "global" and "regional" (European) element of the strategic debate. Therefore, the arms race related to INF became increasingly activated and stirred up. This aspect will be dealt with in the following subsection.

3.2.4 Eurostrategic Weapons

The field of the so-called Eurostrategic weapons is highly controversial for both conceptual and technical reasons. First of all, different definitions of the term *Eurostrategic weapons* have a crucial impact on the way these weapon systems are counted and evaluated. Therefore, much attention should be paid to the problem of definition.

The *SIPRI Yearbook* (1980, p. 175) uses the term *Eurostrategic* to describe nuclear weapons located in and likely to be used in Europe and capable of hitting targets at significant distance within the territory of the opponent. In terms of performance parameters facilitating the distinction of "Eurostrategic" from "tactical" nuclear weapons, missiles and aircraft with a combat radius of about 800 kilometers are regarded as "Eurostrategic." For ship- and submarine-based weapons systems, the line of distinction may be low, at about 400 kilometers (km) according to SIPRI (1980, p. 176). From the NATO point of view, a combat radius of 1,000 km and more is suggested as a criterion to distinguish "Eurostrategic" from "tactical" nuclear weapons (Bundesminister der Verteidigung 1980, p. 29). The IISS *Military Balance* distinguishes, in addition, "tactical nuclear weapons" from "long range theatre nuclear forces" and "medium range theatre nuclear forces" (LRTNF and MRTNF). This has not much influence on the classification of medium-range ballistic missiles, either land or submarine based, and long- or medium-range bomers as "Eurostrategic"; yet difficulties arise with respect to other aircraft. Due to important differences in the evaluation of the combat radius of those aircraft with disputed assignments, the overall figures of Eurostrategic systems will shift significantly. According to the IISS (Military Balance 1980), one had to include not only all of NATO's FB-111A stationed in Europe but also most of the other fighter bombers as well due to exaggerated assumptions regarding the combat radius of these aircrafts; in the 1981 edition of *Military Balance*, however, these figures were corrected, and the combat radius of the F-4 Phantom was adjusted from 2,590 km to 750 km only. Some publications (Lutz 1980a; Lutz 1980b) still report the uncorrected figures causing some controversy among experts (Stratmann 1981).

From the WTO point of view, on the other hand, all forward-based systems (FOBS) of NATO ought to be included into the balance of strategic nuclear weapons. In a TASS commentary of 7 July 1980, the respective numbers given are 784 American FOBS and, in addition, 300 French and British FOBS. Indeed, NATO has, apart from the F-111s, about 1,000 nuclear-capable strike aircraft deployed in the European region, on land bases and on aircraft carriers in the Atlantic and the Mediterranean (SIPRI 1980, p. 176). At least half of them are capable of reaching Soviet territory. The exact accounting of all aircraft assigned to a strategic rather than tactical role, both for NATO and the WTO, would require classified information currently not available for academic research. On these grounds, it can be justified to exclude this category of weapons from the balance for both NATO and WTO.

Finally, to make things even more complicated, there are Eurostrategic systems covered already under SALT I and SALT II. The United States assigns five ballistic missile-equipped, nuclear-powered submarines carrying a total of about 800 Poseidon C-3 reentry vehicles, to the Supreme Allied Commander, Europe. It may be justified not to include these weapons into the balance sheet provided also Soviet submarines with SLBM reaching Western Europe counted under SALT are not included. Also French Eurostrategic forces are not included since they are not subject to NATO command. In 1980, France had eighteen intermediate-range ballistic missiles, sixty-four submarine-launched ballistic missiles, and in addition, around thirty-three Mirage IV-A bombers.

The NATO account does include 64 British SLBMs and 48 Vulcan B-2 bombers. Furthermore, there are at present 156 American F-111s based in Great Britain; they have a range of 5,000 km and are capable of delivering at least two nuclear warheads. Until 1962, the United States had 105 MRBM/IRBMs operational in Europe ("Thor" and "Jupiter"). These were withdrawn in the aftermath of the Cuban missile crisis. The Eurostrategic arsenal of the WTO countries, more precisely: the Soviet arsenal, in 1980, comprised 380 SS-4 MRBMs with a maximum range of about 2,000 km, 60 SS-5 IRBMs with a maximum range of around 3,700 km, and 160 SS-20 IRBMs with a range of about 4,000 km. In addition, there are 60 SS-N-5 SLBMs with a range of around 1,200 km, 318 TU-16 ("Badger") bombers (range 6,500 km), 125 TU-22 ("Blinder") bombers, and 75 TU-22M ("Backfire") bombers (range 9,000 km). This adds up to 268 systems under NATO command and 1,178 WTO systems.

Graph 3.11. Eurostrategic Forces of NATO and WTO (IRBMs and MRBMs)

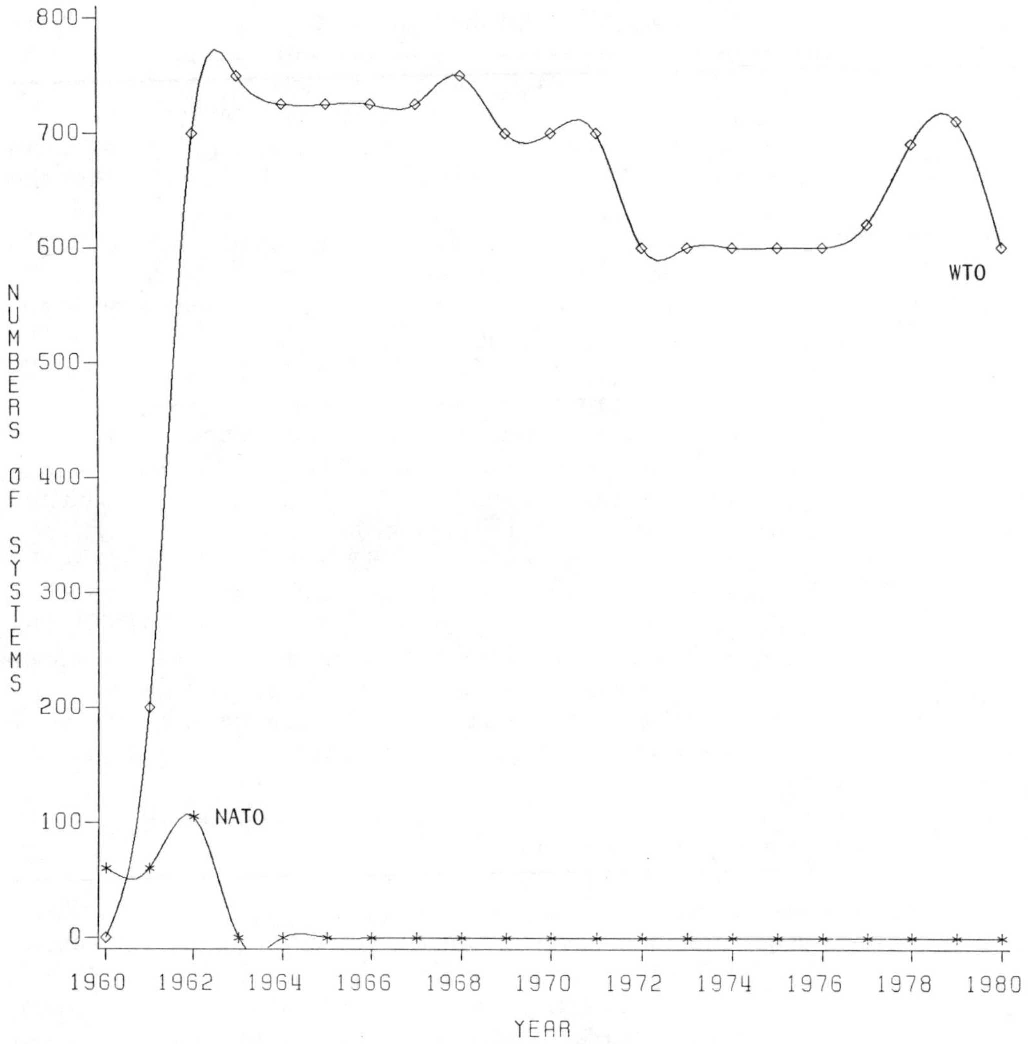
800
700
600
500
400
300
200
100
0
NUMBERS OF SYSTEMS
WTO
NATO
1960
1962
1964
1966
1968
1970
1972
1974
1976
1978
1980
YEAR

Graph 3.12. Eurostrategic Forces of NATO and WTO (SLBMs)

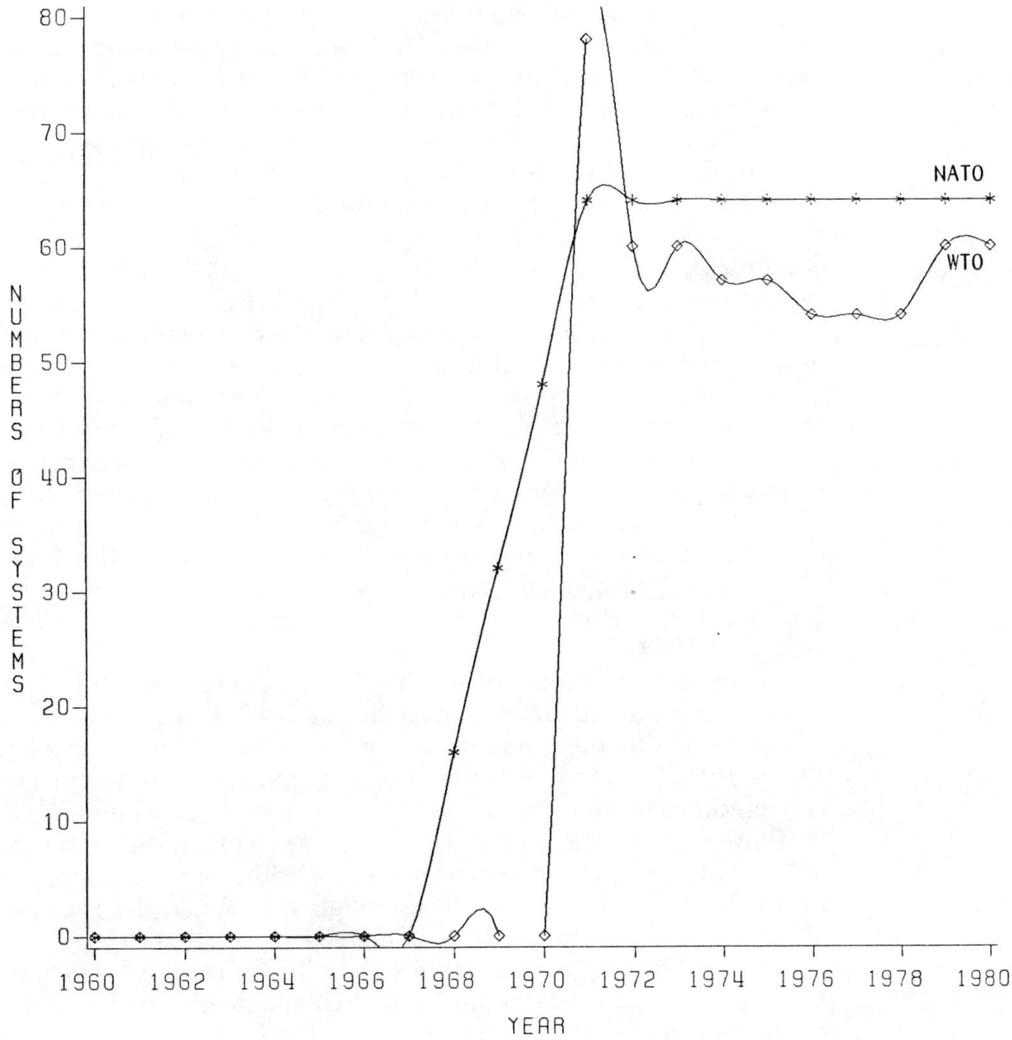
80
70
60
50
40
30
20
10
0
NUMBERS OF SYSTEMS
NATO
WTO
1960
1962
1964
1966
1968
1970
1972
1974
1976
1978
1980
YEAR

These figures were compiled on the basis of various published sources, including the SIPRI Yearbooks, the current issues of the *Military Balance* since 1959, and the FRG *White Book* of 1979. The authors of the present study do not wish to offer any evaluation of these findings with respect to the current discussion on the balance of Eurostrategic weapons. As pointed out before, they believe that very much depends on the choice of definitions (Stratmann 1981, p. 8). Nevertheless, the Soviet superiority in the sphere of MRBMs and IRBMs in Europe cannot be denied.

The dynamics of East-West relations are reflected in the development of Eurostrategic arsenals, as described by the curves in Graphs 3.11 and 3.12. In 1962, following the Cuban missile crisis, the United States moved their MRBMs and IRBMs out of Europe. Ever since then the Soviet Union has enjoyed a considerable superiority in what now is called "Eurostrategic weapons." It is interesting to note that it was not until the middle of the seventies that these facts were "highlighted" and became a crucial issue of the debate on the balance of military power and the limitation of strategic weapons. From a historical point of view, the controversy about Eurostrategic weapons, which started in 1980, is a direct consequence of successful "détente,"; it results from the limitation of and the agreement on certain ceilings regarding strategic nuclear weapons between the Soviet Union and the United States, in 1972 and 1979.

According to the principle of "flexible response," which in 1967 became the official defense doctrine of NATO, any aggression would be met at the appropriate level with the option to escalate the conflict if required. A conventional aggression would be met by conventional means, while a strategic nuclear strike would trigger retaliation by nuclear forces. The crucial concepts in the reasoning of "flexible response" are deterrence, credibility, and incalculability of the risks on the side of any aggressor. When the principle of "massive retaliation" was abandoned in favor of "flexible response" in order to reestablish the credibility of the NATO defense efforts, the United States had lost their monopoly in the sphere of strategic nuclear weapons but still enjoyed a remarkable superiority in terms of numbers of ICBMs and SLBMs. On the conventional level, however, the WTO forces always outnumbered the NATO forces by far, especially with respect to armoured vehicles. In order to ensure the credibility of deterrence at this level, a considerable number of tactical nuclear warheads was stockpiled in Europe. When negotiating the SALT I agreement of 1972 and the 1979 SALT II treaty, the Soviet Union and the United States were not in a position to agree on the nuclear weapons stationed in Europe. The Soviet Union refused to discuss her MRBMs, IRBMs, as well as her bomber force including the "Backfire" bombers, maintaining that these weapons were not "strategic" since they could not reach the American continent. The United States, on the other hand, refused to make their nuclear weapons stationed in

Graph 3.13. Eurostrategic Forces of NATO and WTO (Bombers)

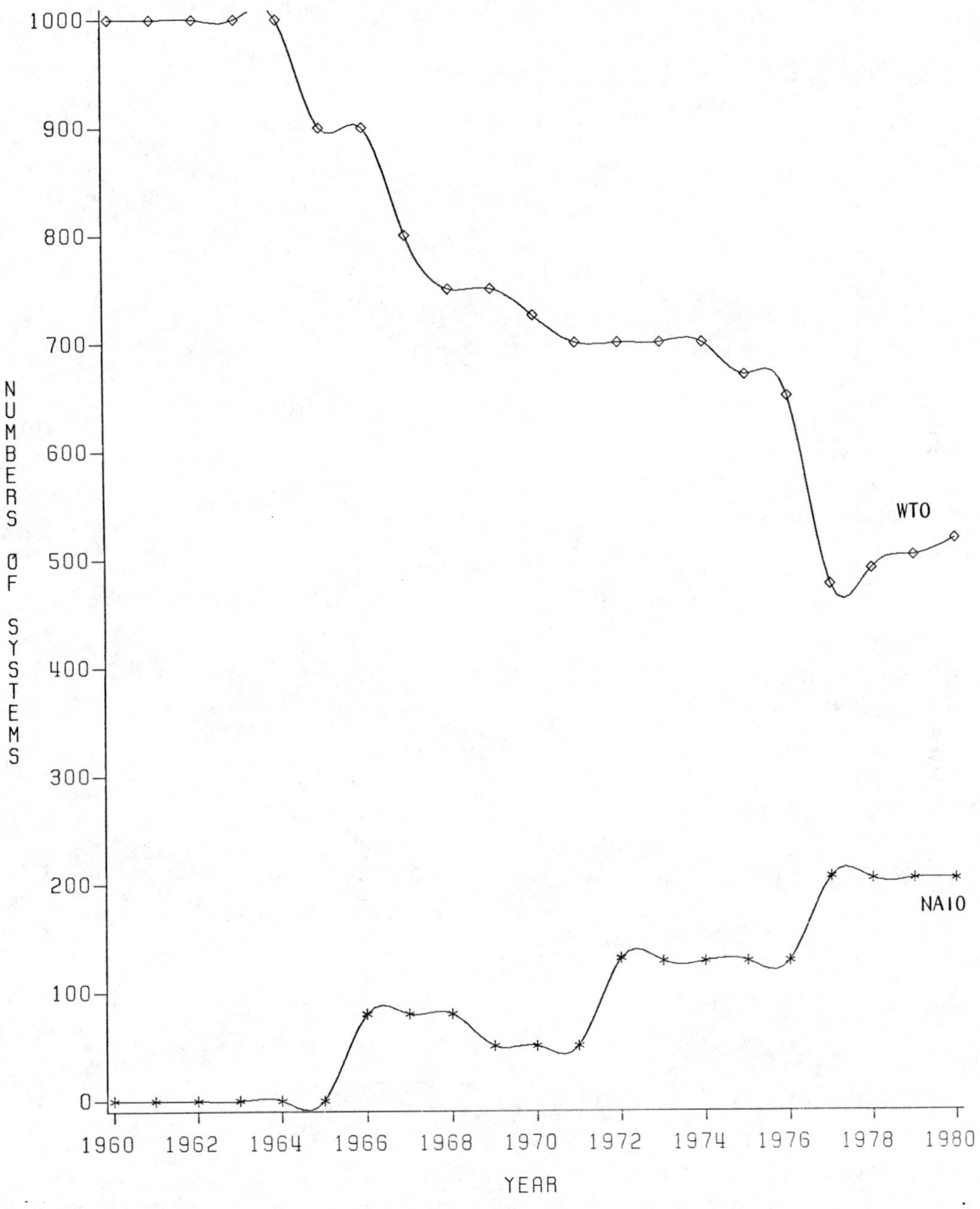
1000
900
800
700
600
500
400
300
200
100
0
NUMBERS OF SYSTEMS
WTO
NATO
1960 1962 1964 1966 1968 1970 1972 1974 1976 1978 1980
YEAR

Graph 3.14. Eurostrategic Forces of NATO and WTO (Total Number of Systems)

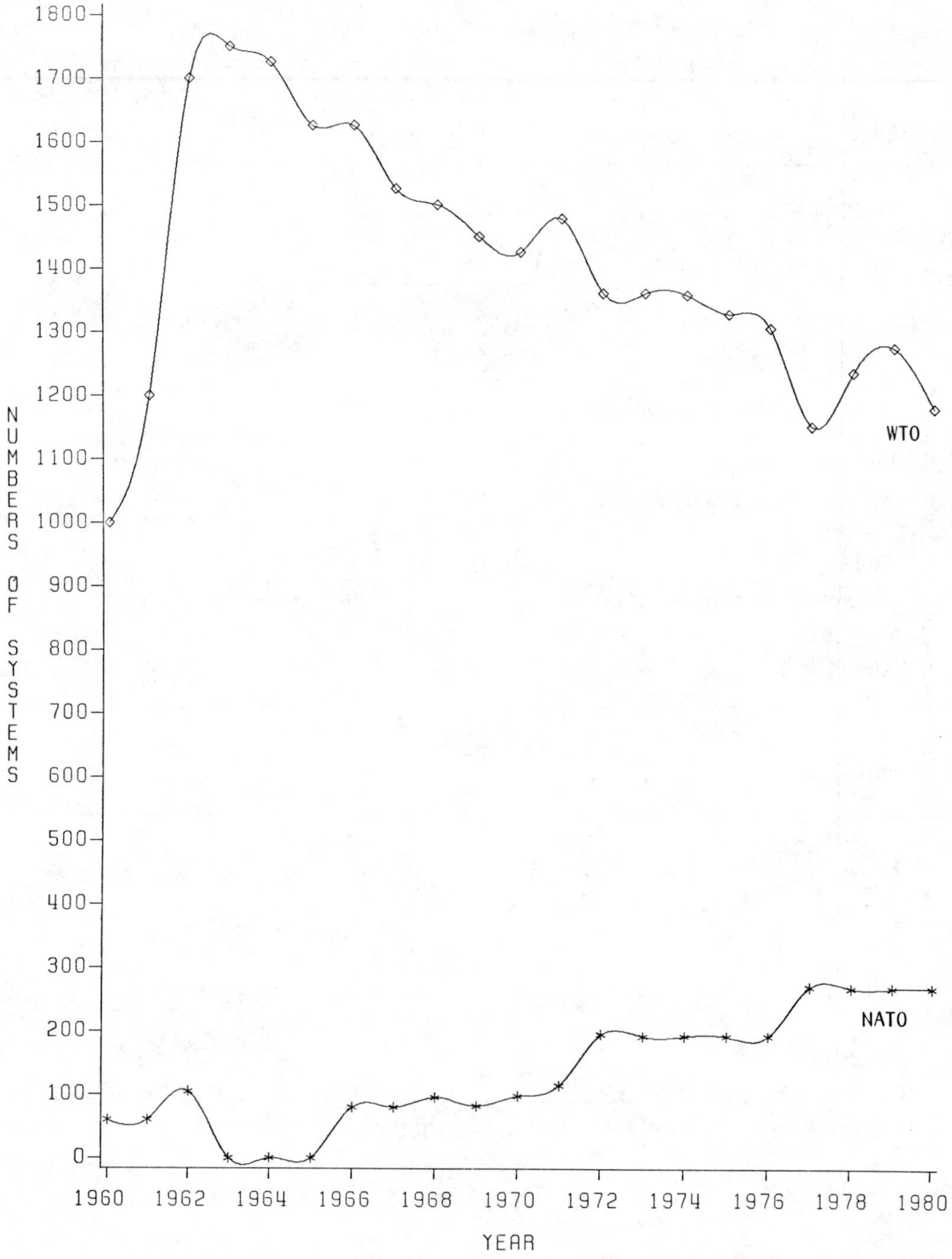
1800
1700
1600
1500
1400
1300
1200
1100
1000
900
800
700
600
500
400
300
200
100
0
NUMBERS OF SYSTEMS
WTO
NATO
1960
1962
1964
1966
1968
1970
1972
1974
1976
1978
1980
YEAR

Europe (in WTO-terminology the so-called Forward-Based Systems) an issue of SALT, although these weapons were regarded as "strategic" from the Soviet point of view as some of them had the obvious capacity to reach Soviet territory. In the last resort, there are geographic asymmetries underlying this controversy, and the geographic asymmetries can in turn lead to asymmetric nuclear risk. While the United States remain in "safe" distance of Soviet IRBMs and MRBMs, their European allies are fully within the reach of these weapons. On the other hand, important sectors of the Soviet territory are located within the combat radius of some of the nuclear delivery systems in Europe operated by US personnel.

Since this problem was not solved in the context of SALT, it was quite natural that the arms race spilled over into what is now called the "Eurostrategic" sphere. In other words, following the success of arms control on the strategic level, a new level between conventional and strategic weapons was introduced; this in fact constituted the price for having excluded some strategic weapons from the SALT negotiations. However, apart from the French IRBMs, NATO did not have any land-based missiles in Europe comparable to the Soviet SS-4 and SS-5 at the time when SALT I was signed. In order to assure the credibility of deterrence on the Eurostrategic level, 75 F-111s were stationed in Great Britain in 1972. Meanwhile, the Soviet Union developed a new IRBM that was labeled by NATO as SS-20. First tests were detected in 1974. The system was introduced in 1976 or 1977, together with the "Backfire" bomber. For NATO, this constituted a qualitative new threat, although the Soviet Union maintains that the primary purpose was not the expansion of her Eurostrategic forces but the substitution of older systems. With respect to performance parameters, however, the SS-20 is superior to any comparable NATO system stationed in Europe. It seems to be generally accepted (SIPRI 1980, p. 178), and confirmed by the Soviets at the occasion of the Brezhnev visit to Bonn in late 1981, that the deployed version carries three MIRVed warheads, thereby boosting the overall number of deliverable nuclear bombs considerably. Alarmed by these events, the NATO heads of state and heads of government, respectively, initiated the Long Term Defense Program of 1977. On 12 December 1979, NATO also decided the modernization of her intermediate-range nuclear forces in Europe by preparing the introduction of 108 Pershing-II-XR missiles (range: 1,800 km) and 464 ground-based cruise missiles (GLCM, range: 2,500 km) for 1983; at the same time, NATO offered negotiations in view of an arms-control agreement that started in Geneva in late 1981.

The relevance of these events for East–West relations and "détente" is utterly severe. With respect to both the introduction of the SS-20 and "Backfire" by the Soviet Union and the proposed and intended stationing of new Pershings and GLCMs in Europe by the United States, "modernization" is a euphemism but hardly an apt description of the process taking place. MIRVing and reloadability, reduced explosive yields plus enhanced radiation and improved precision, easy retargeting and high mobility are new qualitative characteristics of these weapons that point at basic shifts in the strategic evaluation of nuclear strikes currently under way: All these weapons have a salient counterforce capacity. For the European "theatre," these perspectives are even more frightening than from the global "strategic" point of view. The assumption of nuclear weapons guaranteeing the joint survival of nations by the capacity of mutual annihilation is no longer valid if counterforce strategies become an operative military option. Especially the vast increase in nuclear warheads deployed on delivery vehicles of various kinds points at serious preparations for "surgical" strikes against military installations.

Furthermore, it now also seems feasible in principle to limit a nuclear war to Europe. The possibility of decoupling a nuclear confrontation in Europe from the risk of an all-out nuclear war greatly increases the probability of using nuclear weapons. Experts may disagree about these prospects (Stratmann 1981, p. 9), yet the expectations and fears in this respect are quite real and alarming. The future of "détente" in Europe therefore will very much depend on the outcome of efforts undertaken to control the deployment of Eurostrategic weapons, which began in Geneva in the fall of 1981.

3.3 PEACE AND CONFLICT

3.3.1 The Evolution of East-West Relations, 1960–1980

In this section, a kind of "pictorial history" of East-West relations will be presented, based on a graphic representation of the "ups" and "downs" of hostility and friendship between selected countries in the East and the West.

Among the dimensions of East-West relations identified by the content analysis of the statements made at various CSCE meetings, one dimension emerges that was labeled "cooperation and conflict." By contrast to the other dimensions, this dimension refers to the general political and diplomatic climate in relations between countries; it does not reflect specific issues of interaction. Still, "conflict" and "cooperation" are two separate concepts and not simply elements of the same continuum reaching from "maximum conflict" to "maximum cooperation." This is also the way actors apparently perceive East-West relations, as was demonstrated in the factor analysis of the content-analytical data. The following analysis of time-series data on conflictive and cooperative interactions between countries will show that this conception is indeed perfectly in accordance with reality. Interactions between East and West always constitute a mixture of both conflict *and* cooperation. That is why in this section each pair of countries is analyzed in two separate graphs looking at cooperation and conflict between the two states separately.

Interaction between states can be conceived within the framework of events analysis (see Azar and Ben Dak 1975, pp. 2 ff.) as an actor-action-target relationship. Looking at events data means (1) identifying actors and targets, (2) classifying types of actions, and (3) scaling actions or "events" with respect to intensity. The theory and technique of events analysis has been amply discussed elsewhere and does not need further elaboration at this point. The emphasis here is on the analysis of data provided by Azar's COPDAB (Conflict and Peace Data Bank) project. Despite of some shortcomings, these data provide a suitable basis for the analysis of East–West relations in view of the political and diplomatic climate. The COPDAB data are gathered from publicly accessible sources, mostly from newspapers.

The plots presented in this section refer to index values for conflictive and cooperative events, scaled according to intensity and aggregated on an annual basis. When looking at the resulting time-series curves, it must, however, be pointed out that it would not be appropriate to compare the absolute scores for cooperation or conflict among nations because, to some extent, these scores simply reflect different "styles" of foreign-policy conduct rather than different levels of interaction. It also should be noted that the independent press in the West often "produces" events on its own by citing unofficial sources or by conducting specific research. On the other hand, the function of the press is somewhat different in socialist countries. Therefore, the events used in this analysis will not necessarily reflect the respective government's behavior or intentions. Furthermore, it must be borne in mind that if a government wishes to express agreement or disagreement by using subtle signals, these events will not rank as high as the more spectacular kinds of actions preferred by others. Nevertheless, it is legitimate to assume that at least the annual shifts in cooperative and conflictive interactions between nations reflect meaningful changes in policy, taking for granted a certain consistency in the style of foreign-policy conduct.

The graphs presented and commented in the following paragraphs refer to selected pairs of countries. First, the relations between the United States and the Soviet Union will be examined looking at both the cooperative and the conflictive behavior exhibited by each of the two major powers vis-à-vis the opposing power. Following the section regarding US–USSR relations, attention will focus on relations between the Soviet Union and the United Kingdom, France, and the Federal Republic of Germany, respectively.

The United States of America

As the graphs refer to the 1960–1978 period only, it may be useful to briefly summarize the course of East–West relations in the previous postwar years. American-Soviet relations before 1960 were characterized by a policy of containment adopted by the United States and a policy of consolidation of spheres of influence pursued by the Soviet Union. In 1947 the World War II alliance definitively broke down after the failure of the conferences on Germany and the European Recovery Program. The Korean crisis soon put the policy of containment to a hard test. As a new element, the Eisenhower administration (1953–1961) introduced the concept of "roll-back" and "liberation." However, it cannot be denied that in the fifties, some new trends emerged that prepared the ground for a rather different evolution of East–West relations in the period following 1960.

First, the growing strength of the Soviet Union in the field of nuclear strategic weapons appeared to make any confrontation between the two major powers a severe risk not only for the European allies in NATO. There was a growing feeling that any nuclear confrontation would also affect the heartland of the free world, that is, the United States itself. These fears received additional support by events such as the successful launching of the Sputnik in 1957 and additional satellites of the "Lunik" series. In 1961 the Soviet Union tested a 5,000-kiloton superbomb, indicating that she not only possessed adequate delivery capacity for long-distance strikes but also immensely powerful warheads. The shifts in strategic thinking that now took place focused mainly on the credibility of massive retaliation. Nevertheless, any war was still perceived to lead inevitably to a nuclear holocaust.

Second, the United States was not capable of providing any support for the peoples of Eastern Europe when, in June 1953 and again in June and October 1956, they rose against Communist party rule in GDR, Poland, and Hungary. Thus the policy of "roll-back" and "liberation" did not survive its first tests, which was certainly not surprising for the difficulties of such a policy were clear from the beginning. In a hearing before the Committee on Foreign Relations in January 1953, John Foster Dulles (who was to become Secretary of State) declared that "We must always have in mind the liberation of these captive peoples." And he added, "Now, liberation does not mean a war of liberation...." The humiliating fact that no effective aid to liberation movements within the Communist world could be provided without risking a nuclear confrontation very much strengthened the criticism of this kind of policy.

Third, new centrifugal tendencies within the Soviet sphere of influence became evident when after the rejection of Soviet leadership by Yugoslavia in 1948, other Communist party leaders tried to act with some renewed self-assertion, especially after the death of Stalin in March 1953.

In the Soviet Union, the evolution of the international environment caused a steady shift in policy toward the West and the United States. As a concession to the realities of nuclear weapons technology, the XX. Party Congress of the CPSU initiated the policy of "peaceful coexistence," referring to a concept suggested by Lenin. "Peaceful coexistence" mainly meant prevention of nuclear war, intensified contest with capitalism in the social and economic field, aid to liberation movements in the Third World, and continuing ideological struggle without any concessions. Furthermore, ideological differences with China led in 1960 to a schism of the Communist movement, followed by rapidly increasing hostility up to the brink of war.

Nevertheless, the period of the so-called Cold War was never merely a rigid and absolute confrontation of East and West. Again and again attempts to cooperate were made as indicated by successive meetings of foreign ministers and summit meetings. In 1955 the Austrian State Treaty was signed strengthening the hopes that, after all, a constructive common policy of both major powers was possible. However, neither the Soviet nor the American policy were fully consistent with the respective theoretical designs. Schwarz has argued that day-to-day East–West policy is determined by the requirements of specific problems rather than by grand designs (Schwarz 1979a, p. 148); in fact, it seems that these grand designs are hardly more than a kind of an apologetic exercise. Even more than the period of Cold War, the period of "détente" is characterized by cooperation and conflict taking place simultaneously and by fluctuations of changing amplitude and phase-length. The objective of a simultaneous development of cooperation in all fields of international relations and between all European countries was never fully accomplished.

The oscillations of cooperation as represented by the curves of Graphs 3.15 and 3.16 can easily be identified with major events of the sixties and seventies. Several crises affected the level of conflict between the United States and the Soviet Union: the Cuban missile crisis 1962; the Six Day War of 1967; the Middle East crisis of 1970; the October War of 1973; and the involvement of the Soviet Union and her Cuban ally in Southern Africa in 1977 and 1978. Since then, the major issues were disputes over Eurostrategic weapons, Afghanistan, and Poland. It is interesting to note that the Vietnam war hardly affected the level of conflict.

Throughout the sixties, the crises mentioned before also led to a series of meetings and conferences. In 1960 there were discussions on a minor irritant of Soviet-American relations, the question of lend-lease repayment. The Big Four summit meeting in May the same year failed, with the U-2 incident occasioning the Soviet withdrawal from the conference. In 1961, the diplomatic activities were intensified, despite the Berlin crisis. In January discussions took place on the release of the U-2 pilot. In March, meetings were held between the foreign ministers to discuss the situation in Laos.

Graph 3.15. Cooperative Interactions between the United States and the Soviet Union

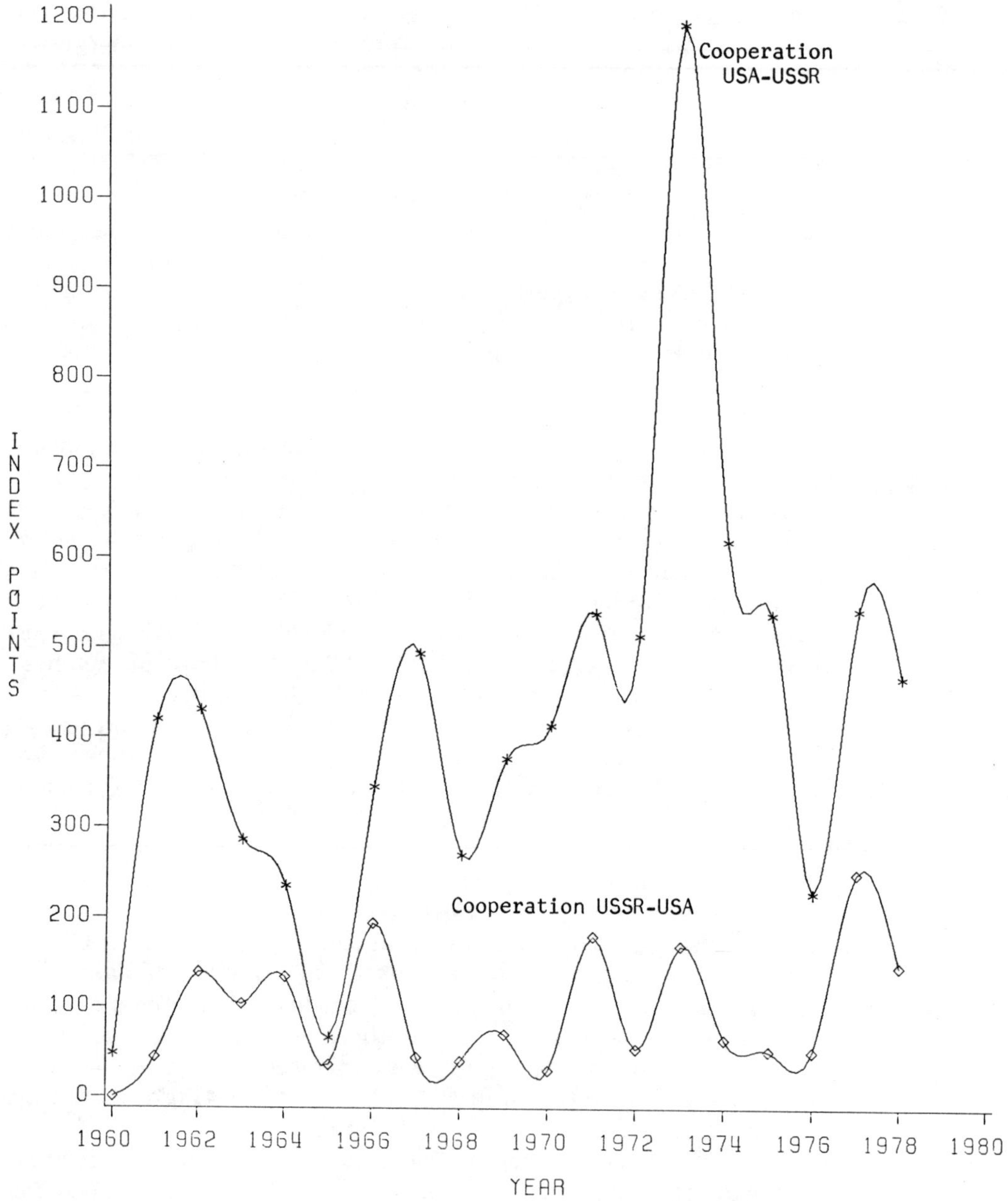
1200
1100
1000
900
800
700
600
500
400
300
200
100
0
INDEX POINTS
Cooperation USA-USSR
Cooperation USSR-USA
1960
1962
1964
1966
1968
1970
1972
1974
1976
1978
1980
YEAR

Graph 3.16. Conflictive Interactions between the United States and the Soviet Union

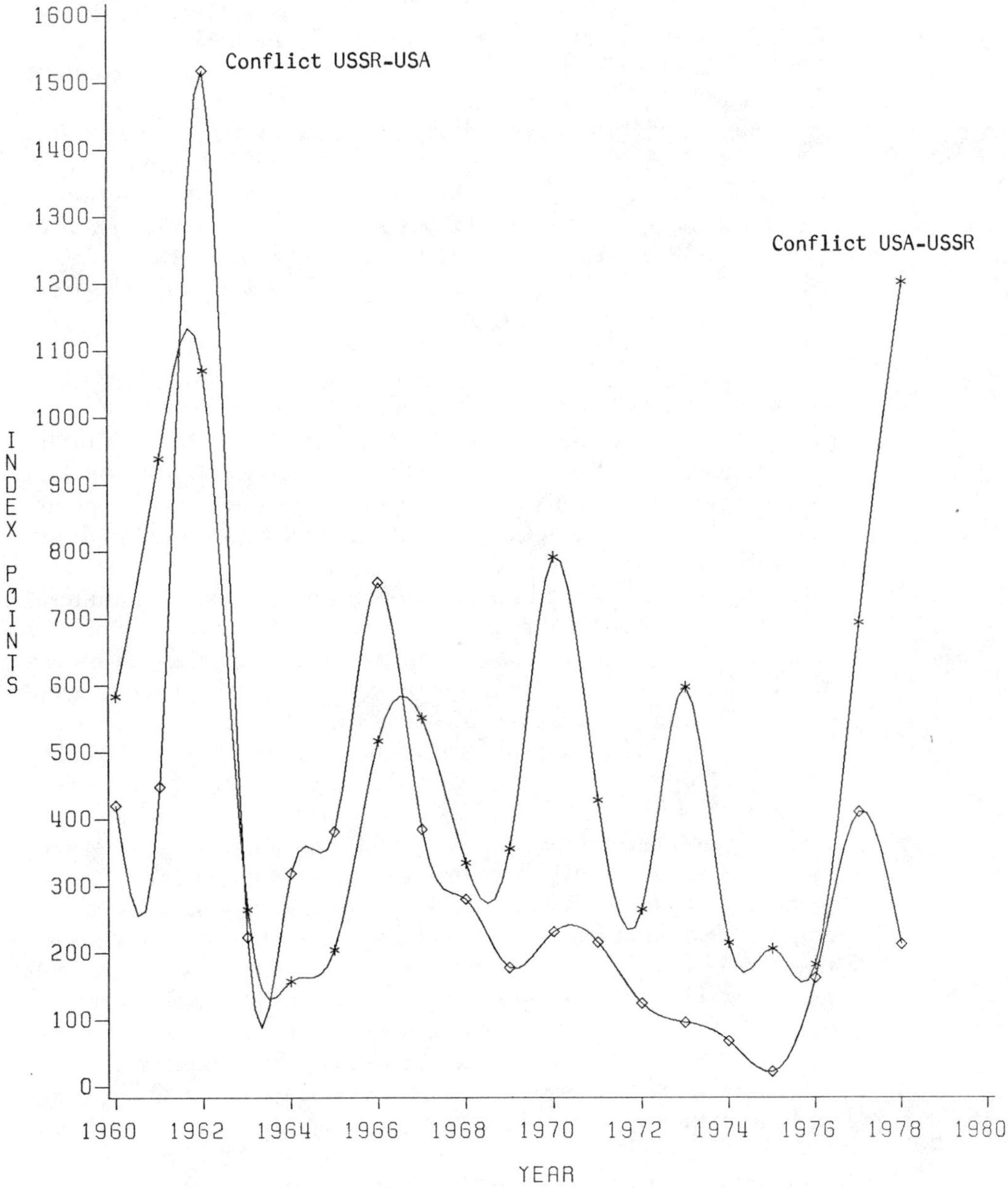
Conflict USSR-USA
Conflict USA-USSR
INDEX POINTS
0
100
200
300
400
500
600
700
800
900
1000
1100
1200
1300
1400
1500
1600
1960
1962
1964
1966
1968
1970
1972
1974
1976
1978
1980
YEAR

In June this trend culminated in a summit meeting between President J.F. Kennedy and Secretary General N.S. Khrushchev who negotiated about the Berlin question and disarmament issues. In August the crisis was further aggravated by the construction of the Berlin wall, but diplomatic efforts to solve the problem continued. In September another Big Four meeting was arranged, and in October Foreign Minister Gromyko met again with President Kennedy. Contacts on the Berlin crisis continued throughout 1962 on various diplomatic levels. But the crucial event of year 1961 of course was undoubtedly the Cuban missile crisis. In many ways, this crisis still affects Soviet-American relations. The solution of the problem became a model of crisis management on the basis of mutual compromise, as, in exchange for the Soviet withdrawal of MRBMs from Cuba, the United States removed their MRBMs from Greece and Turkey.

In 1963 diplomatic activity did not reach the level of previous years; however, three important agreements were concluded before President Kennedy's assassination on November 22: the three years' Cooperation Agreement on Nuclear Research (21 March); the agreement on the so-called Hot Line (20 June); and the Test Ban Agreement (25 July). On 8 November negotiations on Soviet grain purchases were opened, and a contract was signed in January 1964.

During the Johnson administration, after a recession in bilateral relations in 1964 and 1965 due to the changes in leadership in both countries, the policy of cooperation was again stimulated by the Middle East crisis. In 1967 a series of high-level meetings were devoted to this problem, but progress was also made in the arms-control sphere. The nonproliferation negotiations were initiated in October 1966, and the treaty was signed eventually by fifty-nine governments in Moscow in July 1968. Surprisingly, the Vietnam war did not reverse American-Soviet relations. The American military force in South Vietnam was enlarged in 1964 from 16,000 to nearly 25,000 "advisors" to the South Vietnamese forces. In August 1964 American planes raided North Vietnamese installations in retaliation to a North Vietnamese attack on American naval vessels in the Gulf of Tongkin. The successive deterioration of the situation in South Vietnam led to the further "Americanization" of the war in 1965. After February 1965 American planes performed more or less regular bombing raids over North Vietnam, and the number of ground forces expanded until the end of the year to 180,000 men. By 1968 this figure nearly reached 500,000. With his popularity declining rapidly and the end of the war not in sight, President Johnson in March 1968 announced that he would not seek a second term in office. The intervention by Warsaw Pact troops in Czechoslovakia in August 1968 meant an additional serious blow to East–West relations.

In November 1969, however, a new round of arms-control discussions began with preparatory strategic-arms-limitation talks held in Helsinki, followed by the ratification of the nonproliferation treaty a couple of days later, on 24 November 1969. In April 1970 the SALT preliminary talks were resumed in Vienna. The negotiations on the limitation of strategic arms were finally concluded when President Nixon visited the Soviet Union in May 1972. In 1971 three substantive agreements were signed between the Soviet Union and the United States: the multilateral treaty prohibiting placement of nuclear and other weapons on the seabed and ocean floor; the Quadripartite agreement on Berlin stressing once more the responsibility of all four powers for the city, including its Eastern sector; and finally a bilateral agreement on measures preventing the outbreak of nuclear war. The climax of Soviet–American cooperation was reached with the summit meetings of 1972 and 1973, as indicated by the curves in Graphs 2.15 and 2.16.

In his State of the Union Message in January 1970, President Nixon explained his design for a reshaping of Soviet–American relations as passing from "an era of confrontation" to "an era of negotiation." Besides the SALT I agreement and other treaties on cooperation in questions relating to the environment, medical science, technology, and a communiqué on the work of the US–USSR Commercial Commission, the agreements on the prevention of incidents at sea and a declaration on the basic principles of relations between the two countries were the most notable achievements. Interestingly, both parties to the agreement made it clear in the first paragraph, that differences in ideology and in the social systems between the two countries were no obstacles to the bilateral development of normal relations. Among the twelve principles that were supposed to guide relations between the USA and the USSR, the second is perhaps the most important. Both sides "recognize that efforts to obtain unilateral advantage at the expense of the other, directly or indirectly" were inconsistent with the objective of avoiding dangerous situations and preventing the outbreak of nuclear war.

However, efforts to negotiate a trade agreement granting the most-favored nations (MFN) status to the Soviet Union ended unsuccessfully as there was still some opposition in Congress. This issue led to serious controversies in the following years. The list of agreements concluded at the occasion of the summit meetings of June 1973 and June 1974, and the interim period is well documented and needs no detailed discussion (Timberlake 1978). The Agreement on Principles of Relations of 1972 and the Agreement on the Prevention of Nuclear War were put on a serious test in the Middle East crisis of October 1973, four months after the Washington summit meeting.

Obviously, the evolution of these negotiations was based on the practice of establishing linkages between various issues, thereby stimulating compromises. This is most clearly demonstrated in the field of economics. On 8 July 1972, an agreement was reached between the United States and the Soviet Union on the purchase of grain. The related problems referring to shipping rates and the proportion of grain to be shipped in vessels of the respective countries were solved in the maritime agreement negotiated after the grain-purchase agreement and it was signed on 14 October. It was to be implemented retroactively on 1 July 1972. The Soviet grain purchases, furthermore, were to be facilitated by an American 500-million-dollar credit at an interest rate of 6.125 percent. In a Presidential Determination of 18 October 1972, the Export-Import Bank of the United States was requested to guarantee, insure, and extend the necessary credits. All this was surely facilitated by the Soviet determination to solve once and forever the old problem of the lend-lease repayment. This again was facilitated by granting the Soviet Union, on a coeditional basis the most-favored-nation status. Consequently, President Nixon inserted into Title IV of the Trade Reform Act of 1973 (later 1974) a section that would authorize the president of the United States to grant the MFN status to any nation if this was in the American national interest.

Still Congress felt obliged to follow the same line of logic by linking additional issues to the complex web of mutual agreements and understandings, using amendments to the Trade Reform Bill. When finally passed by Congress in late 1974, the Jackson-Vanik amendment on "Freedom of Emigration in East-West Trade" made the granting of the MFN status to the Soviet Union dependent on progress in the field of Jewish emigration. Furthermore, the Stevenson amendment imposed a rigid credit ceiling on Soviet purchases of 300 million US dollars. Thereupon the Soviet Union felt free to cancel the agreement on the settlement of lend-lease debts.

At the Moscow summit of 1974, the Watergate hearings cast a heavy shadow on Soviet-American relations. When President Ford and Secretary General Brezhnev met at the occasion of the signing of CSCE Final Act in Helsinki, the climax of Soviet-American relations had already been passed. At the Vladivostok summit meeting of November 1974, before the debacle caused by the Trade Reform Act, ceilings for strategic nuclear weapons were discussed (SALT II) since the Interim Agreement of 1972 (SALT I) was to expire in 1977. In 1975 and 1976, "détente" became increasingly criticized, mainly because some ambitious expectations regarding human rights and other issues of the third "basket" were not fulfilled. The emigration figures declined, and the Soviet Union did not feel obliged to caution herself with respect to the persecution of dissidents. The term *détente* acquired a negative connotation, most of all during the election campaign of 1976, and President Ford even urged the members of his cabinet to avoid any further use of the word.

When President Carter launched a human-rights campaign and when the Soviet Union suddenly became very active in Africa, new controversial issues were added to the list of unsolved problems.

Since no new SALT agreement could be negotiated until 1977 when the SALT I expired, both governments agreed to abide by its terms until new conditions were negotiated. In fact, on 18 June 1979, SALT II was signed by President Carter and Secretary General Brezhnev in Vienna, but the future of the treaty with respect to the ratification by the United States was unclear. In contrast to Kissinger's confidential diplomacy, the Carter administration felt obliged to fully inform the public on the discussions going on. But contrary to what had been hoped for by President Carter, this did not increase the general trust into the administration's performance; rather the principle of "open diplomacy" triggered fierce controversies about the merits and demerits of the treaty, and eventually congressional approval became insecure. After the Soviet intervention in Afghanistan, the Carter administration decided to postpone the ratification of the treaty.

As has been pointed out previously, most of these events are reflected by the curves displayed in Graphs 2.15 and 2.16, and to some extent explain the specific shape of these curves. In addition, however, the shape of the curves suggests some remarkable comparative findings.

Looking first at the evolution of cooperative relations only, the amplitudes of American behavior vis-à-vis the Soviet Union are much greater than the amplitudes of Soviet cooperation addressed to the United States. In other words, Soviet policy of East–West cooperation is determined by a higher degree of stability and continuity; on the other hand, American cooperative behavior seems to constitute a field where any shifts in the relations between the two major powers are followed by a marked increase or decrease in both the volume and intensity of cooperation, thus producing a dramatic "zig-zag" line characterized by sharp turning points. It is hardly surprising, therefore, that for many Soviet observers the American policy of cooperation is hard to understand given the different "tempers" of foreign-policy conduct. Soviet observers may perceive sudden increases in the level and intensity of cooperation by the US government as an expression of naïve enthusiasm lacking appropriate seriosity; accordingly, a sudden drop in the volume and intensity of cooperation may be perceived as a kind of insolent, uncontrolled, or irrational outlet of hostility not fully compatible with the responsibility and dignity of major-power relations. Although it is hard to offer any reliable evidence of what the Soviet leadership really expects from the United States and although any theories about certain governments being allegedly "disappointed" by the actual course of events (for example, see Hoffmann 1981) are nothing but mere speculation, the observable reality as expressed by the curves representing cooperation between the two major powers does suggest that different styles also imply different normative orientations and expectations.

A similar observation can be made with reference to conflictive relations. There are more turning points from "more conflict" to "less conflict" (and in the opposite direction) in the US behavior vis-à-vis the Soviet Union (eight trend reversals) than in the Soviet conflictive behavior directed against the United States (seven trend reversals). And more important, the amplitudes tend to be more articulate in the American case than in the Soviet case. The degree of hostility expressed by US foreign policy in the late seventies even exceeds the previous maximum level reached in 1962.

Yet there is not only asymmetry between the USA and the USSR; in addition, it can easily be seen that cooperation and conflict in general do not tend to be symmetric. A comprehensive comparative interpretation of the two graphs gives support to the hypothesis that "détente" for the USA practically meant progress in the policy of cooperation with the USSR while the latter did not alter the volume and intensity of her cooperation with the West substantially. On the other hand, "peaceful coexistence" for the Soviet Union meant a decrease of hostility that was not paralleled systematically by a corresponding evolution of the US conflictive behavior. This salient asymmetry between the relative weight of cooperation and conflict in the foreign policies of the two major powers obviously bears an additional potential for mutual misunderstandings and misperceptions.

The United Kingdom

Graphs 3.17 and 3.18 present a summary of cooperative and conflictive relations between the United Kingdom and the Soviet Union. British foreign policy after World War II can be described as an adjustment to a changing international and internal environment, the obvious decline in power being the main feature the United Kingdom experienced during this period. In the field of armaments, Great Britain soon felt the impossibility to compete with the United States and the Soviet Union in the developing new arms race. The obvious limitation to British military power was clearly outlined in the 1957 Defense White Paper. Consequently, the United Kingdom stopped the development of her own strategic missiles in order to purchase American Polaris missiles for the equipment of British-built submarines.

The Nassau agreement of December 1962 clearly finalized the new orientation of British foreign policy; now Great Britain systematically handed over many of her worldwide responsibilities to the United States, enjoying, however, a "special relationship" in return. Since 1947, the transformation of the British Empire into the British Commonwealth, a multiracial group of sovereign states, had continuously limited the British power base and required the definition of a new role for the United Kingdom. While the older Commonwealth members, for example, Australia and New Zealand, still supported the British policy vis-à-vis the Soviet Union, new Commonwealth nations such as Burma, Ceylon, India, and Pakistan were neither sympathetic with nor willing to support the

Graph 3.17. Cooperative Interactions between Great Britain and the Soviet Union

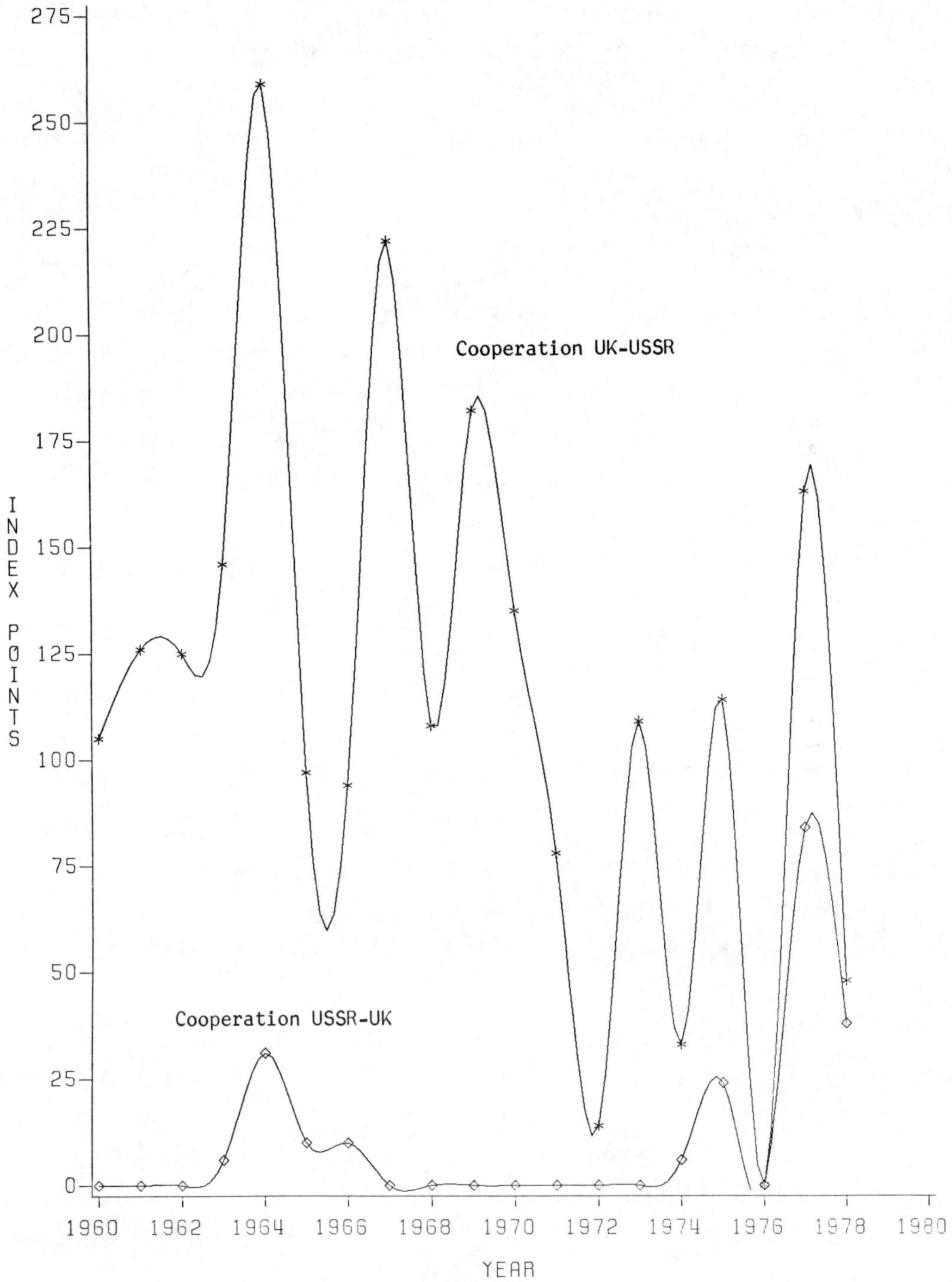
275
250
225
200
175
150
125
100
75
50
25
0
INDEX POINTS
Cooperation UK-USSR
Cooperation USSR-UK
1960
1962
1964
1966
1968
1970
1972
1974
1976
1978
1980
YEAR

Graph 3.18. Conflictive Interactions between Great Britain and the Soviet Union

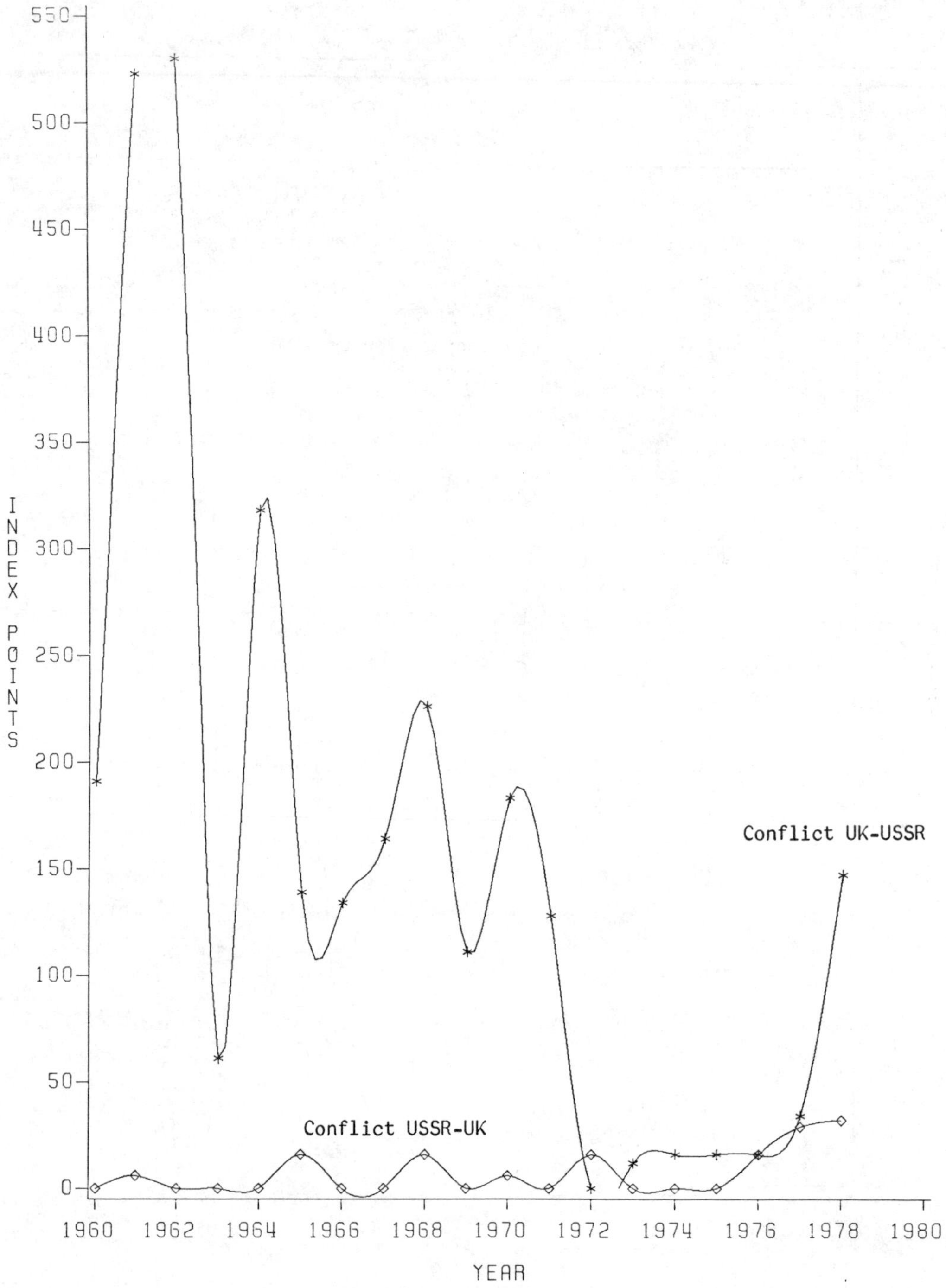
550
500
450
400
350
300
250
200
150
100
50
0
INDEX POINTS
1960
1962
1964
1966
1968
1970
1972
1974
1976
1978
1980
YEAR
Conflict UK-USSR
Conflict USSR-UK

British point of view in the East–West conflict. The ultimate proof of the downgrading of British status since the end of World War II came with the Suez expedition in 1956 when the Soviet Union threatened to use nuclear missiles (Frankel 1975, p. 201) and American disapprovement quickly ended the adventure. Relations with the United States obviously had reached a point where they were more important than the vital waterways to what was left of the British dominion "East of Suez."

Relations with the Soviet Union originally had a central place in British foreign affairs in the post-World War II period. During the war, Britain and the Soviet Union had been treating each other as equals; however, this attitude quickly changed in the fifties. Britain became a minor nuclear power. The British industrial production was constantly falling back while the relative weight of the other European industrialized countries, especially the Federal Republic of Germany, France, and Italy, rapidly grew. Still, influence on American foreign policy was regarded as one of the major assets of British foreign policy. The close relationship between Kennedy and Macmillan supported this view. But once bilateral negotiations of the other West European states with the United States were on their way, a British go-between was no longer necessary. On the other hand, bilateral contacts with France and the Federal Republic of Germany offered a promising alternative perspective.

As a result, the volume of Soviet–British interaction constantly decreased since 1960, both in the conflictive and cooperative sphere. With her military integration in NATO and economic-political integration within the EC after several unsuccessful applications for membership, a considerable share of British–Soviet relations became absorbed by the multilateral frame of interaction. Britain takes a major part in shaping the policies of NATO and the EC vis-à-vis the Soviet Union, but, in contrast to the Federal Republic of Germany and the United States, there are no pressing bilateral problems between the United Kingdom and the Soviet Union that would require special efforts. Vice versa, Graphs 3.17 and 3.18 indicate a similar irrelevance of Great Britain for the Soviet Union; volume and intensity of both cooperation and conflict are strikingly low.

It is interesting to note that one of the first initiatives made in the spirit of what later became the policy of "détente" was a British proposal, the so-called Eden Plan submitted to the Conference of Foreign Ministers in January 1954 and the Geneva summit as the basis of Western proposals. The plan provided for German reunification followed by the establishment of a demilitarized zone in central Europe. In addition to Eisenhower's "open skies" proposal, Eden suggested a joint inspection of forces of East and West in Europe, in fact, an early version of what later was labeled "confidence-building measures." The plan, however, raised fierce opposition by the Federal Republic of Germany; for the same reasons, the Soviet Union found the plan positive (Frankel 1975, p. 201). British-Soviet relations deteriorated as a consequence of the Suez crisis and the Soviet intervention in Hungary in 1956. When Prime Minister Anthony Eden had to resign in January 1957, due to ill health, he was succeeded by Harold Macmillan who launched a new initiative for the improvement of East-West relations when visiting Moscow in 1959. The original Eden Plan had been taken up by the Polish Foreign Minister Adam Rapacki who proposed a limitation of armed forces in certain agreed-upon areas of central Europe. Relations again deteriorated in the course of the Berlin crisis.

When the Labor party came into office in 1964, Soviet-British relations again experienced some progress. Prime Minister Harold Wilson engaged in arms-control negotiations and started an initiative to end the Vietnam war. However, as much as the Soviet Union proved unable to control the North Vietnamese, British diplomacy was incapable of influencing American policies in this respect. The Soviet intervention in Czechoslovakia again severed Soviet-British relations. In 1969 cooperative relations were resumed, but after the 1970 election defeat of the Wilson government, relations with the Soviet Union declined. In 1971, 105 members of the Soviet embassy in London were asked to leave the country; they were presumed to be engaged in illegal intelligence activities. In the meantime leadership in promoting East-West "détente" had been handed over to the Federal Republic of Germany and France and, most of all, to the United States.

The major achievement of the conservative Heath goverment was to gain access to the Common Market. The immediate effects on the British economy were poor, however. When general elections were called for February 1974, Labor again came into office. Harold Wilson unexpectedly announced his resignation on 16 March 1976 and was succeeded by James Callaghan, then foreign secretary, on 5 April. The new government reactivated British-Soviet relations, but the focus was mainly on domestic affairs and relations with the EC. East-West relations had no important position on the British priority list. The 1979 elections brought again a conservative victory. Yet as before, Soviet-British relations were not a primary concern. But due to her specifically Western and anti-collectivist orientation, Prime Minister Margaret Thatcher warmly welcomed the new Reagan administration and the new American attitude toward the Soviet Union. Therefore increasing conflicts in British-Soviet relations are no surprise.

On the whole, the picture presented by Soviet-British relations is considerably distinct from US-USSR relations. US-USSR relations are characterized by a high degree of relevance for reasons of the strategic situation and mutual dependence for survival; yet they exhibit marked variations in both the field of cooperation and the field of conflict. By contrast, Soviet-British relations are mainly determined by a variation of mutual relevance; relevance was clearly declining in the sixties. In the seventies, British relations with the Soviet Union gained again some importance although being far from attracting priority in foreign affairs.

France

French relations with the Soviet Union in many respects resemble British-Soviet relations. As in the case of Britain, other preoccupations had a much more important place in the French foreign-policy priority list than East-West relations. More particularly, the main focus—and maybe obsession—of French foreign policy in the beginning of the sixties was the war in Algeria and the Algerian problem. Yet this problem had some consequences for French-Soviet relations when in 1960 the provisional Algerian government proclaimed by the FLN (Front de la libération nationale) turned for help to Moscow and Peking. Although favoring any anticolonialist movement, Soviet foreign-policy decisionmakers were apparently irritated by the fact that the Algerian revolution was more nationalistic in tone than socialist. Only after assuming power was the FNL finally hailed as a "fraternal party" and its leader Ben Bella awarded the title of a "Hero of the Soviet Union" (Nogee and Donaldson 1981, pp. 136 ff.; Calvocoressi 1968, p. 328 ff.).

The war in Algeria ended and the Algerian problem was solved when in April 1961, in a referendum suggested by French President Charles de Gaulle, the French voters accepted self-government for Algeria. In 1962 negotiations with Algerian FLN leaders were successfully concluded by the Evian Agreement. Quite naturally, after the solution of the Algerian crisis, French-Soviet relations opened new perspectives because, with Algeria removed from the panel of problems, a major obstacle to an improvement of bilateral relations was also removed. Furthermore, the French attitude toward NATO, European integration, and the American involvement in Vietnam at the end of the sixties appeared to converge with the Soviet policy on these issues. Most of all, the increasing unwillingness expressed by the French political elite to accept American leadership in the North Atlantic alliance paved the way for a Soviet-French understanding.

The French policy of self-reliance in matters of national defense already originated in the fifties. France conducted her first nuclear test explosion in 1960 and announced the intention to build an independent nuclear deterrent force ("*force de frappe*"). Consequently, the Soviet-American efforts in the realm of nuclear arms control were regarded as a serious encroachment on the French ambitions for atomic independence. Thus de Gaulle refused to sign the Test Ban Treaty. He also objected to placing parts of the French Mediterranean Fleet under NATO command and insisted on strict equality of France, Great Britain, and the United States in matters of nuclear planning in the alliance. Finally, in 1966, France left the military part of NATO. Although de Gaulle regarded European

Graph 3.19. Cooperative Interactions between France and the Soviet Union

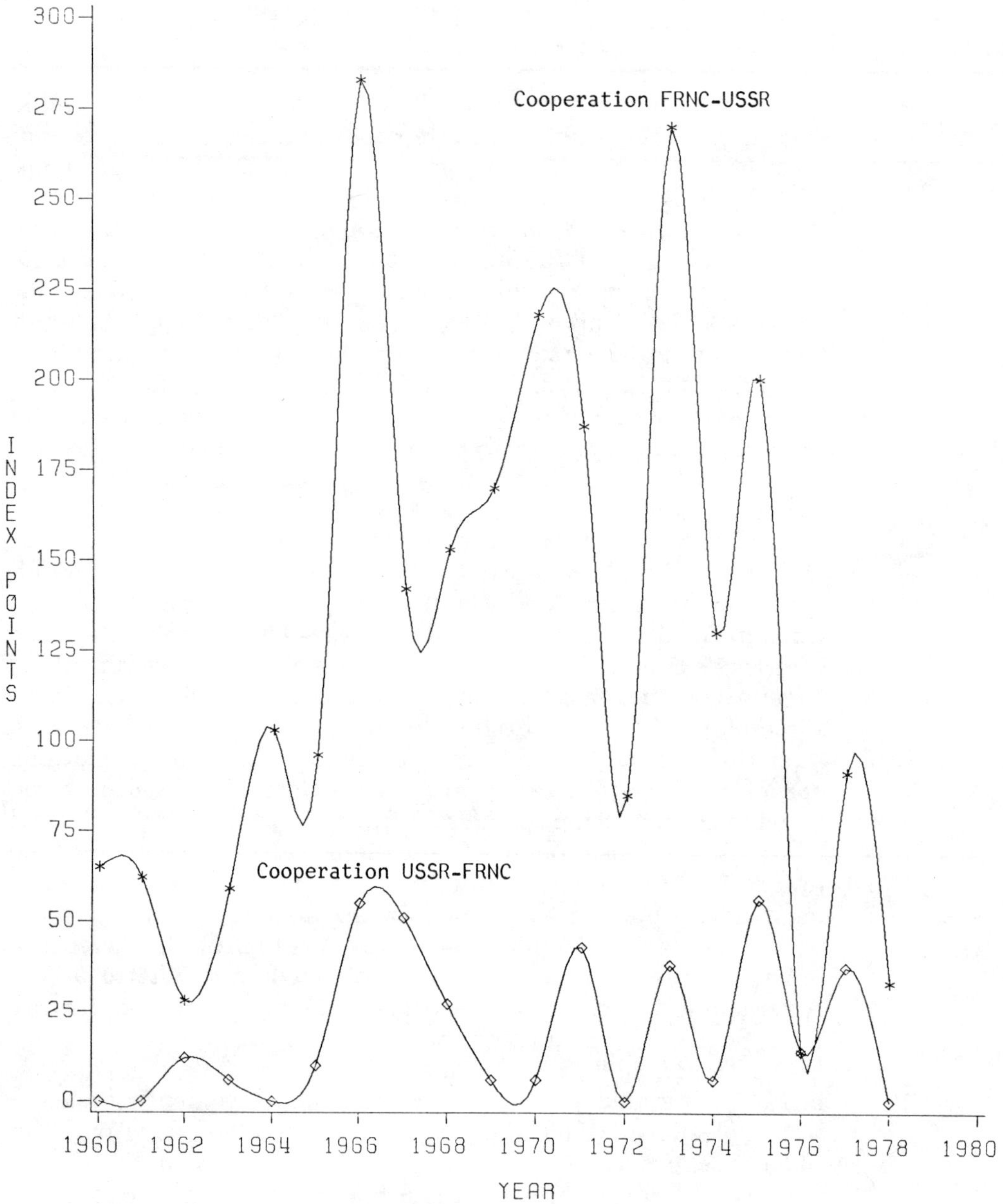
Cooperation FRNC-USSR
Cooperation USSR-FRNC
300
275
250
225
200
175
150
125
100
75
50
25
0
INDEX POINTS
1960
1962
1964
1966
1968
1970
1972
1974
1976
1978
1980
YEAR

Graph 3.20. Conflictive Interactions between France and the Soviet Union

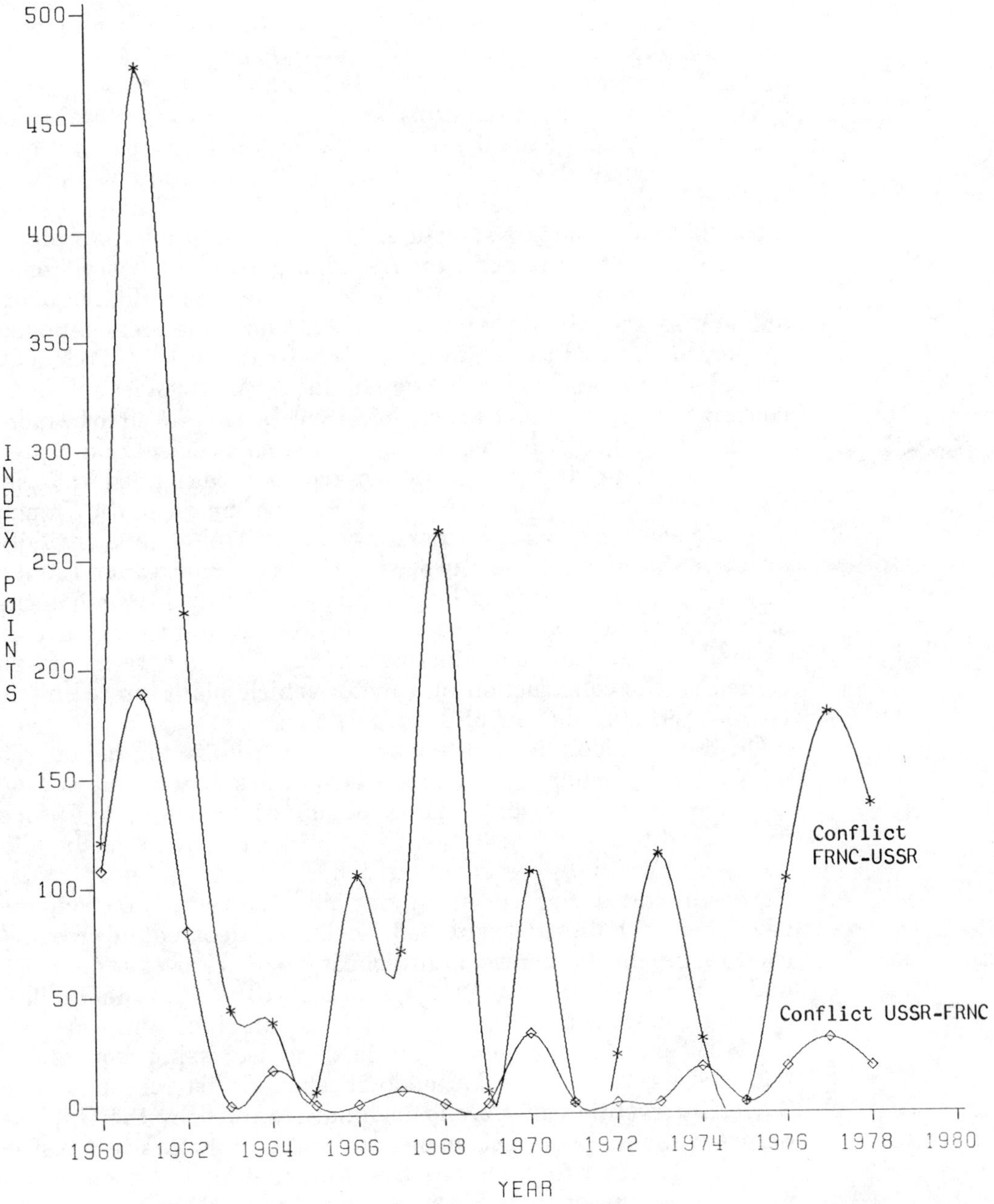
INDEX POINTS
500
450
400
350
300
250
200
150
100
50
0
1960
1962
1964
1966
1968
1970
1972
1974
1976
1978
1980
YEAR
Conflict FRNC-USSR
Conflict USSR-FRNC

integration as a chief instrument of emancipation from major-power dependence, he did not allow the development of any supranational institutions that could possibly curtail French sovereignty. In 1963 and again in 1967, British efforts to join the Common Market were successfully vetoed by France. Britain was always regarded by de Gaulle as a possible bridgehead of American influence in the Common Market.

Thus French–Soviet relations are determined by a plurality of tendencies; some of them are neatly contradictory. It is not surprising therefore that the curves tracing the evolution of cooperation and conflict between France and the Soviet Union indicate a considerably complex structure. The sixties began with a phase of acute hostility, reflecting the Algerian and Berlin crises, immediately followed, however, by a steep decline of conflictive interaction until reaching zero in 1965. At the same time French–Soviet cooperation soared to its climax in 1966. In March 1964, Podgorny visited France and met with de Gaulle. French–Soviet relations continued to prosper as Khrushchev's successors proved to be more flexible. In fall 1964, a French Communist party delegation visited Brezhnev, and a day later a trade agreement was signed in Paris. In March 1965, an agreement was signed on the use of the French SECAM color-television system in the Soviet Union, thus virtually opening the whole East European television market for French technology. Gromyko paid France an official visit in March of the same year, and in October, the French foreign minister Couve de Murville met Brezhnev in Moscow. In May 1966 an agreement was signed on the construction of a motor-vehicle plant, preceding de Gaulle's official visit in Moscow in June.

On this occasion de Gaulle took the opportunity to promote his program of a reshaping of European relations by three steps ("*détente-entente-coopération*"). A reduction of tensions in Europe would lead to a gradual loosening of alliance bonds and the alliances would finally be substituted by a system of independent European states cooperating in matters of security and economic development. Political scientists have largely debated the pros and cons of bipolarity versus multipolarity with respect to security and stability. Their findings do not necessarily support de Gaulle's expectations, but the plan was much too ambitious anyway.

In 1967 and 1968 increasing conflicts and decreasing cooperation indicate a certain perturbation of French–Soviet relations. The Soviet intervention in Czechoslovakia, regarded by the Gaullist minister Michel Debré as a mere "*incident de parcours*" ("a traffic accident"), did in fact demonstrate that the Soviet Union would not tolerate any erosion of the Socialist camp. Furthermore, the events of May 1968 in Paris nearly ended in a turnover of the regime. In the legislative elections of March 1967, the Gaullist coalition won only a narrow victory, and in the aftermath of the student revolt, a series of heavy strikes paralyzed the economy, apparently fueling fears of a Communist take-over in France. Still de Gaulle managed a final landslide victory in the elections held in June 1968. The era ended, however, when his proposals for some very fundamental constitutional reforms were turned down. He resigned in April 1969. Soviet–French relations were still prospering: In May 1968, for example, a large ship-building contract was signed between France and the Soviet Union, despite all difficulties.

In foreign policy and especially French–Soviet relations, the new president of the Republic, Georges Pompidou, had to depart from visions to more pragmatic designs. Two factors now led to a downgrading of France as a cornerstone of Soviet "Westpolitik": First, West German "Ostpolitik" became more attractive for the Soviet Union than any special relations with France; and second, the recent developments in Soviet–American relations that blossomed despite the Vietnam problem offered some interesting new perspectives. The proposed Conference on Security and Cooperation in Europe (CSCE), originally suggested by the Soviet Union in 1966 and renewed in March 1969, was at first met with skepticism in France; nevertheless, France took fully and cooperatively part in the Preparatory Conference held in Helsinki from November 1972 to June 1973. Still, the French concept of "détente" and Soviet designs for "peaceful coexistence" differed in several important matters, most of all in questions of disarmament. From the French point of view, the consolidation of the "force de frappe" and relaxation of tensions in Europe was not a paradox but part of the logic of the process. As Hoffmann put it, "He [Pompidou] pursued de Gaulle's *Ostpolitik* because *détente* made a modicum of West European independence from the United States possible and allowed the East Europeans to receive some Western oxygen into their cage. But such détente was deemed compatible with, indeed dependent on, the overall balance" (Hoffmann 1976, p. 222).

Consequently, France did not participate in the Geneva disarmament talks. SALT was regarded as an exclusive business among major powers, while MBFR, originally a favorite NATO project, was feared to have desastrous effects with regard to asymmetries in the reduction of conventional forces in Europe. French diplomats were also afraid that a demilitarized zone in central Europe would foster neutralist tendencies in the Federal Republic of Germany and also give a new momentum to the neoisolationist mood in the United States. With respect to Europe's future, Pompidou's strategy of "*complément-élargissement-renforcement*" did no longer refer to a system of "fatherlands" reaching from the Atlantic to the Urals but merely to the smaller European Economic Community including also, after all, Great Britain.

In May 1974, Valéry Giscard d'Estaing became President of the Republic, but there was little change in French–Soviet relations. Yet Giscard's concept of "détente" added a new element called the "*détente idéologique*." It implies that, in principle, differences between the social and political systems of European powers were to be taken for granted and were to be respected; however, it also addresses certain limits of ideological struggle, which in practice lead to a strict observance of the principles of nonintervention into internal affairs and political tolerance. This sharply contrasted with the Soviet concept of "peaceful coexistence," which asserts a "continued ideological struggle" as one of its crucial elements. As reflected by the curves, meetings between the French and Soviet leaders on various occasions did in fact result in new peaks of cooperative relations. In 1973, Pompidou paid an unofficial visit to the Soviet Union, while a couple of months later Brezhnev met with Pompidou on a trip to France. France and the Soviet Union signed an agreement on economic cooperation and a contract regarding the construction of an industrial complex in the Soviet Union. In 1974 Pompidou met with Brezhnev on the Crimea, and Brezhnev again paid an official visit to France. The new president, Giscard d'Estaing, met with Brezhnev in October 1975, but increasing strains in relations became obvious. In a more accurate way than any conventional diplomatic analysis, the events-analytical measurement of French-Soviet relations makes clear that, despite occasional peaks in cooperation, the trend of cooperation is clearly declining, and the intensity of conflicts tends to increase. The Soviet intervention in Afghanistan in December 1979 and the dispute between NATO and WTO on INF and FOBs in Europe seem to accelerate this trend.

The Federal Republic of Germany

The Federal Republic of Germany too constitutes a special case in East-West relations. In this country, the early sixties were characterized by a conspicuous reorientation in the relations with the Soviet Union and the other Socialist countries, especially with the GDR. In the fifties, these relations were almost constantly conflictive and subject to all kinds of stresses and strains.

By the treaty of 5 May 1952, the three Western occupation zones had become an independent state, provided the West German government would be willing to join the project of a European Defense Community (EDC). This project was strongly contested by important groups in France and in the West German Bundestag as well. While the Adenauer government was able to mobilize sufficient parliamentary support to overcome opposition by the Social Democrats, especially after the elections of July 1953, the French National Assembly defeated the EDC treaty in August 1954. As a substitute, the Federal Republic of Germany was invited to join NATO and to rearm under the control of the alliance. On 5 May 1955, the treaty was implemented. This course of events was in fact a major success of West German diplomacy, most of all because the NATO allies also pledged to support the policy of reunification of Germany by peaceful means. As the Federal Republic of Germany was now fully integrated into the Western military alliance (and economically within the European Coal and Steel Community and later, within the EEC), the probability for any quick solution to the problem of German reunification faded.

Tensions between the Federal Republic of Germany and the Soviet Union rose when in 1961 the German Democratic Republic sealed the Eastern part of Berlin off from the rest of the city by establishing the Berlin wall. Nonetheless, diplomatic relations with the Soviet Union, which had been established in 1955, continued on a normal base.

Two major internal developments initiated a change in West German foreign policy, culminating finally in the concept of "*Ostpolitik*," as the specific German version of "détente". First, the humiliating defeat of the Social Democrats in the elections of 1957 stipulated a major shift in the party's attitude toward internal and external problems. The new Godesberg program of principles, adopted in 1959, discarded the party's Marxist legacy in favor of a more popular doctrine embracing in fact much of liberal economic thinking and Adenauer's design of foreign policy. Second, the Christian Democrats lost their absolute majority in the Bundestag in the elections of 1961 and had to form a coalition government with the liberal party (FDP). In 1963, Adenauer, aged eighty-seven by this time, retired. In 1965, the CDU lead by Ludwig Erhard, again won the elections, but the second "small" coalition with the liberals lasted only one year.

When the liberals left government in 1966, new elections were held resulting in substantial gains by the Social Democrats, who joined a "grand" coalition government chaired by the Christian Democratic Chancellor Kurt Georg Kiesinger. The Social Democrat Willy Brandt was appointed foreign minister, and he initiated the new "Ostpolitik." Improving relations with the Socialist countries, however, proved to be difficult. The price the Soviet Union asked for normalization of relations appeared to be rather high. It included the recognition of the GDR and the postwar Polish and East German border lines, the signature of the Nonproliferation Treaty, and the annulation of the Munich agreements of 1938. These kinds of concessions were more than what the Christian Democrats were willing to accept. Still, the grand coalition brought about two major shifts in attitude that paved the way for the social-liberal coalition's treaty system. Whereas the Adenauer government had always regarded Soviet concessions with respect to German reunification as the crucial criterion for real "détente", the grand coalition now changed priorities and regarded peaceful reunification as the ultimate result of a long process of a restructuring of Europe overcoming the block structure, beginning with détente in Europe as a first step. Another obstacle, the so-called Hallstein doctrine, was also quietly removed; West German diplomacy so far had always maintained that it would be unacceptable to the FRG if a partner country granted the GDR recognition. Now the East European countries were exempted from the doctrine, while Third World countries still risked a break in diplomatic relations with the FRG in case they recognized the GDR. In 1967 diplomatic relations with Romania were established, and talks were held with Poland, the CSSR, and Bulgaria. Soon the newly evolving "Ostpolitik" experienced a setback by the Soviet intervention in Prague and by the GDR taking some preventive measures demanding, with Soviet consent, her recognition by the FRG as a precondition to any further evolution of diplomatic relations with the Socialist countries.

In the grand coalition, the Social Democrats had demonstrated their capability to assume governmental responsibilities. In the 1969 elections, the Christian Democrats again emerged as the strongest party, but Willy Brandt now managed to negotiate a coalition with the liberals and became the first Social Democratic chancellor. The new cooperation with the former opposition party was initiated when in March of the same year the liberals helped to appoint Gustav Heinemann as the first Social Democratic president of the Federal Republic of Germany. Shortly after assuming power, the new government opened negotiations with the Soviet Union. In the treaty signed on 12 August 1970, the Federal Republic of Germany recognized the Oder-Neisse line as Poland's Western border, while the USSR recognized the Federal Republic of Germany's right to seek reunification of Germany by peaceful means. On 9 November 1972, a treaty was signed with the GDR pledging mutual recognition of sovereignty although not proper diplomatic recognition. Still, this proved to be a practicable *modus vivendi*, and in 1973 both German states were admitted to the United Nations. In the elections of November 1972, the coalition won a substantial majority and the "Ostpolitik" had become quite popular with the electorate, since actual progress had been made in the relations between the two German states, allowing, for example, travels and regular visits on the basis of family ties.

As becomes evident from the curves in Graphs 3.21 and 3.22 the climax in Soviet-West German relations was reached when Willy Brandt was chancellor. This period abruptly ended, and the volume and intensity of Soviet-West German relations drastically declined when, in May 1974, Brandt had to resign.

Brandt's successor, Helmut Schmidt, faced a situation where the tensions between the United States and the Soviet Union were increasing. This put some strains on West German diplomacy. On the one hand, the "Ostpolitik" was implicitly based on comprehensive understanding and coordination with the NATO allies; on the other hand, practical progress in relations with Socialist countries and especially with the GDR, both in the humanitarian and economic fields, were too precious for the Federal Republic of Germany to be used as "bargaining chips" in major-power conflicts. Yet, although the level of cooperative diplomatic activities in relations with the Soviet Union declined since 1974, this process was not paralleled by increasing conflict. On the contrary, the Soviet

Graph 3.21. Cooperative Interactions between the FRG and the USSR

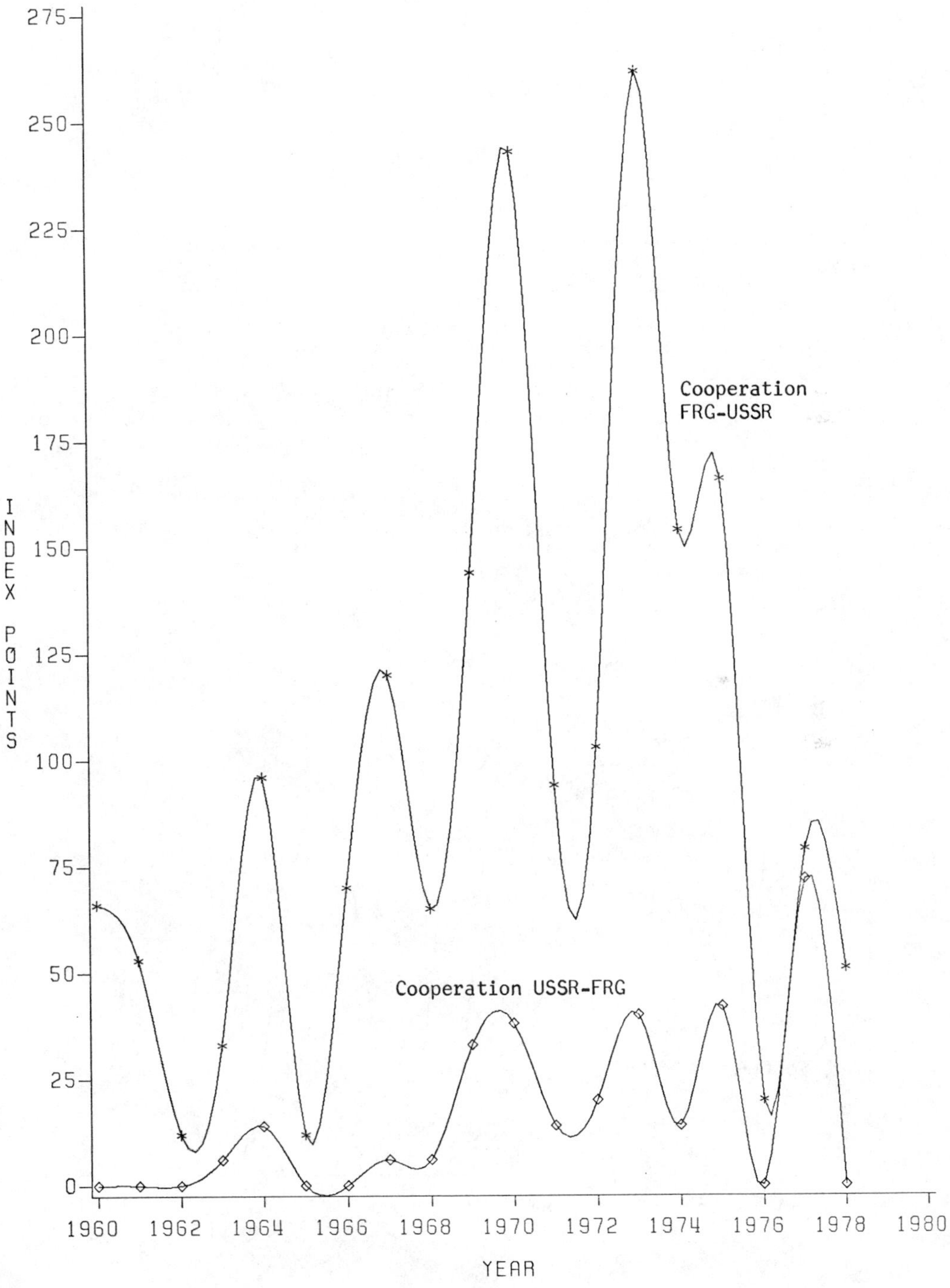
275
250
225
200
175
150
125
100
75
50
25
0
INDEX PØINTS
Cooperation FRG-USSR
Cooperation USSR-FRG
1960
1962
1964
1966
1968
1970
1972
1974
1976
1978
1980
YEAR

Graph 3.22. Conflictive Interactions between the FRG and the USSR

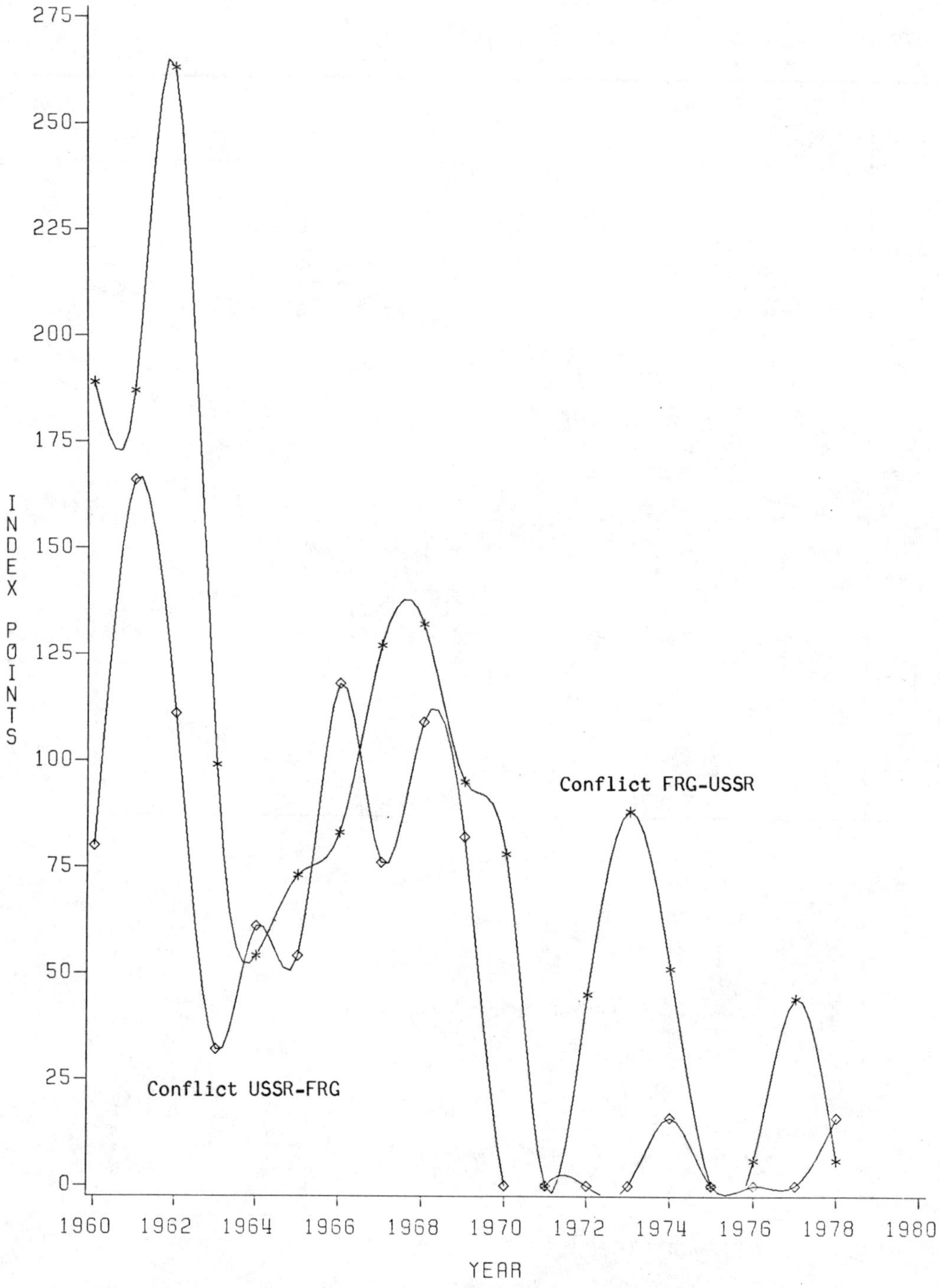
275
250
225
200
175
150
125
100
75
50
25
0
INDEX POINTS
Conflict FRG-USSR
Conflict USSR-FRG
1960
1962
1964
1966
1968
1970
1972
1974
1976
1978
1980
YEAR

Union now intensified cooperative moves addressed to the Federal Republic of Germany. The volume and intensity of USSR–FRG cooperation therefore reached a climax not in the period of nomalization (1969–1974) but in 1977.

Summary

The preceding presentation is limited to four pairs of countries. For reasons of space, no additional analyses of this kind will be presented here; more detailed information about other pairs of countries can be found in Appendix A3.2 where the numerical data for a large number of East–West pairs of countries are listed.

The four analyses presented in this section demonstrate how the evolution of conflict and cooperation between East and West is determined by both specific and general trends. Among the specific trends are shifts in the balance of political parties following elections and changes in the tenure of governmental office. In addition, some countries seem to have quite specific role conceptions in the East–West context, and it can easily be seen that such national-role conceptions remain fairly stable over a considerable period of time; this certainly holds true for the French policy vis-à-vis Eastern Europe, motivated by a need for a relatively independent position within the Western alliance, and it strikingly applies to the concept of "Ostpolitik" as adopted by the Federal Republic of Germany.

However, apart from these "idiosyncratic" determinants, it is possible to discern also salient trends of a more general nature. At least it can be said that the behavior of the states examined in the preceding paragraphs is obviously interconnected: In addition to national peculiarities, they all seem to be subject to a general trend promoting a growth of cooperation and a decrease of conflictivity in the early seventies, followed by a trend reversal between 1974 and 1976. It may be attractive to speculate about the processes and forces underlying this general trend, and there is no want of suggestive explanations. Disappointment about the eventual outcome of East–West relations as contrasted to prior expectations may be a moving force behind the trend reversal observed. Furthermore, extra-European problems and crises seem to have an undeniable impact on East–West relations within Europe. It also seems that US–USSR relations have a kind of pacemaker function, or at least a limiting effect on the latitude of political options available to the other European states in the East–West context. Yet all these speculations are doomed to be somehow idle because they rely on insights rather than on evidence. In order to shed some light on the inherent logic of East–West relations and on the underlying causality, more subtle analyses are required than a mere description of facts. Such analyses will be presented in Chapter 5.

3.3.2 Cooperation and Conflict: Clusters of Nations

In this section the clustering of nations will be examined similarly to the analysis done in Section 2.5. Yet this time the cluster analysis of camps and cleavages in Europe refers to actual behavior and not to perceptions as expressed in diplomatic statements. In other words, the question to be answered by this analysis is, Which groups of countries can be identified as belonging together with regard to their volume of cooperation? And which groups of countries belong together as opponents, that is, as "chronic" conflictive partners?

In order to answer this question, again cluster analysis was applied with the results presented in the form of dendrograms. The raw data of monthly scaled events were pooled for quinquennial periods, from 1960 to 1978 for 870 dyads in each period, that is, relationships among thirty nations (relationships for each of the thirty nations with each other, both as an actor and as a target). In order to trace possible changes in the structure of relationships, a matrix of proximities among the thirty nations in each period, for both conflictive and cooperative relations, had to be computed. After considerable experimentation with various measures of proximity, the following formula was selected:

$$P_{ik} = (I_{ik} / AI_i + I_{ki} / PI_i + I_{ki} / AI_k + I_{ik} / PI_k) / 4$$

In this equation, P is the degree of proximity between nations i and k; I are conflictive or cooperative interactions, respectively, where i and k identify pairs of actors and targets. The term AI is the sum of total actions nation i or k initiates within the system of thirty states, while PI is the sum of actions a state receives as a target. The terms A and P are to signify "active" and "passive," respectively. Thus the formula computes the mean fraction of attention two nations devote to each other. The term P is constrained to values reaching from zero to one. The resulting numerical values are presented in Appendix A3.2. Still these figures are difficult to read. Therefore clusters of nations were computed using the HICLUS procedure incorporated in the Multidimensional Scaling Programs Library (Edinburgh Version, October 1975), as well as the authors' own software. In this procedure, there are two algorithms available for grouping objects or items, the *diameter method* and the *connectedness method.* Both methods have some shortcomings. While the diameter method tends to split objects close in space into different groups, the connectedness method tends to construct one highly homogeneous group of objects, leaving the rest outside the cluster. Therefore, both versions are presented in the subsequent dendrograms. For further information see Appendix A2.5.

Looking first at the structure of cooperative relationships, the comparison of dendrograms for each of the six periods reveals the

Graph 3.23. Clusters of Countries in East–West Interactions, 1960-1964

Cooperation

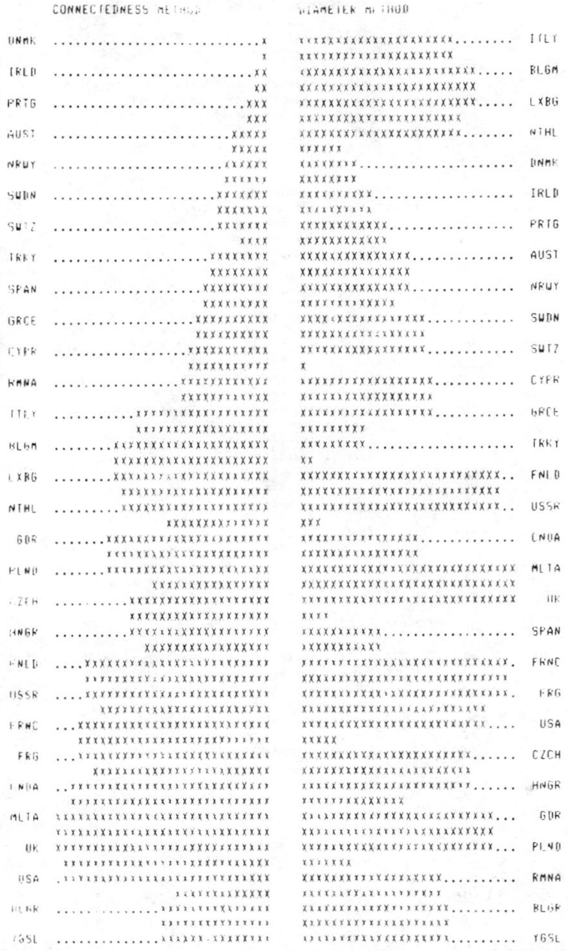
CONNECTEDNESS METHOD
DIAMETER METHOD
UNMK
IRLD
PRTG
AUST
NRWY
SWDN
SWTZ
TRKY
SPAN
GRCE
CYPR
RMNA
ITLY
BLGM
LXBG
NTHL
GDR
PLND
CZCH
HNGR
FNLD
USSR
FRNC
FRG
CNDA
MLTA
UK
USA
BLGR
YGSL
ITLY
BLGM
LXBG
NTHL
DNMK
IRLD
PRTG
AUST
NRWY
SWDN
SWTZ
CYPR
GRCE
TRKY
FNLD
USSR
CNDA
MLTA
UK
SPAN
FRNC
FRG
USA
CZCH
HNGR
GDR
PLND
RMNA
BLGR
YGSL

Conflict

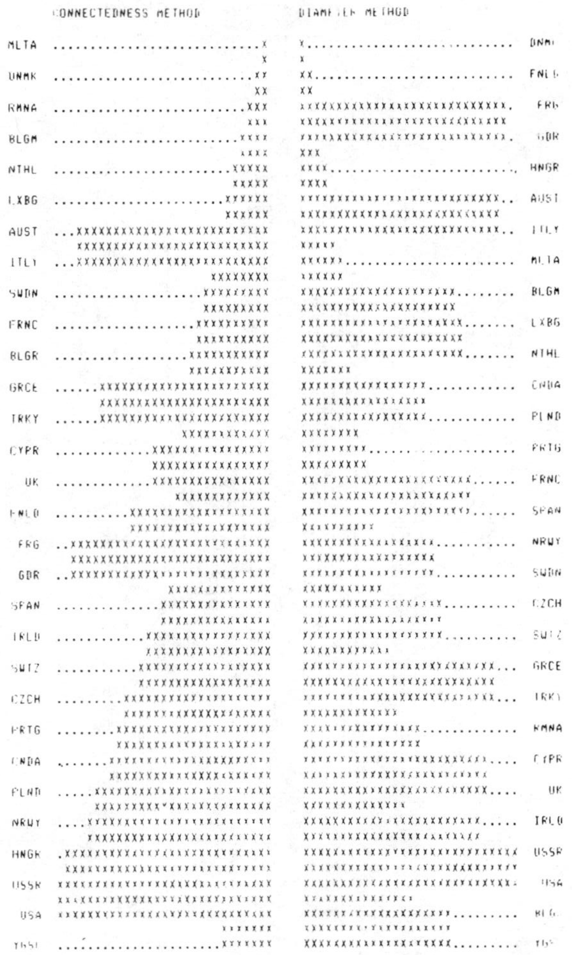
CONNECTEDNESS METHOD
DIAMETER METHOD
MLTA
DNMK
RMNA
BLGM
NTHL
LXBG
AUST
ITLY
SWDN
FRNC
BLGR
GRCE
TRKY
CYPR
UK
FNLD
FRG
GDR
SPAN
IRLD
SWTZ
CZCH
PRTG
CNDA
PLND
NRWY
HNGR
USSR
USA
YGSL
DNMK
FNLD
FRG
GDR
HNGR
AUST
ITLY
MLTA
BLGM
LXBG
NTHL
CNDA
PLND
PRTG
FRNC
SPAN
NRWY
SWDN
CZCH
SWTZ
GRCE
TRKY
RMNA
CYPR
UK
IRLD
USSR
USA
BLGR
YGSL

Graph 3.24. Clusters of Countries in East–West Interactions, 1965-1969

Cooperation

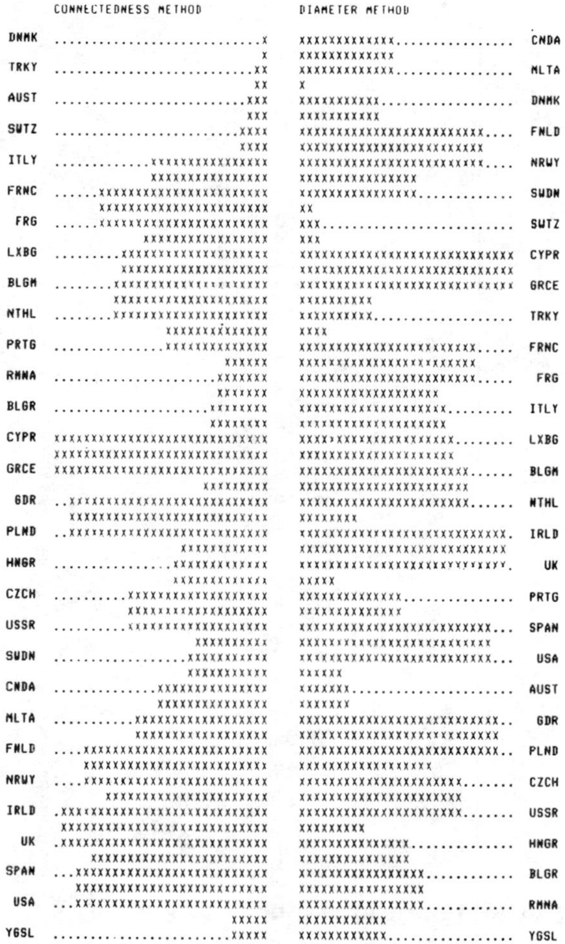
CONNECTEDNESS METHOD
DIAMETER METHOD
DNMK
TRKY
AUST
SWTZ
ITLY
FRNC
FRG
LXBG
BLGM
NTHL
PRTG
RMNA
BLGR
CYPR
GRCE
GDR
PLND
HNGR
CZCH
USSR
SWDN
CNDA
MLTA
FNLD
NRWY
IRLD
UK
SPAN
USA
YGSL
CNDA
MLTA
DNMK
FNLD
NRWY
SWDN
SWTZ
CYPR
GRCE
TRKY
FRNC
FRG
ITLY
LXBG
BLGM
NTHL
IRLD
UK
PRTG
SPAN
USA
AUST
GDR
PLND
CZCH
USSR
HNGR
BLGR
RMNA
YGSL

Conflict

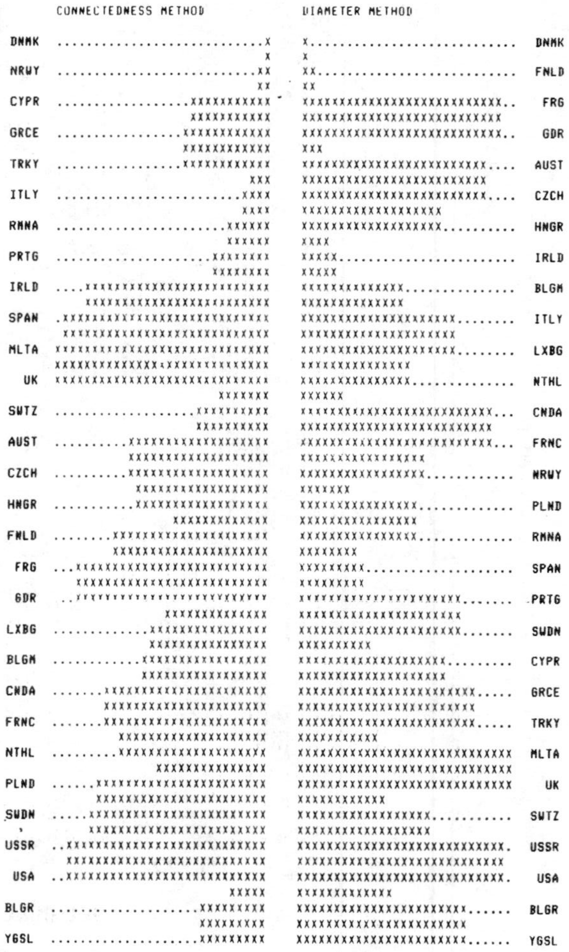
CONNECTEDNESS METHOD
DIAMETER METHOD
DNMK
NRWY
CYPR
GRCE
TRKY
ITLY
RMNA
PRTG
IRLD
SPAN
MLTA
UK
SWTZ
AUST
CZCH
HNGR
FNLD
FRG
GDR
LXBG
BLGM
CNDA
FRNC
NTHL
PLND
SWDN
USSR
USA
BLGR
YGSL
DNMK
FNLD
FRG
GDR
AUST
CZCH
HNGR
IRLD
BLGM
ITLY
LXBG
NTHL
CNDA
FRNC
NRWY
PLND
RMNA
SPAN
PRTG
SWDN
CYPR
GRCE
TRKY
MLTA
UK
SWTZ
USSR
USA
BLGR
YGSL

Graph 3.25. Clusters of Countries in East–West Interactions, 1970-1974

Cooperation

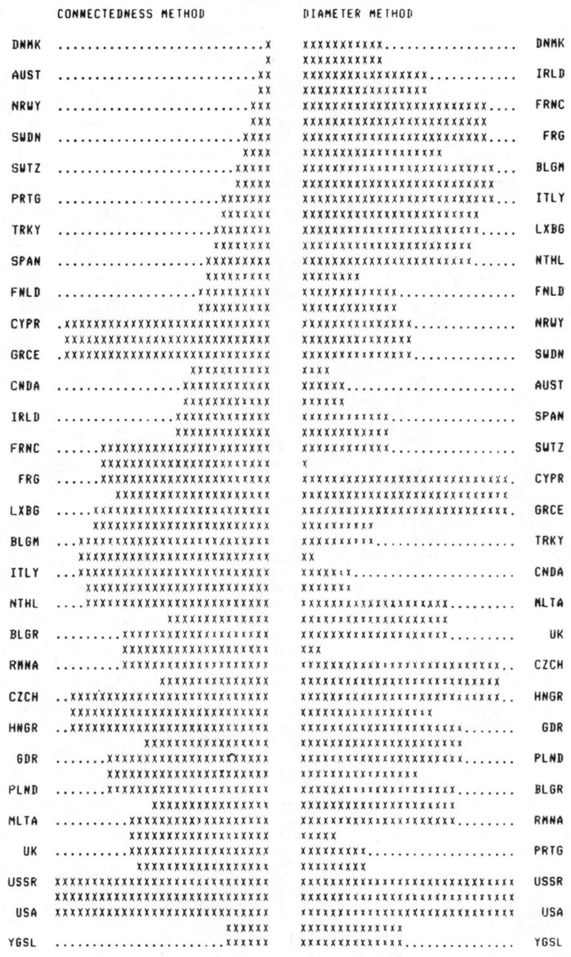

CONNECTEDNESS METHOD
DIAMETER METHOD
DNMK AUST NRWY SWDN SWTZ PRTG TRKY SPAN FNLD CYPR GRCE CNDA IRLD FRNC FRG LXBG BLGM ITLY NTHL BLGR RMNA CZCH HNGR GDR PLND MLTA UK USSR USA YGSL
DNMK IRLD FRNC FRG BLGM ITLY LXBG NTHL FNLD NRWY SWDN AUST SPAN SWTZ CYPR GRCE TRKY CNDA MLTA UK CZCH HNGR GDR PLND BLGR RMNA PRTG USSR USA YGSL

Conflict

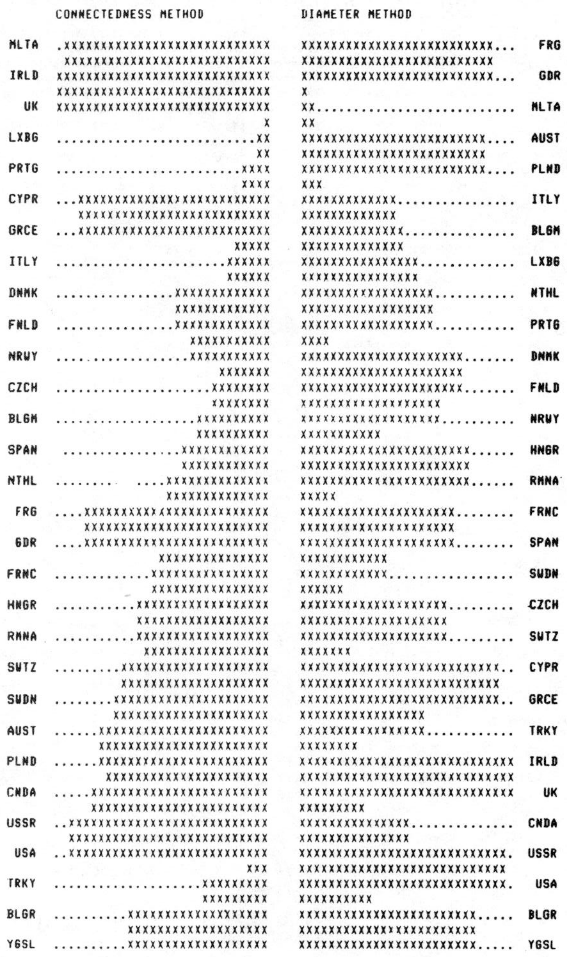

CONNECTEDNESS METHOD
DIAMETER METHOD
MLTA IRLD UK LXBG PRTG CYPR GRCE ITLY DNMK FNLD NRWY CZCH BLGM SPAN NTHL FRG GDR FRNC HNGR RMNA SWTZ SWDN AUST PLND CNDA USSR USA TRKY BLGR YGSL
FRG GDR MLTA AUST PLND ITLY BLGM LXBG NTHL PRTG DNMK FNLD NRWY HNGR RMNA FRNC SPAN SWDN CZCH SWTZ CYPR GRCE TRKY IRLD UK CNDA USSR USA BLGR YGSL

Graph 3.26. Clusters of Countries in East–West Interactions, 1975-1978

Cooperation

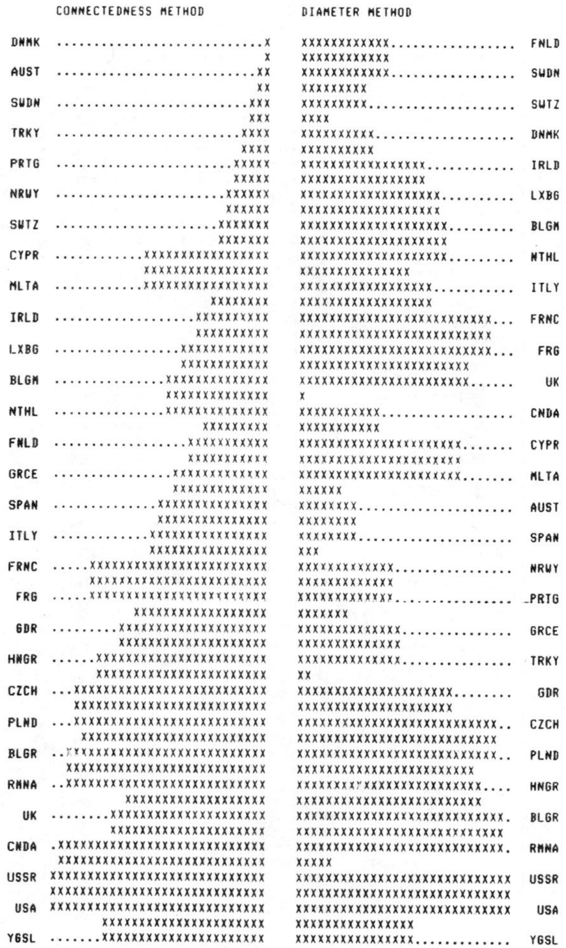
CONNECTEDNESS METHOD
DIAMETER METHOD
DNMK
AUST
SWDN
TRKY
PRTG
NRWY
SWTZ
CYPR
MLTA
IRLD
LXBG
BLGM
NTHL
FNLD
GRCE
SPAN
ITLY
FRNC
FRG
GDR
HNGR
CZCH
PLND
BLGR
RMNA
UK
CNDA
USSR
USA
YGSL
FNLD
SWDN
SWTZ
DNMK
IRLD
LXBG
BLGM
NTHL
ITLY
FRNC
FRG
UK
CNDA
CYPR
MLTA
AUST
SPAN
NRWY
PRTG
GRCE
TRKY
GDR
CZCH
PLND
HNGR
BLGR
RMNA
USSR
USA
YGSL

Conflict

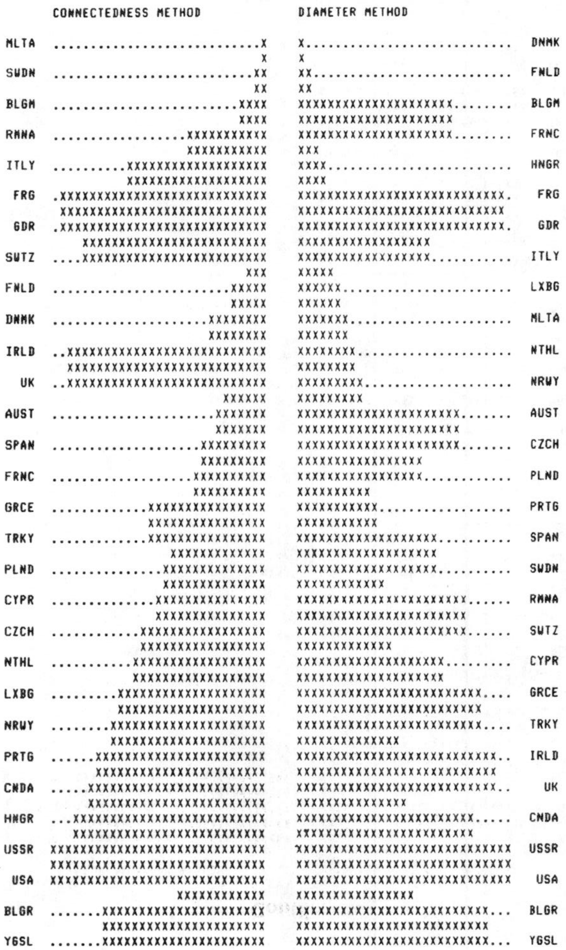
CONNECTEDNESS METHOD
DIAMETER METHOD
MLTA
SWDN
BLGM
RMNA
ITLY
FRG
GDR
SWTZ
FNLD
DNMK
IRLD
UK
AUST
SPAN
FRNC
GRCE
TRKY
PLND
CYPR
CZCH
NTHL
LXBG
NRWY
PRTG
CNDA
HNGR
USSR
USA
BLGR
YGSL
DNMK
FNLD
BLGM
FRNC
HNGR
FRG
GDR
ITLY
LXBG
MLTA
NTHL
NRWY
AUST
CZCH
PLND
PRTG
SPAN
SWDN
RMNA
SWTZ
CYPR
GRCE
TRKY
IRLD
UK
CNDA
USSR
USA
BLGR
YGSL

striking fact that there was little change and a high degree of structural stability in East–West relations. Cooperation closely follows the pattern of alliance membership. Apart from NATO and WTO, smaller clusters of closely interconnected nations emerge such as the Benelux countries and the group of Nordic nations. Other preferential relationships are those between France and the Federal Republic of Germany; between Portugal and Spain; among Canada, the United Kingdom, and the United States; between the GDR and Poland; between Finland and the Soviet Union; between Cyprus and Greece.

In the seventies, however, the increasing cooperation between the two major powers dominates the cluster of cooperative interactions, whereas in the first half of the decade, the EC emerges as a solid block of cooperation. The WTO finds itself split into bilateral pairs of interaction. In the second part of the decade precisely the opposite situation can be observed. When analyzing indicators of political dependency (see Section 3.6), it becomes evident that during the high tide of "détente," the WTO nations directed much of their attention to single partners within or outside the alliance. With increasing tensions, however, the cohesion within the WTO tended to increase.

On the other hand, the identification of clusters of nations bound together in conflictive relationships is a more difficult task, due to the logic of conflicts: Generally, the enemy of one's enemy will very likely become one's friend. Therefore, we would not expect large clusters of nations linked together in conflict, in contrast to the clusters of nations having cooperative interactions. The larger cluster of the East–West antagonism including the Soviet Union and the United States is overlapped by a much larger number of bilateral conflictive relationships between smaller NATO and WTO members. The main conflictive dyads are: the Federal Republic of Germany and the German Democratic Republic, Austria and Romania, Poland and Sweden, Bulgaria and Turkey, Austria and Italy, France and Spain, and Cyprus and the United Kingdom. Not surprising, conflicts within the EC and NATO also result in respective clusters, as, for example, France and Luxembourg; Portugal and the United States; Belgium and the Netherlands; and Greece and Turkey. Conflicts within the WTO do not appear in the data used for this analysis, with the exception of Bulgaria and Yugoslavia, which seem to constitute a stable element within the cluster structure. Still, Yugoslavia is no WTO member.

These observations may suggest the conclusion that it takes more than a decade of East–West interactions to change the structure of relations with regard to cooperation and conflict. These relationships remain overwhelmingly dominated by block loyalties. Yet within NATO and the EC, the plurality of cooperation and conflict is a structural element, hardly to be found in the WTO. While the process of East–West relations in Europe did hardly weaken the cohesion within the WTO, it did nevertheless grant WTO members the possibility of establishing firmer ties with the world outside their camp.

3.3.3 Cooperation and Conflict Among the Thirty-Five CSCE States in the United Nations General Assembly

In the introductory paragraph to the Final Act, the thirty-five governments taking part in the CSCE negotiations reaffirmed their objective of "promoting better relations among themselves and ensuring conditions in which their people can live in true and lasting peace free from any threat to or attempt against their security." The Final Act thus refers to one of the primary objectives pronounced by the United Nations Charter. In his statement made to the 1975 Helsinki meeting of heads of states and governments, UN Secretary General Kurt Waldheim emphasized that there is no contradiction between a regional agreement such as the Final Act and the continuing efforts undertaken by the United Nations. On the contrary, he said, any regional agreement of this sort can offer a basis for world peace.

If this assumption is correct, the amelioration of East-West cooperation will be accompanied by a parallel decrease of the intensity of controversies taking place in the United Nations Assembly and by a growing inclination toward consensual decisionmaking in the General Assembly. On a more operational level, this would imply a broadening scope of congruous voting behavior of the delegates representing the thirty-five CSCE states in the General Assembly.

Based on this assumption, this subsection will present calculations referring to the degree of affinity in voting behavior. The calculations comprise Pearson's product-moment correlation coefficients between pairs of nations computed for roll-call votes in Session 15 through 28 (Newcombe and Wert 1979).* No votes are coded as 0, abstain as 1, and yes as 2. A correlation coefficient close to zero thus means uncorrelated voting; a correlation coefficient of +1 means the voting is always in perfect accordance; if the correlation coefficient is close to −1, the two nations always chose completely opposite points of view. (Values for the 1964 UN General Assembly, XIXth session, were interpolated because no votes were taken.)

Graph 3.27 offers a view on interblock affinities in UN voting behavior, more precisely between the USSR and selected member countries of NATO. All correlations are negative—except the correlations for the years 1971 and 1972 between France and the USSR and for 1971 between the UK and the USSR. Therefore, the basically polarized structure in principle remains constant during the entire period observed. But, on the other hand, it cannot be denied that the intensity of disagreement has somewhat lessened; this

*Data for 1974–1977 communicated by Hanna Newcombe.

Graph 3.27. Interblock Affinities in UN Voting

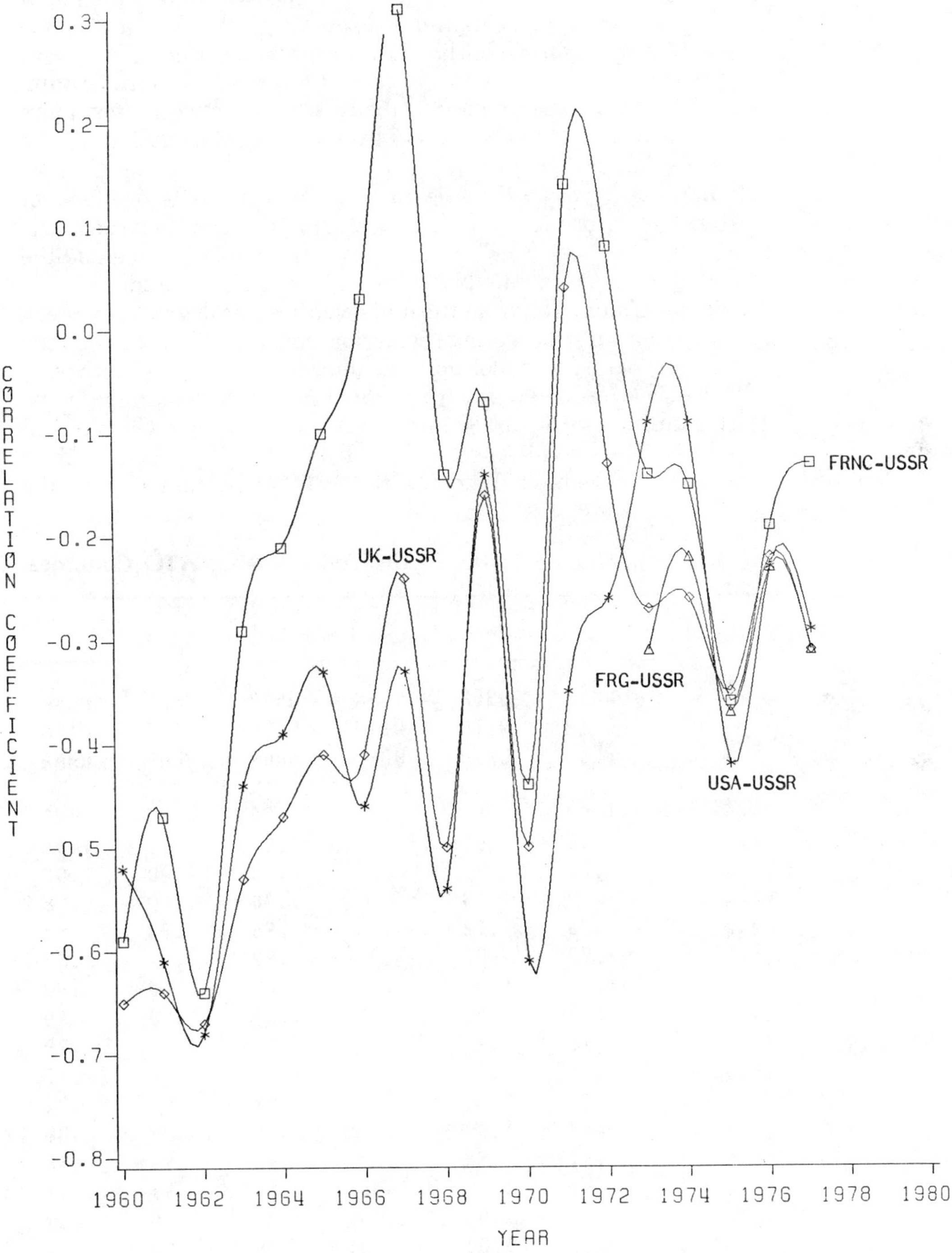

0.3
0.2
0.1
0.0
-0.1
-0.2
-0.3
-0.4
-0.5
-0.6
-0.7
-0.8
CØRRELATIØN CØEFFICIENT
UK-USSR
FRNC-USSR
FRG-USSR
USA-USSR
1960
1962
1964
1966
1968
1970
1972
1974
1976
1978
1980
YEAR

conclusion can be drawn when comparing the coefficients calculated for the early sixties with the coefficients calculated for the seventies. There seems to be a general trend toward a reduction of conflictivity. However, this trend proceeds quite slowly, and so far it does not transform conflict into cooperation, that is, the zero level is transgressed only in the case of France and Great Britain. In the last years, the amount of disagreement between most pairs of nations observed in Graph 3.27 grows again, thus indicating the general crisis of "détente."

It may also be worthwhile to note that the heterogeneity of Western behavior vis-à-vis the Soviet Union was quite large in the late sixties and again in the early seventies when France and the UK adopted a more friendly or less disagreeing attitude vis-àvis the Soviet Union. Yet, from the midseventies, the degree of Western coordination in UN voting behavior conspicuously grows; the curves are neatly parallel or even tend to overlap each other.

This observation can be corroborated further by looking at intrablock affinities within WTO and NATO (Table 3.3 and Graphs 3.28 and 3.29). The two alliances differ strikingly with regard to their internal cohesiveness: Whereas the WTO delegations (with the

Table 3.3. Intrablock Affinities in UN Voting among WTO Countries

year	pairs of countries compared					
	USSR WITH BLGR	USSR WITH CZCH	USSR WITH GDR	USSR WITH HNGR	USSR WITH PLND	USSR WITH RMNA
1960	1.00	.99	.	.99	.99	.99
1961	1.00	1.00	.	1.00	1.00	1.00
1962	1.00	.97	.	1.00	1.00	1.00
1963	1.00	1.00	.	1.00	1.00	.98
1964	.96	.96	.	.96	.96	.93
1965	.92	.92	.	.92	.92	.87
1966	1.00	1.00	.	1.00	1.00	.99
1967	1.00	1.00	.	1.00	.98	.90
1968	.96	.99	.	.99	.99	.78
1969	.96	1.00	.	.96	1.00	.90
1970	.99	1.00	.	.99	.96	.91
1971	.99	1.00	.	.99	.99	.88
1972	.99	.95	.	.96	.94	.48
1973	.99	1.00	1.00	1.00	.99	.71
1974	1.00	1.00	1.00	1.00	1.00	.69
1975	1.00	1.00	1.00	1.00	.99	.71
1976	1.00	.99	1.00	.99	.97	.75
1977	1.00	1.00	1.00	1.00	.98	.63

Graph 3.28. Intrablock Affinities in UN Voting Among NATO Countries (1)

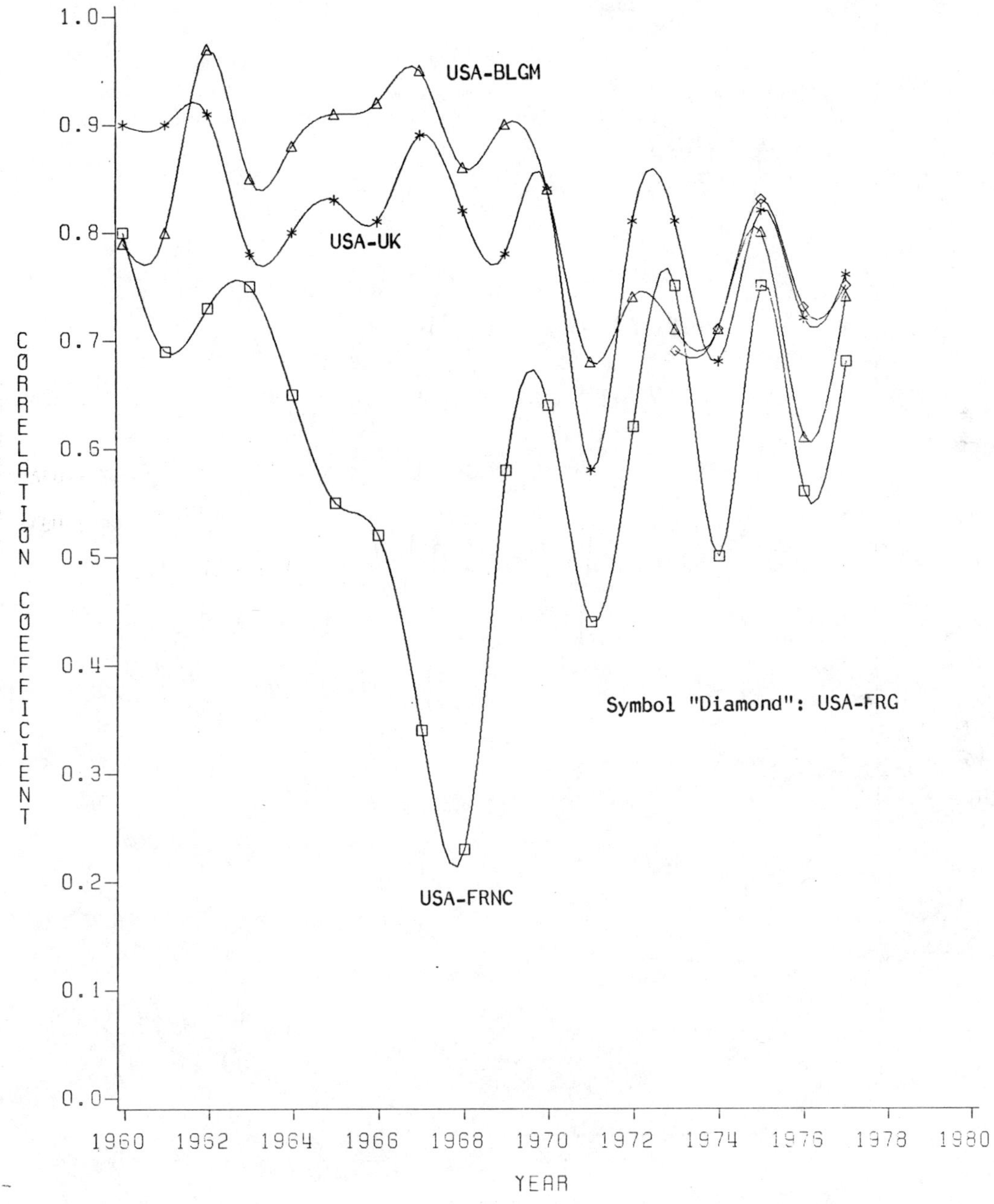
1.0
0.9
0.8
0.7
0.6
0.5
0.4
0.3
0.2
0.1
0.0
CORRELATION COEFFICIENT
USA-BLGM
USA-UK
USA-FRNC
Symbol "Diamond": USA-FRG
1960
1962
1964
1966
1968
1970
1972
1974
1976
1978
1980
YEAR

Graph 3.29. Intrablock Affinities in UN Voting among NATO Countries (2)

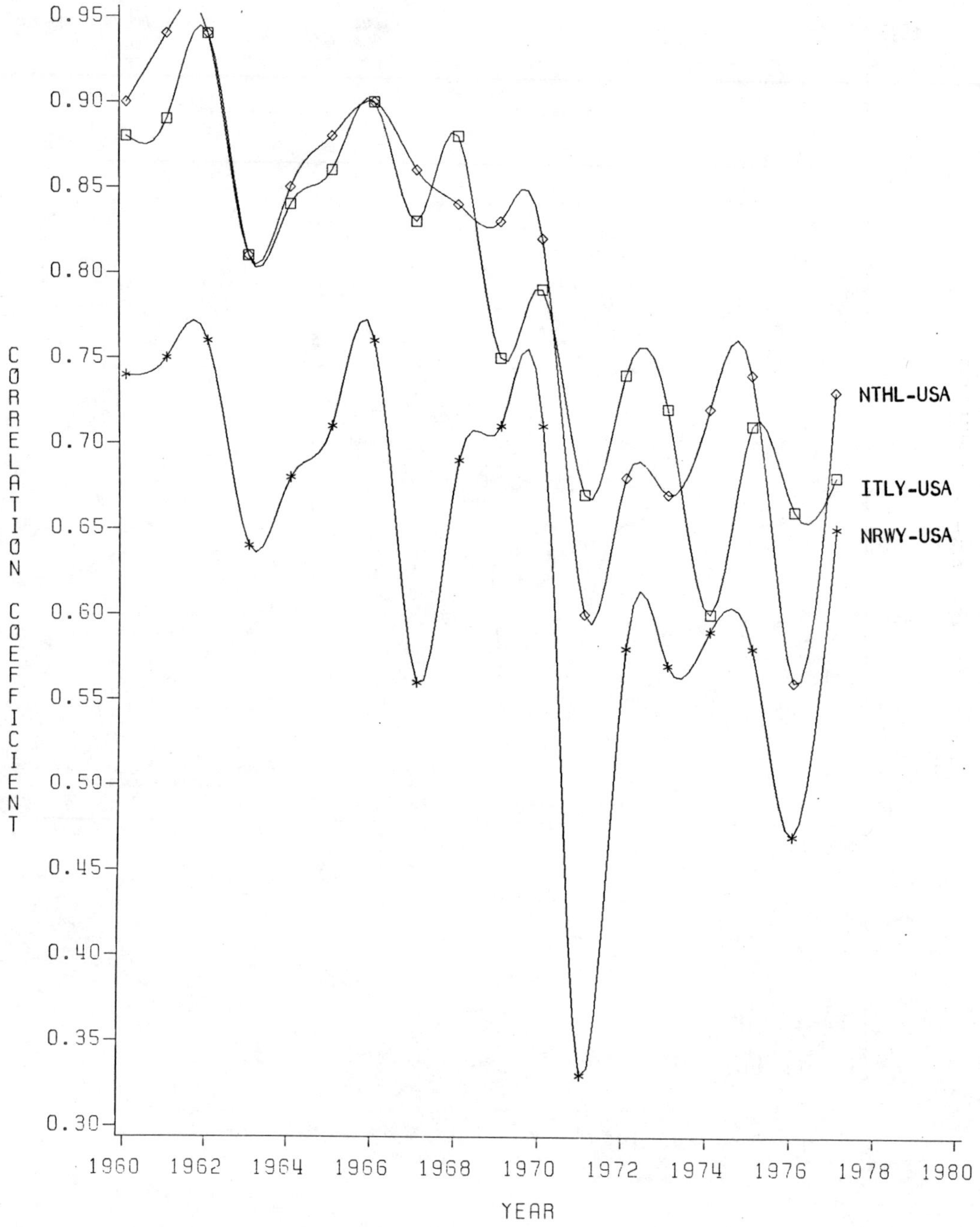
0.95
0.90
0.85
0.80
0.75
0.70
0.65
0.60
0.55
0.50
0.45
0.40
0.35
0.30
CORRELATION COEFFICIENT
1960
1962
1964
1966
1968
1970
1972
1974
1976
1978
1980
YEAR
NTHL-USA
ITLY-USA
NRWY-USA

exception of Romania) constantly vote in complete or nearly complete agreement with the Soviet Union, the picture offered by the NATO groups is considerably more diverse. But still the correlations regarding affinities within NATO are without any exception positive. As will be outlined in Chapter 5, one of the theories proposed about "détente" suggests that the amelioration of East-West relations makes block cohesion less important. If this assumption is correct, the correlation coefficients indicating the agreement of the various countries with their respective block leader would be lower in the seventies than in the sixties. As a matter of fact, this general tendency is to some extent confirmed by the data for the NATO group, and the curve plotted in Graphs 3.28 and 3.29 for six selected pairs of NATO countries indicates a slight inclination from a level of .90 agreement to a level around .70. Within the WTO group of countries, however, intrabloc discipline remains constant and is even improving; as mentioned previously, only Romania clearly shifted from 1.00 full agreement in 1961 to a mere .63 in 1977. There are also slight and symbolic deviations from full agreement by Poland.

To what extent was the group of neutral and nonaligned nations capable of extending their role conception developed within the CSCE framework into the UN General Assembly? This question can be answered by looking at Graphs 3.30 and 3.31. Being neutral or nonaligned obviously does not mean adopting a policy of "equidistance" between the two poles of the East-West confrontation. In the cases of Austria, Sweden, and Finland, all correlations with the United States are positive, and most of the correlations with the Soviet Union are negative. In the case of Yugoslavia precisely the opposite situation can be observed. Yet it is also apparent that these asymmetries to a certain extent are becoming corrected in the course of the late sixties and seventies: Austria's, Sweden's, and Finland's bent toward agreement with the United States voting behavior becomes less marked than in the early sixties, and simultaneously their disagreement with the Soviet Union is becoming less articulate. Correspondingly, the rate of Yugoslavia's opposition to American voting behavior is falling from correlations around −.50 in the sixties to correlations between −.20 and −.10, whereas Yugoslavia's staunch agreement with the USSR (1960: $r=.87$) is being reduced to correlations in the range between .30 and .50. Therefore the conclusion seems to be justified that the N + N countries, in the course of the evolution of East-West relations, cautiously moved toward an intermediate position, however, without disavowing their ideological affinities with the West or (in the case of Yugoslavia) with the East.

The N + N nations never envisaged any blocklike coordination of their policies; yet they tried to find some common approaches to problems of the CSCE. Therefore the question may be asked to what extent this aspiration for a common approach is also reflected in their voting behavior in the UN General Assembly. As

Graph 3.30. Affinities in UN Voting between the United States and Neutral/Nonaligned Countries

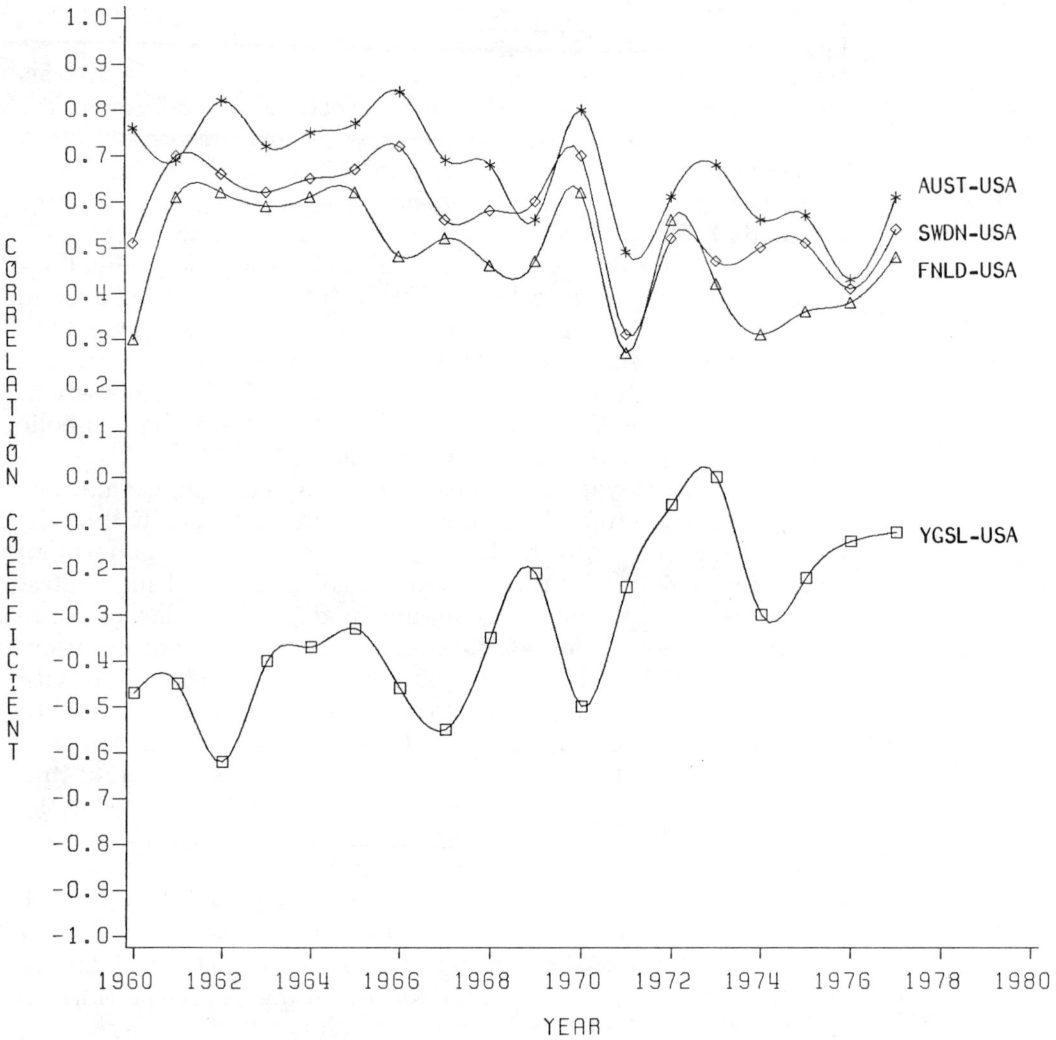
1.0
0.9
0.8
0.7
0.6
0.5
0.4
0.3
0.2
0.1
0.0
-0.1
-0.2
-0.3
-0.4
-0.5
-0.6
-0.7
-0.8
-0.9
-1.0
CORRELATION COEFFICIENT
AUST-USA
SWDN-USA
FNLD-USA
YGSL-USA
1960
1962
1964
1966
1968
1970
1972
1974
1976
1978
1980
YEAR

Graph 3.31. Affinities in UN Voting between the Soviet Union and Neutral/ Nonaligned Countries

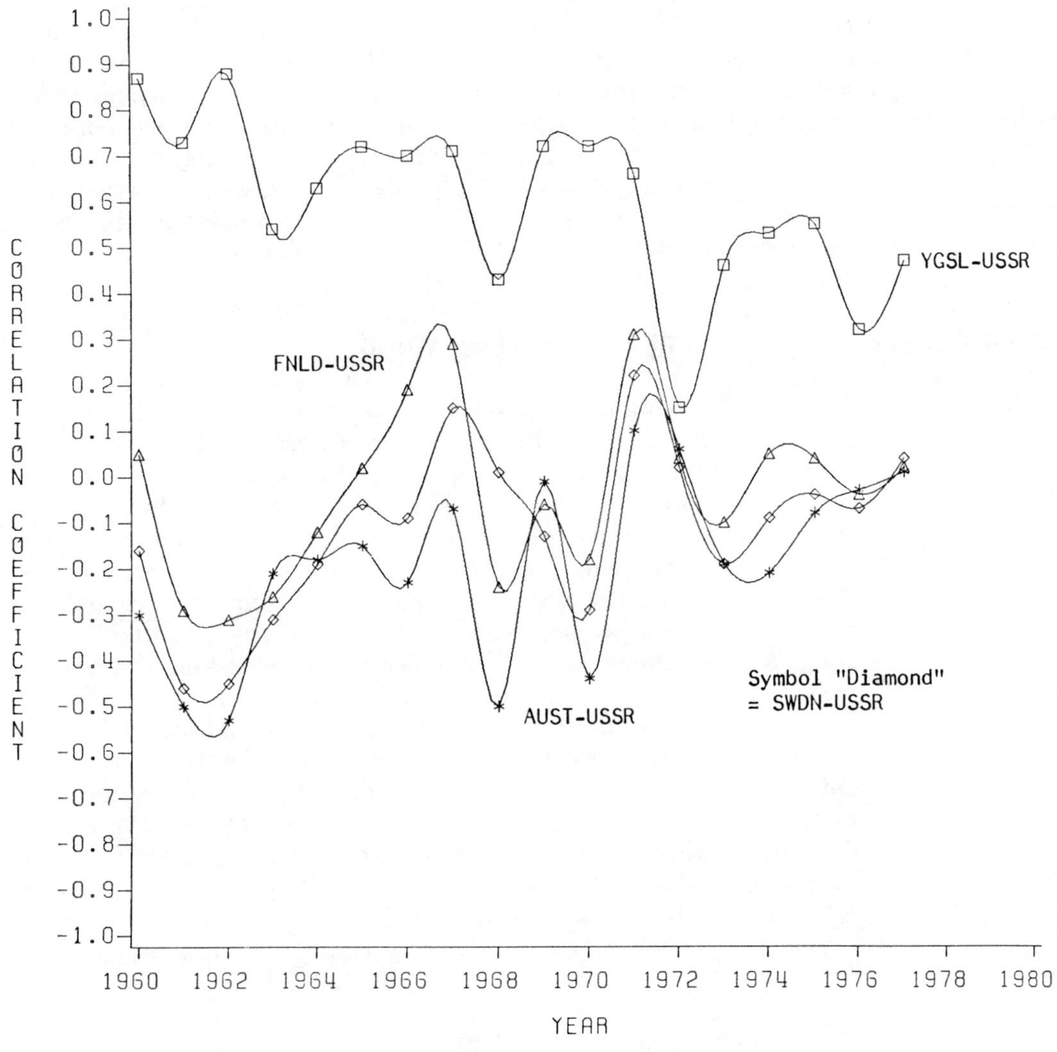
CORRELATION COEFFICIENT
1.0
0.9
0.8
0.7
0.6
0.5
0.4
0.3
0.2
0.1
0.0
-0.1
-0.2
-0.3
-0.4
-0.5
-0.6
-0.7
-0.8
-0.9
-1.0
1960
1962
1964
1966
1968
1970
1972
1974
1976
1978
1980
YEAR
YGSL-USSR
FNLD-USSR
AUST-USSR
Symbol "Diamond"
= SWDN-USSR

can be seen in Graphs 3.32 and 3.33 such a trend can in fact be observed with regard to Yugoslavia's affinities to the other N + N nations. The respective correlation coefficients that were constantly negative in the early sixties are positive in the seventies, and their size is increasing as the process of "détente" evolves. As far as the affinities among Sweden, Finland, and Austria are concerned, it is less obvious to identify any specific trend. The voting affinity between Sweden and Finland has always been considerable due to the framework of Nordic cooperation, and also the level of agreement between Austria, on the one hand, and Sweden and Finland, on the other hand, was quite high during the entire period analyzed. Hence, if there is a process of drawing together the behavior of the various N + N nations, this process mainly concerns the position of Yugoslavia, which underwent a remarkable change in the period observed.

3.3.4 Cooperation and Conflict in the Third World

Although focusing mainly on East-West relations on the European continent and between the two major powers, the Final Act also contains several provisions regarding the Third World and the necessity to promote Third World development. It is obvious that the problems of East-West relations cannot be separated from Third World problems. The two problem areas are closely interlinked. Yet the nature of these linkages is far from being clear. The literature on this subject offers a variety of theories about how East-West relations affect Third World problems and vice versa.

Some authors argue that the Third World will benefit from East-West "détente" by getting access to resources that otherwise are wasted in ceaseless East-West rivalry and accelerated arms race. On the other hand, it is also assumed that activities by the two major powers in regions outside Europe necessarily have repercussions on East-West relations in Europe, in other words, that the evolution of East-West relations is governed by what is sometimes called the "indivisability of détente."

However, other authors straightly contradict this assumption by explicitly pointing at the favorable impact of peaceful coexistence between East and West in Europe on the continued "revolutionary development" in the Third World. In this context, emphasis is also placed on the beneficial impact of the Socialist countries being relieved of their burden to spend a large amount of their attention and resources to their rivalry with the West and thus becoming increasingly more capable to support the "anti-imperialist struggle for liberation from colonialist and neocolonialist rule" by active engagement at various spots in the Third World.

A selection of these theories will be more systematically reported and examined in Chapter 5. At this point, the aim of the following paragraphs is more limited in scope and confined to a merely descriptive presentation of major-power relations with selected

Graph 3.32. Affinities in UN Voting of Neutral and Nonaligned Countries (1)

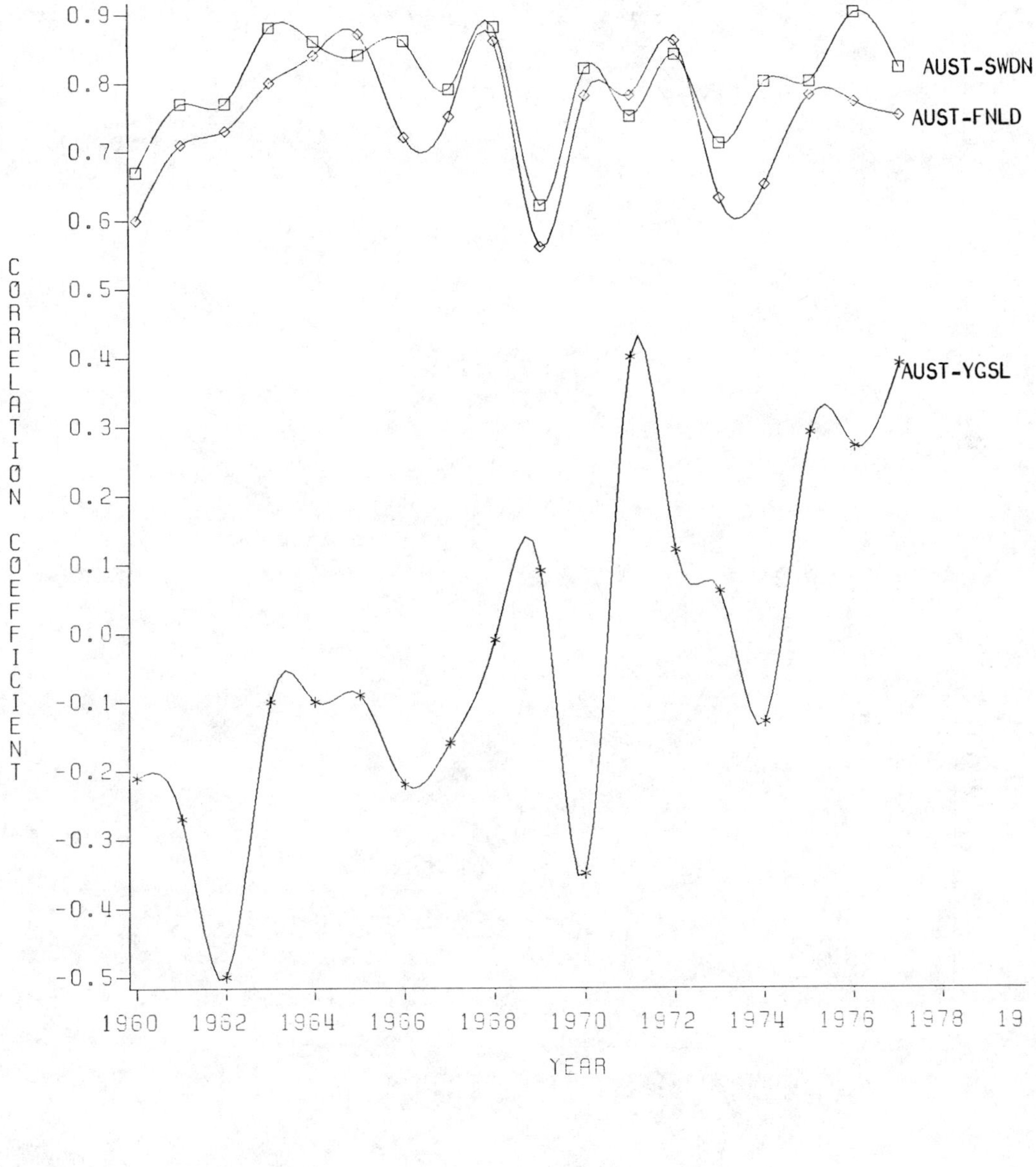
CORRELATION COEFFICIENT
0.9
0.8
0.7
0.6
0.5
0.4
0.3
0.2
0.1
0.0
-0.1
-0.2
-0.3
-0.4
-0.5
AUST-SWDN
AUST-FNLD
AUST-YGSL
1960
1962
1964
1966
1968
1970
1972
1974
1976
1978
19
YEAR

Graph 3.33. Affinities in UN Voting of Neutral and Nonaligned Countries (2)

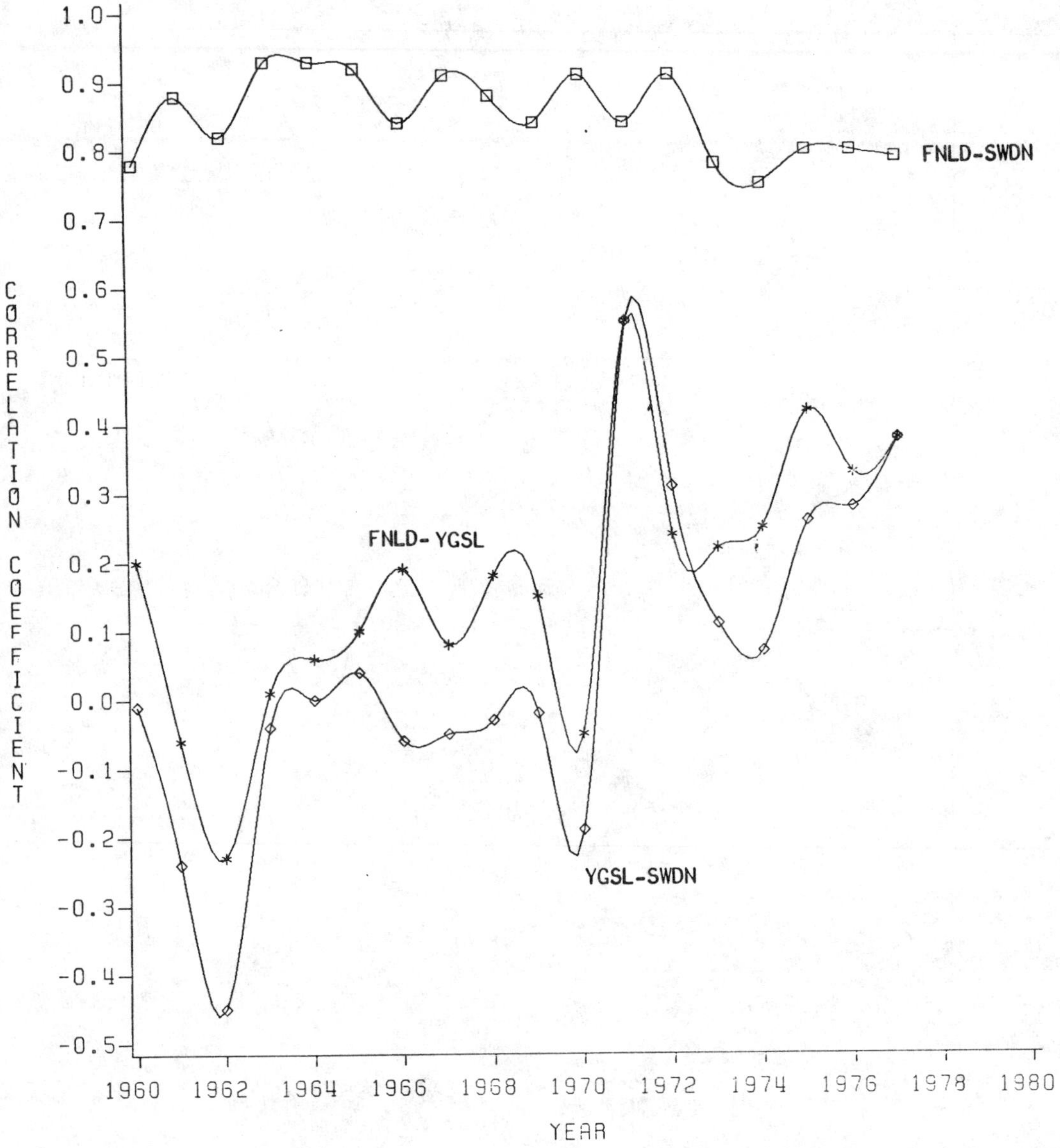

CORRELATION COEFFICIENT
1.0
0.9
0.8
0.7
0.6
0.5
0.4
0.3
0.2
0.1
0.0
-0.1
-0.2
-0.3
-0.4
-0.5
1960 1962 1964 1966 1968 1970 1972 1974 1976 1978 1980
YEAR
FNLD-SWDN
FNLD- YGSL
YGSL-SWDN

Third World regions both in terms of cooperation and conflict. In order to give a comprehensive picture of major-power activities outside Europe, cooperative and conflictive events as reported in the COPDAB data bank are aggregated on an annual basis for each region (Latin America, Africa, Middle East, Asia) separately for the period 1960–1978.

All four graphs (3.34-3.37) make it apparent that the Soviet Union is generally less active in both the cooperative and the conflictive domain than the United States. As has been pointed out in Section 3.3.1, this seems to be a matter of diplomatic style rather than a matter of a generally different significance of the Third World within the global perspective of each major power. (In addition, the difference may also be accentuated by the fact that the data were gathered on the basis of publicly accessible reports; for obvious reasons, US relations with other countries are more amply publicized and exposed to the general public than USSR foreign relations.)

Yet the relative degree of Soviet and American activities is dissimilar from region to region. In the case of Latin America, the frequencies of Soviet viz. American intractions differ most: The curves describing American coopertion and conflict with Latin American countries are clearly separated from the corresponding Soviet curves. This does not mean that Latin America is still the "backyard" of the USA; it simply indicates the continuing importance of geographic and geopolitical neighborhood on the American hemisphere. It should also be noted, however, that the Soviet Union increased her degree of attention paid to Latin America in 1962 and again in the period 1973–1976; the first rise of cooperative Soviet relations with Latin America can be attributed to the sequence of events known as the "Cuban missile crisis"; the second seems to reflect a general reorientation of Soviet foreign policy in the context of "détente," and it is paralleled by a corresponding steep increase of both cooperative and conflictive relations between the USA and Latin America. Whereas prior to 1970 the shape of the curves of US relations with Latin America seems to be independent from the curves indicating Soviet relations, in the period after 1970, the ups and downs become correlated. In other words, as "détente" in the East-West context takes off and progresses, the relations of the two major powers with Latin America become more correlated and are part of an overarching logic.

The picture presented in the case of Asia (excluding Vietnam) is somewhat similar although not as explicit as in the case of Latin America. United States activities are clearly more salient than Soviet activities. Although Vietnam is not included in these data, the Vietnam war had obvious impacts on the American relations with other countries in the region. Yet in the second half of the seventies, a certain convergence seems to be evolving due to a marked reduction in the frequency of US interactions with Asia. Thus in the long run the USSR engagement in Asia seems to be

Graph 3.34. Major-Power Interactions with Latin American Countries

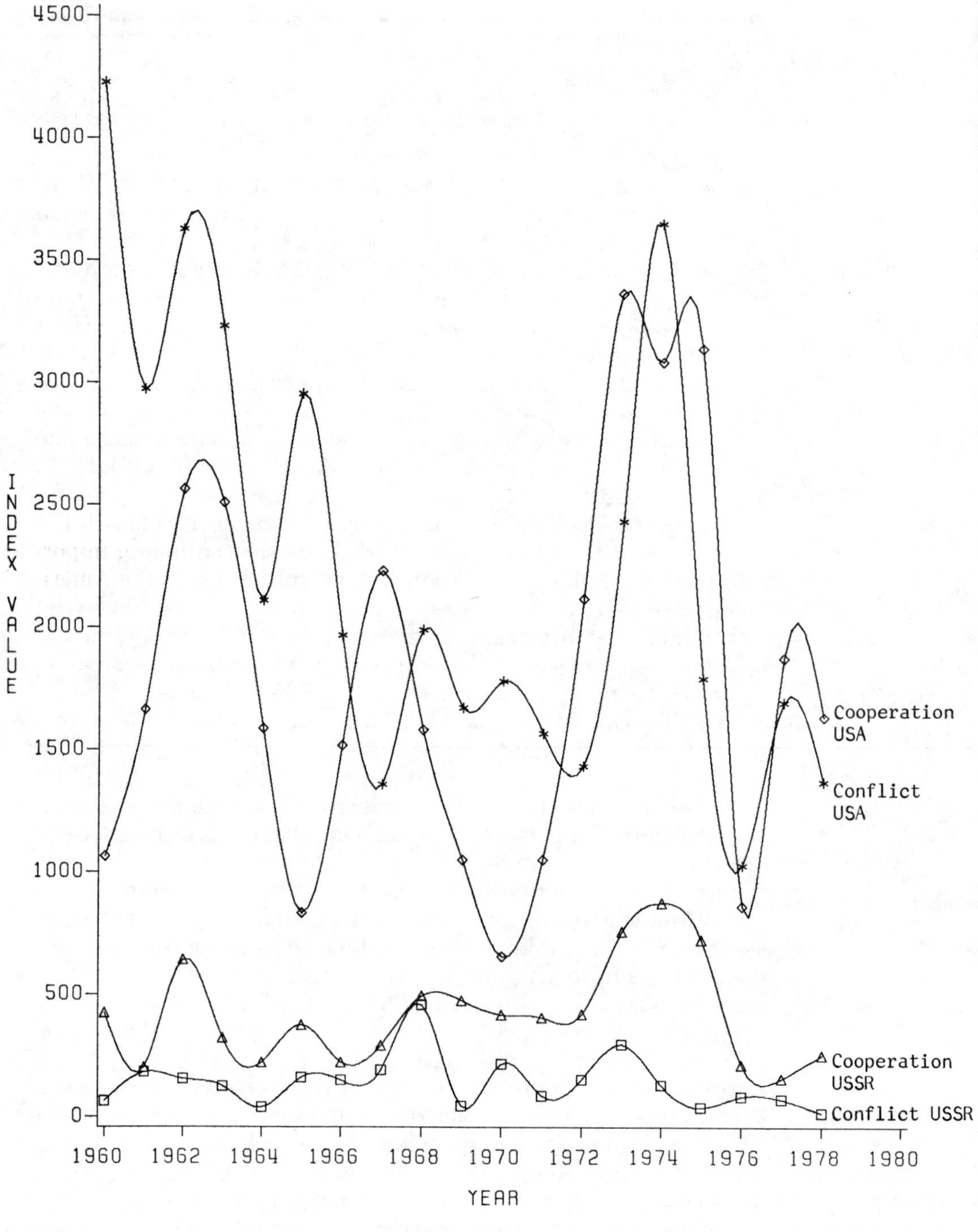
4500
4000
3500
3000
2500
2000
1500
1000
500
0
INDEX VALUE
1960 1962 1964 1966 1968 1970 1972 1974 1976 1978 1980
YEAR
Cooperation USA
Conflict USA
Cooperation USSR
Conflict USSR

Graph 3.35. Major-Power Interactions with Asian Countries (excluding Vietnam)

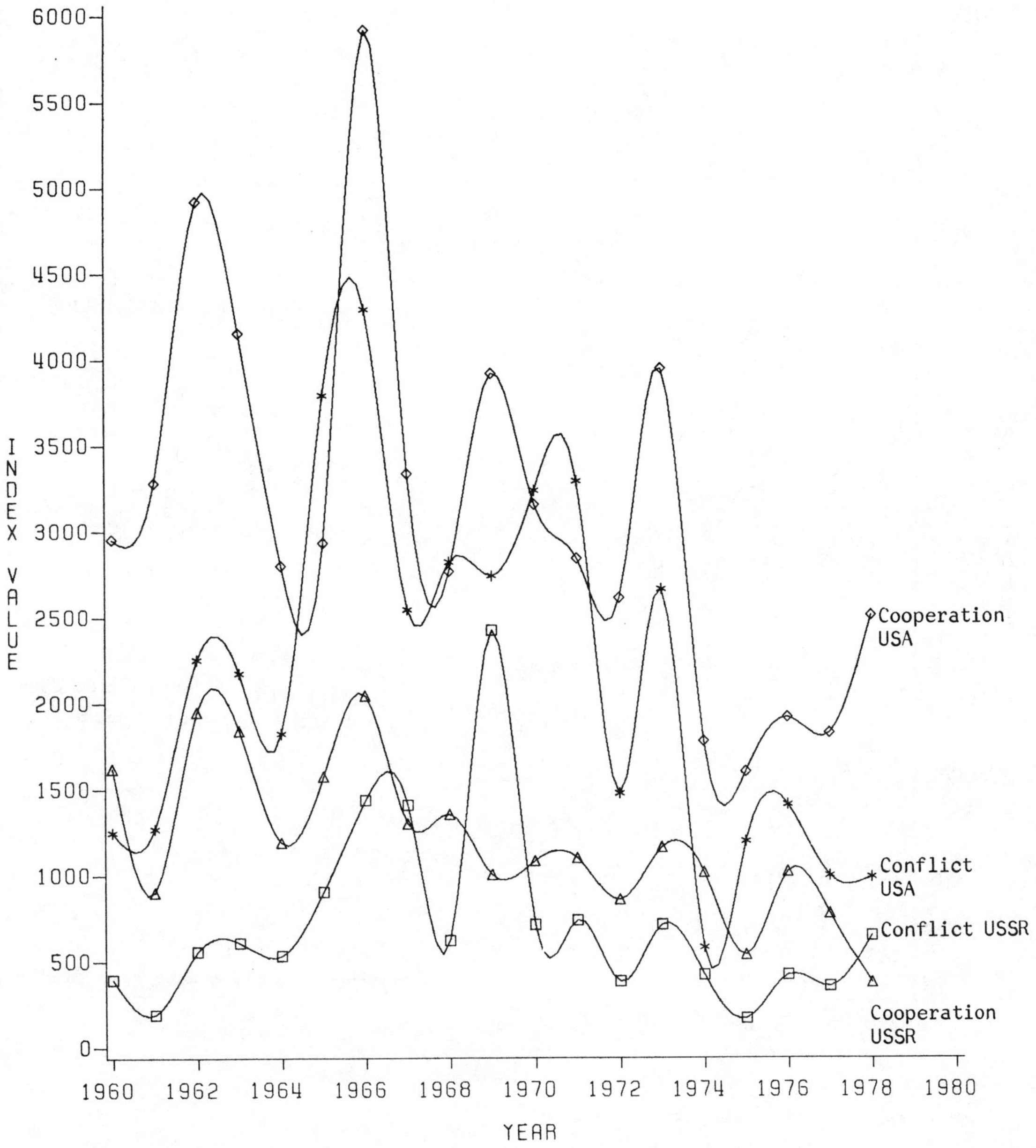
6000
5500
5000
4500
4000
3500
3000
2500
2000
1500
1000
500
0
INDEX VALUE
1960
1962
1964
1966
1968
1970
1972
1974
1976
1978
1980
YEAR
Cooperation USA
Conflict USA
Conflict USSR
Cooperation USSR

Graph 3.36. Major-Power Interactions with African Countries

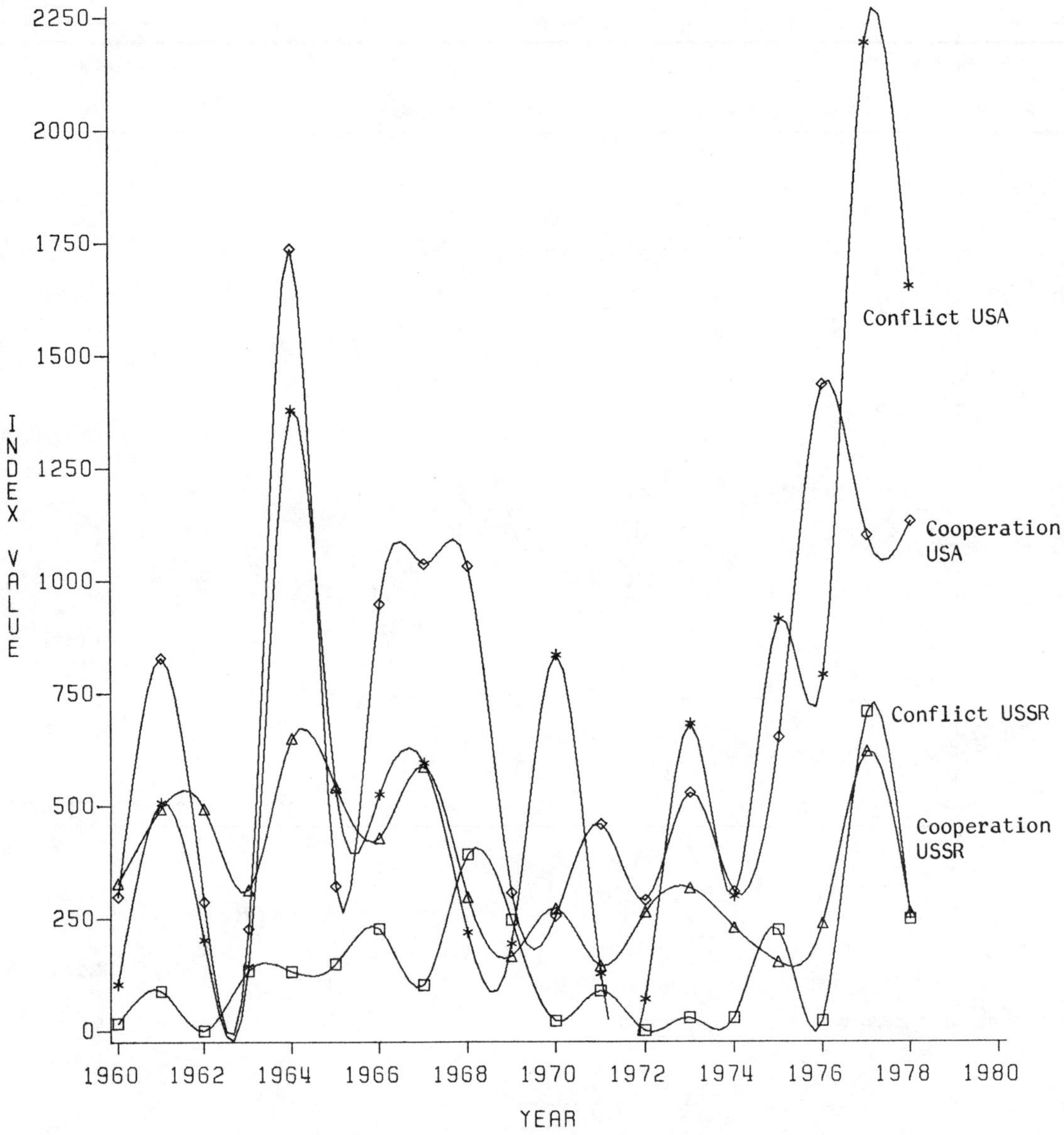
2250
2000
1750
1500
1250
1000
750
500
250
0
INDEX VALUE
1960
1962
1964
1966
1968
1970
1972
1974
1976
1978
1980
YEAR
Conflict USA
Cooperation USA
Conflict USSR
Cooperation USSR

Graph 3.37. Major-Power Interactions with Middle Eastern Countries

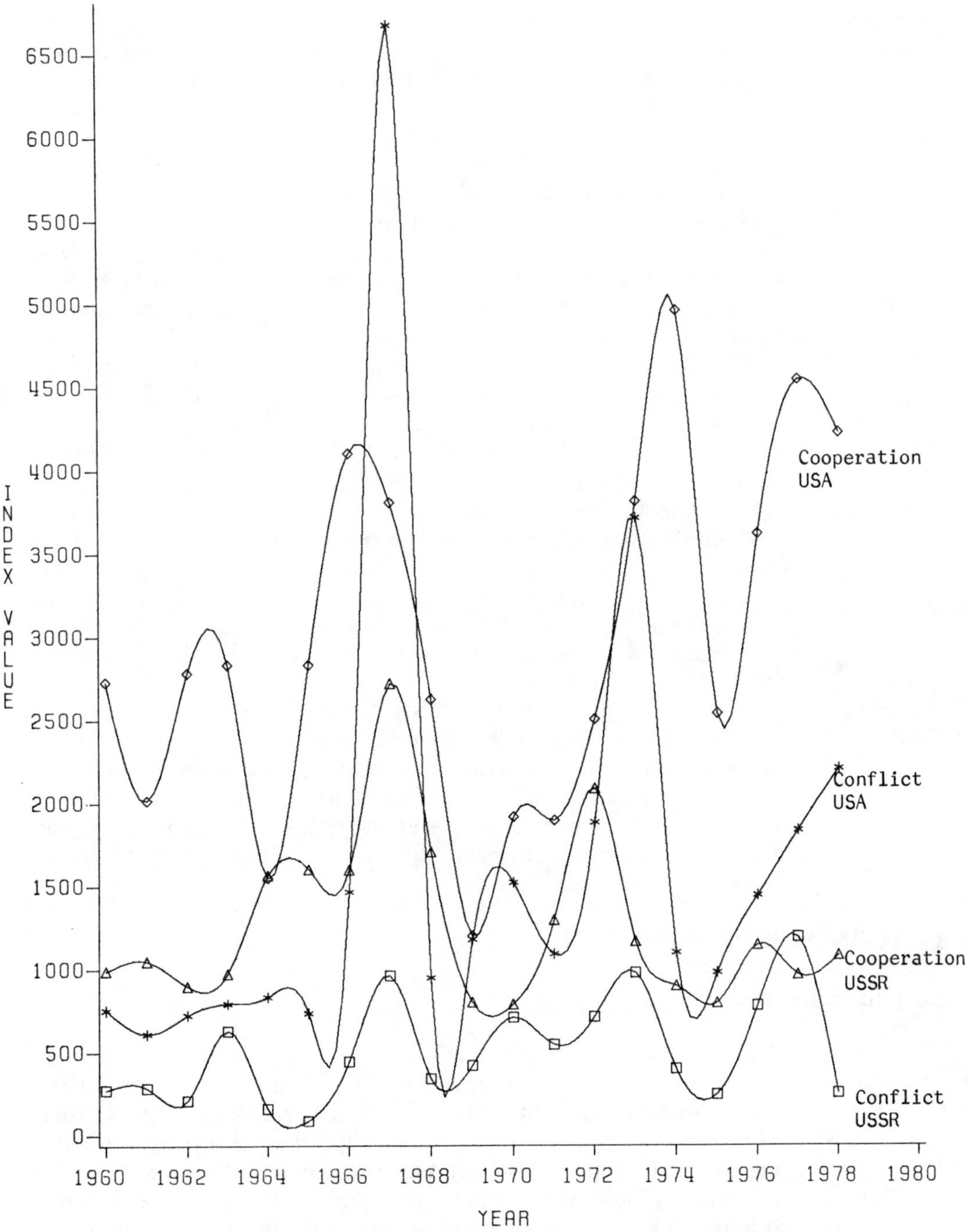
6500
6000
5500
5000
4500
4000
3500
3000
2500
2000
1500
1000
500
0
INDEX VALUE
1960
1962
1964
1966
1968
1970
1972
1974
1976
1978
1980
YEAR
Cooperation USA
Conflict USA
Cooperation USSR
Conflict USSR

more stable and steady than the American engagement.

By contrast to Latin America and Asia, the African and Middle Eastern situation evolved in a much more intricate way reflecting the troublesome fate of these two regions as well as the active involvement of both major powers. Especially in Africa, the erratic oscillations of the curves indicate a high degree of major-power rivalry projected upon this continent. The evolution of East-West "détente" in Europe seems to be directly related to major-power involvement in black Africa. From 1972 both US cooperation and US conflict with Africa is gradually escalating and finally sky-rocking above all thresholds experienced previously, partly in response to the Soviet engagement in Africa following 1976. The picture offered by Graph 3.36 clearly points at a serious process of destabilization taking place in Africa and instigated by East-West rivalry despite (or maybe because of) East-West "détente" in Europe.

The same can be said about the evolution of the situation in the Middle East, which is characterized by "peaks" reflecting the two armed clashes in 1967 and 1973. In the long run, the Soviet Union seems to lose ground as indicated by a certain decrease of her cooperative relations with her Middle Eastern partners. Another striking feature is the sudden and sharp rise of both cooperation and conflictive relations of the USA, in the second half of the seventies. The efforts to reach a certain consolidation in East-West relations in Europe were by no means able to exert any mitigating influence on the Middle East dispute.

In sum, "détente" in Europe cannot be said to have had any beneficial and stabilizing influence on the behavior of the two major powers vis-à-vis the Third World. Their rivalry in regions outside Europe continues either independently of any considerations of East-West "détente" or according to the logic inherent to those extra-European areas of contention. And in some areas, especially in Latin America and in Africa, the major-power confrontation even escalates as "détente" in Europe progresses.

3.4 ECONOMIC COOPERATION

3.4.1 Introduction

When the thirty-five governments taking part in the CSCE negotiations agreed, in the second "basket" of the Final Act, to develop cooperation in the fields of trade, industry, science, and technology and other areas of economic activity, they certainly took into account the existence of obstacles that emerged in more than two decades of Cold War. Apart from the problems and difficulties inherent to any intersystems cooperation, the political and military antagonism in the divided Europe had rapidly spread over to the "nonpolitical" fields of economics, science, and technology.

One of the motives behind this process was the desire, on the part of the West, to deprive the East of an easy access to Western technology and strategically sensitive goods that might have been used for military purposes. One of the instruments set up by the West to control trade and technology transfers to the East was the Coordinating Committee for East-West Trade Policy. (COCOM).

However, as the Cold War postures began to be slowly eroded by what became to be known as the policy of "détente," these and other obstacles were constantly (although not completely) removed. The number of items barred from trade by the COCOM list decreased from over 450 in 1957 to less than 200 in 1976 (Bertsch et al. 1979, pp. 6 ff). This may seem indicative of the new trend.

In order to provide a comprehensive picture of the evolution of East-West relations in the broad field covered by the second "basket," it would be necessary to examine a large variety of types of interactions and cooperation since the Final Act registered several dozens of measures to be taken to improve business contacts and facilities, economic and commercial information, marketing, industrial cooperation, projects of common interest, harmonization of standards, and the like. The detailed description of these and additional specific aspects has been the subject of a large number of specialized studies. In the context of this study, it may be sufficient to look at one single yet representative dimension within the framework established by the second "basket." This will be done by presenting and analyzing data on trade relations. As the majority of measures recommended by the second "basket" in view of improving cooperation in the fields of trade, industry, and technology indirectly or directly refers to the stimulation and promotion of trade, the value of exports may be expected to constitute a reliable indicator of economic cooperation in general. The analysis will shed some light on the development of East-West trade over time and also identify eventual shifts in the clusters of cooperating countries.

3.4.2 The Evolution of East-West Trade, 1960-1980

Graphs 3.38 and 3.39 present time-series data for commercial exchanges between selected pairs of countries in absolute values. (This implies that the figures are *not* at constant prices, that is, not adjusted for inflation, but at current prices.) The overall picture presented by this material exhibits a strikingly conspicuous change in the early seventies when a sudden take-off initiated a period of exponential growth. Between 1960 and 1979, the overall volume of trade between the European Economic Community (EEC) and the Council for Mutual Economic Assistance (CMEA) has multiplied by a factor of more than twenty. American exports to the USSR in 1979 even are a hundred times as large as in 1960, while Soviet exports to the USA multiplied by twenty in the same period. Whatever pair of nations is being considered—the trend is remarkably

Graph 3.38. Monthly Average Exports of EEC to CMEA and CMEA to EEC (in millions of US dollars, at current prices and exchange rates)

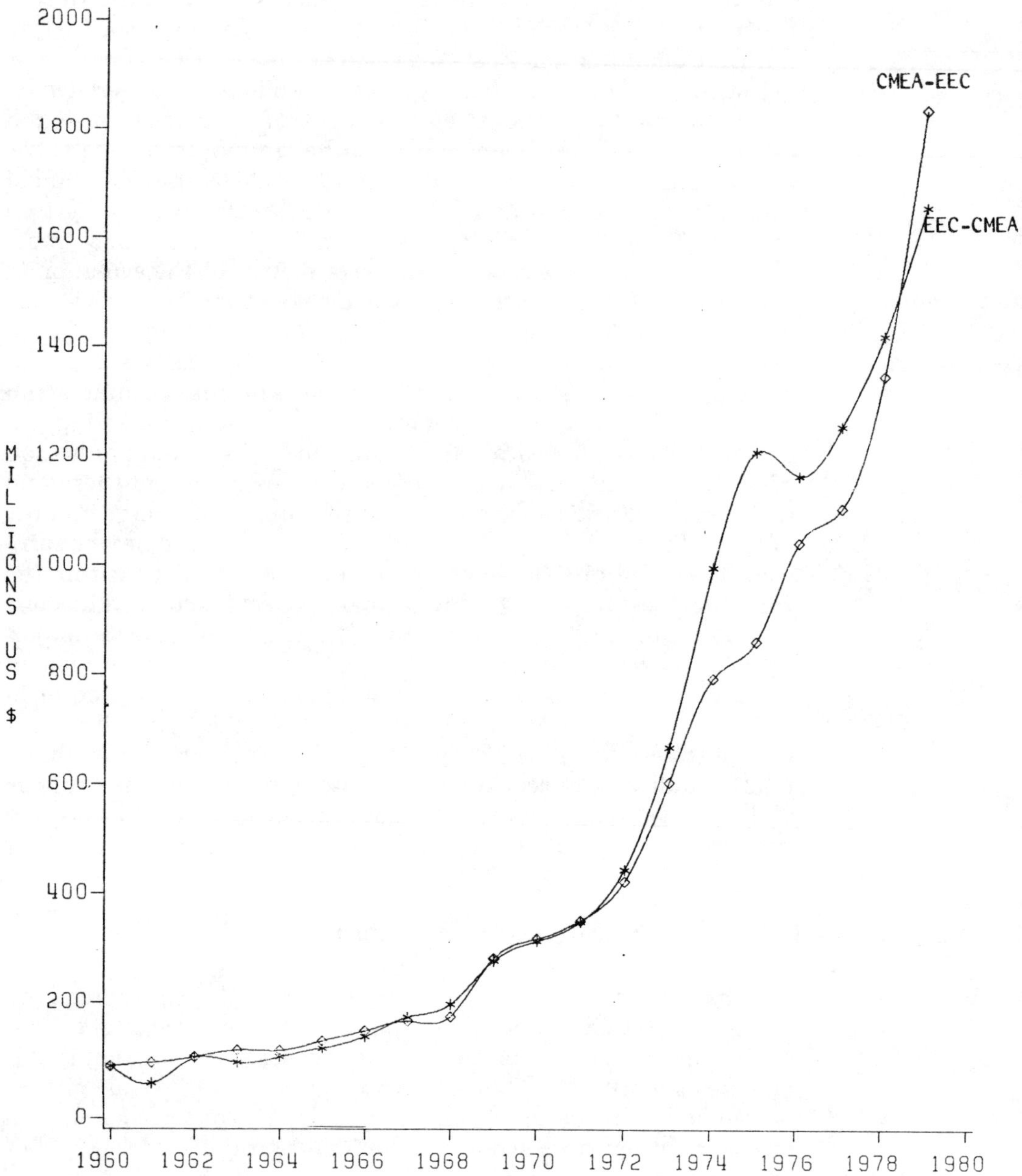

CMEA-EEC
EEC-CMEA
MILLIONS US $
2000
1800
1600
1400
1200
1000
800
600
400
200
0
1960
1962
1964
1966
1968
1970
1972
1974
1976
1978
1980
YEAR

Graph 3.39. Monthly Average Exports of Selected Western Countries to the Soviet Union (current prices and exchange rates)

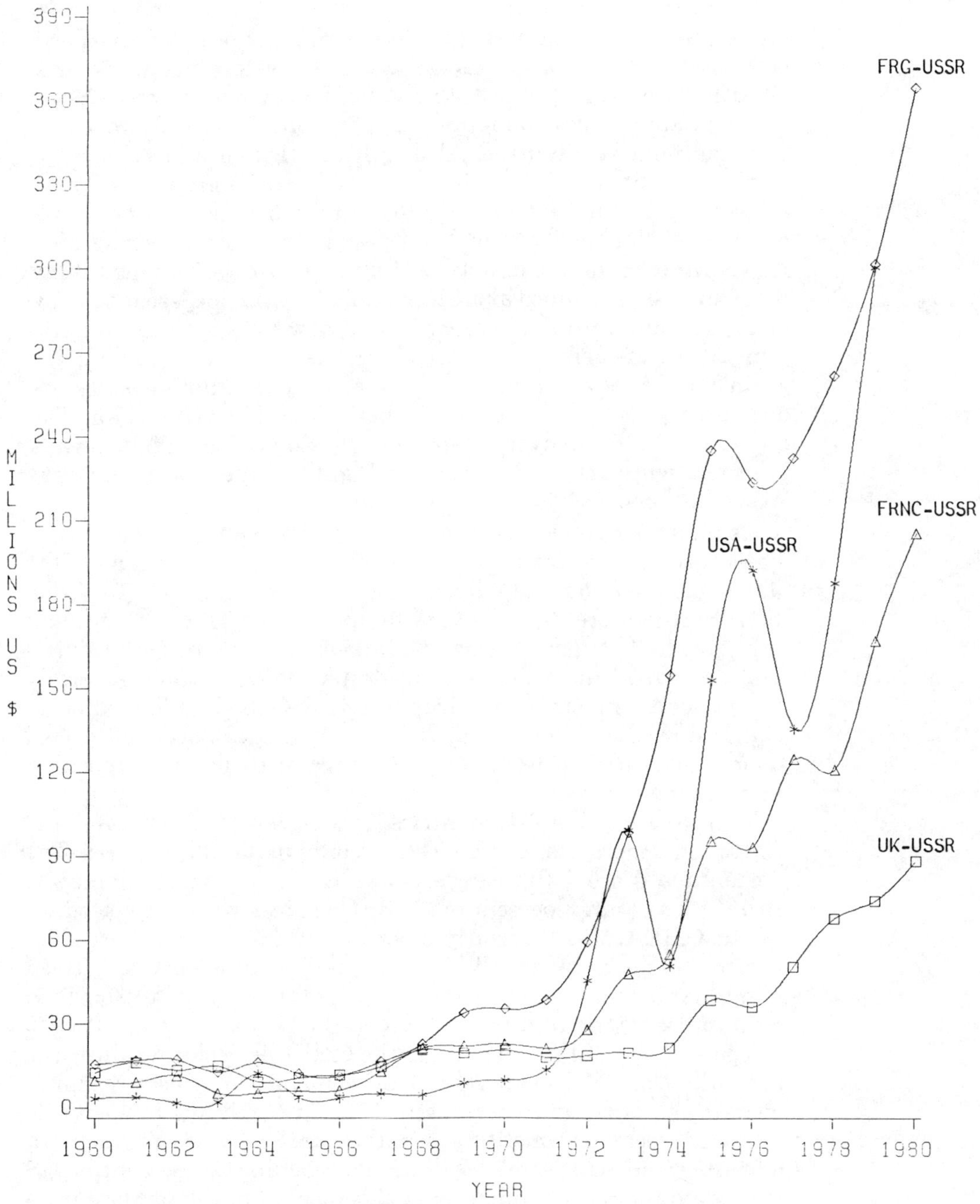
FRG-USSR
FRNC-USSR
USA-USSR
UK-USSR
MILLIONS US $
YEAR
390
360
330
300
270
240
210
180
150
120
90
60
30
0
1960
1962
1964
1966
1968
1970
1972
1974
1976
1978
1980

identical or similar in all cases: a dramatic expansion of the trade volume in the early seventies followed by a steady and steep growth during the whole decade. However, the growth process seems to slow down or even come to a halt in 1979/80.

Scrutinizing individual pairs of nations in a more detailed way offers some interesting insights into a number of specific aspects of East-West relations. Among the four Western countries analyzed in Graph 3.39 and 3.40, the Federal Republic of Germany seems to have been expanding her trade with Eastern Europe at a very fast and steady pace. Although the British and French exports to the Soviet Union also swell, the overall growth is not as decisive as in the case of the FRG. And whereas most countries exhibit regular and gradual increases, the curve representing American exports is characterized by repeated oscillations taking place in two-year intervals. Phases of retrogression seem to coincide each time with the investiture of a new American administration. A crucial aspect of American-Soviet trade is of course the grain purchases by the Soviet Union, which do not depend only on the current harvest results in both the United States and the Soviet Union; the delivery of grain to the Soviet Union has always been and will very likely remain a highly political issue in East-West relations.

As indicated previously, the trends observed on the base of trade data may be distorted or at least exaggerated by the nature of the data that are quoted at current prices and not adjusted for inflation. Furthermore, the absolute figures do not take into account that, due to the massive growth of all economies during the sixties and seventies, the volume of trade tended to expand generally everywhere. The curves in Graphs 3.41 to 3.43 provide further insights since they refer to shares of exports and imports for selected dyads, measured in terms of percentage of their total exports or imports, respectively.

Exports from NATO countries to the Soviet Union and the CMEA in general have increased not only in absolute figures. The percentage share of these exports has also increased considerably. In 1961 less than 2 percent of all EEC exports were accounted for by the CMEA. In 1975 nearly 5 percent of EEC exports were shipped to CMEA countries. When interpreting these curves, keep in mind that the member countries of the EEC increased in 1973 when Britain, Denmark, and Ireland joined the Community. Since 1975 the percentage of EEC exports to the CMEA is declining while the percentage of CMEA exports to EEC countries increased, reaching a share of more than 16 percent in 1979. United States-Soviet trade relations seem to constitute a rather special case. There is an upward trend with some oscillations, reaching 2.5 percent of US exports to the Soviet Union and 6.2 percent of Soviet imports from the United States in 1979. The fraction of US imports from the Soviet Union, however, remained below 1 percent over the whole period of twenty years.

Graph 3.40. Monthly Average Exports of the Soviet Union to Selected Western Countries (current prices and exchange rates)

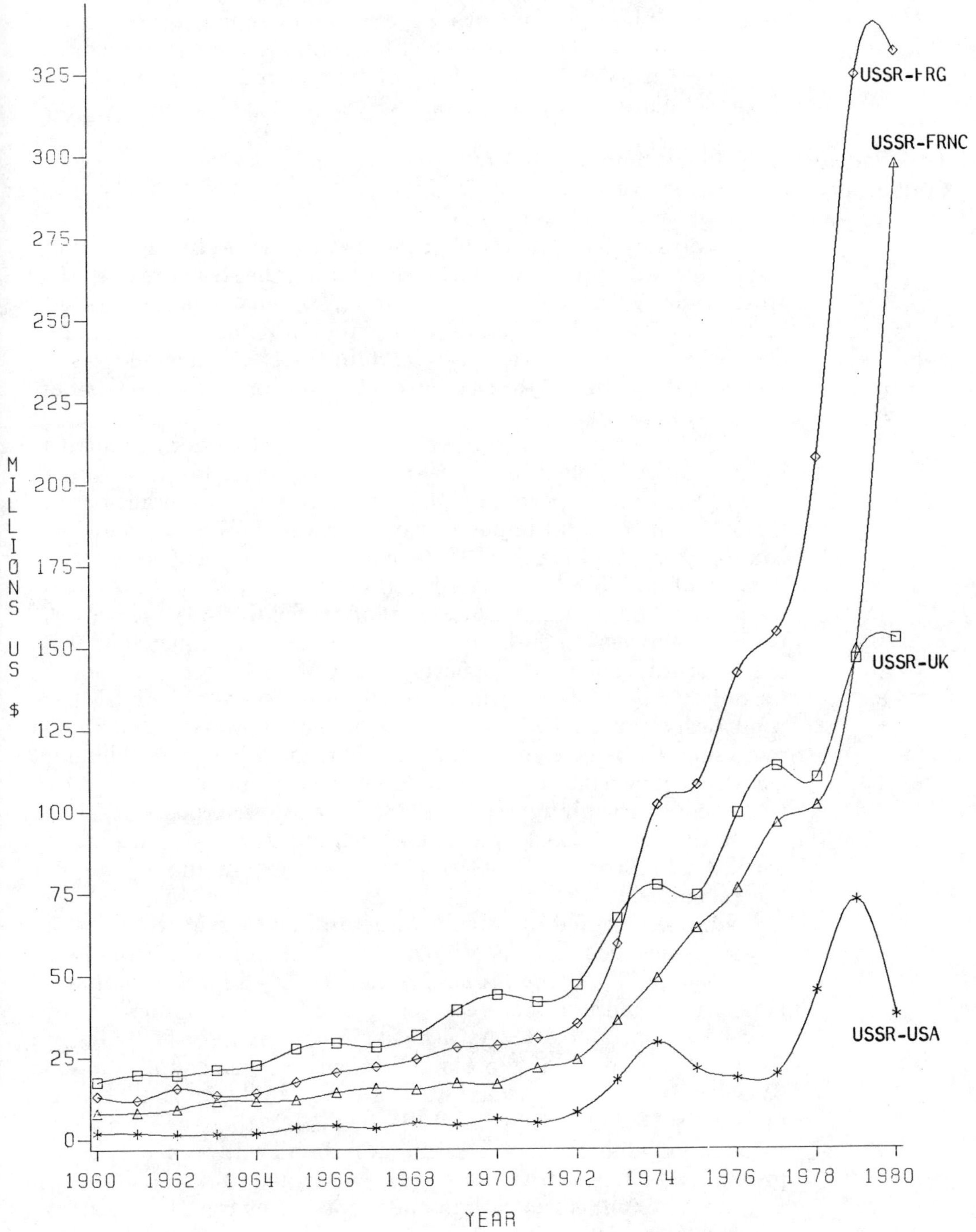
USSR-FRG
USSR-FRNC
USSR-UK
USSR-USA
MILLIONS US $
325
300
275
250
225
200
175
150
125
100
75
50
25
0
1960
1962
1964
1966
1968
1970
1972
1974
1976
1978
1980
YEAR

The most important Western trade partner of the Soviet Union in absolute figures as well as in percentage shares is the Federal Republic of Germany. In 1975, over 3 percent of West German exports were shipped to the Soviet Union, while over 7.6 percent of all Soviet imports came from the Federal Republic of Germany. The share of Soviet exports to the FRG continued to grow, reaching 6 percent in 1979; yet the share of West German exports to the Soviet Union is decreasing since 1975.

3.4.3 Partners in Trade: Some Considerations Concerning the Structure of East-West Trade

The analysis of the material presented in the preceding section allows for two general conclusions regarding the structure of East-West trade. Trade between East and West has remained asymmetric, as far as its importance for the two sides is concerned. Obviously, it has also reached a certain threshold inasmuch as it seems that further expansion of export and import shares is becoming increasingly difficult.

In 1978 the share of exports of industrialized Western countries to the CMEA reached 3.7 percent, which corresponds to 36.8 percent of the total imports of CMEA countries. On the other hand, the share of the total imports of industrialized Western countries coming from the CMEA is 3.0 percent, which corresponds to 26.2 percent of all CMEA exports. In other words, East-West trade is much more important for the East than for the West. However, CMEA countries generally do not take a very active part in extra-systemic trade: The total exports of all CMEA countries accounts for only 9.5 percent of world trade, including trade among CMEA countries. Industrialized Western countries, however, contribute more than 67 percent to the total world trade, whereas developing countries have a share of 23 percent of world trade (11.3 percent by OPEC countries; all figures for 1978). Given these proportions, one can hardly expect East-West trade to change the basic patterns of world trade although East-West trade was expanding rapidly in the seventies.

A suitable method of tracing structural change in transaction flows between countries is offered again by using cluster analysis as in Section 3.3.2. The proximity matrices used for the computation of the dendrograms presented in the following tables can be found in Appendix A3.3 As a measure of proximity for pairs of countries, the mean of exports and imports as percent of total exports and imports, respectively, was used, similar to the formula in Section 3.3.2. As explained in Section 3.3.2., there are two algorithms available for the clustering of nations with respect to their proximity in trade: the connectedness method and the diameter method. The connectedness method tends to construct few clusters thereby ignoring special cases, whereas the diameter method puts the emphasis on particularly close relationship, producing a high

Graph 3.41. Exports from Western Countries and the EEC to the CMEA and the Soviet Union as Percentage of Total EEC Exports and Total Exports of the Respective Western Countries

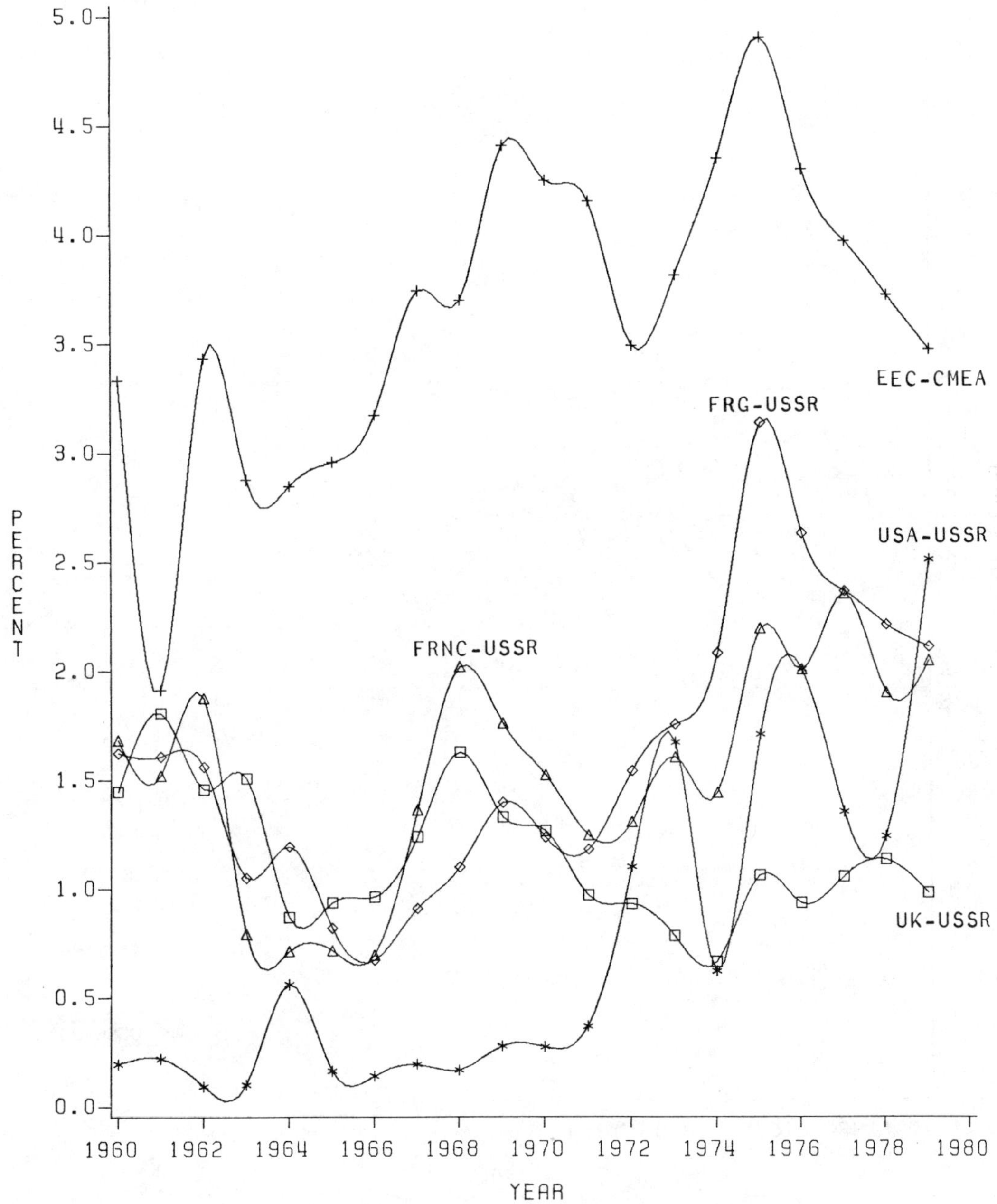
5.0
4.5
4.0
3.5
3.0
2.5
2.0
1.5
1.0
0.5
0.0
PERCENT
EEC-CMEA
FRG-USSR
USA-USSR
FRNC-USSR
UK-USSR
1960
1962
1964
1966
1968
1970
1972
1974
1976
1978
1980
YEAR

Graph 3.42. Exports from the CMEA and the Soviet Union to the EEC and Western Countries as Percentage of Total CMEA and Soviet Exports

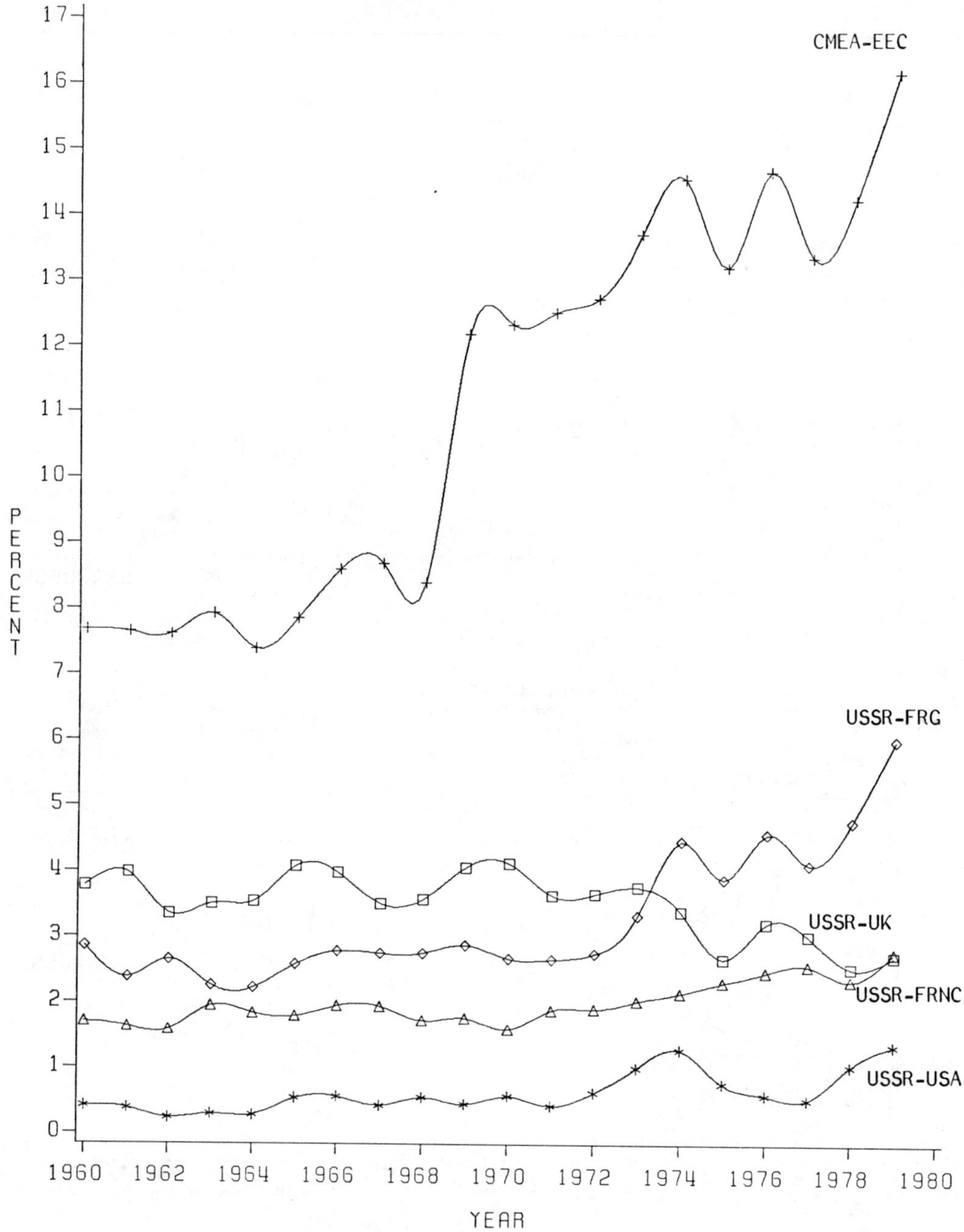
CMEA-EEC
USSR-FRG
USSR-UK
USSR-FRNC
USSR-USA
PERCENT
0
1
2
3
4
5
6
7
8
9
10
11
12
13
14
15
16
17
1960
1962
1964
1966
1968
1970
1972
1974
1976
1978
1980
YEAR

Graph 3.43. Imports of the CMEA and the Soviet Union from the EEC and Selected Western Countries as Percentage of Total CMEA and Soviet Imports, Respectively

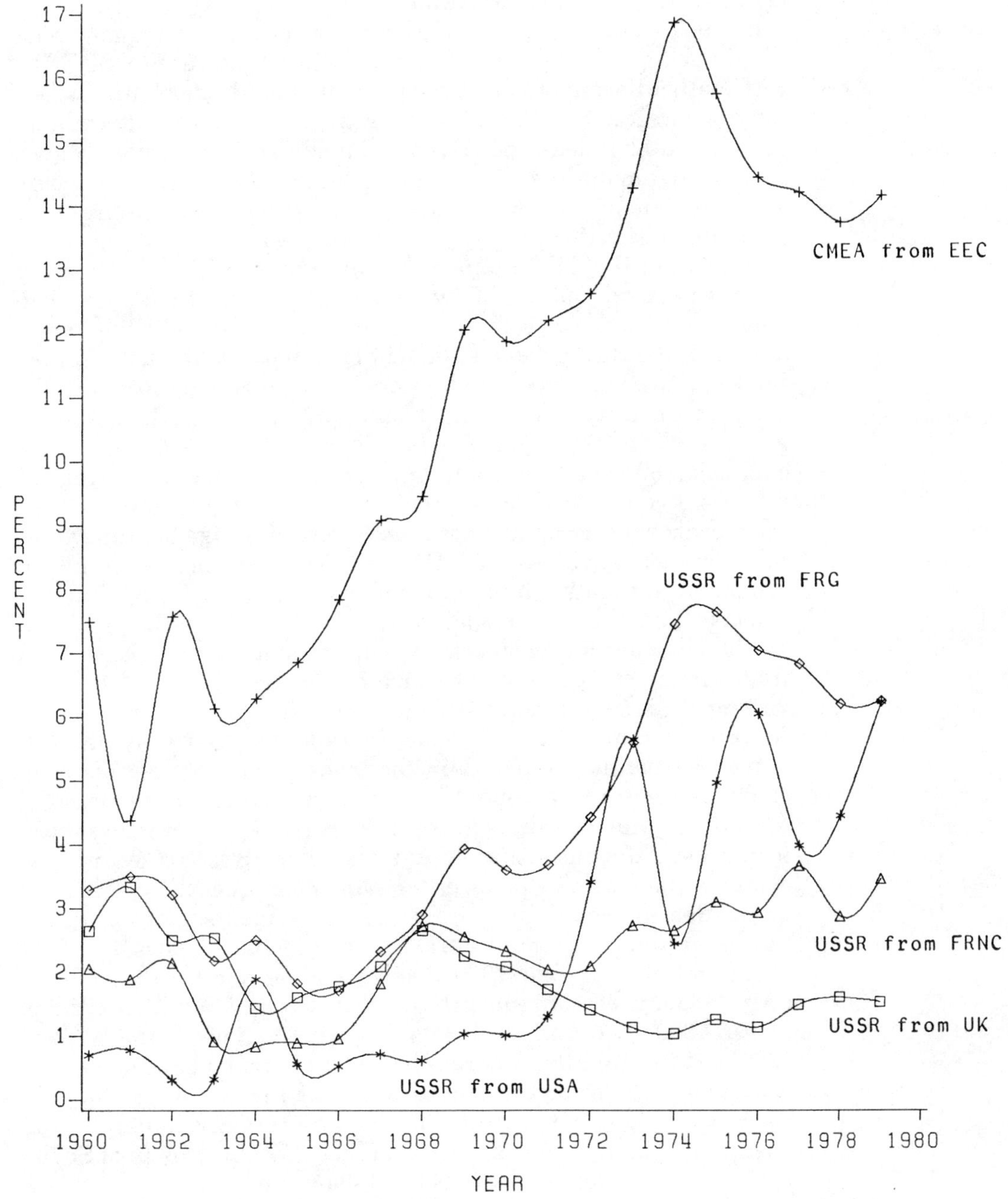
17
16
15
14
13
12
11
10
9
8
7
6
5
4
3
2
1
0
PERCENT
1960
1962
1964
1966
1968
1970
1972
1974
1976
1978
1980
YEAR
CMEA from EEC
USSR from FRG
USSR from FRNC
USSR from UK
USSR from USA

number of relatively small clusters; multiple-group membership will be ignored. The dendrograms were computed for three successive time points: 1965, 1970, and 1975 at the climax of East-West trade. Joint bars of *X* indicate clusters, and the length of the bars signifies the degree of proximity.

In 1965, four major clusters were detected in the commercial exchange among the states that later participated in the CSCE: the EEC with adjacent states (Austria, Switzerland, the Nordic states, Turkey, Greece, and Portugal); the CMEA countries and Finland; the United Kingdom and Ireland; Canada and the United States. Especially among the Nordic countries, among the Benelux countries, and among the CMEA countries trade relationships are close. By 1970, no significant changes had occurred. Only Finland is now approaching the EEC group. Also, in 1975, the situation had not changed considerably. Following the expansion of EEC membership, one would expect both Ireland and the United Kingdom to approach the EEC cluster; still, their links with Canada, the United States, and Spain appear to be more important than those with the European community. Basically the structure of trade in Europe and the North Atlantic area has thus not been affected by the expansion of East-West trade. Only the boundaries separating the clusters become a little bit less salient. According to these findings, the Nordic countries have assumed a sort of bridge-building function between EEC and CMEA, maybe based on geographical proximity, neutrality, and nonmembership in the EEC by Finland, Sweden, and Norway, respectively.

When looking for reasons to explain the stagnation of East-West trade in an era of political cooperation and "détente," the prevailing difference among the economic and political systems is certainly the most crucial element. Trade with centrally planned economies cannot be based on the institutional foundations that characterize trade among Western industrialized countries and most developing countries as well: There is no price system subject to market influences that would allow the Western exporter to evaluate the market's requirements and consequently to shape his production in accordance with these requirements. Currencies are not convertible; this implies trade on a "buy-back" basis or credits in convertible currencies. The debts in convertible currencies of the CMEA countries consequently increased from 7.5 billion US dollars in 1970 to 60.7 billion US dollars in 1978 (Zaleski and Wienert 1980, p. 248). Finally, different levels of economic development in East and West to some extent also impede the exchange of goods; the Soviet Union concentrated on the export of raw materials and energy (electricity, gas, oil). This implies that the growth of Soviet trade with the West so far depended upon the accessibility of low-cost hydrocarbons and electricity.

The second "basket" of the Final Act sums up some of the most important prerequisites for a further expansion of East-West trade relations. Among them are measures aimed at improving working

Graph 3.44. Imports of the EEC and Selected Western Countries from the CMEA and the Soviet Union as Percentage of Total EEC Imports and Total Imports of the Respective Country

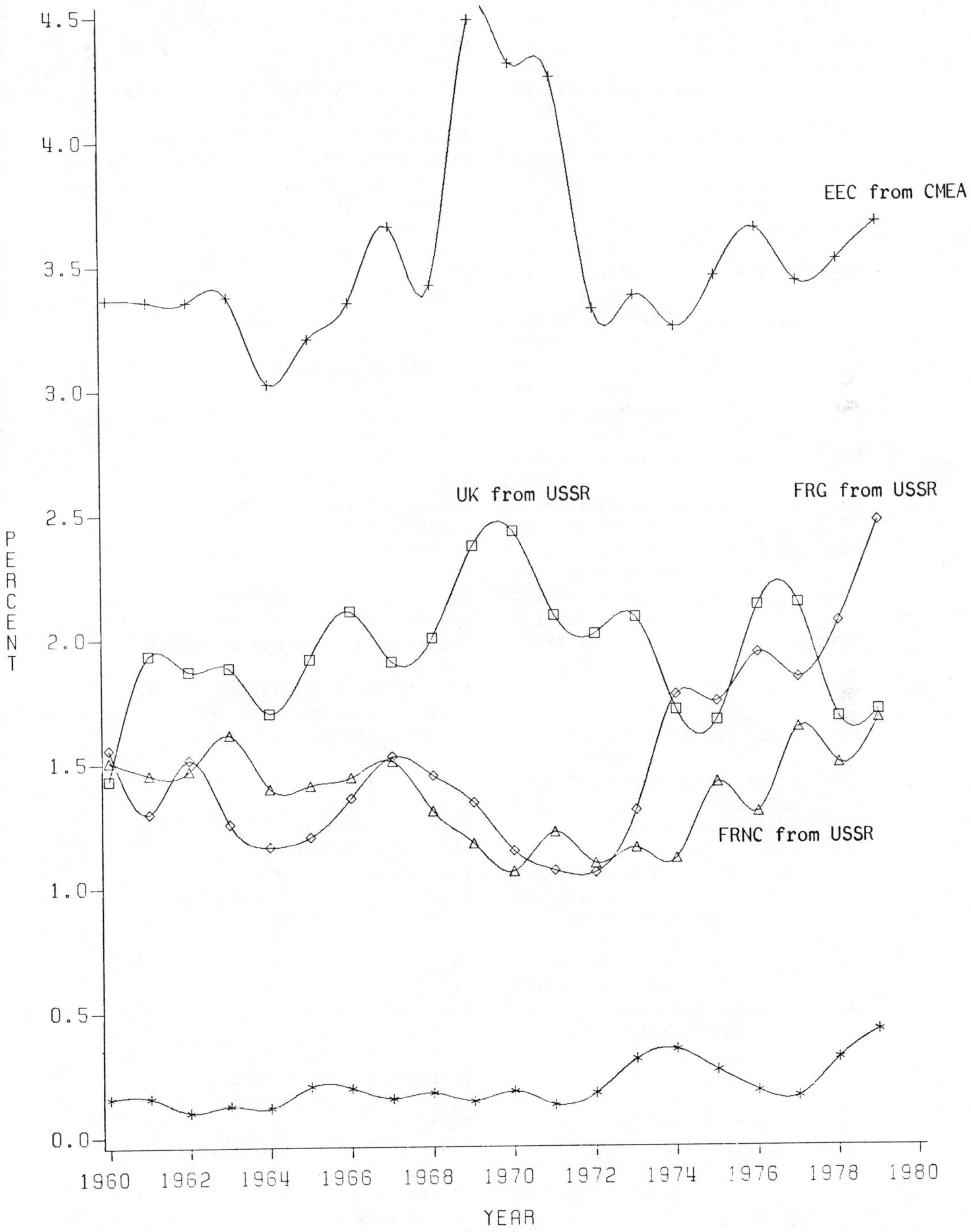
EEC from CMEA
UK from USSR
FRG from USSR
FRNC from USSR
PERCENT
4.5
4.0
3.5
3.0
2.5
2.0
1.5
1.0
0.5
0.0
1960
1962
1964
1966
1968
1970
1972
1974
1976
1978
1980
YEAR

Graph 3.45. Clusters of Countries, Based on Trade Figures for 1965

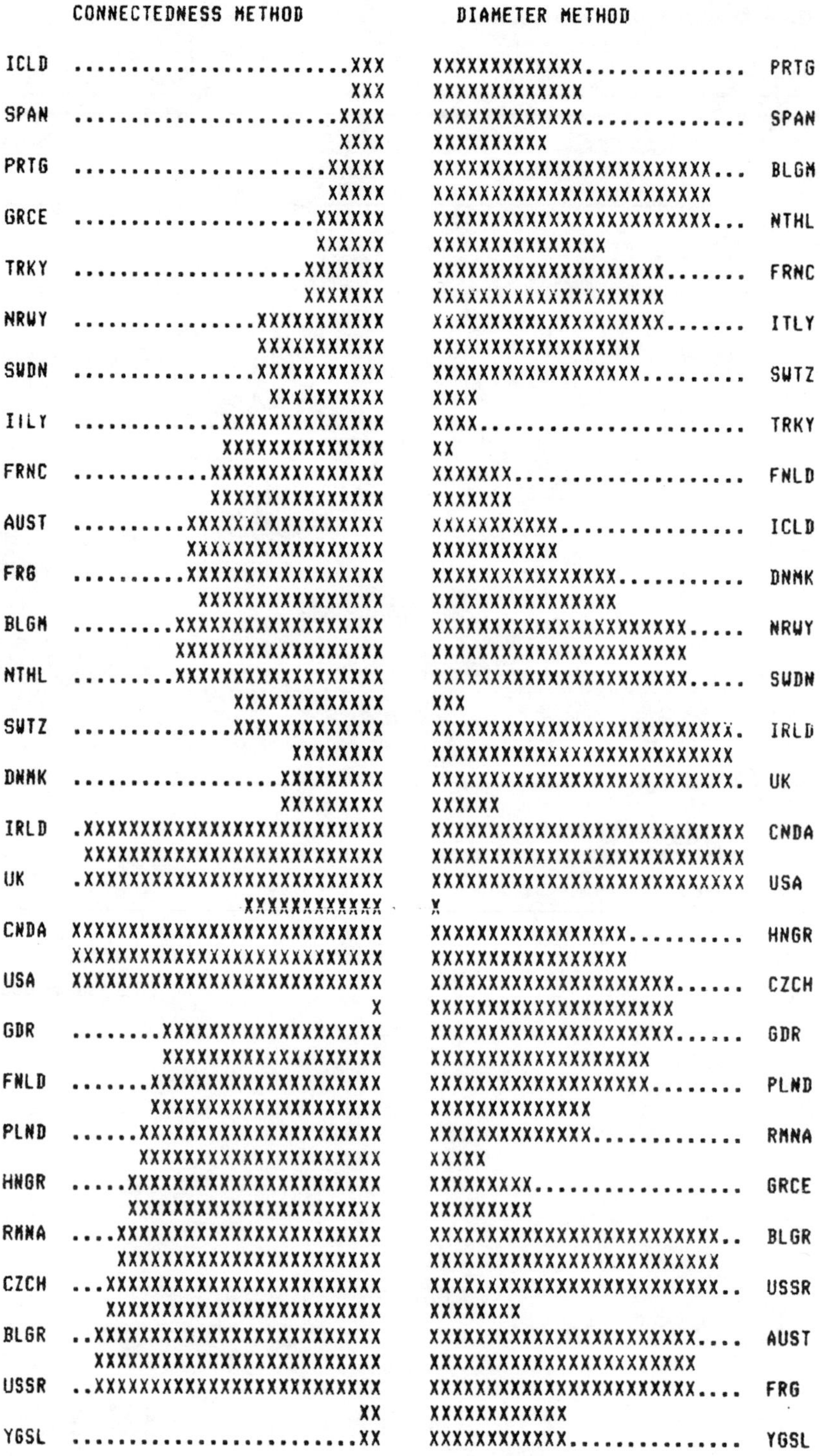
CONNECTEDNESS METHOD
DIAMETER METHOD
ICLD
SPAN
PRTG
GRCE
TRKY
NRWY
SWDN
ITLY
FRNC
AUST
FRG
BLGM
NTHL
SWTZ
DNMK
IRLD
UK
CNDA
USA
GDR
FNLD
PLND
HNGR
RMNA
CZCH
BLGR
USSR
YGSL
PRTG
SPAN
BLGM
NTHL
FRNC
ITLY
SWTZ
TRKY
FNLD
ICLD
DNMK
NRWY
SWDN
IRLD
UK
CNDA
USA
HNGR
CZCH
GDR
PLND
RMNA
GRCE
BLGR
USSR
AUST
FRG
YGSL

Graph 3.46. Clusters of Countries, Based on Trade Figures for 1970

```
      CONNECTEDNESS METHOD                DIAMETER METHOD

ICLD  ..........................X    XXXXXXXXXXXXXXXXXXXXXX.....  FRNC
                                X    XXXXXXXXXXXXXXXXXXXXXX
RMNA  ............XXXXXXXXXXXXXXX    XXXXXXXXXXXXXXXXXXXXXX.....  ITLY
                  XXXXXXXXXXXXXXX    XXXXXXXXXXXXXXX
HNGR  .......XXXXXXXXXXXXXXXXXXXX    XXXXXXXXXXXXXXXXXXXXXXX....  BLGM
             XXXXXXXXXXXXXXXXXXXX    XXXXXXXXXXXXXXXXXXXXXXX
PLND  .....XXXXXXXXXXXXXXXXXXXXXX    XXXXXXXXXXXXXXXXXXXXXXXX...  FRG
           XXXXXXXXXXXXXXXXXXXXXX    XXXXXXXXXXXXXXXXXXXXXXXX
CZCH  ....XXXXXXXXXXXXXXXXXXXXXXX    XXXXXXXXXXXXXXXXXXXXXXXX...  NTHL
          XXXXXXXXXXXXXXXXXXXXXXX    XXXXXXXXX
GDR   ...XXXXXXXXXXXXXXXXXXXXXXXX    XXXXXXXXXXXXXX.............  PRTG
         XXXXXXXXXXXXXXXXXXXXXXXX    XXXXXXXXXXXXXX
BLGR  ..XXXXXXXXXXXXXXXXXXXXXXXXX    XXXXXXXXXXXXXX.............  SPAN
        XXXXXXXXXXXXXXXXXXXXXXXXX    XXXXXX
USSR  ..XXXXXXXXXXXXXXXXXXXXXXXXX    XXXXXXXX...................  ICLD
                               XX    XXXXXXXX
TRKY  ........................XXX    XXXXXXXXXXXX...............  FNLD
                              XXX    XXXXXXXXXXXX
FNLD  ......................XXXXX    XXXXXXXXXXXXXXXXX..........  DNMK
                            XXXXX    XXXXXXXXXXXXXXXXX
DNMK  ................XXXXXXXXXXX    XXXXXXXXXXXXXXXXXXXXX......  NRWY
                      XXXXXXXXXXX    XXXXXXXXXXXXXXXXXXXXX
NRWY  ..............XXXXXXXXXXXXX    XXXXXXXXXXXXXXXXXXXXX......  SWDN
                    XXXXXXXXXXXXX    XX
SWDN  ..............XXXXXXXXXXXXX    XXXXXXXXXXXXXXXXXXXXXXXXXX.  IRLD
                           XXXXXX    XXXXXXXXXXXXXXXXXXXXXXXXXX
SPAN  ....................XXXXXXX    XXXXXXXXXXXXXXXXXXXXXXXXXX.  UK
                          XXXXXXX    XXXXX
GRCE  .................XXXXXXXXXX    XXXXXXXXXXXXXXXXXXXXXXXXXXX  CNDA
                       XXXXXXXXXX    XXXXXXXXXXXXXXXXXXXXXXXXXXX
BLGM  ...........XXXXXXXXXXXXXXXX    XXXXXXXXXXXXXXXXXXXXXXXXXXX  USA
                 XXXXXXXXXXXXXXXX    X
ITLY  ..........XXXXXXXXXXXXXXXXX    XXXXXXXXXXXXXXXXXX.........  AUST
                XXXXXXXXXXXXXXXXX    XXXXXXXXXXXXXXXXXX
AUST  .........XXXXXXXXXXXXXXXXXX    XXXXXXXXXXXXXXXXXX.........  SWTZ
               XXXXXXXXXXXXXXXXXX    XXXXXXX
FRNC  ........XXXXXXXXXXXXXXXXXXX    XXXXXXX....................  TRKY
              XXXXXXXXXXXXXXXXXXX    XXX
FRG   ......XXXXXXXXXXXXXXXXXXXXX    XXXXXXXXXXXXXXXX...........  HNGR
            XXXXXXXXXXXXXXXXXXXXX    XXXXXXXXXXXXXXXX
NTHL  ......XXXXXXXXXXXXXXXXXXXXX    XXXXXXXXXXXXXXXXXXXX.......  CZCH
                   XXXXXXXXXXXXXX    XXXXXXXXXXXXXXXXXXXX
SWTZ  .............XXXXXXXXXXXXXX    XXXXXXXXXXXXXXXXXXXX.......  GDR
                         XXXXXXXX    XXXXXXXXXXXXXXXXXXX
PRTG  ..................XXXXXXXXX    XXXXXXXXXXXXXXXXXXX........  PLND
                        XXXXXXXXX    XXXXXXXXXXX
IRLD  .XXXXXXXXXXXXXXXXXXXXXXXXXX    XXXXXXXXXXX................  RMNA
       XXXXXXXXXXXXXXXXXXXXXXXXXX    XXXXXXXXXX
UK    .XXXXXXXXXXXXXXXXXXXXXXXXXX    XXXXXXXXXXXXXXXXXXXXXXXXX..  BLGR
                     XXXXXXXXXXXX    XXXXXXXXXXXXXXXXXXXXXXXXX
CNDA  XXXXXXXXXXXXXXXXXXXXXXXXXXX    XXXXXXXXXXXXXXXXXXXXXXXXX..  USSR
      XXXXXXXXXXXXXXXXXXXXXXXXXXX    XXXX
USA   XXXXXXXXXXXXXXXXXXXXXXXXXXX    XXXXXXXXXXXXX..............  GRCE
                             XXXX    XXXXXXXXXXXXX
YGSL  .......................XXXX    XXXXXXXXXXXXX..............  YGSL
```

Graph 3.47. Clusters of CSCE Countries, Based on Trade Figures for 1975

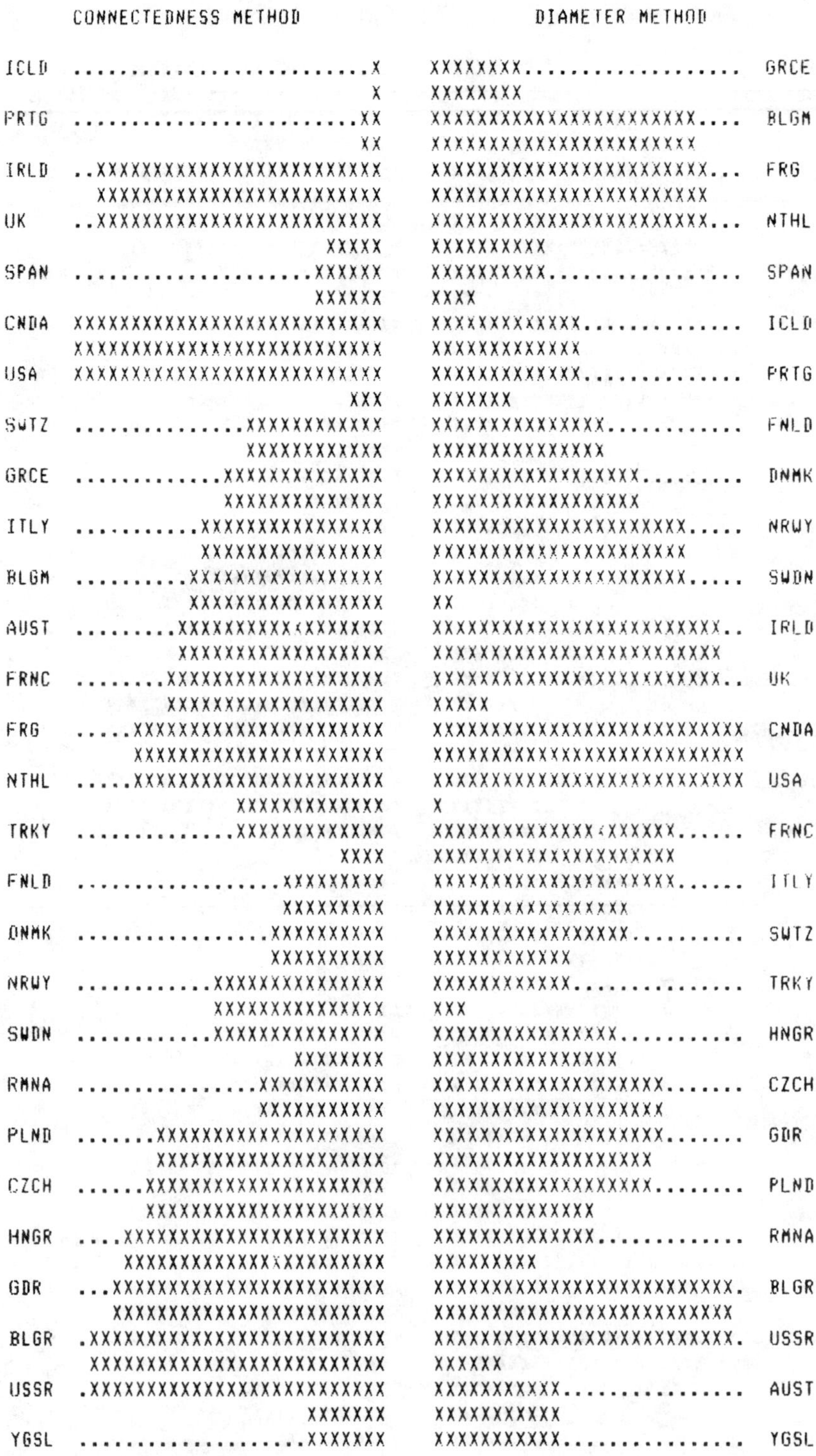
CONNECTEDNESS METHOD
DIAMETER METHOD
ICLD
PRTG
IRLD
UK
SPAN
CNDA
USA
SWTZ
GRCE
ITLY
BLGM
AUST
FRNC
FRG
NTHL
TRKY
FNLD
DNMK
NRWY
SWDN
RMNA
PLND
CZCH
HNGR
GDR
BLGR
USSR
YGSL
GRCE
BLGM
FRG
NTHL
SPAN
ICLD
PRTG
FNLD
DNMK
NRWY
SWDN
IRLD
UK
CNDA
USA
FRNC
ITLY
SWTZ
TRKY
HNGR
CZCH
GDR
PLND
RMNA
BLGR
USSR
AUST
YGSL

conditions of representatives of foreign organizations, enterprises, firms and banks; providing the necessary information on legislation; the establishment of permanent representation and offices; access to statistical data; and facilitation of commercial contacts and marketing. The implementation of these and other measures does not seem to be a goal that will be reached easily in the foreseeable future.

3.4.4 The Transfer of Technology

Among the issues dealt with in the second "basket," scientific and technological cooperation has an important place. The Final Act puts much emphasis on the desirability of such cooperation and asserts that it is essential "to promote the sharing of information and experience, facilitating the study and transfer of scientific and technological achievements, as well as the access to such achievements on a mutually advantageous basis."

The transfer of technology in fact constitutes a major dimension in East–West relations where a considerable change took place in the course of the process called "détente." This is clearly demonstrated by Graphs 3.48 to 3.50, which present the evolution of East–West transfers of research-intensive products or, more precisely, of those products that are listed as so-called SITC-7 products according to the OECD nomenclature.* As the graphs show, there was a sudden trend reversal in the early seventies (1971), comparable to and even more articulate than in the case of exports presented in Subsection 3.4.2. The growth of the transfer of technology was, however, markedly asymmetric; obviously much more technology was transferred from the West to the East than vice versa. The volume of SITC-7 goods acquired by the East is constantly about six times as large as the corresponding figure for technology transfers from the East to the West.

In the period 1960–1979, the total volume of SITC-7 exports of the EEC to CMEA countries has multiplied by a factor of more than twenty (from 309 million US dollars in 1960 to 6.9 billion US dollars) in 1979. Comparing the technology-transfer behavior of selected Western countries also draws attention to strong differences existing among NATO countries. Quite remarkably, the Federal Republic of Germany always was the chief furnisher of technology to the East, and the CMEA countries seemed to have preferred the FRG as their favorite supplier in this field. The volume of SITC-7 goods sold to the East by the FRG exceeds the volume of US technology exports by a factor of approximately 4.

Another interesting observation can be made with reference to the last period considered in this study. As can be seen from Graph 3.49, the pace of technology transfers generally slowed down in the

*SITC-7 refers to items listed in Section 7 of the Standard International Trade Classification; Section 7 comprises machinery and transport equipment.

Graph 3.48. SITC-7 Exports from the EEC to CMEA and from CMEA to EEC (current prices and exchange rates)

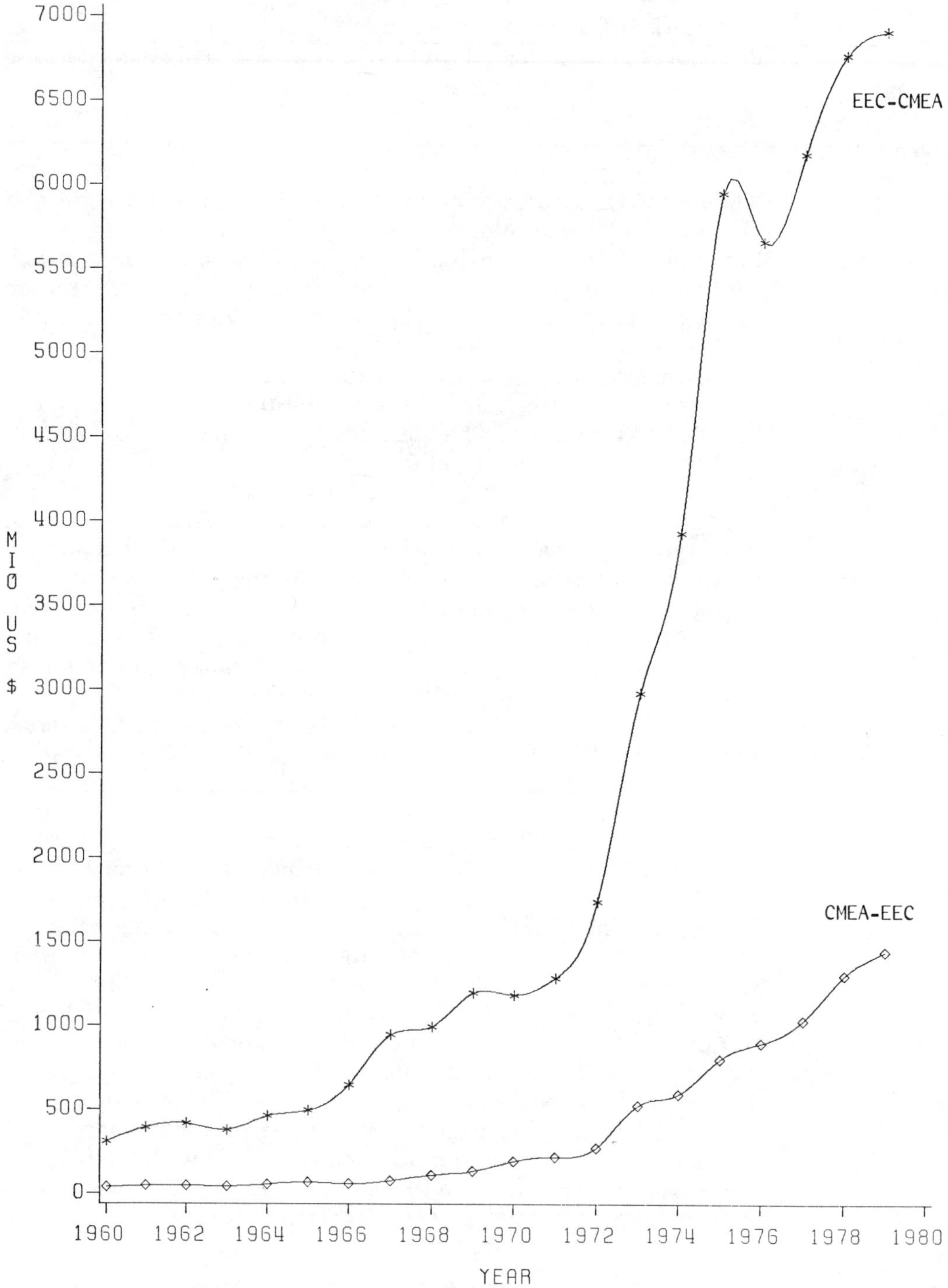
7000
6500
6000
5500
5000
4500
4000
3500
3000
2500
2000
1500
1000
500
0
MIØ US $
EEC-CMEA
CMEA-EEC
1960
1962
1964
1966
1968
1970
1972
1974
1976
1978
1980
YEAR

Graph 3.49. SITC-7 Exports from Selected Western Countries to the Soviet Union (current prices and exchange rates)

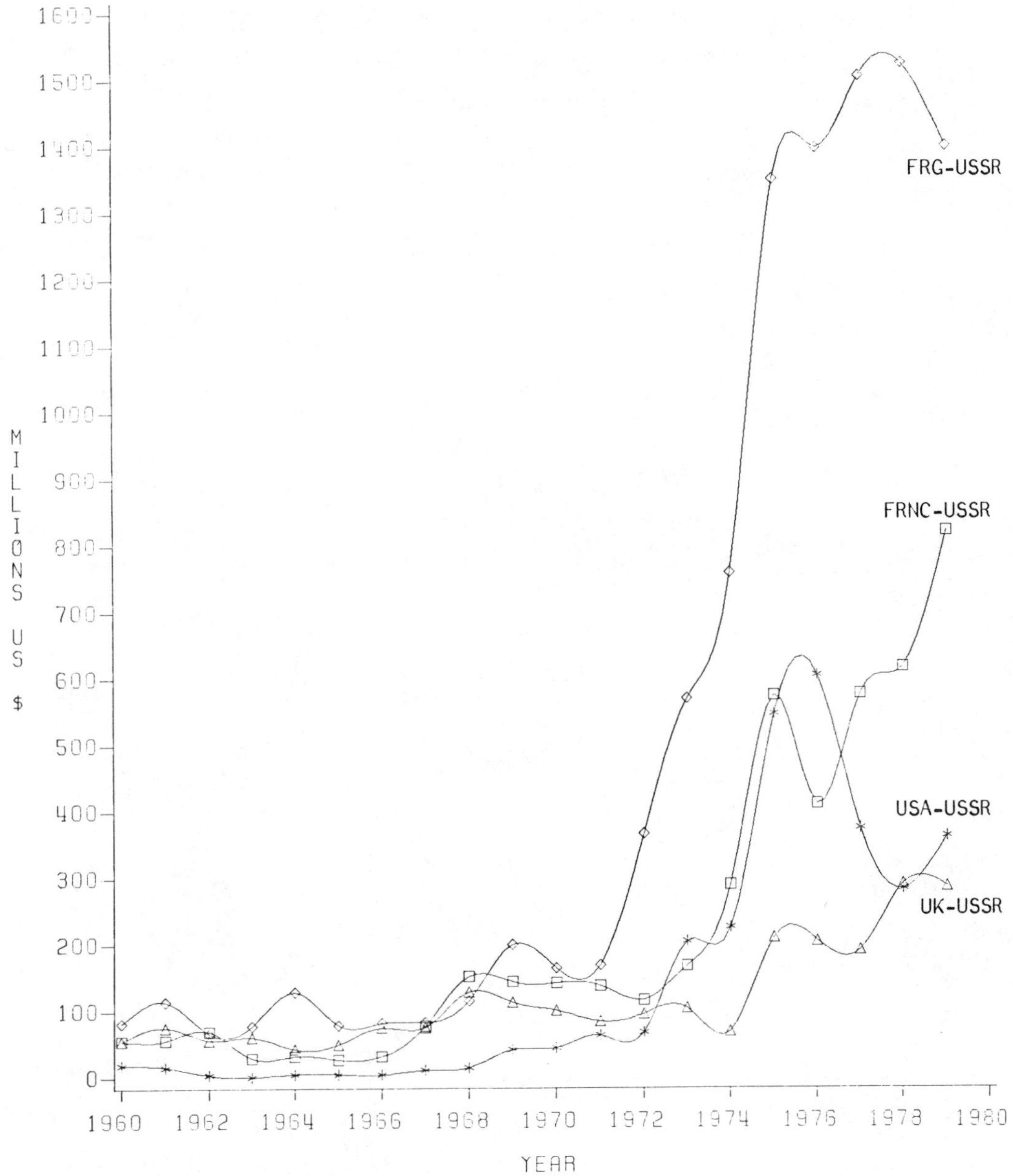
1600
1500
1400
1300
1200
1100
1000
900
800
700
600
500
400
300
200
100
0
MILLIONS US $
1960
1962
1964
1966
1968
1970
1972
1974
1976
1978
1980
YEAR
FRG-USSR
FRNC-USSR
USA-USSR
UK-USSR

Graph 3.50. SITC-7 Exports from the EEC and Selected Western Countries as Percentage of Total Exports to the CMEA and the Soviet Union

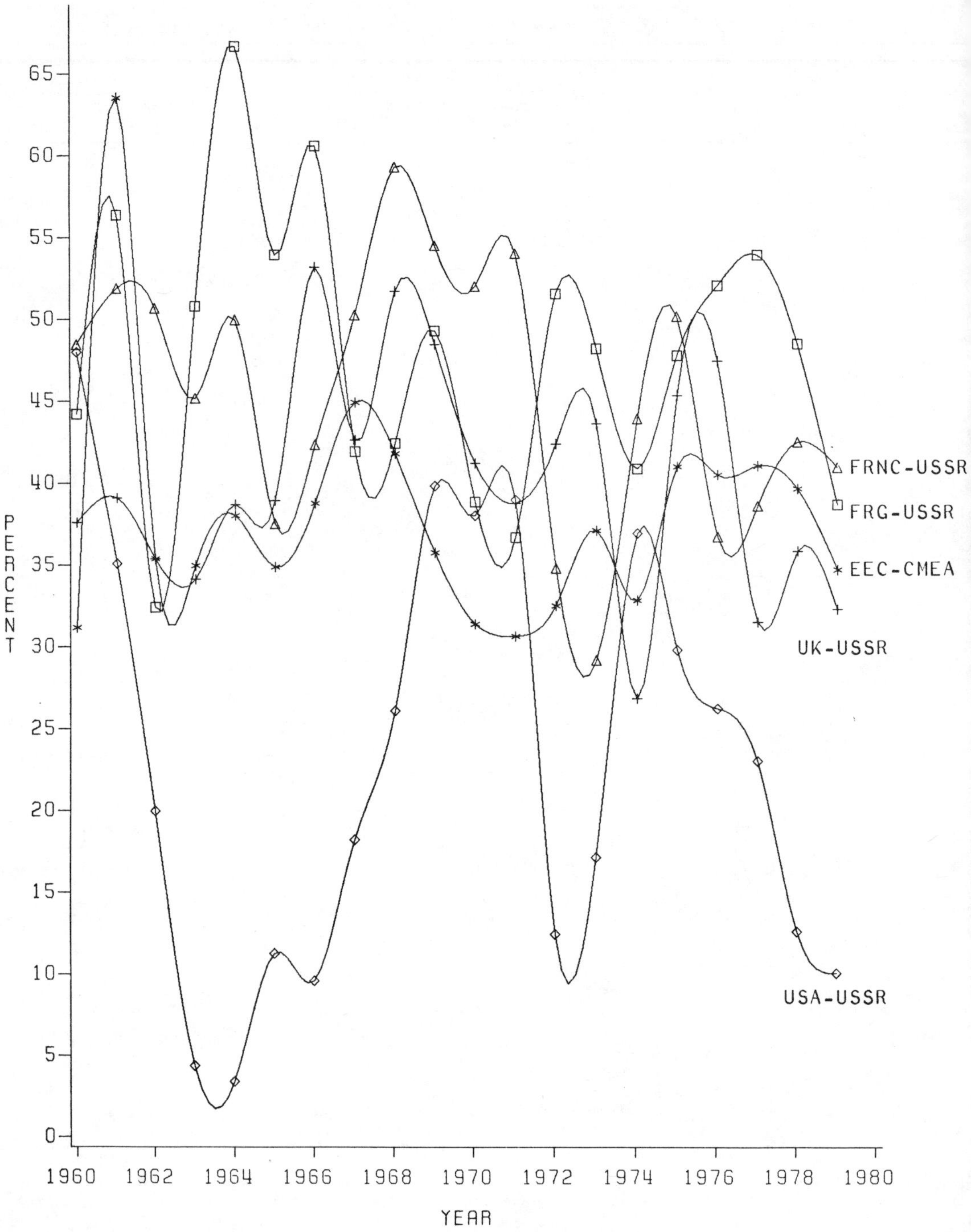

PERCENT
65
60
55
50
45
40
35
30
25
20
15
10
5
0
1960
1962
1964
1966
1968
1970
1972
1974
1976
1978
1980
YEAR
FRNC-USSR
FRG-USSR
EEC-CMEA
UK-USSR
USA-USSR

second half of the seventies and experienced even some retrogression in the years 1978 and 1979. It seems that, after the acute and rapid increase in the early seventies, some saturation has been reached. For a variety of reasons—mainly financial and political—the West was no longer in a position to supply technology as generously as it did before.

As a matter of fact the United States, although a leading country in this field, seems to have been rather reluctant to engage in unconditional supply of technology for the benefit of their ideological rivals. This reluctance is also indicated by the dramatic drop of the US curve after 1976 when Soviet and Cuban support for some revolutionary governments and liberation fronts in Eastern and Southern Africa led to a major "crisis of détente"; the United States obviously tends to fine-tune their volume of technology transfers to the East in a way not indifferent to the overall political relationship.

What is the impact of this transfer of technology on the economics of the Socialist countries? In the Soviet Union, Hungary, and Bulgaria, the imports of technology were not able to offset the trend toward decreasing growth rates of the economy. In the cases of the GDR and Czechoslovakia, however, small improvements were made. At least in the case of the GDR, these may be attributed to trade links with the West since the so-called inner-German trade profits from EEC regulations. Poland and Romania were able to increase the growth rates considerably; in both cases this can be attributed to increasing trade with the West and the purchase of high-technology and research-intensive products (Table 3.4).

At the same time the CMEA countries accepted a massive inflow

Table 3.4. Growth Rate of GNP and Net Hard Currency Indebtedness

	ave. p.c. growth of GNP (%)		net hard currency indebtedness (bill. US$)	
	1960-1970	1970-1977	1970	1978
USSR	5.8	4.4	1.8	17.2
Poland	5.2	6.3	1.0	16.8
Romania	7.7	9.9	1.1	4.4
GDR	4.2	4.9	1.1	8.2
CSSR	3.8	4.3	0.3	2.0
Hungary	5.4	5.1	0.7	5.7
Bulgaria	7.4	5.7	0.9	3.4

Source: World Bank Atlas, for per-capita growth of GNP; Zaleski/Wienert (1980, p.248), for net hard currency indebtedness.

of credits in convertible currency. This had to be done on an enlarged scale when the economic recession in many Western countries, 1974 and 1975, in the aftermath of the first oil crisis, destroyed the hopes of the CMEA countries that the accelerated modernization of their industry could be financed with the revenues from the goods manufactured on the newly imported equipment and sold on Western markets. Since the disruption of world trade in the consequence of exploding energy prices severed the competition on Western markets enormously, the chances for an expansion of CMEA exports of manufactured and semimanufactured products in the West vanished.

Yet rising oil prices partly offset these unfavorable effects. Since the middle of the seventies, SITC-3* imports of the EEC countries from the CMEA countries have been increasing rapidly. Most important are the SITC-3 imports of the Federal Republic of Germany from the Soviet Union, followed by Soviet energy exports to France. Because of the North Sea oil that made Britain self-sufficient in the energy field, the British SITC-3 imports from the Soviet Union have reached a point of saturation since 1977. The American SITC-3 imports from the Soviet Union remained negligibly low (Tables 3.51 and 3.52). In other words, the SITC-3 exports from CMEA countries represent a kind of a mirror image of their imports of SITC-7 goods. The East exchanges technology from the West against energy. Of course, this type of exchange has always been "mutually advantageous"; otherwise, it would not have taken place. Yet it is highly asymmetric, reflecting also different levels of economic development.

Such an asymmetric structure carries the risk of being destabilized by a fear of becoming vulnerable to outside pressure. Especially in the West some doubts are being expressed about whether it is really appropriate to rely so heavily on Soviet energy exports. Among the scenarios quoted in the public discussion on this problem, the possibility is mentioned that the Soviet Union might be tempted in a crisis situation to use the "oil weapon" in much the same way as demonstrated by the OPEC countries in 1973. Furthermore, some experts think that very soon the Soviet Union will herself become a net oil importer; yet the respective assumptions are quite controversial (cf. Schneider 1980, p. 211; Goldman 1980).

At any rate, future progress in the field of East-West exchange of technology for energy requires a considerable amount of mutual trust, given the delicate structure of this exchange. It is hard to see this prerequisite being strengthened in the early eighties. Quite the contrary may be true, thus severly jeopardizing the evolution of East-West relations in this field.

*SITC-3 refers to hydrocarbons.

Graph 3.51. SITC-3 Exports from EEC to CMEA and from CMEA to EEC (current prices and exchange rates)

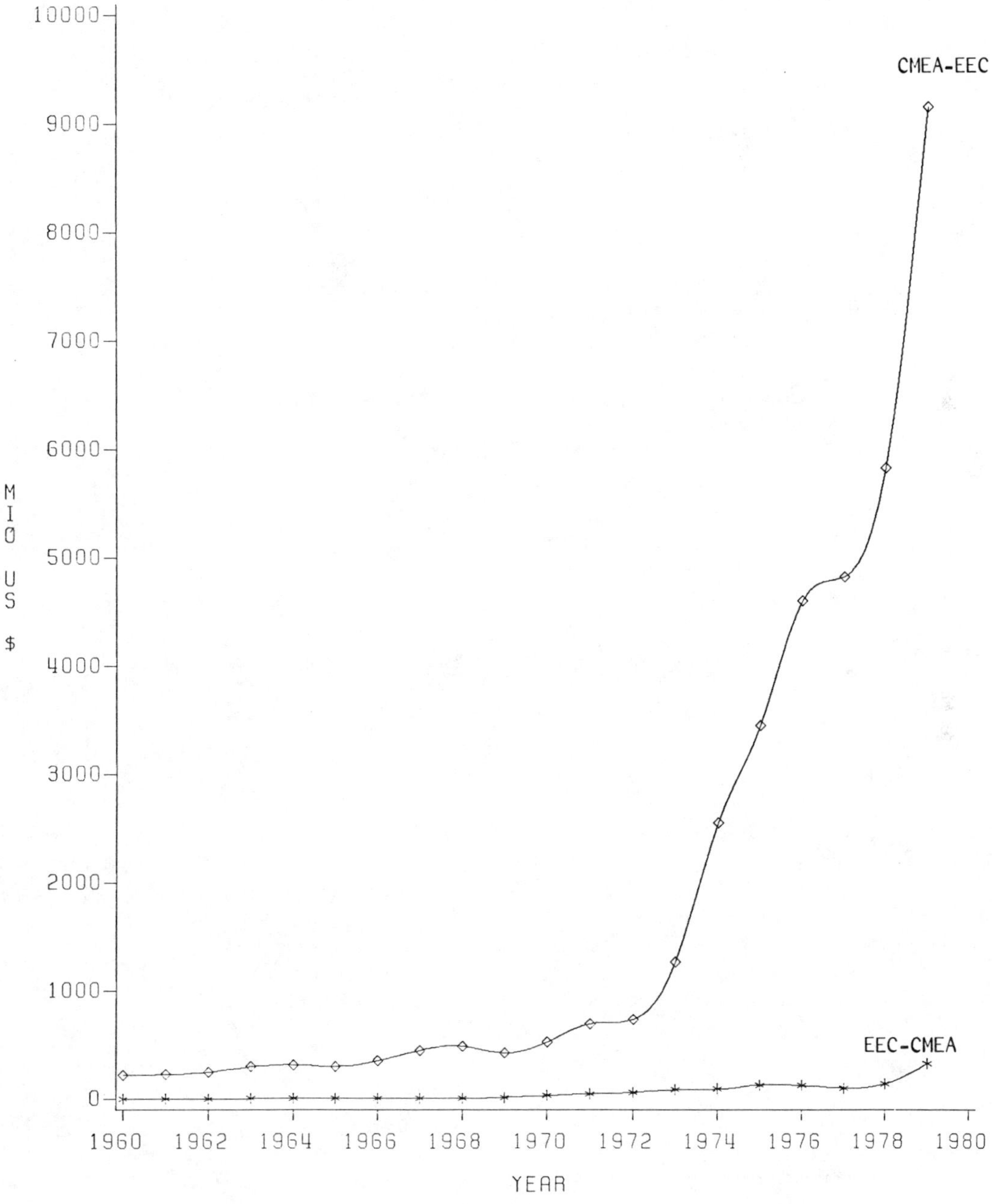
CMEA-EEC
EEC-CMEA
10000
9000
8000
7000
6000
5000
4000
3000
2000
1000
0
MIO US $
1960
1962
1964
1966
1968
1970
1972
1974
1976
1978
1980
YEAR

Graph 3.52. SITC-3 Exports of the Soviet Union to Selected Western Countries (current prices and exchange rates)

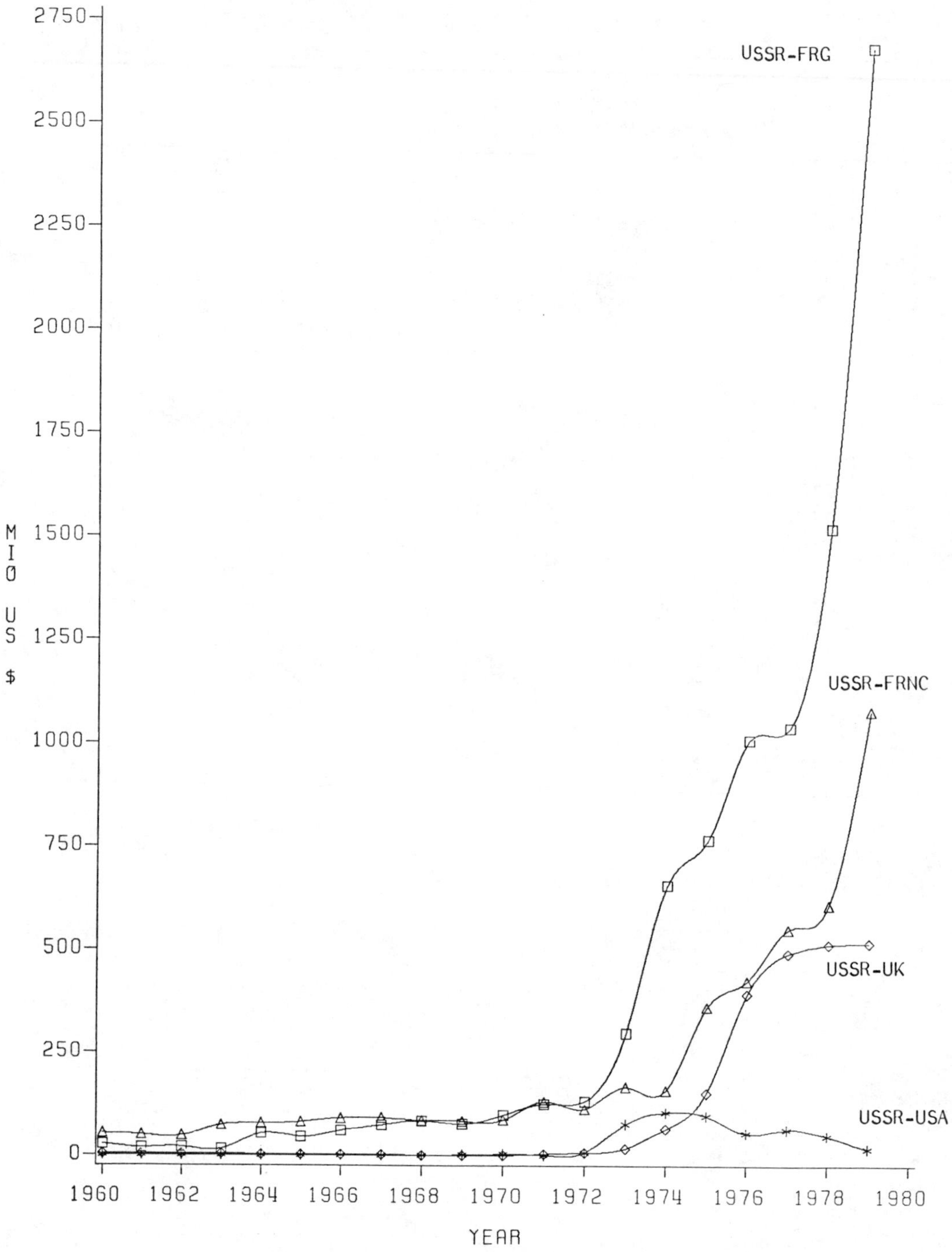
2750
2500
2250
2000
1750
1500
1250
1000
750
500
250
0
MIO US $
USSR-FRG
USSR-FRNC
USSR-UK
USSR-USA
1960
1962
1964
1966
1968
1970
1972
1974
1976
1978
1980
YEAR

3.5 HUMAN RIGHTS AND CONTACTS

3.5.1 Introduction

In the Helsinki Final Act the issue of human rights is mentioned in the context of the principles guiding relations, and most of the third "basket" concerns questions of human contacts between people and humanitarian problems. The participating states agreed to improve the possibilities for contacts and regular meetings on the basis of family ties, the reunification of families, and the facilitation of marriages between citizens of different countries. Travel for personal and professional reasons is to be encouraged as well as measures aimed at the general improvement of conditions for tourism. Agreement was also reached on the facilitation of meetings among youth and the exchange in the sphere of sports. Furthermore, contacts among governmental and nongovernmental institutions of the participating states, respectively, were encouraged. Another important aspect of the third "basket" is the question of information exchange. The participating nations agreed to encourage the circulation, access to, and exchange of information of all kinds. Also general cooperation in the field of information and the working conditions for journalists is to be improved.

The following subsections present data on limited, albeit vital, aspects only of human rights and human contacts. They are not supposed to constitute a definitive solution to the measurement problem in this highly controversial field.

As a matter of fact, the concepts used in this section may constitute the most difficult concepts if one tries to observe and to measure what in reality is meant by these concepts. The difficulty originates in the existence of many fundamental disagreements over the definition and meaning of those concepts, especially with regard to the criteria according to which "violations" or "respect" for human rights can be said to exist. In addition, what is called "human rights" covers a wide variety of values, comprising at least six different aspects: equality of economic and social conditions, provision of minimum economic and social conditions, respect for cultural diversity, group self-determination, political participation, and political freedom and repression (cf. McCamant 1981). Each element requires a different measurement scheme; it cannot be the task of the present study to provide such a comprehensive effort of measurement and data gathering.

3.5.2 Indices of Political Rights and Civil Liberties

A solution of the problem of measurement in the field of human rights has been suggested by the *Comparative Survey of Freedom* (Gastil 1978) comprising two indices, the index of political rights and the index of civil rights. Both indices are based on expert judgment ratings. They rank countries from 1 (highest degree of liberty) to 7 (no liberties). The construction of each index is based on a large number of facts that can be observed but hardly quantified. For rating the level of political rights, countries are assigned a value of 1 if they have a fully competitive electoral process and if those elected really hold power. Factors leading to lower values include, for example, extreme economic inequality, illiteracy, or intimidating violence and other shortcomings of effective competitive rule or obstacles to regular power transfer. Lowest ratings are assigned to countries with no institutionalized public influence on government and politics.

The second scale provides ratings for civil liberties. Countries ranking at scale value 1 are characterized by freedom of the press, absence of censorship, legal protection of individual civil rights, and absence of prosecution for political opinion or faith. There is free selection of residence and education, while the right of private ownership is generally respected. In countries ranking at scale value 2, there is a stronger authoritarian tradition with respect to jurisdiction and government, or the democratic infrastructure is less institutionalized. The authors of the *Comparative Survey of Freedom* have rated nations since 1973. (For a more detailed discussion of previous efforts in this respect and for additional methodological aspects, see Gastil 1978).

Several authors have expressed severe criticism with regard to these indices pointing at their culture-bound nature and at problems of reliability and reproducability of the findings ((McCamant 1981; Scarritt 1981; Scoble and Wiseberg 1981). However, while alternative approaches to the measurement of human rights are available, it is impossible to find also corresponding data collected in a cross-national perspective. For this reason, the following tables refer to Gastil's *Comparative Survey of Freedom* indices being well aware of the weakness inherent to this approach.

Table 3.5 presents time-series of index values for countries broken down by groups of countries (NATO, WTO, and neutral and nonaligned nations and those not members in the two military organizations mentioned before). For each set of nations, group means are computed. The progress documented by the evolution of index values for the NATO group are largely due to the democratization process, which took place in Portugal, and to the fall of the Greek military regime in 1974. As far as civil rights are concerned, there have been slight setbacks in the Federal Republic of Germany, France, and Italy. According to Gastil, in these countries opposition to the government or to the symbols of the system seems to be less acceptable as in the more traditional democracies, the United States and England. In the WTO group, there has been a slight amelioration in civil-rights situation as a result of specific policies in the GDR, Poland, and Hungary. Especially opposition of the churches in the GDR to compulsory premilitary training in high schools has been handled by the authorities with considerable care. In the Soviet Union, however, political rights declined some-

Table 3.5. Political and Civil Rights in CSCE Countries

COUNTRY	POLITICAL RIGHTS 1973	1974	1975	1976	1977	1978	1979	CIVIL RIGHTS 1973	1974	1975	1976	1977	1978	1979
BLGM	1	1	1	1	1	1	1	1	1	1	1	1	1	1
CNDA	1	1	1	1	1	1	1	1	1	1	1	1	1	1
DNMK	1	1	1	1	1	1	1	1	1	1	1	1	1	1
FRNC	1	1	1	1	1	1	1	2	2	2	2	1	1	2
FRG	1	1	1	1	1	1	1	1	1	1	1	1	1	2
GRCE	6	7	2	2	2	2	2	6	5	2	2	2	2	2
ICLD	1	1	1	1	1	1	1	1	1	1	1	1	1	1
ITLY	1	1	1	1	2	2	2	2	2	2	2	1	1	2
LXBG	2	2	2	2	2	1	1	1	1	1	1	1	1	1
NTHL	1	1	1	1	1	1	1	1	1	1	1	1	1	1
NRWY	1	1	1	1	1	1	1	1	1	1	1	1	1	1
PRTG	5	5	5	5	2	2	2	6	6	3	3	2	2	2
TRKY	3	2	2	2	2	2	2	4	4	3	3	3	3	3
UK	1	1	1	1	1	1	1	1	1	1	1	1	1	1
USA	1	1	1	1	1	1	1	1	1	1	1	1	1	1
	1.80	1.80	1.47	1.47	1.33	1.27	1.27	2.00	1.93	1.47	1.47	1.27	1.27	1.47
BLGR	7	7	7	7	7	7	7	7	7	7	7	7	7	7
CZCH	7	7	7	7	7	7	7	7	7	7	6	6	6	6
GDR	7	7	7	7	7	7	7	7	7	7	7	7	7	6
HNGR	6	6	6	6	6	6	6	6	6	6	6	6	5	5
PLND	6	6	6	6	6	6	6	6	6	6	6	6	5	5
RMNA	7	7	7	7	7	7	7	6	6	6	6	6	6	6
USSR	6	6	6	7	7	7	7	6	6	6	6	6	6	6
	6.57	6.57	6.57	6.71	6.71	6.71	6.71	6.43	6.43	6.43	6.29	6.29	6.00	5.86
AUST	1	1	1	1	1	1	1	1	1	1	1	1	1	1
CYPR	2	2	4	4	3	3	3	3	3	4	4	4	4	4
FNLD	2	2	2	2	2	2	2	2	2	2	2	2	2	2
IRLD	1	1	1	1	1	1	1	2	2	2	2	1	1	1
LICH														
MLTA	1	1	1	1	1	2	2	2	1	1	1	2	2	2
MNCO														
SANM														
SPAN	5	5	5	5	5	2	2	6	6	5	5	3	2	3
SWDN	1	1	1	2	1	1	1	1	1	1	1	1	1	1
SWTZ	1	1	1	1	1	1	1	1	1	1	1	1	1	1
VATC														
YGSL	6	6	6	6	6	6	6	6	6	6	6	6	5	-5
	2.22	2.22	2.44	2.56	2.33	2.11	2.11	2.67	2.56	2.56	2.56	2.33	2.11	2.22

how when the authorities stepped in against opposition from dissidents and human-rights groups. In the third set of countries, the democratization in Spain produced an improvement, while the 1974 events in Cyprus are negatively reflected in the data.

3.5.3 Human Rights in the Perspective of Amnesty International

Although Amnesty International (AI) is not interested in systematically collecting data on the human-rights situation, the annual reports published by this organization do contain a considerable amount of information useful for the purpose of this study. The following evaluation of the human-rights situation in selected countries taking part in the CSCE negotiations (listed in alphabetical order) presents some qualitative rather than quantitative insights; it is based on recent issues of Amnesty International Report.

The major concern of AI in the last decade with respect to *Bulgaria* has been the legislation restricting freedoms guaranteed in the Constitution, with the effect of making some types of reference to these freedoms a public offense. For instance, the distribution of leaflets criticizing the official economic policy would result in a four and a half years sentence of imprisonment. Also, all kinds of nonofficial contacts with foreigners are likely to be prosecuted. Attempts to leave the country without official permission (which is rarely granted) are punishable by up to five years of imprisonment and a fine. There have also been numerous allegations of ill-treatment of prisoners and torture of criminal and political prisoners. Furthermore, AI reports on cases of systematic prosecution of ethnic and religious minorities in Bulgaria such as Turks and Moslems.

In *Cyprus*, AI notes that since the hostilities of 1974, still a considerable number of people are missing. An independent Committee on Missing Persons to investigate the fate of missing people, both Turkish and Greek, is to be established following a proposal by the Secretary General of the United Nations.

Within the unofficial *Czechoslovakian* human-rights movement, Charta 77, a Committee for the Defense of the Unjustly Persecuted (VONS), was established in 1978 in order to monitor violations of human rights in Czechoslovakia. Ten of its members were arrested in May 1979 and charged for actions hostile to the interest of the state. Various efforts by AI to observe trials were prevented by government authorities. Since the events of 1968, the imprisonment of people making use of their right of freedom of expression has been a regular practice in Czechoslovakia according to AI. Also Roman Catholic priests apparently were subject to harassment on the charge of being obstructive against governmental supervision of churches and religious societies or illicit trading of religious literature. Furthermore, there are complaints about ill-treatment of prisoners.

The main concern of AI in the *Federal Republic of Germany* relates to conditions of imprisonment of people suspected or convicted of politically motivated crimes. The authorities were urged to abolish solitary confinement and small-group isolation as regular forms of imprisonment. AI also criticized changes in the legislation in connection with the persecution of terrorism that could be used to restrict the freedom of speech.

In *France* AI focused its attention on the treatment of conscientious objectors. A further issue of concern is the relatively suppressive reaction of French authorities against the self-determination movements of Bretons, Corsicans, and others.

In the *German Democratic Republic*, AI reports that a considerable number of people are imprisoned under laws explicitly restricting the use of the human right to leave the country granted in the Final Act of Helsinki. The attempt of crossing the border without permission (*Republikflucht*) can result in a sentence of up to five years' imprisonment. When the Final Act was fully published also in the GDR, the number of people filing an application for permission to leave the country increased considerably. Most of these applications, however, are turned down. Individuals applying repeatedly for a visa and insisting on their right to leave the country on the grounds of the international human-rights covenants that were also ratified by the GDR, are frequently arrested on charges such as interference with public activity or incitement hostile to the state, and public degradation. Appealing to organizations outside the GDR in order to gain support can result in charges of "activities directed against the GDR or other peace-loving nations." Also, the distribution of information considered officially as discrediting the GDR will lead to a prosecution by the authorities. Exact figures on political prisoners in the GDR are not available.

In *Greece*, AI deplores the treatment of Jehovah's Witnesses imprisoned due to their refusal to do military service. In 1977 the government introduced a law offering conscientious objectors the alternative of unarmed military service for twice the regular duration. Since Jehovah's Witnesses refused to do any kind of military service, including unarmed service, this has not solved the problem.

The chief concern of AI with respect to *Hungary* relates to legislative measures restricting the freedom of expression and the imprisonment of people attempting to exercise their right to freedom of movement.

The *Republic of Ireland* was affected in some ways by the events in neighboring Ulster. After AI submitted to the government of the Republic a report of a mission that concluded that people detained on suspicion of politically motivated crimes had been ill-treated by the police during 1975–1977, the government set up an independent committee for the investigation of the respective allegations.

In connection with the persecution of terrorism in *Italy*, AI has expressed concern about lengthy periods of detention of prisoners while the judicial investigations were unduly protracted. There were also problems with regard to the treatment of conscientious objectors.

Detention and even mass detention has been a regular practice in *Poland* as a means employed by the authorities to cope with unofficial demonstrations. AI also reports police brutality and the open abuse of the judicial system for the purpose of suppressing critical attitudes. The evolution of the social and political situation since summer 1980 had a positive effect on the human-rights situation at least in the beginning. Recent outlooks are not so favorable.

Romania is reported to prohibit the exercise of many human rights, especially the right to emigration and freedom of religious belief. Members of Protestant Evangelical communities have been exposed to severe persecution by the authorities, including detention and police brutality. With respect to the types of punishment, there seems to be a trend to replace prison sentences by corrective labor "without deprivation of liberty." Also confinement to psychiatric institutions appears to have taken place. Although there are no formal provisions for banishment in Romanian law, authorities admitted unofficially that an unspecified number of strikers were "banished."

In *Spain*, the process of democratization during the late seventies brought considerable constitutional and judicial reforms, the most notable achievement being the new constitution substituting General Franco's Fundamental Laws. It abolishes the death penalty, except under military law in time of war. Also the use of torture and inhuman and degrading punishments are now explicitly prohibited. The right of association and the right to strike were also recognized, while the period of preventive detention was limited to seventy-two hours. Nevertheless, AI had reasons to complain about cases of nonapplication or incomplete application of the new norms. There were even allegations and charges of torture against police officers.

In *Switzerland*, AI's major concern in the seventies was the imprisonment of conscientious objectors. Efforts regarding the introduction of an alternative civilian service were not successful; in 1977 a public referendum turned down a proposal regarding a respective amendment to the Constitution, while the number of conscientious objectors was growing.

In *Turkey*, AI accused the sometimes inhumane and degrading treatment of prisoners. There have also been occasional informations on the use of torture in Turkish prisons, before and after the takeover of the government by the army. The measures taken to control growing terrorism have undoubtedly severed the complete situation. There have been continuing reports on the persecution of members of the Kurdish minority or of people charged with "making propaganda for separatism" by merely recognizing the Kurds as a separate ethnic group.

According to AI reports on the *Soviet Union*, the persecution of people holding views disapproved by the authorities, whether political, religious, or nationalist, is a common practice. This includes harassment, arrest, trials, imprisonment and detention in psychiatric institutions or exile. Since the signing of the Final Act of Helsinki, groups have been set up in the Soviet Union concerned with the monitoring of the human-rights situation. The authorities have been especially busy since 1975 in controlling these groups and prohibiting their activities by all means available. The charge of "anti-Soviet agitation and propaganda" apparently allows to persecute any opinion deviating from the official views.

In the *United States of America*, AI inquired into allegations of political motivation for criminal charges. American Indians, blacks, and illegal immigrants from Mexico seem to be more often convicted than other groups of the population, and there are charges regarding false testimony induced by the prosecuting authorities.

In the *United Kingdom*, various measures in connection with the fighting of terrorism caused concern by AI. In particular, AI expressed criticism about the emergency legislation, the detention of prisoners for prolonged periods, and the operation of the nonjury courts set up to try suspected terrorists. AI also commented on the conditions in the Maze prison in Belfast.

In *Yugoslavia*, the majority of prisoners of conscience taken care of by AI were charged with "hostile propaganda." Especially sensitive issues in this respect are the relationship between the national groups and ethnic minorities. The measures applied to the control of alleged separatist tendencies do not always meet internationally accepted standards of just treatment of prisoners and fair trial. A few cases of detention in psychiatric clinics are also investigated by AI.

As indicated at the beginning of this subsection, it is hard to draw any reliable and representative conclusions, on the base of *AI Reports*, on the comparative state of human rights in the thirty-five countries involved in CSCE negotiations, due to the fact that these reports are case oriented rather than systematically evaluating the situation by quantitative means. Nevertheless, the material offered by AI is quite meaningful and pertinent in the context of this study. It can easily be seen that since the beginning of the CSCE negotiations, the situation in the field of human rights underwent considerable change. In the West significant progress took place. In the East too the fact that the CSCE drew attention to the problems of human rights had a noteworthy impact; however, this impact occurrs to have a somewhat ambivalent nature: At some places and with respect to some aspects of the human-rights question, it led in fact to some forms of liberalization or at least to a certain relaxation; yet, the active concern for human rights, and especially the initiatives to promote the cause of human rights systematically by organizational measures undertaken by new movements within and outside the countries concerned, also led to a tendency to backfire giving rise to more intensive vigilance on the part of the authorities now militating against what they call "antigovernmental propaganda."

3.5.4 Political Rights and Economic Rights

As has been pointed out in Subsection 3.5.1, the concept of "human rights," for many reasons, represents a highly controversial issue. In principle, all governments claim to respect human rights fully and comprehensively. Yet when it comes to define the concept, differing and fundamentally diverging views tend to prevail. In particular, governments in Socialist countries accuse Western conceptions to be rooted in "bourgeois" bias and thus of being incapable of taking into account the crucial aspect of material welfare. Authors in Socialist countries therefore recommend considering the provision of minimum social conditions a primary element of human rights; the appropriate indicator they suggest is the rate of unemployment: The smaller the percentage of unemployed personnel, the better the human rights are implemented, as in the case of Socialist economies, in which the right to work constitutes an officially guaranteed human right. They point out that, furthermore, the case of human rights is materialized best in the Socialist system. This line of reasoning, although quite selective in its view of "material welfare" by avoiding any comparison of standards of living, is taken up in this subsection, with a look at unemployment figures for countries in the West. The authors of this study do not share this point of view since we feel that the picture offered by unemployment figures would be rather incomplete if neglecting the fact that in Western countries, social security is widely guaranteed by unemployment-insurance schemes providing unemployment pay that exceeds by far the average salary of a Soviet worker.

On the other hand, according to the Western concept, the main values implied by the meaning of human rights pertain to political freedom and absence of repression. One of the appropriate indicators to measure the degree of human rights existing in a country therefore is the absence of political sanctions: The smaller the number of sanctions, the better the state of human rights. Therefore, in this subsection, the annual number of political sanctions in Socialist countries will be used as an indicator. These data refer to simple numbers of events without scaling for intensity and are taken from the events data bank of the *World Handbook of Political and Social Indicators* (Taylor 1981).

The evolution of the state of human rights as reflected in these two differing conceptions are presented in Graphs 3.53–3.56. Looking first at Western unemployment figures, one has to draw the conclusion, in terms of the Socialist conception of human rights, that the situation in the West constantly declined. The economic recession following the oil crisis of 1973 caused a massive increase of unemployment exceeding, in 1977, the 7 percent level. A similar

Graph 3.53. Unemployment in NATO Countries and Neutral/Nonaligned Countries as Percentage of Total Labor Force

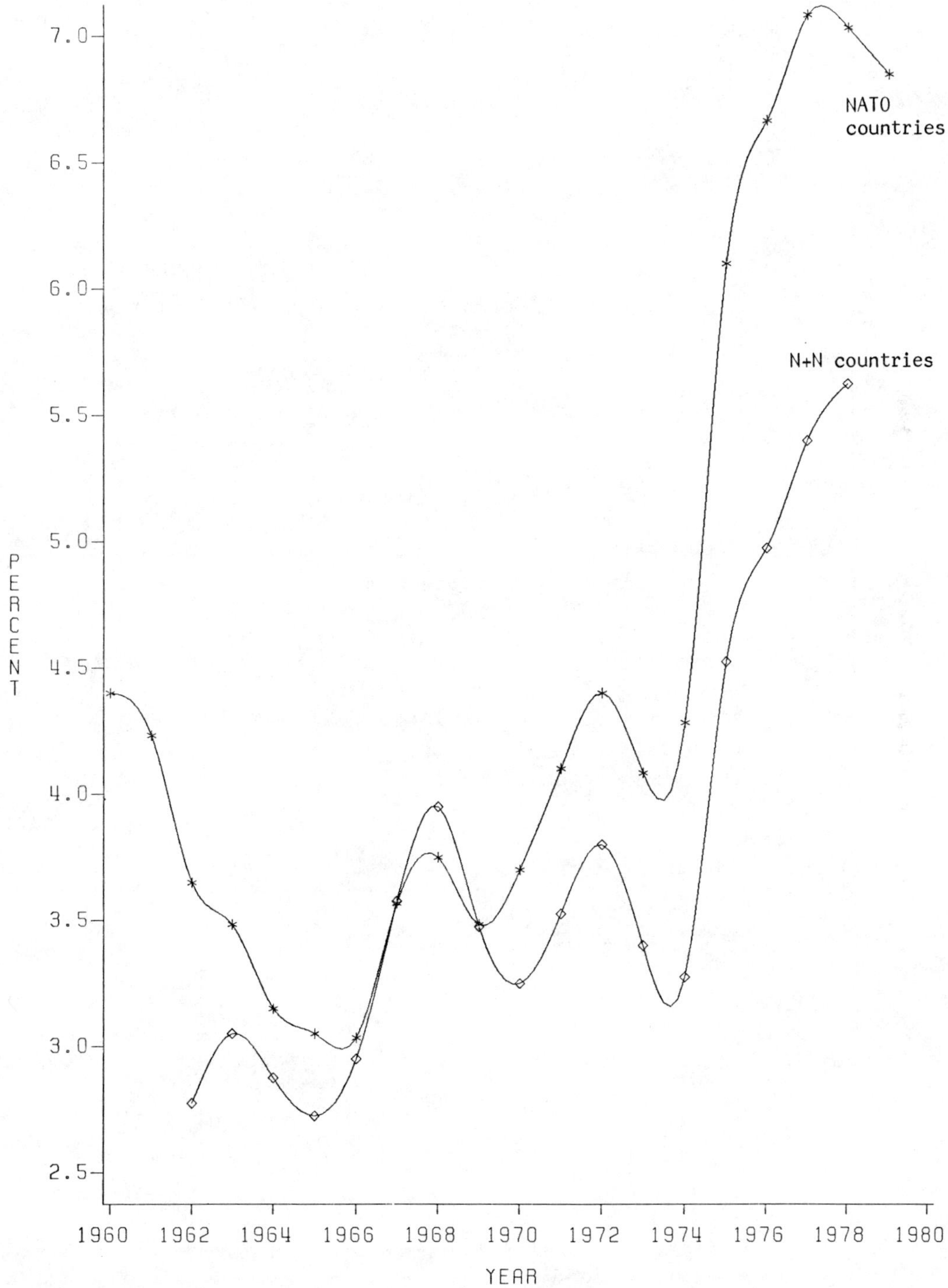
7.0
6.5
6.0
5.5
5.0
4.5
4.0
3.5
3.0
2.5
PERCENT
1960
1962
1964
1966
1968
1970
1972
1974
1976
1978
1980
YEAR
NATO countries
N+N countries

Graph 3.54. Unemployment in Selected Western Countries as Percentage of Total Labor Force

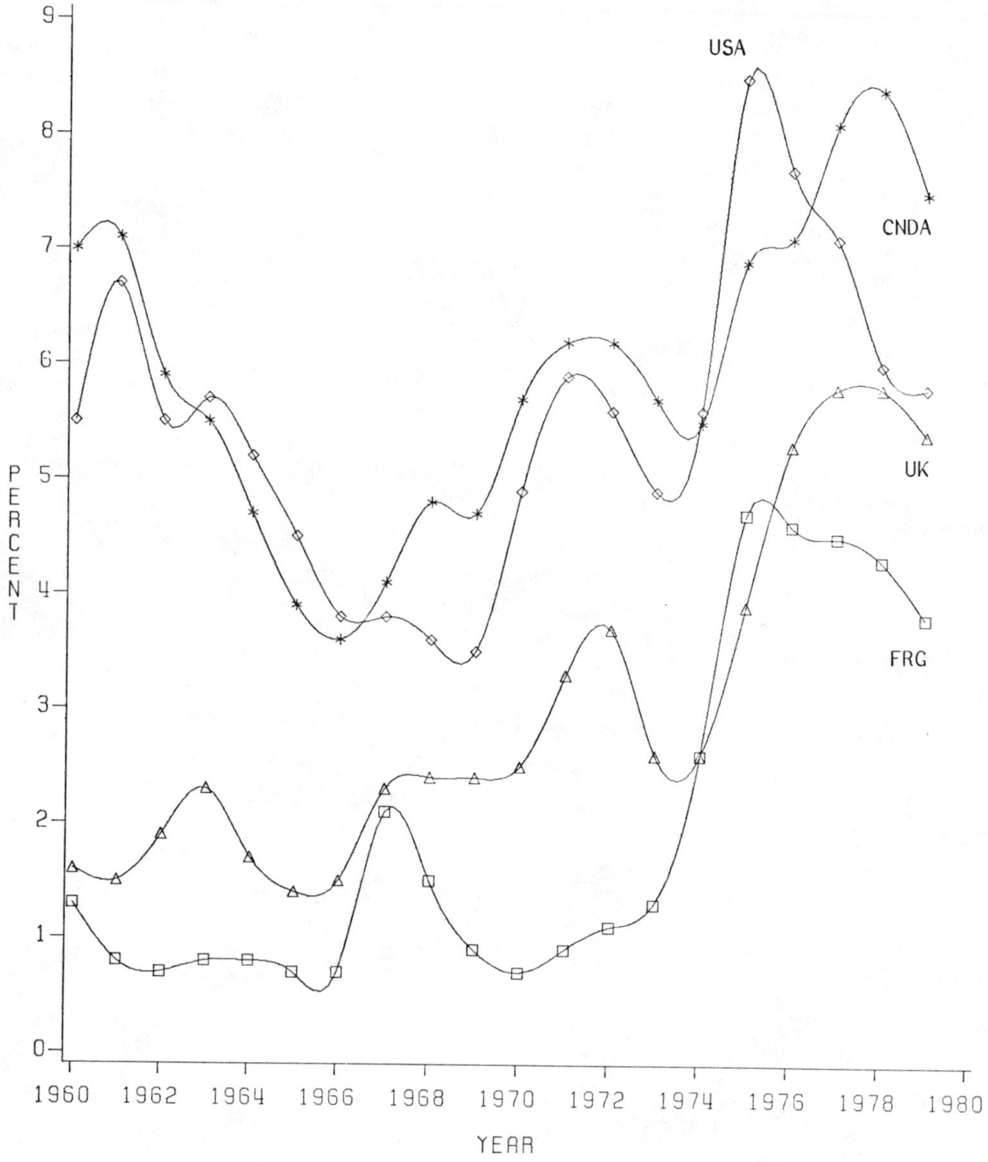
USA
CNDA
UK
FRG
PERCENT
0
1
2
3
4
5
6
7
8
9
1960
1962
1964
1966
1968
1970
1972
1974
1976
1978
1980
YEAR

Graph 3.55. Number of Political Sanctions in WTO Countries (2)

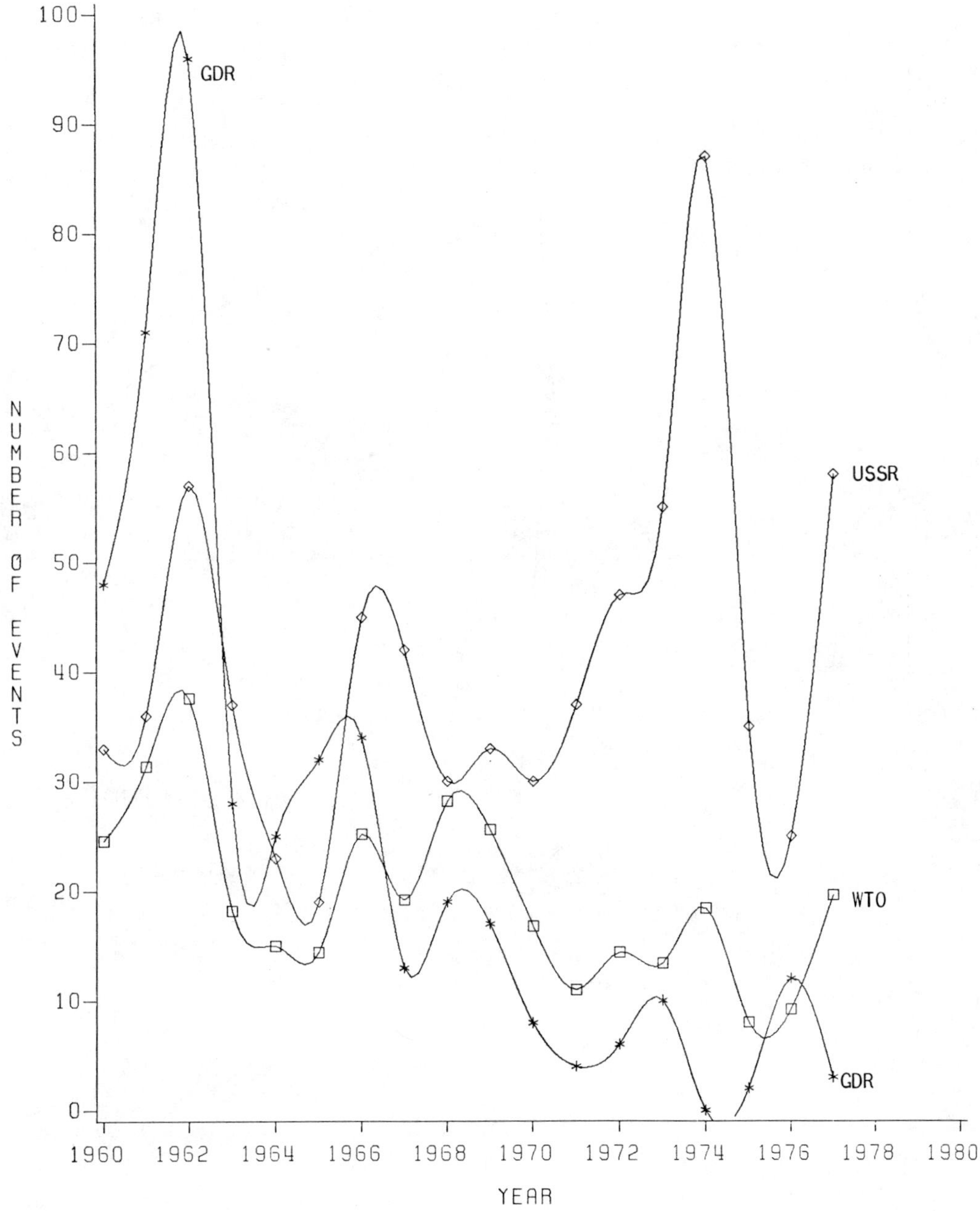
GDR
USSR
WTO
GDR
NUMBER OF EVENTS
0
10
20
30
40
50
60
70
80
90
100
1960
1962
1964
1966
1968
1970
1972
1974
1976
1978
1980
YEAR

Graph 3.56. Number of Political Sanctions in WTO Countries (1)

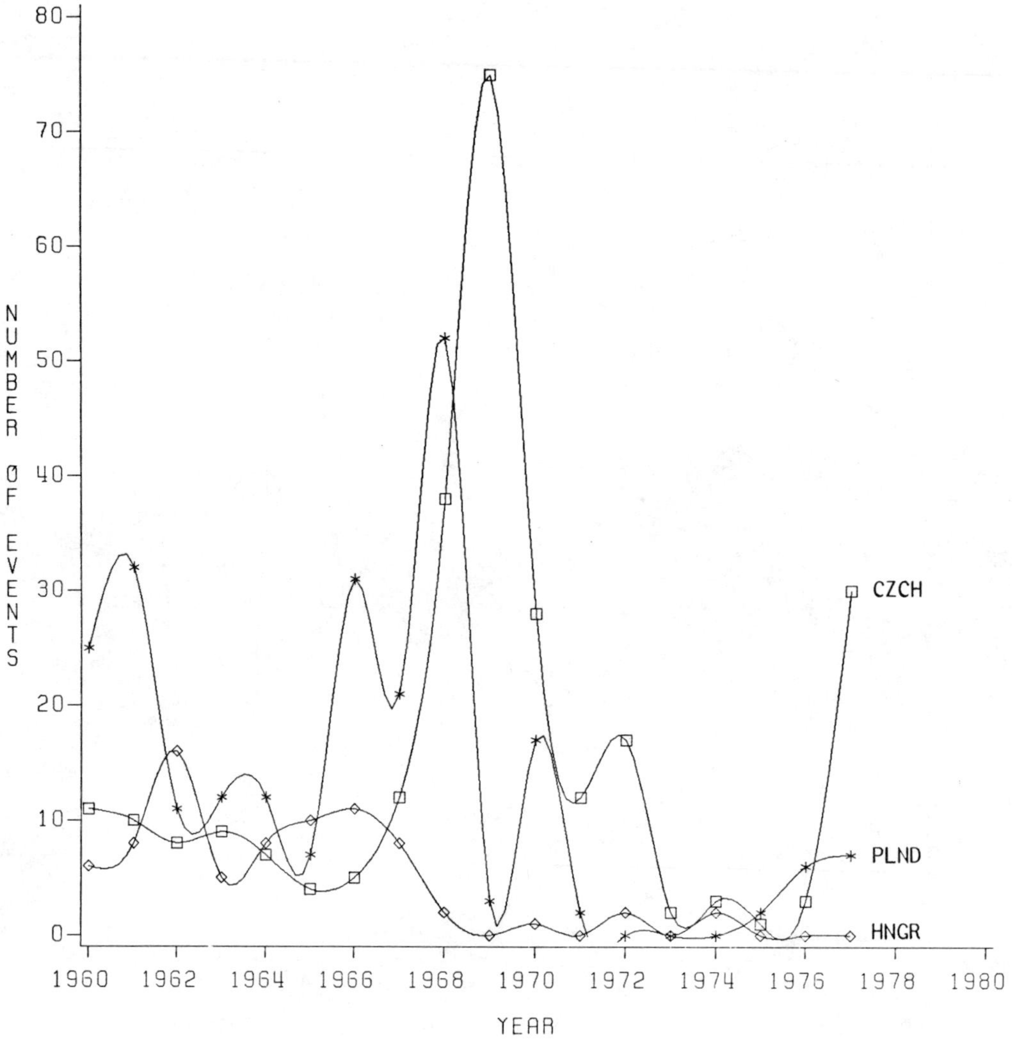
NUMBER OF EVENTS
YEAR
CZCH
PLND
HNGR
0
10
20
30
40
50
60
70
80
1960
1962
1964
1966
1968
1970
1972
1974
1976
1978
1980

picture is offered by the curve representing the evolution of unemployment figures in N + N countries. Using a more refined analysis and looking at certain countries individually, one can easily see that the impact of the general recession affected all countries practically at the same time (1974); however, some countries managed to recover sooner (USA, FRG) than other countries (Canada, UK). This does hardly reflect any difference in cherishing the values of human rights. It is a mere function of the degree of adaptability and flexibility of the respective economies and cannot be linked in any meaningful way with the evolution of East–West relations.

On the other hand, there seems to be a definitive interrelation between the evolution of the human rights situation in the East, as measured by Western indicators, and the progress of "détente." Looking at the aggregate number of political sanctions reported for all WTO countries (Graph 3.55, curve identified with square symbols), one can easily detect a general tendency toward a certain relaxation. Although the frequency of governmental sanctions in the domestic sphere is oscillating, the basic trend observable since the midsixties points at a lessening of repressive governmental activities. In 1971 and 1975, the number of such sanctions was lowest; this coincides with two important events characterizing the evolution of "détente." Yet at the end of the period observed (1977), the number of sanctions is again growing.

When examining the curves plotted for individual countries, however, some exception from this trend can be discerned. In the Soviet Union the frequency of political sanctions was extremely high immediately prior to the signing of the Final Act, in 1975, and again in 1977. In Czechoslovakia, the 1968 events were followed by an unprecedented rise in repressive activities in 1969, and a new wave of political repression was initiated in 1977. Only in the case of the GDR "détente" seems to have had a lasting and beneficial impact; here, the number of repressive sanctions that in 1962 had reached a record level, steadily declined. The least repressive country, measured by this approach, is Hungary, which, since the beginning of the seventies, exhibits extremely low values on this scale.

3.5.5 East–West Tourism

In the Final Act, the signatories expressed their desire to contribute to understanding among peoples and envisaged contacts between people, among other measures, as a suitable way to contribute to the attainment of these aims. In particular, the Final Act says that "the participating States consider that tourism contributes to a fuller knowledge of the life, culture and history of other countries, to the growth of understanding among peoples, to the improvement of contacts and to the broader use of leisure; they intend to promote the development of tourism, on an individual or

Graph 3.57. Visitors from Western Countries to the Soviet Union

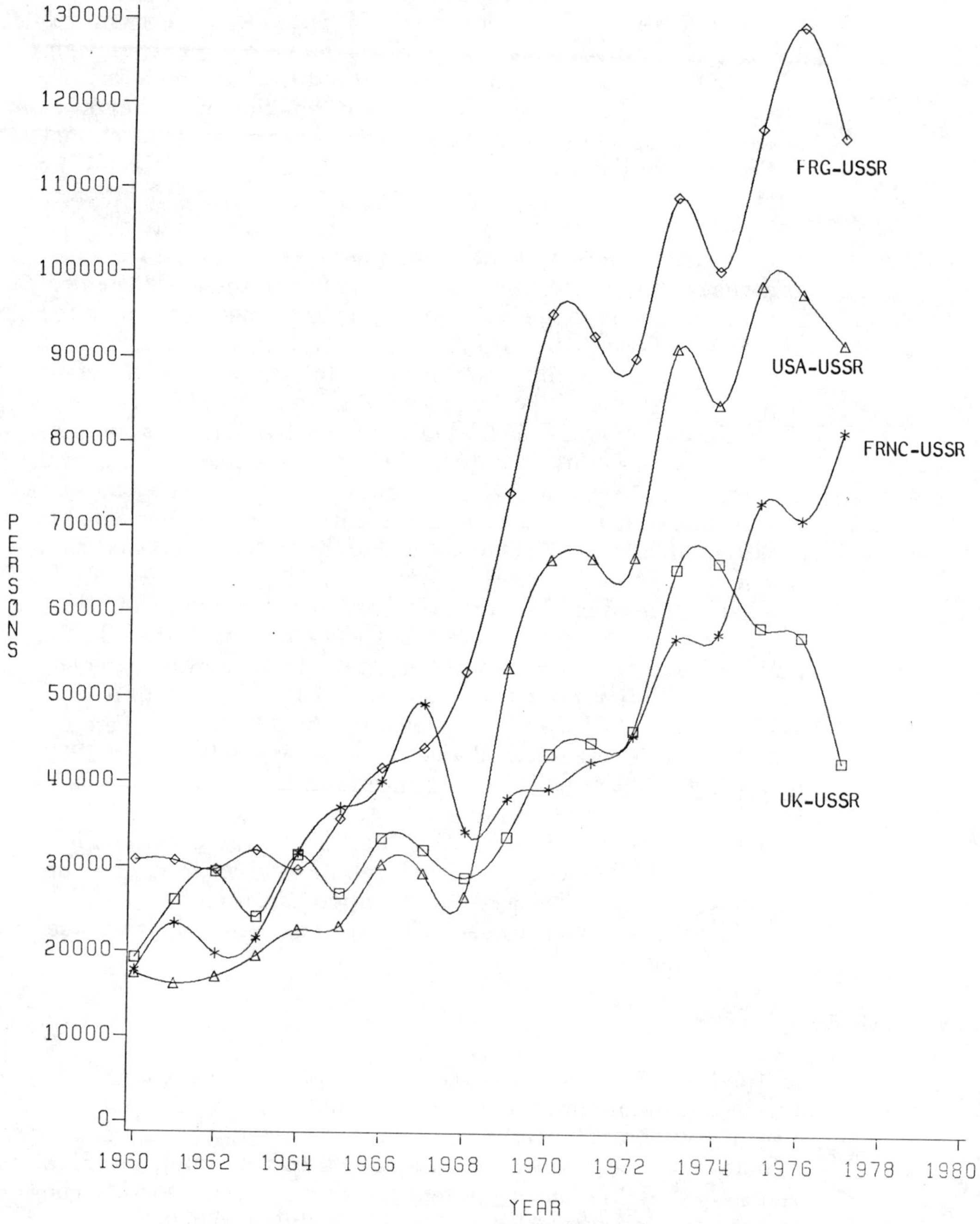
130000
120000
110000
100000
90000
80000
70000
60000
50000
40000
30000
20000
10000
0
PERSØNS
1960
1962
1964
1966
1968
1970
1972
1974
1976
1978
1980
YEAR
FRG-USSR
USA-USSR
FRNC-USSR
UK-USSR

Graph 3.58. Visitors from Socialist Countries to the FRG

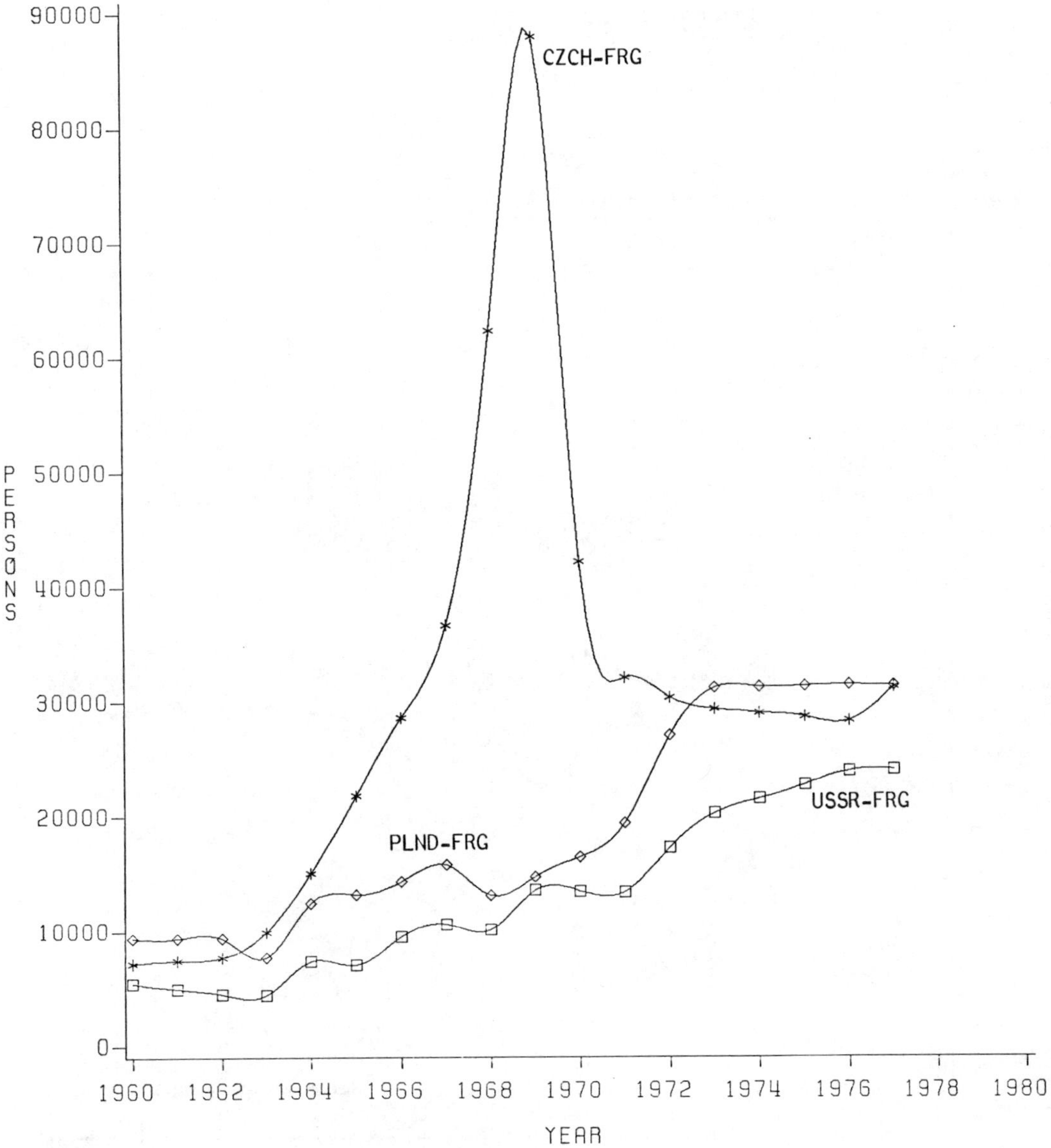
90000
80000
70000
60000
50000
40000
30000
20000
10000
0
PERSONS
CZCH-FRG
PLND-FRG
USSR-FRG
1960
1962
1964
1966
1968
1970
1972
1974
1976
1978
1980
YEAR

Graph 3.59. Exchange of Visitors between the GDR and the FRG

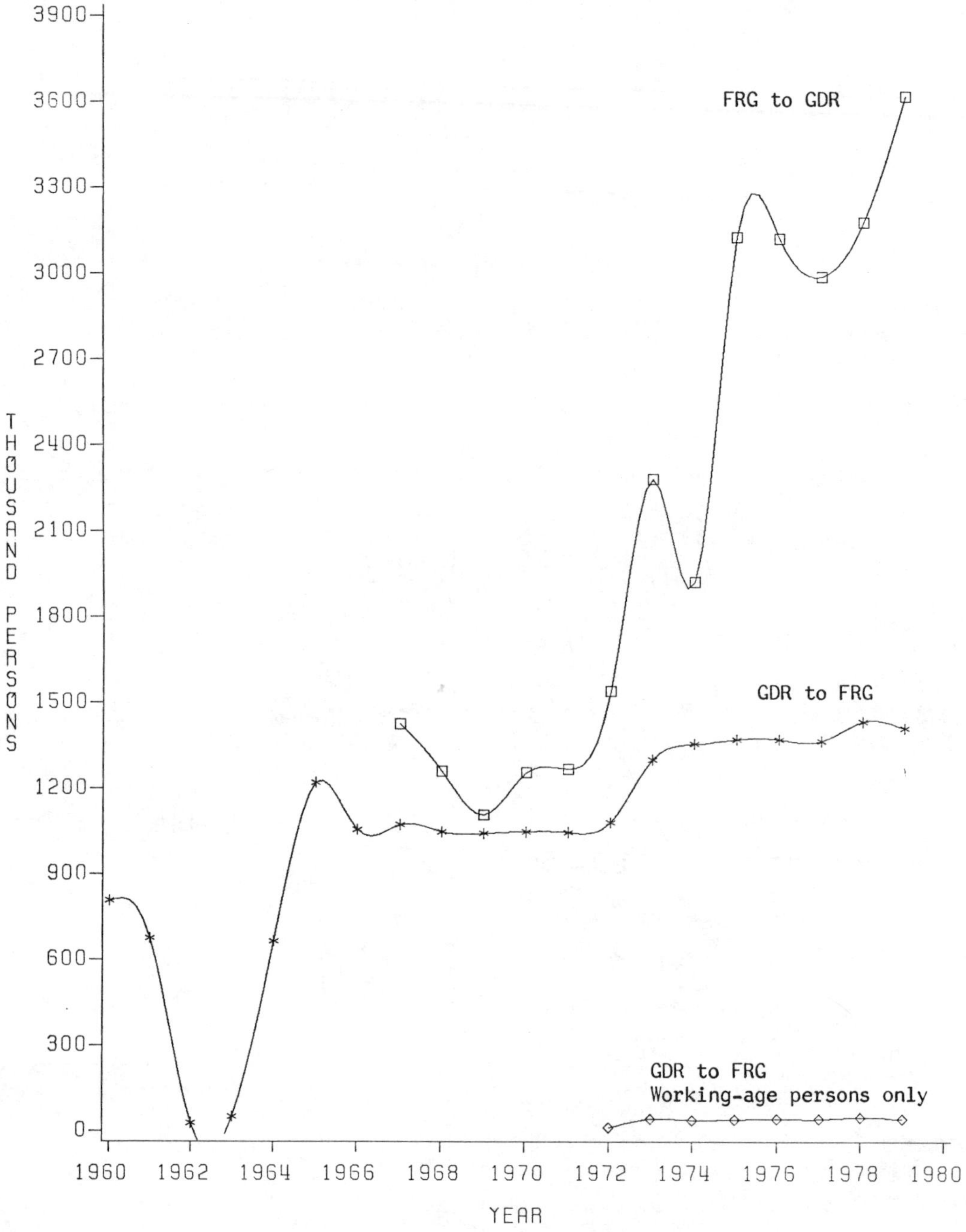
3900
3600
3300
3000
2700
2400
2100
1800
1500
1200
900
600
300
0
THOUSAND PERSONS
FRG to GDR
GDR to FRG
GDR to FRG
Working-age persons only
1960
1962
1964
1966
1968
1970
1972
1974
1976
1978
1980
YEAR

collective basis." To what extent did the evolution of "détente" eventually advance the growth of East–West tourism? This question is answered by Graphs 3.57–3.59.

Before interpreting these graphs, however, one has to bear in mind the inherently different proportion of tourism from the West to the East and vice versa. Generally, the number of tourists from the West visiting countries in the East is between six and seven times larger than the corresponding figures for the flow of tourists in the opposite direction. The structure of tourism in Europe is therefore characterized by conspicuous asymmetry. This asymmetry can partly be ascribed to financial reasons, more precisely to problems of convertibility of East European currencies. In addition and maybe more important, the fact that only a small number of tourists from socialist countries get an opportunity to visit countries outside the WTO region certainly reflects the well known differences in the economic and social systems of the East and the West and the specific way in which authorities in Socialist countries handle applications for traveling abroad. By contrast to the assumptions underlying the recommendations laid down in the Final Act, setting right the asymmetry is not a matter of formalities and their simplification on the part of the countries *receiving* visitors but rather a matter of granting citizens in Socialist countries access to the necessary travel documents and exit visa.

As far as tourism from the West to the East is concerned, the statistics clearly indicate a marked increase of the flow of tourists. The decisive expansion took place prior to the signing of the Final Act, in the late sixties and early seventies. It may as much reflect the change in political atmosphere as the rapid economic development in the West that allowed for amazing growth rates of tourism in general. It should also be noted that at the end of the period observed, there is a tendency toward diminishing frequencies of tourists visiting the Soviet Union.

On the other hand, the frequency of visits to Western countries by citizens of Socialist countries seems to be much more subject to political determinants. The soaring rise of the numbers of Czechoslovak citizens traveling to the Federal Republic of Germany and to Western countries in general in 1968 and 1969 is obviously closely connected with the events in Czechoslovakia in August 1968 and thereafter, and the many persons leaving their country did so hardly for tourism reasons. Tourism originating in Poland and the Soviet Union is characterized by a more steady evolution based on very small growth rates and contained within well-defined limits reached in the midseventies and not transgressed since.

Travel between the Federal Republic of Germany and the German Democratic Republic seems to be virtually controlled by politics. This is strikingly obvious in the case of GDR visitors to the FRG. The evolution of Westbound "inner-German" tourism starts at point zero in 1962/63, after the construction of the Berlin wall by the GDR, when the GDR authorities sealed off their population from their West German relatives. After a certain normalization, the GDR authorities also managed to keep the frequencies of visits to the West constantly stable for a period of more than six years; between 1974 and 1976 they agreed to increase the number of exit visas somewhat, yet stabilizing the frequency again carefully on the new level. Similarly, Eastbound travel is also determined by political factors. Agreements negotiated by the FRG government in view of facilitating visits to the GDR promptly resulted in substantial growth rates.

In conclusion, the evolution of tourism very much bears the articulate handwriting of politics. The "growth of understanding among peoples" seems to depend more on the growth of intergovernmental "détente" than vice versa, as was hoped for by the authors of the Final Act.

3.5.6 Migration from East to West

In the 1975 Final Act, the thirty-five participating states pledged "to deal in a positive and humanitarian spirit with the applications of persons who wish to be reunited with members of their family." The progress made with regard to the reunification of families is generally considered as one of the substantial and major achievements of the CSCE. Although the evolution of "détente" is still far from bringing about free movement of people, it cannot be denied that in the absence of the new quality of East-West relations developed in view and in the context of the CSCE, it would hardly have been possible to improve the situation in the field of family reunification to the extent accomplished in the past ten years.

The oscillations of the curves presented in Graphs 3.60 and 3.61 clearly mirror the ups and downs of political tension and "détente." For instance, emigration from Poland to the Federal Republic of Germany was based on special bilateral agreements regarding Polish citizens of German origin; a similar arrangement was negotiated with Romania and the Soviet Union. On the basis of such agreements, a considerable number of persons were given permission to leave the respective countries during the seventies. On the other hand, the volume of emigration from Czechoslovakia to the Federal Republic of Germany decreased significantly after 1969, thus indicating that unless there are special arrangements made on the political level, there is little chance for mobility from East to West.

Emigration from the Soviet Union to the West—with the exception of citizens of German origin, practically exclusively by Soviet citizens of Jewish origin—also entirely depends on the evolution of the political "climate" and on political decisions made within the overall context of the evolution of East-West relations in general. Following a marked increase of the number of Jewish emigrants permitted to leave the Soviet Union in the late sixties and early seventies, the respective figures declined again after 1973, when the US government, on the basis of the Jackson Amendment

Graph 3.60. Migration from Eastern Europe to the FRG

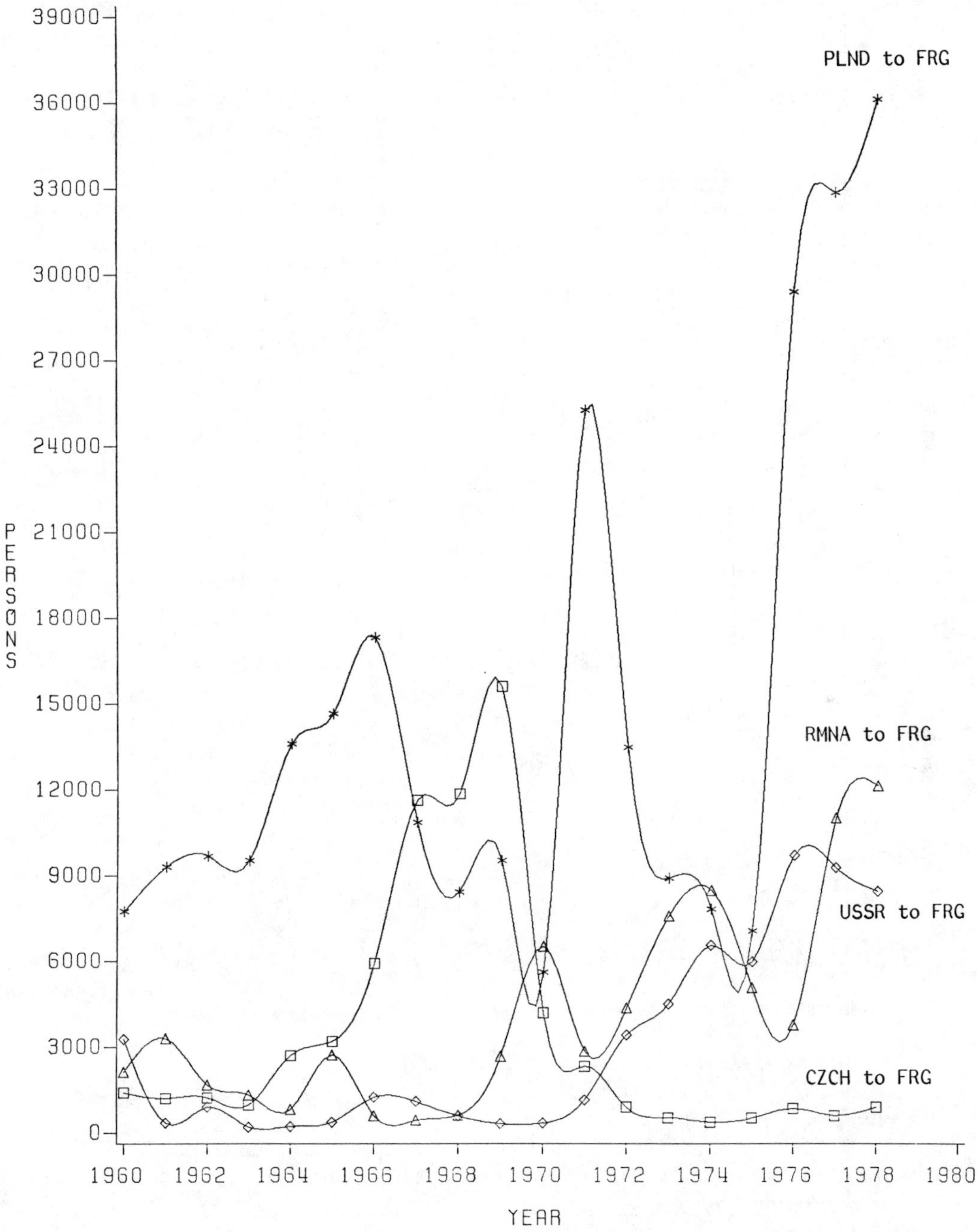

39000
36000
33000
30000
27000
24000
21000
18000
15000
12000
9000
6000
3000
0
PERSONS
PLND to FRG
RMNA to FRG
USSR to FRG
CZCH to FRG
1960
1962
1964
1966
1968
1970
1972
1974
1976
1978
1980
YEAR

Graph 3.61. Migration from the GDR to the FRG and from the USSR to Israel

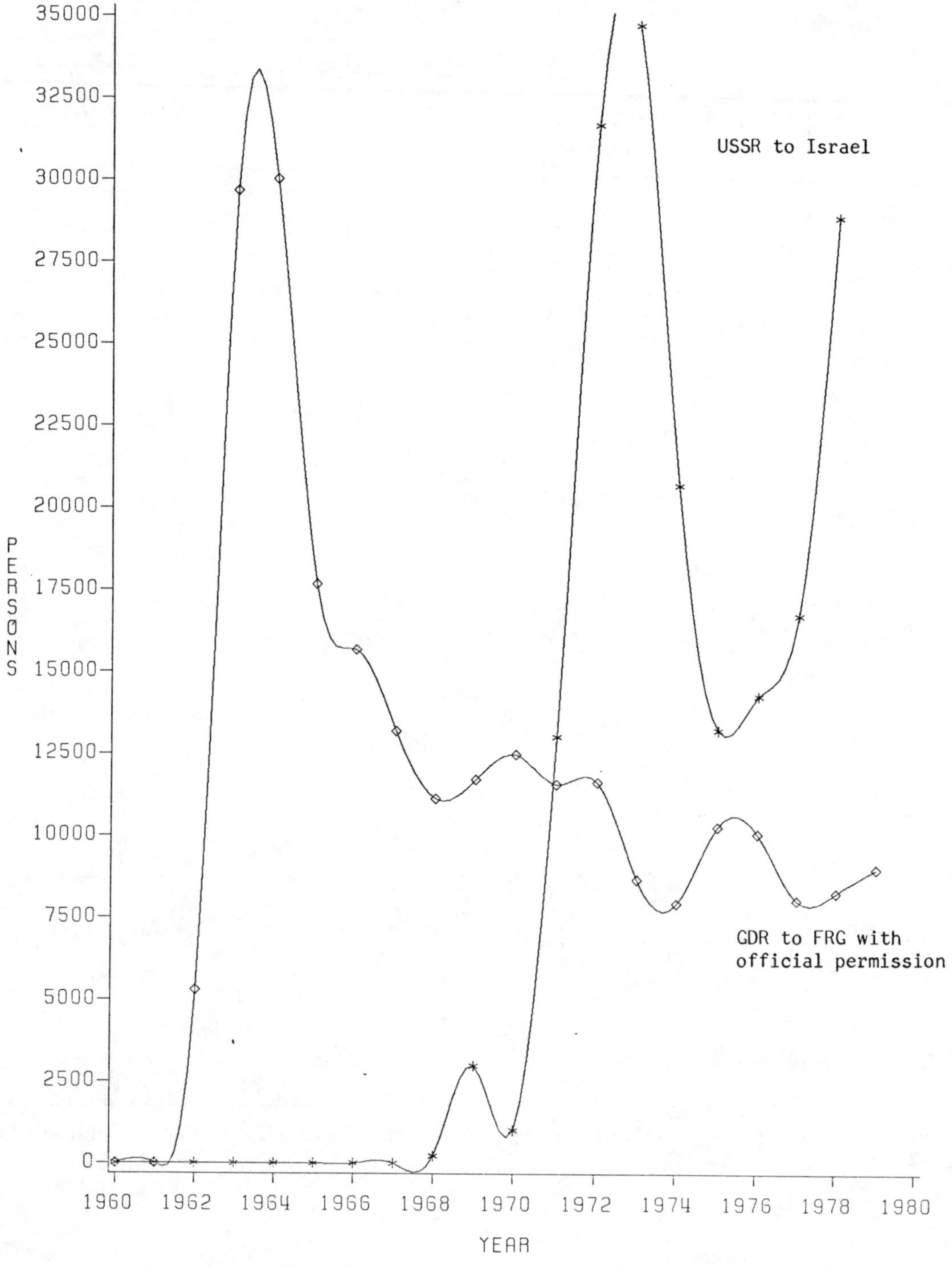
35000
32500
30000
27500
25000
22500
20000
17500
15000
12500
10000
7500
5000
2500
0
PERSONS
1960
1962
1964
1966
1968
1970
1972
1974
1976
1978
1980
YEAR
USSR to Israel
GDR to FRG with
official permission

to the Trade Reform Bill, tried to establish a linkage between the granting of the most-favoured-nation status to the USSR and the facilitation of Jewish emigration by Soviet authorities. The situation improved again, however, in the late seventies, obviously due to careful political "fine-tuning" of the issue by Soviet policy. This political fine-tuning is being done irrespective of the importance of the issue itself, which, for thousands of persons, constitutes a most pressing matter; between 1968 and 1978, 177,463 Soviet Jews were given permission to emigrate, while more than 400,000 persons filing applications were not granted a positive response by Soviet authorities. For these persons, the situation of course is still far from being satisfactory. Nevertheless, some progress was made, and it must not be underestimated.

3.6 SOVEREIGNTY AND INDEPENDENCE

Repeatedly and quite remarkably, CSCE delegates refer to concepts such as "sovereignty" and "independence." As was pointed out in the factor analysis reported in Section 2.4, this dimension also emerges as one of the crucial and central dimensions underlying the whole notion of East–West relations. It is therefore imperative to look at it more closely and to try to determine *how much* independence or dependency each country enjoys or suffers from and to what extent the structure of dependency relationships among the thirty-five European countries was subject to *change* in the course of the process of "détente."

However, it is obvious that these concepts are extremely difficult to grasp operationally. They are, by their very nature, extremely fuzzy and difficult to locate in political reality although they have a high symbolic value and are constantly being referred to and although international law offers precise definition at least for the term *sovereignty*. The following attempts to measure the relative degree of independence or dependency of the thirty-five CSCE nations and to identify shifts in the dependency structure requires, therefore, certain reservations, although we, the authors, having studied a wide variety of alternative approaches, feel that the solutions suggested in this section represent the optimum solution to be found under these circumstances. Two approaches will be used.

The first approach starts from the assumption that the structure of interactions among countries is somehow related to the structure of dependencies existing among these countries. A concentration of interactions of a particular country on another country means that there is a special relationship between them; it also means that these two countries are interdependent. Irrespective of whether this interdependency is a good thing or a bad thing, it will be difficult for any of the countries concerned to untie itself from this special relationship; more precisely, any step toward detaching itself from this special relationship will involve certain political costs. Therefore, if one wishes to determine the degree of independence or dependency of a country, one has to ascertain to what extent the external relations of the country concerned deviate from a completely equal distribution of interactions on all other countries. This can be done by examining the distribution of dyadic interactions as reported in Azar's COPDAB (Conflict and Peace Data Bank) dataset, which comprises all events taking place between 134 nations. If a country had an ideally equal distribution of external relations, the total amount of interactions with the outside world would be evenly distributed among the remaining 133 countries (indicated by the maximum value of 100 percent); if, on the other hand, its external relations were fixed on one single partner country from which it would completely depend, the corresponding percentage figure would be extremely low. The results of the analysis of the COPDAB data based on these assumptions are presented in Table 3.6. The data refer to political and diplomatic interactions in both the cooperative and conflictive domain.

At a first glance, no coherent trend can be discerned. Some countries succeeded in increasing the degree of dispersion of their external relations, thus diminishing their degree of dependency. Other countries seem to have undergone a process of concentration of their external relations on fewer partners. For some countries the degree of dispersion remained practically constant that is, change of no more than 5 percent or below) from the early fifties to the late seventies. These findings may be summarized as suggested in Table 3.7. The majority of countries were in a position to increase their degree of independence. In three cases only the trend points at the opposite direction (Spain, Greece, and Norway); these three countries share in common their rapid pace of modernization, which also implied an intensification of external relations mainly with a few key partner countries.

Which countries profited most from "détente" in terms of gaining more independence? Obviously, some NATO allies (Canada, the Benelux countries, Denmark, and the FRG) were able to increase considerably their rate of dispersion. Among the Socialist countries, Yugoslavia and Romania achieved the highest rate of change favoring independence; this obviously reflects the articulate policy of emancipation skillfully practiced by these two countries. It is interesting to note that among the WTO member countries, the German Democratic Republic and Bulgaria also succeeded in obtaining a broadened scope for international activities. In the case of the GDR, this reflects the fact of universal recognition obtained as one of the first breakthroughs of the post-Cold War type of East–West relations. The recognition of the GDR, as a matter of fact, constitutes one of the crucial successes made by the Socialist countries under the auspices of the new policy of "détente" and "peaceful coexistence."

However, one must also bear in mind that there is little impact of "détente" on the dependency structure of the other WTO coun-

Table 3.6. Dispersion of External Interactions as Percentage of Total Possible Interactions (based on COPDAB Cooperative and Conflictive Events)

country	period					
	1950-54	1955-59	1960-64	1965-69	1970-74	1975-78
USA	96	99	96	94	96	91
Canada	40	57	46	55	61	69
United Kingdom	87	85	83	87	92	82
Ireland	22	24	21	6	39	44
Netherlands	47	57	51	60	63	60
Belgium	40	43	51	56	65	59
Luxembourg	27	24	36	40	48	46
France	75	77	82	79	85	78
Switzerland	35	34	33	38	38	34
Spain	50	31	45	48	45	44
Portugal	32	40	34	26	45	47
FRG	63	62	73	80	83	72
GDR	33	43	37	36	67	50
Poland	38	51	52	53	42	37
Austria	37	31	33	26	38	34
Hungary	37	40	47	47	41	36
CSSR	38	57	59	59	48	39
Italy	53	59	62	66	70	58
Malta	--	--	--	22	26	76
Yugoslavia	49	56	49	61	58	80
Greece	40	44	32	32	34	34
Cyprus	--	--	26	30	33	82
Bulgaria	28	42	45	50	47	38
Romania	25	37	39	59	55	44
USSR	70	86	81	86	79	76
Finland	19	19	21	31	31	40
Sweden	42	51	37	36	45	45
Norway	39	43	28	28	32	31
Denmark	35	44	30	36	51	49

Values were computed according to the following formula:

$$\text{Dispersion}_i = (\text{Links}_i/133)\ 100$$

For country *i*, the number of "links" with the rest of the world is computed and expressed as a percentage of the total possible "links" with all 133 other countries. A "link" is any interaction in the respective quinquennial period with one of the other 133 states in the system, as reported in COPDAB. If this interaction took place, a "link" between these two states is regarded as established and counts for the above computation.

Table 3.7. Summary List of Countries, by Direction of Change in the Dispersion of Their External Relations, 1950–1978

dispersion increasing (more independence)	dispersion decreasing (more dependency)	dispersion stable (change $\leq$ 5%)
Cyprus (+ 56%)	Norway (- 8%)	USA
Malta (+ 55%)	Spain (- 6%)	United Kingdom
Yugoslavia (+ 31%)	Greece (- 6%)	Italy
Canada (+ 29%)		France
Ireland (+ 22%)		Switzerland
Belgium (+ 19%)		Sweden
Luxembourg (+ 19%)		Austria
Romania (+ 19%)		Poland
GDR (+ 17%)		Hungary
Portugal (+ 15%)		CSSR
Denmark (+ 14%)		
Netherlands (+ 12%)		
Finland (+ 11%)		
Bulgaria (+ 10%)		
FRG (+ 9%)		
USSR (+ 6%)		

tries. The positions of Poland, Hungary, and the CSSR remained practically unchanged. The same must be said about NATO's medium-sized members (France, UK, and Italy). Generally speaking, some members of the Western alliances and some specific countries such as the GDR were able to profit most from the policy of "détente."

Yet it would be misleading to generalize the trend discerned in Table 3.6. A more refined analysis of Table 3.7 would yield findings that shed a light on the recent development of East-West relations: In most cases, the degree of dispersion of external interactions was growing up to the midseventies, reaching its climax in the 1970–1974 period. In the succeeding period, however, many countries experienced a decrease of dispersion, that is, the degree of independence was reduced again. This evolution is in accordance with many aspects of East-West relations, which, as it seems, were subject to a kind of trend reversal in the midseventies.

A second approach for measuring the degree of independence of the countries participating in CSCE negotiations more specifically looks at the relationship between each country and the respective major power (US or USSR) representing the leader of the "camp" or "block" the country belongs to. In other words, the question to be asked is, To what extent do the European countries orient themselves toward the respective "block" leader? And to what extent was there any change in this dependency structure? This question can easily be answered by calculating for each country the share of cooperative interaction exchanged with the respective "block" leader (as percentage of the total amount of external interactions of the country concerned). The calculations presented in Tables 3.8 and 3.9 again refer to COPDAB data.

The picture offered by these tables plainly indicates that in both East and West, all countries reduced their share of interaction exchanged with their respective "block" leader. There is not any single exception from this obvious trend. Some countries even reduced their "special relationship" with either the USA or the USSR quite drastically from 1950 to 1978: In 1950, Canada exchanged 29 percent of her interactions with her "giant neighbor"; yet by 1978, the corresponding figure had dropped to 11 percent. Considerable rates of reduction can also be observed in the cases of the Netherlands (from 12 percent to 4 percent), France (from 16 percent to 5 percent), the Federal Republic of Germany (from 16 percent to 7 percent) and Denmark (from 13 percent to 3 percent). Among the Socialist countries, the shift in emphasis devoted to relations with the USSR was high with regard to Hungary (from 16 percent to 10 percent), the GDR (from 16 percent to 9 percent), and Romania (from 12 percent to 8 percent).

Generally speaking, NATO countries reduced their relations with the USA to a larger extent than the WTO countries in their relations with the USSR. This difference in trend is indicated by the mean value that declined from 13 percent in 1950 to 6 percent

Table 3.8. Share of Cooperative Interactions Exchanged Between NATO Countries and the USA (Percentage of Sum Total of All Cooperative Interactions), 1950–1978*

country	period					
	1950-54	1955-59	1960-64	1965-69	1970-74	1975-78
Canada	29	23	13	11	6	11
Netherlands	12	4	4	2	3	4
Belgium	8	2	4	2	2	4
Luxembourg	3	1	1	-	1	2
France	16	11	10	3	4	5
Portugal	12	3	6	9	10	8
FRG	16	12	12	6	5	7
Greece	11	9	12	10	14	11
Norway	6	5	3	8	2	6
Denmark	13	4	5	4	2	3
mean	13	7	7	6	5	6

*Computed on the basis of COPDAB index values of cooperative interactions, aggregated for quinquennial periods.

Table 3.9. Share of Cooperative Interactions Exchanged Between WTO Countries and the USSR (Percentage of Sum Total of All Cooperative Interactions), 1950–1978*

country	period					
	1950-54	1955-59	1960-64	1965-69	1970-74	1975-78
Poland	13	18	8	12	9	10
Hungary	16	11	5	12	10	10
CSSR	10	7	8	16	11	10
Bulgaria	15	13	11	9	7	11
GDR	16	13	14	12	8	9
Romania	12	11	7	8	5	8
mean	14	12	9	12	8	10

*Computed on the basis of COPDAB index values of cooperative interactions, aggregated for quinquennial periods.

in 1978, that is, by more than half, in the case of the NATO countries, whereas the corresponding figures for WTO countries show a slightly less articulate trend (from 14 percent to 10 percent, that is, less than one-third). But in either "block," the degree of orientation toward the central "pole" has become markedly weaker in the course of "détente."

Additional insights can be obtained when looking more closely at the temporal sequence of this evolution. In this respect, three interesting observations can be made: First, the decisive shift in orientation did not occur in the years generally considered to constitute the culmination period of "détente" but prior to this period in the second half of the fifties in the case of NATO and in the early sixties in the case of WTO. In other words, it is not the policy of "détente" that triggered a mild process of "dissolution" of block structures and of emancipation from major-power leadership; this process seemed to occur independently from the policy of "détente." Yet, second, the culmination of the state of relative independence as measured by the degree of concentration of relations with the respective major-power partner was reached, in either alliance system, in the first half of the seventies. This coincides with the peak of "détente" according to the generally prevailing judgment offered in the context of contemporary history interpretations. Third, it cannot be denied that in the late seventies there seemed to be indications pointing at a certain trend reversal in both East and West. The relative importance of the two major powers seems to become revived to some extent. This finding also corroborates interpretations prevailing in current discussions about the renewed significance of alliance systems.

A corollary analysis is offered in Graphs 3.62 and 3.63 presenting the evolution of the percentage shares of interactions taking place within each "block" and between the "blocks," excluding the two "block" leaders in order to avoid distortions in the pattern. Obviously, no specific trend can be discerned. There is no long-term trend, within NATO, to decrease the share of intrablock contacts or to increase the share of cooperation with Socialist countries, nor is there any similar tendency on the part of the WTO countries. The two alliance systems, irrespective of the role of the "block" leaders, seem to constitute firmly established frames of reference of a very durable nature.

Yet it makes sense to interpret some of the oscillations of the curves by attributing them to the changing nature of East-West relations. As indicated in Graph 3.63, the WTO countries, in the early seventies, greatly increased their share of interactions with the West, and they obviously did so at the expense of intrablock interactions. This evolution seems to have given rise to the need for more coordination, thus leading to renewed efforts to intensify interactions within the Socialist "camp"; by 1974 the situation was brought back to normalcy, that is, to proportions customary prior to the take-off of "détente."

Graph 3.62. Cooperative Interactions of NATO Countries with "Camps" as Percentage of Total Cooperative Interactions of NATO Countries (Excluding the United States)

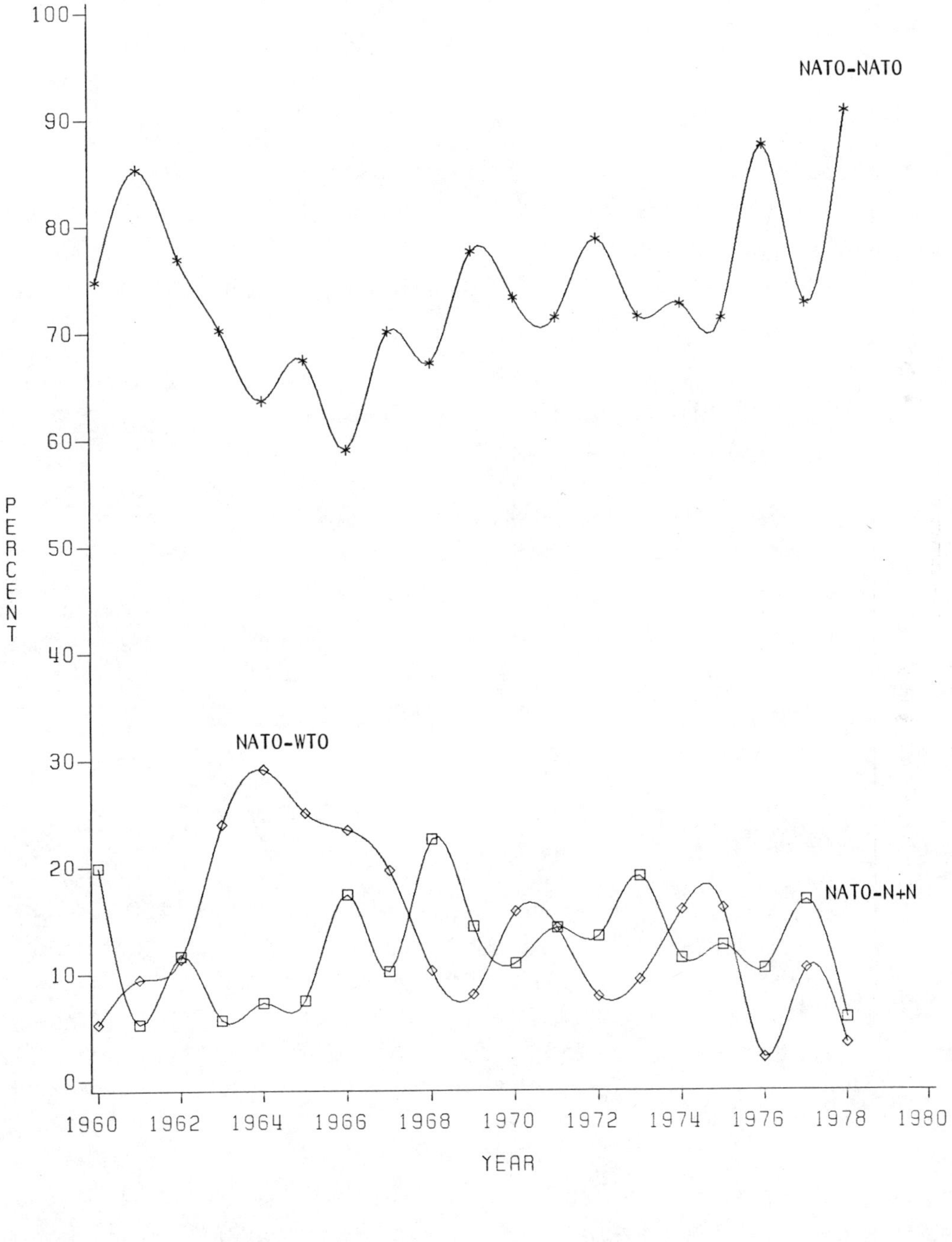

100
90
80
70
60
50
40
30
20
10
0
PERCENT
NATO-NATO
NATO-WTO
NATO-N+N
1960
1962
1964
1966
1968
1970
1972
1974
1976
1978
1980
YEAR

Graph 3.63. Cooperative Interactions of WTO Countries with "Camps" as Percentage of Total Cooperative Interactions of WTO Countries (Excluding the Soviet Union)

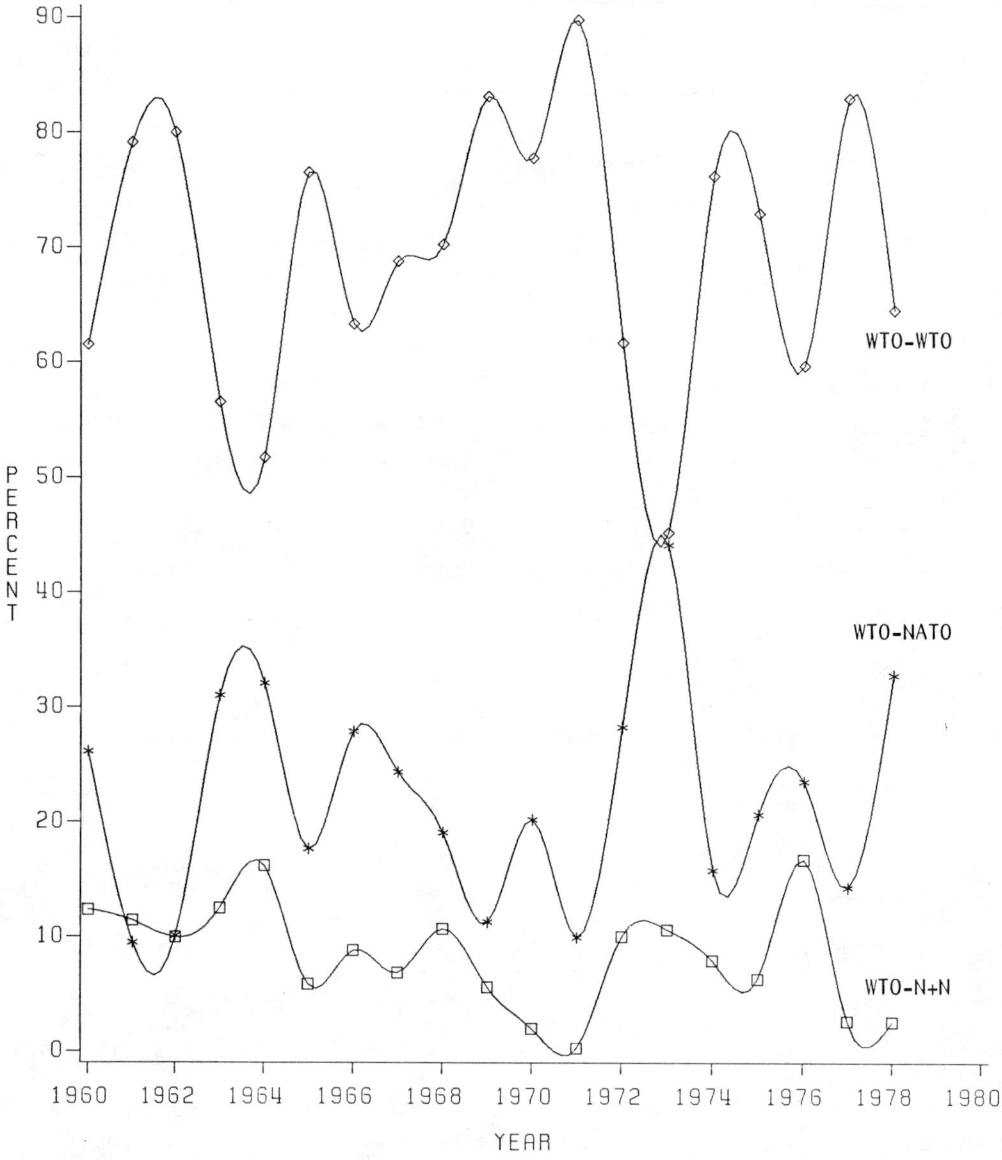

90
80
70
60
50
40
30
20
10
0
PERCENT
WTO-WTO
WTO-NATO
WTO-N+N
1960
1962
1964
1966
1968
1970
1972
1974
1976
1978
1980
YEAR

Chapter 4

A Comprehensive View of East–West Relations: Changing Perceptions and Changing Realities

4.1 INTRODUCTION: A DESCRIPTIVE ANALYSIS IN THE PERSPECTIVE OF SELECTED GROUPS OF COUNTRIES

In the preceding chapters, East–West relations in Europe were examined with regard to two aspects: In Chapter 2 the question was raised of how the thirty-five governments involved in the CSCE negotiations perceive East–West relations, what elements of East–West relations they consider to be relevant, and to what extent there are variations and changes in these perceptions. Chapter 3 presented insights into and evidence of the real developments as they can be observed by using hard (or as hard as possible) indicators and monitored by time-series data.

Now, in Chapter 4, an effort will be made to combine the two approaches by asking, What does the "reality" of East–West relations look like when perceived in the varying perspectives of the governments concerned? How much "détente" was there when evaluating East–West relations from the vantage point of different conceptions of "détente"? The reason for designing this combinatory view is obvious: Political relationships such as "détente" and tension are highly subjective and, by their very subjectivity, constitute a reality different from —and maybe more relevant than—the "reality" of international relations as presented by "plain facts" alone. In order to understand the dynamics of East-West relations, it is indispensable to take into account the subjective element of perceptions that sets the standards for the positive or negative evaluation of the "real" development in East-West relations.

The analysis is carried out by computing index values for each national perspective. Technically speaking, the individual national perceptions of what East–West relations mean are used as weights to determine the relative importance of the indicators included in the index. If a government thinks that armaments or disarmament constitute a major element of East–West relations, then armaments data, or military-budget data, and so on, will weight high, accordingly. If, however, a government thinks that the human-rights issue is a major element of East–West relations, indicators regarding the fulfilment of human rights or human contacts must be included. Based on the content analysis done previously, a subjective East–West index can now be calculated for each national perception individually. And, as there are five content analyses for each country (namely, for two Helsinki, two Belgrade, and the Madrid statements) it is possible to make use of five different sets of weight.

The East–West Index (EWI) is an index computed for each country or groups of countries on the basis of five indicators corresponding to the five master dimensions indentified previously (see Section 2.4.7); the indicators are weighted according to the share of attention they have been given by the heads of delegation in Helsinki, Belgrade, and Madrid. The values for each national perception are calculated according to the following formula:

$$\mathrm{EWI}_{ik} = x1_{ik} \cdot \mathrm{I1} + x2_{ik} \cdot \mathrm{I2} + x3_{ik} \cdot \mathrm{I3} + x4_{ik} \cdot \mathrm{I4} + x5_{ik} \cdot \mathrm{I5}$$

In the following analysis, EWI is the index, computed for $i = 3$ groups of countries (NATO, WTO, N + N) and $k = 5$ different views (Helsinki, Belgrade, and Madrid statements). The x terms are the weights, and the I terms are the indicators. The indicators are standardized to values ranging from 0 to 100. The sum of weights will always add up to 1.0; thus the index EWI will theoretically range from 0 to 100. In addition, the index is also calculated for the "objective" development of East–West relations with every weight equal to 20. The weights for the selected groups of countries (NATO, WTO, N + N) are identical to the mean percentages of attention shares on the five master dimensions of East–West relations (see Section 2.4.7).

The five master dimensions included into the index according to the perceptive weights are based on the type of measurement developed in Section 3. Peace and conflict is represented by the sum of American and Soviet cooperative interactions with each other minus the sum of conflictive interactions, assuming that for all groups of countries, the political climate between the major powers is of utmost importance. Economic cooperation is the sum of percentage shares of exports and imports as fractions of total exports and imports, respectively, for the trade between the EEC and the CMEA. Disarmament and security is measured in terms of NATO plus WTO military expenditure. As the choice of suitable indicators in the field of Human rights and human contacts is difficult and controversial, two solutions are presented. From the NATO perspective and the perspective of N + N countries, the situation with respect to political and civil rights in the WTO countries is the focus of interest; therefore this dimension is represented by the number of political sanctions. As in WTO perspective, the economic situation is of overriding concern, the mean rate of unemployment as percentage of the total labor force in Western and neutral countries was selected as an appropriate indicator.

Finally, sovereignty and independence is operationalized by calculating the fraction of cooperative interactions of WTO countries (excluding the Soviet Union) exchanged with NATO countries. The assumption underlying this particular operationalization is that for NATO countries as well as the neutral and nonaligned countries, the problem of independence and sovereignty of allies of the Soviet Union has been a major cause of concern, with the events of 1956 and 1968 in mind. It is no secret at all that sovereignty and independence in Socialist countries are limited by the common interest of the Socialist community, according to current political doctrine of the Soviet Union and her allies.

The values for all these indicators are standardized (by assigning the value of 0 to the minimum value observed and the value of 100 to the maximum value observed in the period 1960–1980). In the case of the Human Rights master dimension, the first index is the mean of five indicators using political sanctions as a measure for human rights, while the second index incorporates unemployment in NATO countries (see Table 4.1). Weighting the resulting index values with the percentages of attention computed in Chapter 2 yields time series representing individual perceptions of the performance of East-West relations according the views expressed at the CSCE meetings of Helsinki 1973, Helsinki 1975, Belgrade 1977–1978, and Madrid 1980.

4.2 EAST-WEST RELATIONS IN NATO PERSPECTIVES

Describing the evolution of East-West relations in terms of perceptions applied by NATO countries and expressed at the Helsinki, Belgrade, and Madrid CSCE meetings, yields quite suggestive results. In 1973 and 1975 the main emphasis was on disarmament and security (more than 30 percent), followed by a considerable share of attention devoted to peace and conflict (more than 20 percent), while economic cooperation attracted 16 and 18 percent, respectively, and the human-rights issue accounted for a share of

Table 4.1. Weights for the Computation of Curves Representing the Evolution of East–West Relations as Perceived by Three Groups of Countries.

					Human Rights		
		Disarmament/ Security	Peace/ Conflict	Economic Cooperation	(Political Sanctions)	(Unemploy- ment)	Sovereignty/ Independence
NATO	1973	.35	.24	.16	.13	---	.12
	1975	.31	.23	.18	.14	---	.14
	1977	.25	.21	.24	.23	---	.07
	1978	.22	.11	.24	.35	---	.08
	1980	.30	.15	.13	.29	---	.13
WTO	1973	.33	.28	.23	---	.06	.09
	1975	.27	.30	.23	---	.06	.14
	1977	.44	.13	.22	---	.09	.11
	1978	.45	.11	.25	---	.12	.07
	1980	.45	.22	.17	---	.08	.08
N+N	1973	.28	.30	.17	.08	---	.16
	1975	.18	.31	.22	.11	---	.16
	1977	.30	.19	.22	.15	---	.14
	1978	.24	.14	.28	.26	---	.08
	1980	.36	.27	.12	.13	---	.12

13 percent in 1973 and 14 percent in 1975, sovereignty for 12 percent in 1973 and 14 percent in 1975. According to what has been expressed at the 1977 Belgrade meeting, the fraction of attention devoted to the human-rights issue (at the expense of the disarmament question) meant a very significant change. Economic cooperation too attracted considerably more attention (24 percent), while sovereignty accounts for only-half of the percentage observed prior in 1975 (7 percent). In 1978 the importance of the human-rights issue (35 percent) was further emphasized, while the attention devoted to peace and conflict seems to have been declining. In the 1980 Madrid meeting, disarmament became the favorite focus of attention again (30 percent), nearly matched by human rights (29 percent). To what extent does this shifting perception make any difference when reporting the course of events in East-West relations in the two decades prior to 1980?

Graph 4.1 offers an answer to this question. Irrespective of the perception adopted, the evolution during the sixties is generally evaluated in a rather homogeneous way. The picture becomes different, however, in the seventies, depending on the perception and expectations the governments of NATO countries were starting from. If seen in the perspective adopted at the 1973 Helsinki meeting, the progress of "détente" appears to be rather modest; the respective curve constantly ranks lowest. The most optimist evaluation of the evolution of East-West relations, from the NATO point of view, is produced if one adopts the perspective expressed in the 1978 statements. The most recent evaluation (based on the perception expressed in the Madrid opening statements of 1980) again yields a rather pessimistic picture. Although the curves representing the evolution of East-West relations in terms of different perceptions constantly parallel to each other, one cannot fail to observe that the shifts in perception always also mean a radical shift in the evaluation of the reality perceived. Speaking in general terms, the NATO countries tended to underestimate the progress of "détente" when East-West relations were improving (1973-1975), and they tended to perceive the past in a more favorable perspective when there was a stagnation or even deterioration of current East-West relations (1977-1980), thus adding a kind of a "perceptive swing" to the real development.

Interestingly, according to NATO perception, considerable progress was achieved already in the 1963-1965 period, when interactions between East and West became more friendly. There was a first severe crisis of "détente" in the late sixties, reaching its low ebb in 1968, but thereafter, the curves indicate a straight improvement leading to the climax of East-West "détente" in 1973 which, in turn, was followed by another one in 1975. However, the development of East-West relations since 1976 resulted in a dramatic deterioration, leading to a level of "détente" similar to the one already reached prior to 1970, that is, before the beginning of

Graph 4.1. East-West Relations in NATO Perspective

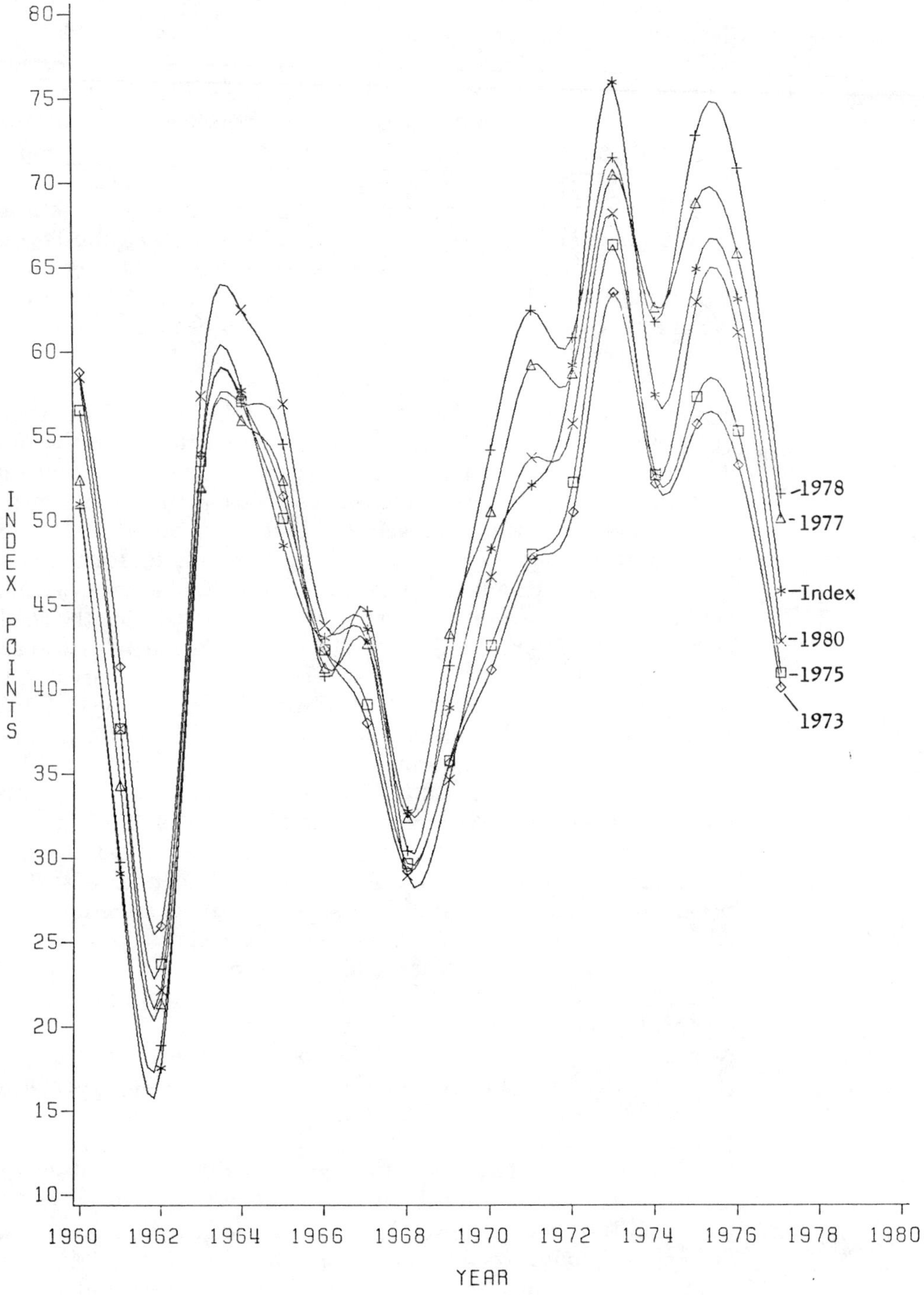
80
75
70
65
60
55
50
45
40
35
30
25
20
15
10
INDEX POINTS
1960
1962
1964
1966
1968
1970
1972
1974
1976
1978
1980
YEAR
1978
1977
Index
1980
1975
1973

the CSCE negotiation. Seen against this background, it is not surprising therefore, that some commentators believe that the world is facing a new cold war.

4.3 EAST–WEST RELATIONS IN WTO PERSPECTIVE

The attention profile prevailing in the perspectives adopted by WTO countries is determined by the importance of the disarmament-and-security issue that was given a share of 33 percent in 1973 and no less than 44 percent in 1980. Other salient issues, as seen in the WTO perspective, refer to peace and conflict and economic cooperation while human rights was never given much attention.

Comparing the evolution of East–West relations as perceived in the WTO perspective (Graph 4.2) with the results of the analysis carried out in the previous section points at two major differences. First, the variation among the five sets of perceptions is a little bit larger in the case of the WTO perceptions than in the case of the NATO perceptions. Second, and more important, the amplitudes of the ups and downs of East–West relations are decisively stronger in the case of WTO than in the case of NATO: The rise and fall of "détente," in the WTO perspective, is characterized by a process of mighty change and dramatic revulsion of the political climate.

Among the different views adopted by the WTO countries between 1973 and 1980, the perceptions expressed in the 1975 statements offer the most optimistic picture whereas the 1977, 1978, and 1980 perceptions suggest a much more sober evaluation of reality. As in the case of NATO, this may reflect a certain disappointment about evolutions that took place in this crucial period, and it seems that this attitude led to a kind of downgrading of both past experience and present reality.

It is also interesting to note that the governments of WTO countries evaluate the sixties in a similar way as do the governments of NATO countries, except for a more radical evaluation of the state of East–West relations in 1968/69. The climax of "détente," in this perspective, also took place in 1973, but the consecutive evolution, according to WTO perception, is characterized by a stupendous deterioration resulting in a state of affairs similar to the one experienced in the early sixties and at the time of the 1968 events in Czechoslovakia. Still, the index calculated for the most recent year included in this time series (1978) points at the possibility that the decline of "détente" has come to a halt.

4.4 EAST–WEST RELATIONS IN N+N PERSPECTIVE

The perceptions held by the governments of N + N countries lead to the conclusion that the latest perception (that is, the one ex-

Graph 4.2. East-West Relations in WTO Perspective

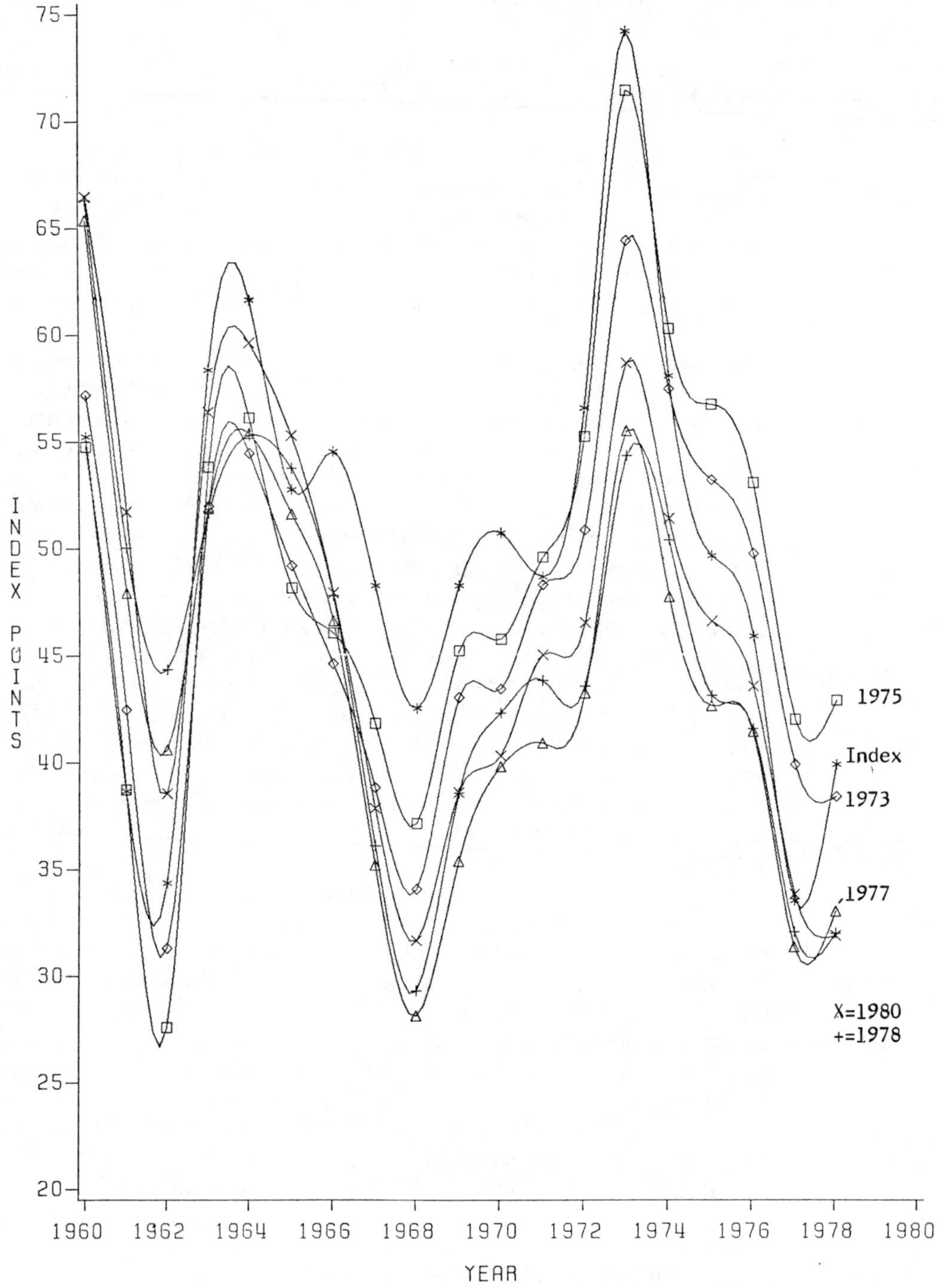
75
70
65
60
55
50
45
40
35
30
25
20
INDEX POINTS
1960 1962 1964 1966 1968 1970 1972 1974 1976 1978 1980
YEAR
1975
Index
1973
1977
X=1980
+=1978

Graph 4.3. East–West Relations in the Perspectives of Neutral and Nonaligned Countries

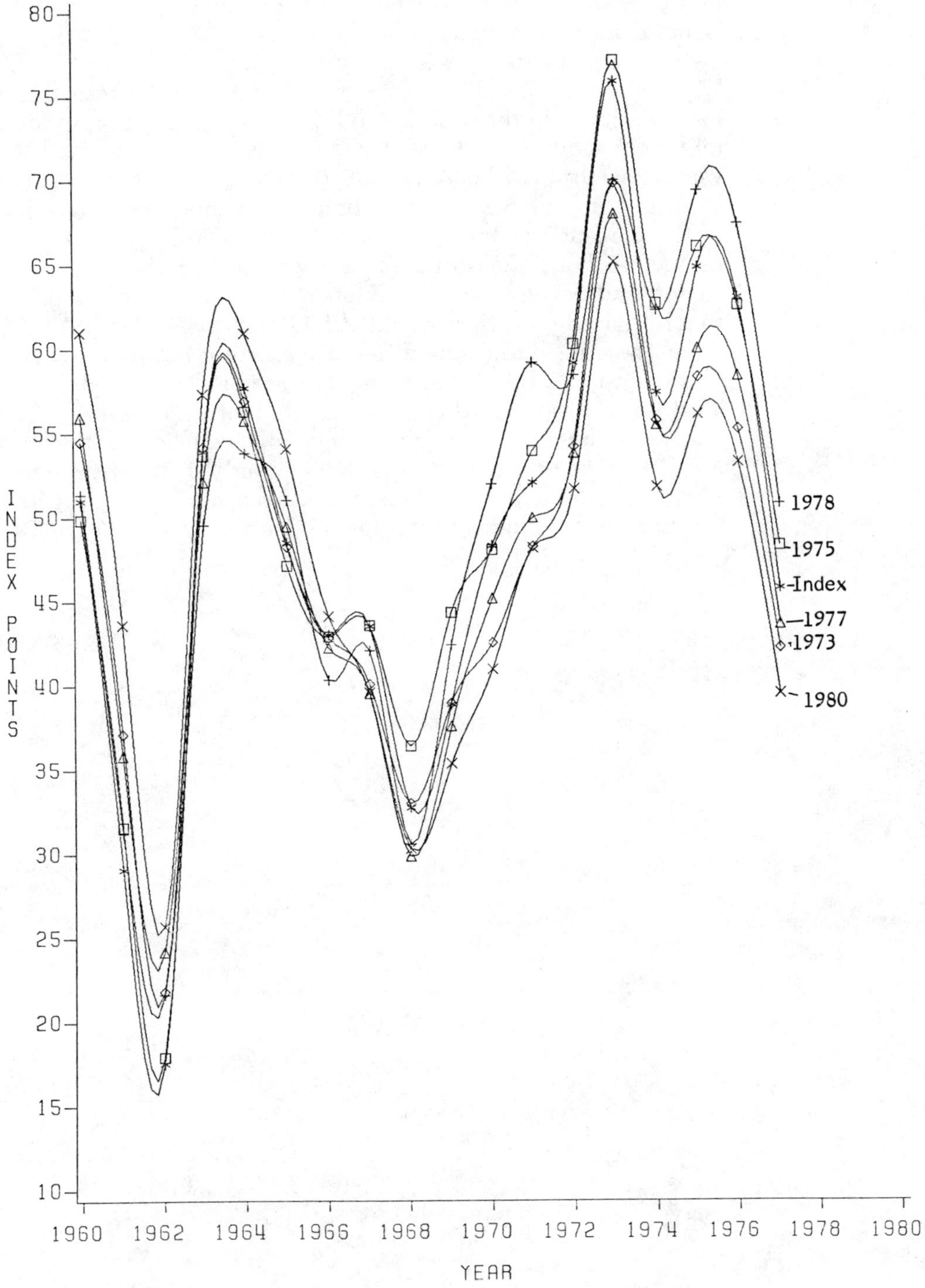
80
75
70
65
60
55
50
45
40
35
30
25
20
15
10
INDEX POINTS
1960
1962
1964
1966
1968
1970
1972
1974
1976
1978
1980
YEAR
1978
1975
Index
1977
1973
1980

pressed in 1980) yields the least favorable picture of East–West relations. The view adopted by N + N countries are heavily based on the issue of disarmament and security and peace and conflict, and only at the 1978 Belgrade meeting was emphasis put on the issue of human rights.

The shape of the curves offering a "pictorial history" of East–West relations based on these perceptions closely resembles the ones observed in the case of NATO countries. The amplitudes are relatively modest, and the decline of "détente" perceived in the years 1976 and 1977 does not go so far as perceived by WTO countries. In sum, the N + N perception hardly presents an alternative to the perceptions employed by NATO and WTO countries. With respect to both the shifts in perceptions and the evaluation of trends and developments in East–West relations, it appears to be roughly similar to the one identified with regard to NATO.

On the other hand, the difference existing between NATO perceptions and WTO perceptions must not be dramatized. East and West largely agree in their interpretation of the evolution of East–West relations. In particular, they fully coincide in their views about climax and low-ebb point. They only differ with regard to their judgment about the severity of the repeated crises of "détente," the East being slightly more pessimistic than the West.

Chapter 5

Reexamining Some Theoretical Assumptions about "Détente"

5.1 MAJOR THEORIES OF "DÉTENTE": A BRIEF INVENTORY

5.1.1 Introduction

Although the basic thrust of this study aims at description and not at explanation, the widespread and many-faceted discussion about the innerlogic of East–West relations and the premises and consequences of détente cannot be ignored. All statesmen involved in the diplomacy of East–West relations explicitly or implicitly start from, and act according to, theoretical assumptions, that is, assumsumptions of causal relationships between motives and East–West cooperation. And they also imply assumptions and expectations about the impact of specific policies chosen in the East–West context. It is also quite significant that the Helsinki Final Act itself presents assumptions of this kind, for example, in the introduction to the second "basket"; the text adopted in Helsinki presents the list of suggestions regarding cooperation with the following statement:

> The participating States, convinced that their efforts to develop cooperation in the field of economics, of science and technology and of the environment contribute to the reinforcement of peace and security in Europe and in the world as a whole....

In other words, it is assumed that cooperation in specific "non-political" fields will have a positive and beneficial impact on the state of East-West relations in the political sphere as well as on world peace in general.

Causal assumptions of this kind are even more often and more explicitly expressed by scholars studying the reasons and conditions conducive to or inhibiting the progress of East-West cooperation. There exists an ever-growing body of academic literature on the subject of East-West relations. A selected bibliography by Schwarz and Lutz (1980) lists about one thousand books and articles. Most of the literature, notwithstanding its enormous diversity, simply deals with the question of "Why détente?" or, in another version, "Why not more détente?".

It cannot be denied that the theoretical explanations offered by all these numerous studies do seem a little bit repetitive. As a matter of fact, the majority of these studies consider the same or similar "causes" of "détente," however, proposing different and sometimes contradicting hypotheses as to the meaning and relevance of these "causes." It may seem desirable and feasible therefore to sum up systematically the major theoretical assumptions about East-West relations as expressed by both diplomatic "practitioners" and academic students of East-West relations, in other words, to present a brief and structural inventory of the major theoretical propositions discussed so far.* This will be done in this chapter by distinguishing three groups of propositions that are of interest in this context: (1) hypotheses regarding international premises of political "détente," (2) hypotheses regarding domestic ("intrasystem") requirements of political "détente," and (3) hypotheses regarding the interrelations between political "détente" and East-West relations in other ("non-political") fields.

5.1.2 Propositions Regarding International Requirements of Political "Détente"

The overwhelming majority of theoretical contributions for understanding East-West relations explains "détente" as the result of the shifting balance of forces. This approach is dominant in the literature published in Socialist countries. The main hypothesis put forward by both official spokesmen and scholars in Socialist countries points at the ongoing change in the balance of force in favor of socialism on the global and European scale, which has led the Western countries to mitigate their "aggressive" policies directed against the Socialist countries and, in their view, thus

*The authors wish to express their gratitude to Professor Kjell Goldmann who in his important studies on this subject (Goldmann 1974, 1979, 1980) made pioneering contributions toward a systematic and intelligently compelling clarification of the various theoretical approaches. His contributions have been extremely crucial also for the present inventory of hypotheses, although this inventory uses a different rationale.

constitutes a necessary prerequisite of "détente" (Lebedev 1978, ch. II; Cherkasov and Proektor 1978, p. 307; Koloskov 1978, pp. 27 ff.; Pastusiak 1978; Müller and Neubert, and Pirsch 1980, p. 109; Friedliche Koexistenz in Europa 1977, pp. 59-69; Arbatow and Oltmans 1981, pp. 84 ff.). In this perspective, the balance of forces, or, in Soviet terminology, the change in the "correlation of forces" in favor of the East is the key variable. Some authors also suggest that this shift of power virtually forced the Western countries to adopt a policy of "détente" (Konfrontation, Entspannung, Zusammenarbeit 1979, p. 23). This first hypothesis can be represented and summarized by the following arrow diagram:

Hypothesis 1

change in the correlation of forces in favor of Socialist countries —+→ "détente"

This hypothesis can be specified depending on how the "correlation for forces" is conceptualized. Some authors tend to emphasize the military aspects; in their view, "détente" is the outcome of the Soviet Union and the Warsaw Treaty Organization countries catching up in the field of armament and military preparedness, in other words, the outcome of the shift in the strategic balance of power (Morawiecki 1977, p. 111). Other authors offer more comprehensive conceptualizations of "power" or "forces" envisaged by this hypothesis, and some also give suggestions regarding indicators suitable for measuring the "correlation of forces." A study published in the GDR (*Friedliche Koexistenz in Europa 1977, p. 65*) suggests index values for the production of electrical power, steel, and fertilizer. One Soviet author (Koloskov 1978, pp. 27–28) more amply proposes to take into account indicators such as size of territory, population, industrial production, industrial growth rates, and share of world industrial production. On the other hand, according to this view, deadlocks and setbacks of "détente" have to be attributed to attempts made on the part of the West to reverse the "historic dynamics of the change of the correlation of forces" (Samoschkin and Gantman 1980).

In discussions in the West, there is a corollary hypothesis to hypothesis 1. It basically confirms the propositions put forward by official spokesmen from Socialist countries, evaluating things quite differently, however. This is the so-called Finlandization hypothesis, which suggests that the Soviet build-up in the field of armaments does not aim at launching a war of aggression but rather aims at making war unnecessary by creating a power situation in which West European governments will deem it prudent to accept Soviet guidance (Luttwak 1979; Knight 1980). There are several variations of this Finlandization hypothesis. They may be summed up in two groups, the first group assuming that "Finlandization" of Western Europe by means of superior power has already become an established fact as in Finland, the second group assuming the Finlandization strategy as a great design underlying Soviet foreign policy but still having the logical status of wishful thinking.

Authors in Socialist countries do not expound, however, on whether the shift in the "correlation of forces" led to an overall equilibrium between East and West or whether it produced a net advantage in favor of the East. The concept of "parity" is rarely used, but it can at least be found in official Soviet statements that are explicitly addressed to a Western audience (Mateew 1981); there is no clear evidence as to its precise meaning in the context of Soviet political and strategic thinking (Wettig 1981, pp. 92–105).

Western authors tend to be more specific about this question. Jacobsen (1980, p. 80) and Link (1980, p. 151), for instance, propose that a power equilibrium and symmetry of parity are a necessary prerequisite for "détente" and for coexistence without resorting to military force. More specifically, other authors emphasize that without reaching approximate parity in strategic weapons with the United States, the Soviet Union would have been reluctant to accept any deals from a position of perceived inferiority (Simes 1980).

An empirical study by Goldmann [1974, ch. 5; see also Goldmann (1979, pp. 88–90)] tends to support this proposition:

Hypothesis 2

balance of military power $\xrightarrow{+}$ "détente"

Whereas in hypotheses 1 and 2 the balance or "correlation" of power has the weight of an independent, explanatory variable, one might ask on which additional variables in turn this variable will depend. Some of these variables explaining the balance of power will be dealt with in Section 5.1.3. (hypothesis 9); they belong to the domestic or intrasystems domain. However, some additional variables clearly refer to the intersystems level. One such variable is the political independence of the Third World, which, in a Socialist perspective, weakens the power of the West due to the loss of the colonies and thus strengthens the power of the East (Pastusiak 1978). According to this approach, this development is further promoted and strengthened by the increasing degree of solidarity among Third World countries in their struggle against "imperialism" (Kulish 1977):

Hypothesis 3

decolonization and Third World solidarity $\xrightarrow{+}$ shift in the correlation of forces in favor of Socialist countries $\xrightarrow{+}$ "détente"

On the other hand, many Western authors tend to identify the balance of military power as an exclusive matter of US-USSR relations. In their view, "détente" (or tension) on a global scale as well as on a European scale is affected and determined by US-USSR relations (Sonnenfeldt 1977/78; Ropers 1980b, p. 843); "détente" in Europe thus represents a mere function of major-power relations.

Hypothesis 4

US-USSR relations $\xrightarrow{+}$ East-West relations in Europe

In this view, the improvement of East-West relations in Europe during the period called "détente" can be attributed to a prior improvement of US-USSR relations. More specifically, the process of "détente" is closely tied to the benefits, both regional and global, that the superpowers expect to derive from it (Andrén, 1980, p. 90).

In this context, the question arises whether East-West confrontations outside Europe can affect "détente" in Europe. Some authors think they do. Bindschedler (1978) says that conflicts outside Europe inevitably increase the level of conflict in Europe too because European politics are part of global politics. Hart (1979) maintains that all extra-European conflicts tend to spread also to Europe. A conceptual framework is developed for the analysis of the spread of war.

Hypothesis 5

conflict outside Europe $\xrightarrow{-}$ "détente" in Europe

Other authors (Wiberg 1979) think, however, that events outside Europe and the Middle East area do not seem to affect tension and "détente" in Europe greatly.

A related line of arguments leads to the individuality thesis, which asserts that "détente" cannot and must not be divided geographically; if there is no "détente" in one region of the world, there will also be no "détente" in other parts of the world. A more general version of this hypothesis suggests an interrelationship between conflict or "détente" within Europe and conflict or "détente" outside Europe (Nastasescu 1980; Hoffmann 1981).

Hypothesis 5a

conflict/"détente" outside Europe $\xrightarrow{+}$ conflict/"détente" in Europe
conflict/"détente" outside Europe $\xleftarrow{+}$ conflict/"détente" in Europe

However, the opposite assumption can also claim a certain plausibility: According to this assumption, as the main protagonists become preoccupied with a crisis outside Europe, the pressure on Europe is relieved (Goldmann 1974, p. 96). Some authors more specifically argue that for the US, the Vietnam war was a crucial incentive to engage in a policy of "détente" in Europe, and similar arguments are put forward with reference to the USSR, which, according to this concept, had an interest in promoting "détente" in Europe in order to be able to spend more attention and resources to the growing conflict with China (Schissler 1980, p. 13).

Hypothesis 5b

conflict outside Europe $\xrightarrow{+}$ "détente" in Europe

Yet in an empirical study, Goldmann (1974, p. 93–96) found that any of these interpretations of internationl relations of the past three decades is going too far. Tension in Europe did not decrease because of crises elsewhere but rather in spite of them. Therefore hypotheses 5 and 5a, in a cautious interpretation, may be said to constitute a null hypothesis, that is, it may seem legitimate to propose that the two types of conflicts (or of "détente") tend to occur independently from each other.

In a more general version, the theoretical perspective envisaged by these hypotheses draws attention to the concept of bipolarity and bipolarization. As Goldmann (1974, pp. 114–118) points out, the scholarly literature on the effect of bipolarization upon tension and "détente" is quite controversial, and a systematic inventory of all possible relationships between two variables yields a set of (at least) six variations of the depolarization hypothesis (for further bibliographical reference, see Goldmann 1974, pp. 118–130).

Hypothesis 6 (a–f)

a. bipolarization $\xrightarrow{+}$ tension

b. bipolarization $\xrightarrow{-}$ tension

c. bipolarization $\xrightarrow{\circ}$ tension

d. bipolarization $\underset{+}{\overset{+}{\rightleftarrows}}$ tension

e. bipolarization $\underset{+}{\overset{-}{\rightleftarrows}}$ tension

f. bipolarization $\underset{+}{\overset{\circ}{\rightleftarrows}}$ tension

The empirical testing of these hypotheses leads to the conclusion that there exists in fact a negative correlation between European military bipolarization and tension according to variant 6b. In other words, the higher the degree of bipolarization, the more tension decreases (Goldmann 1974, pp. 159). A more refined interpretation of appropriate data may suggest that also variant 6e may offer a suitable explanation. According to this approach, tension is increased for some particular reason with bipolarization as a result; yet this does not lead to a further increase in tension but to a "détente," which brings about depolarization.

Finally, it is possible to develop a hypothesis focusing on the sequence of initiatives and responses made on the progress of "détente." The question is whether it might be possible to ascribe initiatives clearly to one particular side and to identify the other side as the responsive partner. Based on this idea, Schwarz (1979, p. 53) suggests that Western policy of "détente" is a function of Soviet initiatives:

Hypothesis 7

Soviet initiatives —+→ Western responses

In other words, the process of "détente" rather than being an outcome of "Ostpolitik" designed by Western governments constitutes a result of Soviet "Westpolitik."

A less specific version of the theoretical approach used in hypothesis 7 offers a more comprehensive look at the phenomenon of reciprocity and reactivity in general by assuming that political processes such as "détente" tend to have their own momentum and an inner logic. Starting from the spiral-process model discovered by students of arms races and conflict-escalation processes, theorists advocating this approach suggest that the process of *de*escalation follows a similar pattern. Therefore, the process of escalation could simply be converted in direction for the benefit of both opponents. If reciprocity leads to escalation, reciprocity must also promote deescalation. The idea of turning the escalation ladder upside down has been presented most comprehensively in the books and a series of articles by the American social psychologists Osgood (1962a, 1966, 1969) and Etzioni (1962). Both authors propose small conciliatory steps to be taken by one side and reciprocated by accommodative steps by the other side, to be followed by additional "rounds" of small-step conciliatory actions, thus building up mutual trust and opening prospects for a more effective overcoming of hostility and tension.

Hypothesis 8

small conciliatory action —+→ small conciliatory
of one side ←+— action of other side

Empirical examinations of the reciprocation hypothesis (Gamson and Modigliani 1971; Sullivan 1976, pp. 277–300) have shown that, in the relationship between the two major powers, refractory actions by one side have, for the most part, been met with belligerent reactions by the other side; on the other hand, conciliatory actions have been met by a high percentage of accommodative responses. Hence there is good reason to conclude that the basic assumption of the reciprocity-reactivity theory holds true (for a more ample discussion of this approach, see Frei 1980, pp. 18–26). It may even be assumed that cooperative moves tend to reinforce themselves; therefore, as one author assumes, the process of "détente" tends to become continuous (Haftendorn 1975, p. 231).

5.1.3 Intrasystems Requirements of Political "Détente"

Many authors focus on domestic (or internal or intrasystems) variables operating within the political, societal, and economic systems of the countries involved in the process of "détente." According to this second theoretical perspective, these intrasystems variables create a momentum of their own, producing an interest in peaceful coexistence and thus triggering the process of "détente."

The major theoretical thrust outlined in this context aims at supporting the "correlation of forces" hypothesis (see hypothesis 1) by additional domestic variables. The general hypothesis asserts that the "correlation of forces" has shifted in favor of socialism because intrasystematic problems and difficulties of all kinds weakened the Western countries and because, for systemic reasons, the overall military and economic strength grew faster in countries belonging to the Socialist system. Yet, the second part of the hypothesis is rarely explained in detail; authors in Socialist countries obviously tend to emphasize the first part of the hypothesis, stressing the importance of the domestic crises that trouble the capitalist nations, especially the United States (Arbatow and Oltmans 1981, p. 87).

Hypothesis 9

decline of capitalism	—+→	change in the correlation of forces in favor of socialism	—+→	"détente"

Most authors advocating this general hypothesis tend to elaborate it further by drawing attention either on additional variables that in turn cause capitalism to decline or on indicators suitable for measuring what is being meant by "decline of capitalism." Thus the major refinements added to this hypothesis point at (1) the decline of production in capitalists countries (to be measured by the number of unemployed); (2) the growth of class contradictions and class struggle (to be measured by the frequency of strikes); (3) governmental crises; and (4) the progress made by Communist parties and other left-wing forces in many capitalist countries (*Friedliche Koexistenz in Europa* 1977, pp. 69–71; Kulish 1977; Cherkasov and Proektor 1978, p. 309).

It is hardly surprising that Western authors do not always agree with this point of view. Some argue that domestic factors in fact do affect the government's willingness to engage in a policy of "détente"; but in their view the relationship is different: The weaker and the more unstable the domestic economy, the more there are political and social tensions that in turn make domestic policy a paramount preoccupation of the governments concerned, thus leaving little room and little incentive for a policy of "détente." In addition, Western authors argue that economic stagnation, instability and crises may also give rise to feelings of fear of becoming vulnerable to external influence. Governments struggling with problems of their countries' economy are afraid of becoming the object of exploitation by their external opponent who may be tempted to abuse the temporary weaknesses and dilemmas. On the other hand, it is proposed that a policy of "détente" in foreign affairs requires domestic stability both politically and economically.

Hypothesis 10

domestic stability (political, economic) $\xrightarrow{+}$ "détente"

Authors concentrating on this hypothesis (for example, Teunissen 1980, p. 21) wish to assert its validity for all countries independently of their political and social system. Other authors, even if they hesitate in making their theory as explicit and specific, at least agree that there are close causal relationships between the domestic social development and the development of East-West relations (Greven 1976, p. 282) in both Eastern and Western countries.

A different theoretical approach is presented by authors who perceive dire economic necessities to be the main motive of the decrease in tension and of the growth of cooperation. This assumption seems to be quite popular not only in scholarly literature but also in newspaper comments and political discussions about "détente." The approach is usually applied unilaterally with regard to the East although it would be feasible to develop a similar hypothesis with regard to the West too. The popular assumption, formulated as a hypothesis, asserts that "détente" is an outcome of the Soviet Union's and the other Socialist countries' desire to get access to Western products, especially Western technology and know-how (Bell 1977, p. 6; Thalheim 1980; Simes 1980).

Hypothesis 11

need of Socialist countries to import Western technology $\longrightarrow$ "détente"

Yet a critical examination of this hypothesis cannot ignore the relative unimportance of overall Soviet imports. Measured in terms of percentage of the gross national product (GNP), Soviet imports of Western technology account for 1.5 percent only (Stehr 1980,

p. 17); also in other Socialist countries the respective percentage figures are low (Bethkenhagen et al. 1980, p. 11). This proportion will hardly support the hypothesis that economic and technological necessities have become crucial factors in shaping the Soviet Union's conduct of external affairs.

5.1.4 The Consequences and Inner Logic of "Détente"

A large body of hypotheses is devoted to the consequences and the inner logic of "détente" referring to the impact political "détente" has on cooperation in other, "nonpolitical" fields and vice versa, and pointing also at the impact of "détente" on the political and economic state of affairs in various national and international contexts.

When in the late 1960s the process of "détente" began, many Western statesmen expressed the hope that the relaxation of tension between the two systems would have an impact on the political structures inside the two systems, especially on the Socialist system. The promoters of the new "Ostpolitik" in the West German Social-Democratic party coined the slogan of *"Wandel durch Annäherung"* ("change through rapprochement"), summing up the general hypothesis that an increase in East-West cooperation would lead to a certain liberalization inside the Socialist countries.

Hypothesis 12

"détente" $\xrightarrow{+}$ liberalization in Socialist countries

In the meantime grave doubts have been expressed by many scholars about the validity of this hypothesis (Schwarz 1979b, p. 278 and 295; Füllenbach and Schulz 1980, p. 359). Today certainly nobody would propose it with the same degree of emphasis as fifteen years ago. Yet in the discussions about "détente" it still persists, and it is appropriate therefore to mention it in the present context.

A similar hypothesis draws attention to the internal cohesion of the "blocks" in East and West. It argues that the more there is "détente," the more block cohesion will decrease.

Hypothesis 13

"détente" $\xrightarrow{+}$ decrease of block cohesion (politically and economically)

This hypothesis too seems to find no corroboration by the empirical facts. Independently, whether one looks at the alliance structure (Ropers 1977, p. 491 ff.; Schwarz 1979b, p. 295) or at the trade-flow structure within and between the two blocks (Greven 1976, p. 271 ff.), little or virtually no evidence can be discovered that would support the assumption expressed by this hypothesis. As Goldmann (1974, p. 159) indicates, if there is any relationship between tension and bipolarization (or "détente" and decrease of bipolarization) at all, this relationship is reverse, that is, the tighter the bipolarization, the higher the tension; when in a time-series analysis, bipolarization is lagged the relationship tends to disappear but not when tension is lagged.

A look at the empirical facts so far available may even suggest that the impact of intersystems "détente" on the structure within the system tends to be quite contrary to what has been assumed by the two hypotheses. Instead of promoting increased openness, permeability and liberalization, the growth of intersystems "détente" seems to have given rise to feelings of becoming destabilized. Particularly in Socialist countries the progress of international "détente" was followed by a tendency of the governments to accentuate political "delimitation" (*Abgrenzung*). The more intersystems cooperation grows, especially in the economic field, the more the wish for political "delimitation" becomes articulate and even predominant, thus signaling a certain critical boundary of the range of actions available to East–West cooperation and "détente" (Brock 1976, p. 213; Jacobsen 1976, p. 438).

Hypothesis 14

"détente" $\xrightarrow{+}$ "delimitation" (increasing impermeability of Socialist systems)

A related although eventually different line of arguments is proposed by authors (for example, Weltman 1979) who start from the assumptions expressed in hypothesis 11, tending, however, to put hypothesis 11 (need of Socialist countries to import Western technology as a prime motive for the policy of "détente" adopted by the East) in a different context. In their view, the motive underlying the policy of peaceful coexistence promoted by the Soviet Union and her allies, in fact, is the pressure for economic development calling for massive and continuous infusions of Western capital and expertise; a policy of accommodation with the West is seen as a necessary precondition for being able to benefit from such an infusion. Yet, in contrast to the plain assumptions underlying hypothesis 11, this policy is, in the last resort, not motivated by the willingness to improve the living conditions of Socialist economies; the ultimate aim of this policy is seen as part of a Soviet strategy to acquire new capabilities that directly affect the Soviet international power position and may be used later for promoting Soviet expansion. This in turn would almost certainly signal the end of "détente." In other words, "détente" is assumed to be self-destroying in the long run, and the policy of relaxation of tension adopted by the Socialist countries is interpreted as a mere tactical device for gaining a one-sided advantage. "Détente" thus appears to be a clearly transitory phase in intersystems relations.

Hypothesis 15

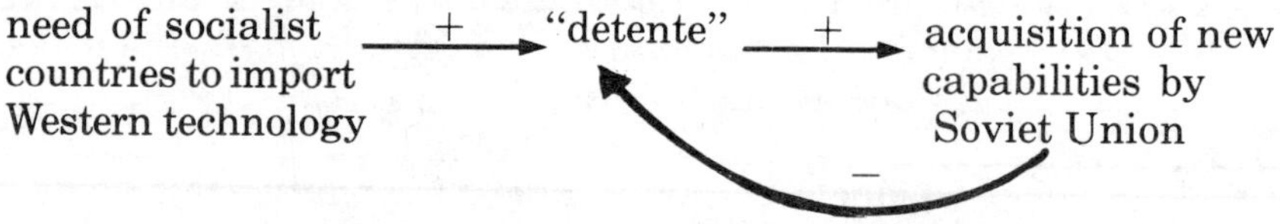
need of socialist countries to import Western technology
+
"détente"
+
acquisition of new capabilities by Soviet Union
–

Some authors starting from observations summed up in hypothesis 14 go even further and end up with a more general hypothesis suggesting a growth of follow-up problems caused by "détente"; the difficulties arising from these follow-up problems in turn would then backfire on "détente," thus slowing down and maybe also completely halting and renewing its progress (Jütte 1979, p. 156).

Hypothesis 16

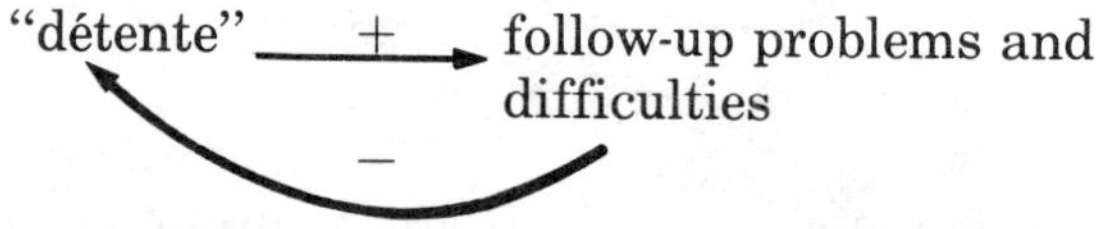
"détente"
+
follow-up problems and difficulties
–

More specifically, one might suggest the hypothesis that there is a negative-feedback process at work here (Goldmann 1981) because some of the expectations held in the first phase of "détente" were not fulfilled, and "détente" did not yield what some people had been hoping for. The level of expectations thus would constitute a crucial intervening variable explaining why the process of "détente" ultimately tends to destabilize and to reverse itself, thus constituting a process according to the general concept of the "law of rising expectations."

Hypothesis 16a

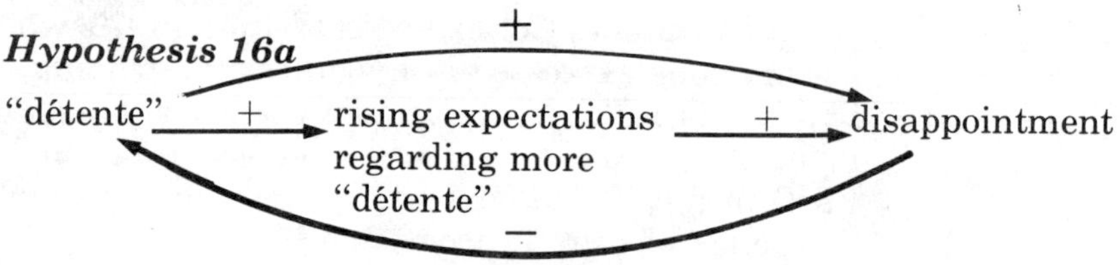
+
"détente"
+
rising expectations regarding more "détente"
+
disappointment
–

One follow-up problem arising out of the process of "détente" can be seen in the crisis behavior of the major powers in regions outside Europe. According to theories developed in Socialist countries, "détente" in Europe definitively does not mean giving up active support for national liberation movements (or what is being defined as "national liberation movements" by Soviet authorities) in the Third World. On the contrary, Soviet authors underline the fact that in their opinion, peaceful coexistence creates the most favorable conditions for accelerating the national liberalization struggle outside Europe (see Kipp 1978, p. 198; Müller, Neubert, and Pirsch 1980, p. 121). Thus the position held by authors in Socialist countries does not differ from the critical observations made by Western authors who claim that political, economic, and military activities of the Soviet Union and her allies in Africa, Asia, and Latin America amounts to an exploitation of favorable opportunities offered by "détente." Assuming that the more that an accommodation with the West required a low-key policy in Europe, the greater was the Soviet inclination to demonstrate advances in other areas of the world (Simes 1980), the hypothesis therefore links "détente" with crises in regions outside Europe.

Hypothesis 17

"détente" in Europe —+→ East-West confrontations and crises in the Third World

The only difference exists with regard to the type of "feedback" that might be expected from this fact: Whereas authors in Socialist countries usually do not comment on this question, Western authors tend to identify this fact as one of the major obstacles to the further progress of "détente" because, as they argue, "détente" has to be indivisible and because the confrontation and even escalation of a policy of confrontation outside Europe cannot go hand in hand with further steps of "détente" in Europe.

Hypothesis 17a

"détente" in Europe —+→ East-West confrontation and crises in the Third World
"détente" in Europe ←−— East-West confrontation and crises in the Third World

Another problem widely discussed in the literature about "détente" concerns the relationship between political "détente" and disarmament. It has been noted by many authors that the progress in political "détente" basically did not affect the ongoing arms race. This factual statement is hardly doubted by any author, and after all, it cannot be denied that neither in the West nor in the East the arsenals are growing and the amount of resources spent for military purposes are rapidly increasing everywhere, irrespective of the ups and downs of political "détente" (Ropers 1980b, p. 838; Väyrynen 1977a, p. 65). Yet there is disagreement about the meaning of this fact and about the consequences for the overall process of "détente."

Hypothesis 18

"détente" —+→ armaments

According to one hypothesis (18), "détente" leads straight to new and additional armaments. The rationale for this hypothesis is seen either in the need for a kind of power-political "reinsurance" in order to avoid risks that might loom in the process of "détente"; in other words, hypothesis 18 implies that the willingness of the parties concerned to agree on a policy of "détente" depends essentially on the availability of tension reescalation options. "Détente" will work only if the governments involved feel strong and confident enough and only if their security requirements are met by the possibility of escalating if necessary, in case of a failure of the efforts made with a view to a relaxation of tension (Kaltefleiter 1976). This assumption is sometimes called the "two-pillars theory" (Väyrynen 1977*a*, p. 65). Another line of reasoning justifying this hypothesis draws attention to the interest of the two major powers to maintain and to strengthen their leadership position in their respective alliances; therefore, the more "détente" grows, the more resources they will spend in the armaments sector for the sake of their position within each of the two blocks (Väyrynen 1977, p. 225).

Seen in this perspective, nonprogress in the field of disarmament and arms control would not affect progress in the field of political "détente"—and maybe it would, on the contrary, facilitate it. The "feedback" of the growth of armaments would therefore be either neutral or positive.

Hypothesis 19

"détente" $\xrightarrow{+}$ armaments

$\xleftarrow{0/+}$

Other authors, not surprisingly, stress exclusively the negative consequences of armaments in "détente." They are afraid that the lack of progress in military "détente" may have a harmful impact on the development of the "détente" process (Gantman 1977, p. 11; Dobrosielski 1977, p. 9); Arbatow and Oltmans 1981, p. 338).

Hypothesis 19a

"détente" $\xrightarrow{(+)}$ armaments

$\xleftarrow{-}$

Yet, as Goldmann (1979, pp. 88-90) points out, universal propositions of this kind are untenable because some arms are in some circumstances more destabilizing than others.

The opposite approach to the whole problem suggests that "détente" leads—or necessarily must lead—to disarmament, that tensions cause an acceleration of the arms race (Wiberg 1979). This constitutes the (negative) corrollary hypothesis to hypothesis 18, mentioned previously.

Hypothesis 18a

"détente" $\xrightarrow{-}$ armaments

tension $\xrightarrow{+}$ armaments

Yet in view of the disappointing developments in the field of disarmament, most authors are too cautious to propose this hypothesis in such a blunt form. A more refined version of hypothesis 18a says that "détente" is a necessary although not sufficient condition for disarmament and arms control (Väyrynen 1977, p. 225). Authors from Socialist countries tend to combine this hypothesis with hypothesis 19a: "Détente" in military affairs is not possible without political "détente"; however, political "détente" cannot be successful unless it is paralleled and supported by military "détente" (Jahn 1977a, p. 71). This type of conditional statement confirms Goldmann's argument that it is hardly useful to work with universal propositions linking together "détente" and disarmament in a simplistic fashion.

A considerable part of theoretical efforts made in view of explaining "détente" refers to the relationship between political "détente" and cooperation in other (sometimes called "nonpolitical") fields . Basically there are three possible ways of linking together these two groups of variables: A first version of the hypothesis proposes a spill-over effect of the "nonpolitical" cooperation on political "détente," thus triggering and surely also strengthening and promoting "détente." This approach has been widely maintained by the so-called functionalist and neofunctionalist schools of thought (see Frei 1980, pp. 13–18). The second version asserts the opposite relationship: Progress (or its contrary) in the field of political "détente" determines progress (or its contrary) in all other fields. The first version reflects what might be called the "liberal assumption" (Jodice and Taylor 1981; Weede 1981; Stehr 1980, p. 16 ff.; Czempiel et al. 1980, p. 46). It is also expressed in the preamble of the third "basket" of the Final Act, which declares:

> The participating States, Desiring to contribute to the strengthening of peace and understanding among peoples and to the spiritual enrichment of the human personality without distinction as to race, sex, language or religion; Conscious that increased cultural and educational exchange, broader dissemination of information, contacts between peoples, and the solution of humanitarian problems will contribute to the attainment of these aims....

The second version corresponds to the classical "mercantilist model" (Jodice and Taylor 1981), which assumes the primacy of politics over all other forms of intersocietal relations and according to which the political "climate" of "détente" would determine the size and growth of trade relations and cooperation in other "nonpolitical" fields (Link 1980, p. 196–199; Stankovsky 1980, p. 535; Baumer and Jacobsen 1980, p. 572; Schneider 1980, p. 205).

One author very aptly summed up the main perspectives used in this context by distinguishing what he calls the "cold war strategy" from the "détente strategy." The first strategy implies that the reduction of political conflict will lead to an increase of cooperation; the second strategy proposes that cooperation leads to a reduction of political conflict (Nygren and Lavery 1981, p. 2).

However, the literature also suggests a third version of the preceding hypothesis ascribing the relationship between cooperation and "détente" a "dialectic" nature, or, to put it more simply, proposing that there is an interactive relationship between the two variables. This version seems to be preferred by authors from Socialist countries (Hinkel and Nicolai 1978, p. 13; Friedliche Koexistenz in Europa 1977, p. 169; Spröte 1980). One of them (Kusnezow 1975, p. 51 ff.) laconically asserts: "Trade promotes peace—peace promotes trade." Other authors from Socialist countries seem to have an inclination toward the first version, or they point at the increasing "international division of labor" that would facilitate intersystems approximation and contribute to containing political confrontation (Cherkasov and Proektor 1978, p. 310; Lomejko 1980, p. 95). Furthermore, they suggest that the law of the "multiplier effect" is valid for intersystems cooperation as well as for intrasystems processes (Frei 1980, p. 14).

Summing up the concepts discussed so far, the three versions can be represented as follows:

Hypothesis 20

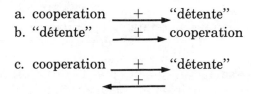

a. cooperation $\xrightarrow{+}$ "détente"

b. "détente" $\xrightarrow{+}$ cooperation

c. cooperation $\underset{+}{\overset{+}{\rightleftarrows}}$ "détente"

Although these three versions are quite encompassing and exhaustive, some authors still prefer to conceptualize the relationship between the two variables in a less simplistic and more refined, that is, conditional form. Hinkel and Nicolai (1978, p. 13) start from the "dialectic" assumption expressed by hypothesis 20c but add that in the whole complex interplay, of all variables, in the long run, the political factors are of overriding importance. Others (for example, Dobroczynski 1980, p. 117) think that cooperation is a necessary but not sufficient condition for "détente"; this statement constitutes a specification of hypothesis 20a (see also von Bredow 1979, p. 174). Western authors generallly assume that although, according to hypothesis 20b, political developments basically determine cooperation, the latter cannot be explained completely by political factors because it has its own momentum and furthermore depends on additional factors outside the field of politics such as the general level of economic well-being (Link 1980, p. 195; Knirsch 1980, p. 667). The motives shaping cooperation in the field of trade and other fields may also be independent from political motives (Jahn 1977, p. 186).

There is no need to rely on the degree of plausibility only inherent to each of the three versions of this hypothesis. At least as far as the field of East–West trade relations is concerned, ample empirical evidence offers an opportunity to draw more solid conclusions. Jodice and Taylor (1981), testing the "mercantilist," hypothesis, conclude that the process of "détente" has not fundamentally altered the patterns of intra- and interbloc trade; similar results are reported by Weede (1981) and Thalheim (1980). However, confronting empirical results for the hypotheses 20a and 20b, the general conclusion is that "détente" and tension is more suitable for explaining cooperation than vice versa (Goldmann 1980, p. 44); there seems to be a large concensus that hypothesis 20a is untenable (von Bredow 1979, p. 167 ff.) and that a simplistic projection of "functionalist" paradigms makes no sense in the context of contemporary East-West relations (see Frei 1980, p. 14 ff.). Similar findings are reported about the impact of cultural relations and tourism on political "détente" (Ropers 1980a, p. 703). Looking at interactions more comprehensively and generally, Nygren and Lavery 1981, pp. 20-32) found out that in American-Soviet relations conflict-solving interaction or a policy of "détente" usually precedes cooperation-creating interaction, whereas in Soviet-French relations, the two types of interaction occurred relatively independently of each other (Nygren and Lavery 1981, p. 36). Examining the relationship between state interaction, that is, intergovernmental acts and gestures, and societal interaction such as trade flows Nygren and Lavery (1981, p. 54) also confirmed that business relations were initiated mainly as a result of conflict-solving interaction and the withdrawal of export restrictions.

The controversial nature of the relationship expressed by the three versions of hypothesis 20 gave incentives to develop more complex lines of reasoning. Perhaps some of them are more appropriate to cope with the ambivalent character of the impact trade relations have on political "détente." One such line of reasoning suggests that increasing interactions in the field of trade may give rise to feelings of dependency and threat perceptions and thus have a negative impact on the further development of political "détente" (Jacobsen 1976, p. 417 and 438; Burzig 1977, p. 215). Why does economic cooperation have such an impact under some circumstances but not under other circumstances? Clearly, there must be an intervening variable affecting the positive or negative nature of the outcome. This variable is probably symmetry-asymmetry (Frei 1980, pp. 15-18). If economic cooperation grows symmetrically, no one has to be afraid of being exploited or threatened by increasing dependence; in this case there is true interdependence (Jütte 1979, p. 159), which in turn promotes mutual confidence. However, if it leads to an asymmetric structure, the result is different and fosters the inclination to safeguard one's position by military means (Burzig 1977, p. 215), that is, by compensating asymmetry and economic weakness by additional efforts in the field of armaments and military preparedness and by emphasizing political differences through a policy of "delimitation" (Jacobsen 1976, p. 438). The symmetry/asymmetry hypothesis, even if justified by different causal chains, seems to be widely accepted (Wiberg 1979).

Hypothesis 21

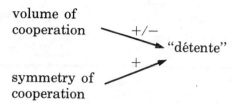

volume of cooperation —(+/−)→ "détente"

symmetry of cooperation —(+)→ "détente"

Therefore, in order to link cooperation to the progress or stagnation of "détente," it is necessary to consider both volume and symmetry -asymmetry of cooperation.

In a more general perspective, the theoretical ideas expressed in hypotheses 18–21 may be summed up as a kind of balance-imbalance problem inherent to all forms of social interaction. This problem has been amply and thoroughly studied in the field of integration theory (see Frei 1980, pp. 9–13). Its principal hypothesis is basically that progress in a set of social interaction cannot be achieved or will be doomed to a deadlock if progress of interaction is not taking place on several dimensions simultaneously. Applied to the current problem of East-West relations, this abstract concept would mean that "détente" progresses if and only if all dimensions (or all "baskets") are developed simultaneouosly. Imbalance, on the other hand, leads to a crisis of "détente."

Hypothesis 22

balance of progress in different fields —(+)→ "détente"

"Détente," in other words, would be indivisible not only with regard to its global scope but also with reference to the various subject matters that constitute fields of interest in East-West relations. Limited "détente," on the other hand, would in the long run hardly have any prospects for success because "détente" involves a unity of various aspects.

This hypothesis is often further elaborated with special attention to the imbalance between "political détente" and progress in the field of disarmament. The proposition suggests that the continuation of the arms race finally jeopardizes "détente" although substantial progress is being made in the political field and in improving the general atmosphere between East and West (Arbatow and Oltmans 1981, p. 338). The imbalance hypothesis thus constitutes a more general version of what has been mentioned in the context of hypothesis 20a.

5.2 TESTING SOME THEORIES

5.2.1 Introduction

Developing theories about the causes and consequences of "détente" is one matter; it is quite another to find out which of these theories are true and which are not. Some of the hypotheses reported in Section 5.1 have been subject to rigorous empirical testing by other authors; yet the empirical knowledge available so far is limited to a small fraction of these hypotheses. This study does not and cannot aim at giving ample and complete empirical evidence for the great number of remaining hypotheses.

However, as it presents a data base for monitoring the development of East–West relations, it may seem suitable for testing at least some of the hypotheses discussed so far. It may therefore be worthwhile to make an empirical contribution to the further understanding of the inner logic of "détente". This will be done here in using the data gathered in this study* and to calculate Pearson's product-moment correlation coefficients for various pairs of time-series variables covering the periods 1960–1980. The authors are well aware of the fact that this type of analysis does not provide more than quite limited results, the main reason being that correlation coefficients (if significant at all) do not necessarily reflect functional relationships or even causality. Whether the empirical regularities identified by correlation analysis are to be considered as meaningful, trivial, or even spurious remains a matter of theoretical interpretation.**

5.2.2 Empirical Evidence Regarding International Requirements of "Détente"

According to hypotheses 1 and 2 outlined in Section 5.1.2, the progress of "détente" is to a large extent determined by the military balance or imbalance between the two major powers. These hypotheses can be easily tested by correlating the behavior of the USA and the USSR with various indicators for military strength. The results of this computation are presented in Table 5.1.

Looking first at the determinants of US cooperative behavior, it can easily be seen that the inclination of the United States to

*For the sources, see Table 3.1; for a detailed description, see Chapter 3.

**For several reasons more technical in nature, no multivariate analysis (partial correlations, multiple regression, or path analysis, to mention a few) was applied to the data. With $N = 21$ only (in the case of missing data and lagged variables again smaller), the ratio of *data points* available for estimating statistical parameters (e.g., beta values) to *model variables* becomes increasingly unfavorable in complex models. Most hypotheses tested in this section are only bivariate, anyway. Since the task of this study was not theory-building, the computation of Pearson's product-moment correlation coefficients should suffice. In contrast to multivariate analyses, an obvious advantage of correlation coefficients is easy comprehension for those readers not familiar with statistical techniques.

Table 5.1. Relationship Between US and USSR Behavior and Various Indicators of Military Strength

	US behavior		USSR behavior	
number of	cooperative	conflictive	cooperative	conflictive
US bombers	-.38	-.03	-.10	.50
USSR bombers	.47*	-.21	.42*	-.32
US submarines	.40*	-.28	.20	-.52*
USSR submarines	.41*	.01	.30	-.46*
US SLBMs	.46*	-.28	.20	-.52*
USSR SLBMs	.46*	.05	.32	-.44*
US ICBMs	.38	-.32	.22	-.50*
USSR ICBMs	.54**	-.14	.14	-.60*
US delivery systems	.34	-.34	.21	-.45*
USSR delivery systems	.54**	-.08	.21	-.57**
US warheads	.46*	-.08	.29	-.48*
USSR warheads	.38	.13	.32	-.44
US military expenditure	:09	-.09	-.14	-.06
USSR military expenditure	.54**	-.09	.27	-.54

In all the following tables, the significance levels of correlation coefficients are indicated by asterisks. Correlation coefficients are a measure of the quality of a relationship between two variables according to regularities in the respective data. Correlation coefficients are defined for values between −1 and +1, whereby −1 would indicate a strong reciprocal relation and +1 a strong proportional relation. Values around zero indicate the absence of any regular pattern in the data. The significance of a correlation coefficient refers to the probability that the observed empirical regularities do in fact represent characteristics of the data and not merely incidental results of the sampling procedure, that is, the collection of data. The concept of statistical significance is based on assumptions originating in the theory of probabilities. Very briefly, the idea is that with more or other data (for example, data collected for monthly instead of yearly time points in the case of this study) there is a chance that the results could change more or less. A significance level of 1 percent (two asterisks) indicates that the observed regularities have only a 1-percent probability of being merely results of the sampling procedure (or, that they could be reproduced using additional or different data with a chance of 99 percent); a significance level of 5 percent would guarantee the reproduction of similar results with a mere 95-percent probability, respectively (one asterisk).

cooperate is positively and significantly related with the number of ICBMs and delivery systems acquired by their Soviet opponents. It is also related with the USSR military expenditures. The respective correlation coefficents are mostly near .5, which means that the relationships between the variables observed are moderately strong. This finding seems to support the theory put forward by authors from Socialist countries who suggest that it is the newly acquired strength of the "Socialist camp" that forces the West to adopt a moderate and cooperative position.

This hypothesis is further corroborated by the coefficients computed by correlating US/USSR ratios with US cooperative behavior (Table 5.2). The coefficient obtained for the US-USSR ratio of nuclear delivery systems is negative (−.48), that is, the less favorable the ratio for the US is, the more cooperatively the US behaves.

The "correlation-of-forces" hypothesis may also be supported by the fact that all correlation coefficients are higher for US cooperative behavior than for Soviet cooperative behavior. In other words, whether the USSR is more or less willing to cooperate is not to the same extent determined by the power relationship as is the case for US cooperative behavior.

When looking at the conflictive behavior, however, the picture becomes somewhat different. On the American side, the correlation coefficients are generally low and often close to zero; there is a weak or zero relationship therefore between armaments and US cooperative behavior. On the other hand, the Soviet conflictive behavior is associated with the armament dynamics, as the correlation coefficients (most of them in the .45 to .60 region) indicate. The more armaments, the less conflictive Soviet behavior becomes. The results obtained for the ratios (Table 5.2) emphasize these findings. Here, rather high positive correlations (.63 and .5), all of them significant, were found. The more the power ratios are in favor of the US, the more conflictive the USSR behave, or, to put it negatively, according to the logic of the historical trend that exhibits an overall decline of the ratio and favors the USSR: The

Table 5.2. Relationship Between US and USSR Behavior and Military Ratios

ratio US/USSR for	US behavior		USSR behavior	
	cooperative	conflictive	cooperative	conflictive
delivery systems	-.48*	.08	-.07	.63**
warheads	-.32	-.12	-.04	.50*
defense expenditure	-.48	.08	-.35	.48
ICBMs	-.39*	.16	.08	.75**

less the power relations favor the US, the less the USSR behaves in a conflictive way.

What do these findings mean when trying to draw general conclusions against the background of the theories outlined in Section 5.1.2? Two conclusions suggest themselves: First, the same alteration in power relationship affects the US and the USSR differently. "Détente," on the US part, obviously means more cooperation and less change in the level of conflictive behavior, whereas for the USSR, "détente" means a decrease in conflictivity without spectacular changes in the level of cooperation. This general feature has already been taken note of in the descriptive analysis presented in Chapter 3 (Section 3.3). It can now be confirmed again in the context of the present analysis.

Second, it cannot be denied that the progress of "détente" goes hand in hand with a relative decline in US power. The "correlation-of-forces" hypothesis thus seems to contain a grain of truth—and maybe even more than just a grain.... On the other hand, the same findings may of course also be used for supporting the balance-of-power hypothesis 2, suggesting that an equilibrium or parity of power is a necessary prerequisite for "détente." As the power ratios were moving from a state of affairs favoring the US (with a ratio of more than 5:1 in 1962) to ratios around 1:1 in 1980, that is, to a state of equality, the progress of "détente" can also be attributed to the steady shift of the power ratio toward the point of equality. The question of whether the correlation-of-force hypothesis or the power-parity hypothesis finally comes out to be more solidly founded could only be settled if there were empirical evidence for a complete reversal of the power ratio beyond the point of parity toward Soviet superiority. (In that hypothetical situation, there must either be an extremely high degree of "détente" forced on the West, according to the correlation-of-forces hypothesis, or again a high degree of conflict, according to the power-parity hypothesis.)

Another problem regarding the international requirements of East–West relations concerns the question of to what extent the relationship of the two major powers determines the rest of East–West relations, particularly between the less powerful European countries. As pointed out in hypothesis 4, some authors seem to assume that "détente" in Europe entirely depends on the state of major-power relations. This hypothesis can be examined by correlating US viz. USSR behavior (both cooperative and conflictive) with the relations between some selected West European countries and the USSR (Table 5.3); a more refined analysis correlates the relations *between* selected countries in East and West Europe with the relations between the two major powers (Table 5.4). These correlations are also calculated for time-lagged data.

If hypothesis 4 were true, the growth of cooperation and the decrease of conflictivity between the two major powers would precede the corresponding development in the relations between other

Table 5.3. Relationship Between US and USSR Behavior (Time-lagged) and Behavior of Selected West European Countries and the USSR

	US behavior directed to USSR								USSR behavior directed to USA							
	cooperative				conflictive				cooperative				conflictive			
time lags	t	t-1	t-2	t-3	t	t-1	t-2	t-3	t	t-1	t-2	t-3	t	t-1	t-2	t-3
cooperation between:																
UK and USSR	-.08	-.48*	-.15	-.42*	.03	-.05	.36	.16	.12	-.14	.09	-.16	.18	.31	.62**	.24
USSR and UK	.05	-.13	.22	.22	.16	-.28	-.11	-.18	.59**	.11	.02	-.20	-.04	-.14	-.04	-.24
France and USSR	.47*	-.07	.17	-.36	-.17	-.38	-.17	-.07	.21	-.32	.54*	-.13	-.22	-.24	-.04	-.01
USSR and France	.38	-.12	.23	-.15	-.12	-.26	-.38	-.45*	.39*	-.28	.43	-.11	.02	-.09	-.27	-.26
FRG and USSR	.68**	.28	.31	-.06	-.05	-.31	-.02	.02	-.02	-.06	.25	-.12	-.46*	-.36	-.09	-.21
USSR and FRG	.51*	.04	.51*	.13	-.05	-.42*	-.00	-.11	.36	-.23	.09	-.19	-.32	-.36	-.24	-.23
conflict between:																
UK and USSR	-.27	-.44*	-.58**	-.37	.53**	.35	.22	.17	-.08	-.31	-.15	-.19	.70**	.15	.56**	.31
USSR and UK	-.11	-.05	-.07	-.36	.27	-.18	-.34	-.21	-.18	-.31	-.11	-.07	-.14	-.18	-.28	-.11
France and USSR	-.00	-.35	-.37	-.01	.61**	.18	-.21	-.36	-.01	-.39	.08	-.29	.40*	.05	.07	-.34
USSR and France	-.18	-.32	-.36	.52*	.53**	.22	-.03	-.04	-.23	-.35	-.49*	.01	.39	.01	.03	-.30
FRG and USSR	-.18	-.31	-.58**	-.62**	.42*	.40	.17	.06	-.23	-.28	-.20	.02	.71**	.36	.27	.36
USSR and FRG	-.37	-.52*	-.52*	-.51*	.27	.17	.06	-.07	-.18	-.33	-.11	.22	.58**	.27	.48*	.36

Table 5.4. Relationship Between US and USSR Behavior (Time-lagged) and Behavior Between Selected Countries in East and West Europe

	US behavior directed to USSR								USSR behavior directed to USA							
	cooperative				conflictive				cooperative				conflictive			
time lags	t	t-1	t-2	t-3	t	t-1	t-2	t-3	t	t-1	t-2	t-3	t	t-1	t-2	t-3
cooperation between:																
FRG and GDR	.59**	.72**	.41	.38	-.13	-.26	-.33	-.04	.04	.31	.19	.06	-.53**	-.53*	-.47*	-.36
GDR and FRG	.51*	.45*	.18	.32	.09	-.28	-.40	-.15	.01	.14	-.06	-.04	-.34	-.49*	-.48*	-.37
France and GDR	.45*	-.00	.20	.02	.06	-.34	.03	.24	-.09	-.07	.15	-.32	-.33	-.26	-.12	.03
GDR and France	-.49	.06	.46*	.35	-.10	-.46*	-.06	.47*	.08	-.16	.47*	-.16	-.22	-.31	-.21	.09
FRG and Poland	.38	.23	.34	.27	-.25	-.49*	-.16	.14	.05	-.06	.04	.19	-.36	-.29	-.34	-.08
Poland and FRG	.47*	.11	.08	-.02	-.12	-.43*	-.01	.17	.02	.07	.13	-.16	-.30	-.26	-.13	-.04
conflict between:																
FRG and GDR	-.30	-.20	-.43*	-.04	.45*	.11	-.25	.06	-.10	-.20	-.10	.24	.72**	.01	.01	.46*
GDR and FRG	-.13	-.18	-.52*	-.07	.49*	.07	-.31	-.11	-.27	-.09	-.35	.07	.41*	.02	-.04	.14
France and GDR	-.16	-.39	-.31	-.27	.28	-.12	-.21	-.20	-.10	-.22	-.00	.14	.18	.08	.01	.01
GDR and France	-.11	-.14	-.44*	-.33	.48*	.51*	.19	-.01	-.15	-.15	-.40	-.05	.86**	.26	.18	.03
FRG and Poland	.12	.23	.00	-.10	-.27	-.05	.15	-.13	-.25	-.27	-.38	.53*	-.25	-.08	-.08	-.08
Poland and FRG	-.13	-.45*	-.46*	-.38	.33	.15	.12	-.13	-.19	-.40*	-.07	.22	.40*	.08	.55*	.13

European countries and the major power of the opposite camp. As a result of such a hypothetical sequence, the correlation coefficient for time-lagged data would be higher than the correlation coefficients obtained for time *t*. However, as can be seen in Table 5.3, this is generally not the case. Although in some instances high correlations for time-lagged relationships seem to indicate a lead of major-power "détente," it is hard to find a general trend that would support the hypothesis.

Yet some precautions suggest themselves: It is obvious that the relationship between conflictive policies is stronger than the relationship between cooperative policies. In other words, if "détente" between the two major powers makes progress, it does not necessarily imply a systematic, homogeneous increase of cooperation, simultaneous or time-lagged, between the other Western countries and the USSR. However, any escalation of conflictivity between the two major powers is immediately (that is, at time *t*) followed by a corresponding increase of conflict between West European countries and the USSR. Western solidarity, in other words, works better in situations facing conflict than in periods of "détente."

When analyzing these data, one has to bear in mind that they are aggregated on an annual basis only. Thus when speaking about "simultaneous" developments, one does not exclude the possibility of certain temporal sequences of causes and events as suggested by hypothesis 4, provided such sequences take place at a much more accelerated rhythm, that is, in a way observable only by looking at data aggregated on a monthly or even weekly basis. Any statements made about problems of time lags and leads, therefore, refer to what can be observed on the basis of annual data only; a more detailed analysis would be required for definitively confirming or disconfirming the hypothesis.

Whereas Table 5.3 looks at the relationships between selected medium-sized Western countries and major-power "détente," Table 5.4 carries the analysis one step further by correlating the relations between selected pairs of nonmajor powers in East and West with major-power relations. Again it is hard to find any general trend that would confirm hypothesis 4. It is interesting to note, however, that FRG–GDR relations are much closer connected with major-power relations than the relations between other East–West pairs of nations. This is not surprising since the "German question" and the delicate relationship between the two German states constitute an important and sensitive focus and testing ground for major-power rivalry and "détente." Some strata in West German public opinion wish to see the Federal Republic of Germany develop a special relationship with the German Democratic Republic and decoupling this relationship from the rest of the world; this wish obviously does not reflect reality, but it can be easily understood as a natural (although, as the data suggest, not very realistic) reaction to the uneasy feelings raised by the awareness of being dependent on the whims of major-power relations. Again high and significant correlations are more often found for relations at time *t* and rarely for relations between time-lagged data. Again therefore the original hypothesis 4 cannot be confirmed.

Hypothesis 5 asserts a causal relationship between conflicts outside Europe and conflicts within the East–West system of Europe. This hypothesis can also be tested on the basis of events data. The main question to be asked is whether or not "détente" is indivisible, that is, whether or not conflictive activities by major powers in extra-European regions do affect relations between these major powers themselves. As any wholesale examination of this hypothesis might be misleading, the following analysis will proceed stepwise by region. Furthermore, the problem will be subdivided, looking first at the extent to which the two major powers are mutually engaged in Third World regions, and, second, analyzing the correlations between their behavior in Third World regions on the one hand and their mutual relationship within the primary East–West context on the other.

Graph 5.1 presents summary models of the relationship between the activities (both cooperative and conflictive) of the United States and the Soviet Union in four Third World regions. Obviously, any generalization would be inappropriate; the salient differences observed between the individual regions confirm that it is appropriate to approach the problem region by region.

Asia seems to be the region where major-power activities take place in a rather synchronized way: The more the US becomes involved in Asian conflicts, the more the Soviet Union does ($r = .58$); and the more the United States gives support to Asian "clients," the more the Soviet Union deploys parallel activities ($r = .75$), and vice versa. A similar tendency can be observed in Africa. It is also interesting to note that in Asia the correlations measuring the relationship between major-power activities are higher for cooperative relations than for conflictive relations; in Africa, conflictive activities by the two major powers correlate higher ($r = .61$) than cooperative activities ($r = .41$). The picture offered by the graphs regarding Asia and Africa strongly contrasts to the claims expressed by the Non-Aligned Movement to keep the Third World out of major power rivalry. In Asia and Africa the two major powers obviously act, with precision and jealous attention, along the same lines of conflictive interference and cooperative engagement.

Yet the picture looks somewhat different in the case of Latin America and the Middle East. In Latin America, US cooperative activities correlate with Soviet cooperative activities ($r = .62$), but for the remaining relationships among the four variables, no significant correlation can be observed. This finding may be explained by the fact that Latin America, to some extent, still constitutes a kind of an American "sphere of interest" leaving little opportunity for outside powers to interfere. Yet the high correlation between US and USSR cooperative activities in Latin America indicates that this situation may be changing rapidly; the

Graph 5.1.: Relationship between major power activities in Third World regions.

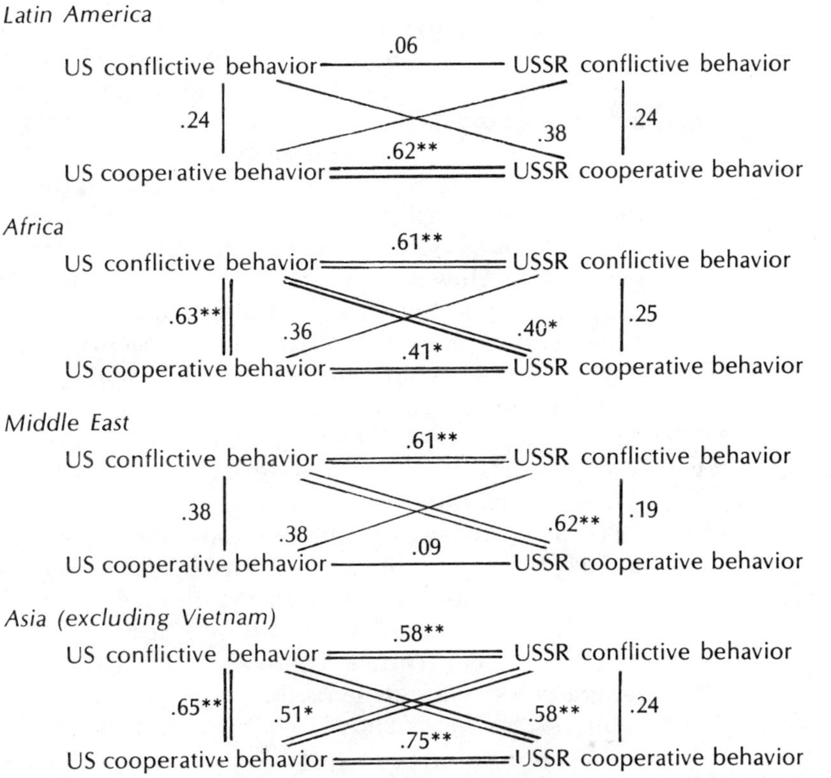
Latin America
US conflictive behavior
USSR conflictive behavior
US cooperative behavior
USSR cooperative behavior
.06
.24
.38
.24
.62**
Africa
US conflictive behavior
USSR conflictive behavior
US cooperative behavior
USSR cooperative behavior
.61**
.63**
.36
.40*
.25
.41*
Middle East
US conflictive behavior
USSR conflictive behavior
US cooperative behavior
USSR cooperative behavior
.61**
.38
.38
.62**
.19
.09
Asia (excluding Vietnam)
US conflictive behavior
USSR conflictive behavior
US cooperative behavior
USSR cooperative behavior
.58**
.65**
.51*
.58**
.24
.75**

Note: The figures labeling the arrows refer to Pearson's product-moment correlations. Arrows representing significant relationships are doubled.

high correlation points at efforts made by the Soviet government to get involved in Latin America by offering cooperation in various fields. The most important recipient is still Cuba.

As far as the Middle East is concerned, a certain degree of parallel activities by the US and the USSR cannot be denied, although the correlation coefficients obtained are only moderate. However, in the conflictive domain the "mirror-image" type of correspondence between American and Soviet hostile acts directed against Middle East countries appears in a marked way ($r = .61$).

Having thus clarified the degree of major-power competition in both conflicts and cooperation with the Third World countries, the question now can be asked to what extent this engagement is affecting "détente" between the US and USSR directly, as proposed by hypothesis 5 and its variations. The four variables examined previously (US cooperative behavior, US conflictive behavior, USSR cooperative behavior, USSR conflictive behavior) now are correlated with American–Soviet relations (both cooperative and conflictive) and analyzed separately according to origin and target of the respective cooperation and conflict). In addition, the values for the previous variables are lagged in order to identify the temporal sequence of any relationship observed. The results of this comprehensive analysis are summarized in Tables 5.5 to 5.8.

The correlations presented in Tables 5.5–5.8 do not suggest any clear-cut general trend. Nevertheless, a series of significant correlations leads to the conclusion that cooperative or conflictive relations between the United States and Latin America are not irrelevant to the Soviet Union: When the United States increased their rate of conflict with Latin American countries, the Soviet Union adopted a more hostile attitude toward the USA two or three years later. However, when the USSR increased cooperation with Latin America, the effects on major-power relations were ambiguous. The explanation is that until recently Cuba was the only Soviet "bridgehead" in the Western Hemisphere and thus the favorite and single target of American hostility in the region.

Similar processes can be identified in Africa. Although the number of significant correlations is small (5) and the strength of the correlations observed never reaches the .5 level, the evidence may be sufficient to conclude that major-power commitments in Africa have some impact on US–USSR relations.

In the Middle East, on the other hand, major-power engagements in both the cooperative and the conflictive field tended to promote US–USSR cooperation. There are similar trends in Asia, but here, major-power engagements also often and significantly exerted incentives for increasing US–USSR hostility.

As the findings presented by the region-by-region approach are rather heterogeneous, it may be convenient to scrutinize the empirical evidence found in a more comprehensive manner by simply looking at the number of significant correlations. This is demonstrated in Table 5.9.

As the theoretical maximum number for each type of correlation is 16, the number of significant correlations eventually observed may seem rather modest. In fact, the empirical investigation conducted on the basis of events-data time series does not lend support to the hypothesis that any engagement or intervention of any major power in the Third World must automatically lead to a corresponding improvement or deterioration of US–USSR "détente." Hence the more cautious version of this hypothesis is: US–USSR relations often are not unaffected by the activities deployed by the two major powers in Third World countries.

Furthermore, a conclusion regarding the nature of this impact may seem legitimate: Third World activities by major powers more often affect the cooperative dimension of American–Soviet relations than the conflictive dimension (6 versus 4 significant correlations). In other words, the major-power rivalry in the Third World to some extent reduces the prospects for US–USSR cooperation, but it does not necessarily fuel US–USSR escalation or trigger steps beyond decisive new thresholds of the major-power conflict. Major power

Table 5.5. Relationship Between Major-Power Activities in Africa (at t_o, t-1, t-2, t-3) and Bilateral Relations Between the USA and the USSR

	US behavior directed to Africa								USSR behavior directed to Africa							
	cooperative				conflictive				cooperative				conflictive			
time lags	t	t-1	t-2	t-3	t	t-1	t-2	t-3	t	t-1	t-2	t-3	t	t-1	t-2	t-3
US behavior directed to USSR:																
cooperative	-.11	-.32	-.11	-.05	.13	-.24	-.10	.21	-.19	-.37	-.46*	-.40	-.04	-.21	-.05	.03
conflictive	-.03	.12	.40	.22	.27	.29	.12	.48*	.18	.23	-.21	-.10	.05	.39	.18	.24
USSR behavior directed to USA:																
cooperative	.27	-.01	.24	-.21	.49*	.16	.31	-.12	.24	.06	-.19	-.43*	.47	-.08	.02	.13
conflictive	-.06	.16	.05	.03	-.11	.00	.02	.00	.49*	.39	.22	.31	-.05	-.07	-.05	-.00

Table 5.6. Relationship Between Major-Power Activities in the Middle East(at t_o, t-1, t-2, t-3) and Bilateral Relations Between the USA and the USSR

	US behavior directed to the Middle East								USSR behavior directed to the Middle East							
	cooperative				conflictive				cooperative				conflictive			
time lags	t	t-1	t-2	t-3	t	t-1	t-2	t-3	t	t-1	t-2	t-3	t	t-1	t-2	t-3
US behavior directed to USSR:																
cooperative	.32	.15	-.36	-.27	.46*	.08	.04	-.00	-.07	.16	.07	-.07	.51*	.38	.16	.26
conflictive	.15	.02	-.09	.20	.14	-.14	-.19	.20	-.22	-.14	-.04	-.02	.01	.19	-.16	.00
USSR behavior directed to USA:																
cooperative	.34	.06	-.49*	.24	.06	-.18	-.24	-.35	-.11	-.08	-.33	-.45*	.33	.22	-.34	-.07
conflictive	.01	-.24	-.16	.20	-.12	-.23	-.29	-.22	-.00	-.02	-.15	-.22	-.24	-.35	-.48	-.23

Table 5.7. Relationship Between Major-Power Activities in Asia (at t_o, t-1, t-2, t-3) and Bilateral Relations Between the USA and the USSR

	US behavior directed to Asia								USSR behavior directed to Asia							
	cooperative				conflictive				cooperative				conflictive			
time lags	t	t-1	t-2	t-3	t	t-1	t-2	t-3	t	t-1	t-2	t-3	t	t-1	t-2	t-3
US behavior directed to USSR																
cooperative	.01	-.10	-.30	-.34	-.09	-.08	.24	.15	-.34	-.28	-.43*	-.41	-.05	-.10	.07	.07
conflictive	.28	-.12	-.45*	-.47*	-.09	-.25	-.15	-.26	-.08	-.21	-.12	-.34	-.07	.01	-.16	-.14
USSR behavior directed to USA:																
cooperative	.25	-.24	-.32	-.38	.11	-.07	-.34	-.40	.02	-.11	-.43*	-.17	.05	-.35	-.05	-.39
conflictive	.62**	.10	-.06	.12	.24	-.03	-.26	-.28	.62**	.05	.29	.42	.05	-.14	-.19	-.28

Table 5.8. Relationship Between Major-Power Activities in Latin American Countries (at t_o, t-1, t-2, t-3) and Bilateral Relations Between the USA and the USSR

	US behavior directed to Latin America								USSR behavior directed to Latin America							
	cooperative				conflictive				cooperative				conflictive			
time lags	t	t-1	t-2	t-3	t	t-1	t-2	t-3	t	t-1	t-2	t-3	t	t-1	t-2	t-3
US behavior directed to USSR:																
cooperative	.67**	-.01	-.32	-.39	-.18	-.24	-.48*	-.50*	.49*	.09	.04	-.04	.21	.16	-.11	.06
conflictive	-.02	-.46*	-.48*	.35	.09	-.03	-.16	-.22	-.16	-.53*	-.25	.25	.01	-.21	-.17	-.19
USSR behavior directed to USA:																
cooperative	.20	-.34	-.05	.21	-.21	-.17	-.18	.31	-.18	-.35	.04	.32	-.19	.05	-.69**	.20
conflictive	-.01	-.03	-.22	.34	.37	.24	.54*	.59*	-.09	-.49*	-.16	-.04	-.06	-.03	-.38	-.11

policies *within* the different regions of the Third World however appear to be closely related or even coordinated (see Graph 5.1).

The hypotheses on the relationship between "détente" and the alliance structure will not be examined here. As was pointed out previously, the most global version of this approach focuses on the issue of bipolarization, and there is a considerable amount of disaccord about how bipolarization affects "détente" or tension (hypotheses 6, parts a–f). In this context, the question might be asked to what extent the degree of bipolarization manifest in the two aliance systems of NATO and WTO is related to the evolution of "détente." This question will be answered in Section 5.2.4 in connection with the opposite hypothesis 13, which proposes that the evolution of "détente" will result in a decrease of block cohesion.

Looking at the theories on escalation and de-escalation suggesting processes of reactivity and response as the driving forces in East–West relations, it is possible to test also some of their important assumptions by confronting them with time-series data of cooperation and conflict. By introducing time lags, the temporal sequence of cooperative and conflictive moves can be identified. According to hypothesis 7, it is Soviet initiatives that determine the nature and pace of East–West relations, the West being merely responsive. Table 5.10 demonstrates to what extent this assumption is correct.

If hypothesis 7 were to be confirmed, the correlation coefficients for time-lagged Soviet behavior (at time $t-1$, $t-2$, $t-3$) would have to be higher than the coefficients for Soviet behavior taking place simultaneously (that is, in time t). This is generally not the case, and it is hardly possible to identify a Soviet lead either in the cooperative domain or in the conflictive domain. Only American reactions two and three years after Soviet initiatives ($t-2$ and $t-3$) indicate a noticeable relationship with Soviet behavior. If the Soviet Union adopts a cooperative strategy, the United States two or three years later reacts by decreasing her conflictive behavior; if the Soviet Union decreases her share of conflictive moves, the United States three years later reacts by also behaving in a less conflictive way.

Yet, the data suggest a definitive interrelation between the behavior patterns of East and West, maybe even a kind of mirror-image reciprocity, as proposed by hypothesis 8. This is at least suggested by the correlation coefficient obtained for time t (that is, for behavior taking place simultaneously in both East and West). A considerable number of these correlations are significant with values around and above .5. If the Soviet Union behaves in a cooperative way, the Western powers are highly responsive and assume a similar attitude, and vice versa. USSR–UK relations seem to deviate a little bit from this trend but are still in line with the overall hypothesis.

The low values for the lagged data suggest that no obvious direction can be found in this relationship; except for US–USSR

Table 5.9. A Summary of Significant Correlations Found for the Impact of Major-Power Relations with Third World Countries on US–Soviet Relations*

	behavior directed towards Third World countries			
	US behavior		Soviet behavior	
	cooperative	conflictive	cooperative	conflictive
US behavior directed to USSR:				
cooperative	1	4	3	1
conflictive	4	1	1	0
Soviet behavior directed to USA:				
cooperative	1	1	3	1
conflictive	1	2	3	0

*The Theoretical maximum number of significant correlations in each case is 16.

Table 5.10. Time-lagged Relationships Between Soviet "Westpolitik" and Western Responses

Behavior of Western countries:	Soviet behavior							
	cooperative				conflictive			
	t	t-1	t-2	t-3	t	t-1	t-2	t-3
cooperative:								
USA	.43*	.08	.25	-.06	-.21	-.14	-.20	-.31
United Kingdom	.22	-.29	.08	.25	-.34	-.05	-.08	.03
France	.63**	-.21	.38	.03	-.40*	-.44*	-.38	-.13
Federal Republic of Germany	.61**	.14	.25	.23	-.41*	-.19	-.10	.01
conflictive:								
USA	.26	-.02	-.43*	-.45*	.50**	.05	-.28	-.48*
United Kingdom	-.18	-.08	-.15	-.02	-.18	-.14	-.16	-.08
France	-.16	-.10	-.02	-.23	.78**	.51*	-.07	-.26
Federal Republic of Germany	-.18	-.20	-.35	-.34	.76**	.53**	.17	-.22

relations, it does not matter whether it is the Soviet Union that makes a cooperative initiative followed by a corresponding Western response or whether this reactive process works the other way around. The process unfolds practically simultaneously if one looks at the data aggregated for annual periods. (The question has to be left open whether a more refined analysis based on monthly or weekly data would produce different results.)

Another conclusion which can be drawn from Table 5.10 concerns the different impact of cooperative and conflictive moves. The correlation coefficients obtained when comparing cooperation here with cooperation there are generally low, and they are lower than the coefficients comparing mutual behavior in the conflictive domain. Thus it seems that in East–West relations, it is "easier" to escalate (that is, to respond to conflictive acts by own conflictive behavior) than to deescalate (that is, to respond cooperatively to cooperative moves). This finding corroborates a well-known theory developed, in view of interindividual relations, in the social-psychological laboratory (Jenkins 1969). It certainly constitutes a general characteristic of any interactive situation on any level. Generally speaking, escalation occurs much more promptly and more quickly than deescalation and "détente." This finding presents an important limitation to expectations based on hypothesis 8.

5.2.3 Empirical Evidence Regarding Internal Requirements of Political "Détente"

To what extent do intrasocietal variables create a momentum of their own, and to what extent do they in fact facilitate the explanation of the ups and downs of East–West relations? In Section 5.1.3 various hypotheses suggesting specific relationships between internal factors and the progress of "détente" were mentioned. Some of them will now be subject to an empirical examination.

According to Socialist authors, the change of the "correlation of forces" in favor of the Socialist camp being the main reason for the West's policy of "détente" in turn depends on the "decline of capitalism," of a systemic crisis deeply embedded in the capitalist system (hypothesis 9). Taking unemployment in the United States as an indicator representing the "crisis of capitalism" and correlating unemployment time-series data with time-series data for three selected indicators representing US "détente" policy vis-à-vis the Soviet Union, yields results that can be interpreted easily (Table 5.11).

There is a rather high negative correlation between unemployment in the US and US military expenditure, but unemployment correlates extremely low and almost not with behavioral indices. The first finding suggest that—contrary to some assertions still propagated by parts of the literature—the United States does *not* try to mitigate economic problems by increasing her defense budget and thereby yield to pressures exerted by the "military-

Table 5.11. Relationship Between Unemployment in the US and Three Selected Indicators for US Behavior Toward the USSR

	US military expenditure	cooperative acts by US directed to USSR	conflictive acts by US directed to USSR
unemployment in USA	-.70*	.09	.03

industrial complex"; rather, both unemployment and decreasing defense expenditure (or full employment and increasing defense expenditure) seem to have a common cause, namely, military needs or a decline in military demands on the economy such as experienced after the Vietnam war. The second finding is of course the lack of any meaningful relationship between the "crisis of capitalism" and the intensification of cooperation or a decline in conflictivity expressed by the US. Therefore, the assumption expressed in hypothesis 9 cannot be confirmed.

The same data for the interaction variables can also be used to test the opposite hypothesis, which argues that in case of domestic difficulties Western governments very much hesitate to engage in East-West cooperation for the fear of the opponents being tempted to abuse temporary weakness (hypothesis 10). Correlating US military expenditure and US behavior directed to the USSR with selected indicators for domestic instability (Table 5.12) does not yield clearly conclusive results. American conflictive activities toward the USSR seem to be completely unaffected by the domestic climate in the United States; no significant correlations can be found in this respect (last column). However, as far as the American cooperative activities are concerned, some meaningful correlations occur, and all of them—except the correlations for the US rate of inflation—are negative: The more frequent expressions of collective protest, the less frequent the number of American cooperative acts directed at the Soviet Union. This seems to be in accordance with hypothesis 10 and therefore contradicts the assumption underlying hypothesis 9. Yet some caution may be appropriate in this case, referring to the behavior of one single country only. As a matter of fact, the American domestic scene during the period of the Vietnam war was largely characterized by rapidly spreading mass protest, which in turn receded into the background after the end of the war; at the same time the process of East-West "détente" took off. Hence the correlations observed in Table 5.12 may simply reflect a historical coincidence of two otherwise unrelated trends.

As indicated in hypothesis 11, some authors argue that the progress of "détente" is simply an outcome of economic necessities,

Table 5.12. Relationship Between Domestic Stability and Instability in the US and Three Selected Indicators for US Behavior with Regard to the USSR

	US military expenditure	cooperative acts by the USA directed to USSR	conflictive acts by USA directed to USSR
demonstrations in USA			
at t_0	.08	-.28	-.20
at t-1	.17	.27	-.03
riots in USA			
at t_0	.38	-.19	.06
at t-1	.64**	-.33	-.13
attacks in USA			
at t_0	-.05	-.66**	-.23
at t-1	.02	-.51*	-.22
collective protest in USA			
at t_0	.25	-.41*	-.14
at t-1	.45*	-.11	-.13
US inflation rate			
at t_0	-.09	.45*	-.07
at t-1	-.28	.19	-.08

Note: the variable "collective protest" is the aggregate sum of the values observed for the variables "protest," "riots," and "attacks," according to Taylor 1981.

especially in the case of the Soviet Union where the need to mitigate economic setbacks and difficulties of all kinds by getting access to Western economic resources, mainly Western technology, leads to a more moderate attitude and cooperative behavior with regard to the West. An attempt to test this hypothesis is presented in Table 5.13.

All correlations between indicators for Soviet economic growth and Soviet defense expenditures are negative although very low. Soviet cooperative acts directed to the United States correlate negatively with the indicators for Soviet economic growth, and the correlations for time-lagged relationships between the two variables are clearly significant. The conclusion that, with increasing economic success, the Soviet Union loses interest in her cooperation with the United States would be misleading, however. Obviously the Soviet Union engaged in a cooperative policy vis-à-vis the United States because she expected some economic benefit from this behavior. Some economists regard declining growth rates

Table 5.13. Relationship Between Soviet Economic Growth and Soviet Behavior with Regard to the US

	USSR military expenditure	cooperative acts by USSR directed to USA	conflictive acts by USSR directed to USA
growth of Soviet GDP			
at t	-.28	.03	.26
at t-1	-.25	.09	.11
at t-2	-.23	-.54*	-.22
growth of Soviet GDP p.c.			
at t	-.23	-.02	.23
at t-1	-.19	.08	.06
at t-2	-.17	-.52*	-.24

in the Soviet Union, which began in the early sixties, as signs of severe economic difficulties. The historical coincidence with "détente"—or rather, "peaceful coexistence"—appears to be more than just a lucky chance.

A more refined analysis can be offered by looking at the transfers that took place in the field of technology. This can be done by correlating data on the American–Soviet and FRG–Soviet flow of technology on the one hand with Soviet behavior vis-à-vis the USA and the FRG on the other hand. Tables 5.14 and 5.15 display some very high and significant correlations between these two variables. The most obvious and salient conclusion to be drawn from these results is that the more the Soviet Union reduces her conflictive attitude vis-à-vis the United States and the Federal Republic of Germany, the more technology transfers to the Soviet Union take place subsequently.

It is, however, a different question whether these correlations can also be attributed a causal or even intentional meaning—in other words, whether it is appropriate to interpret the close and significant relationships found by statements such as "The Soviet Union received more technology transfers *because* she behaved less conflictively" or even "The Soviet Union reduced her conflictive attitude vis-à-vis the West *in order* to benefit more from technology transfer." Any such conclusion would require empirical proofs of a very different kind (sources on policy statements by the Soviet leadership). It may be noted that in the case of FRG–USSR relations (Table 5.15), there are also moderately strong and highly significant negative correlations between technology transfers with a lead of one or two years and the level of conflictivity.

Table 5.14. Relationship Between US-USSR Technology Transfers and US-USSR Relations (at t+3, t+2, t+1, t, t-1, t-2, t-3)

	US behavior directed to USSR		USSR behavior directed to USA	
	cooperative	conflictive	cooperative	conflictive
US SITC-7 exports to USSR				
at t+3	.71**	-.24	.11	-.51**
at t+2	.72**	-.23	.24	-.47*
at t+1	.39*	-.16	.04	-.47*
at t	.24	-.13	.11	-.37
at t-1	.08	.09	.29	-.21
at t-2	.13	.46*	.42*	-.14
at t-3	.07	.65**	.30	-.12

This finding may recommend a more cautious and less speculative interpretation. The respective correlations are even positive in the case of the US. Still, there are very high correlations between US cooperative behavior vis-à-vis the USSR and subsequent US technology transfers, corroborating the results of Table 5.13.

These findings, in sum, suggest that the rapid growth of technology transfer coincides indeed with "détente". However, the somewhat simplistic assertions of hypothesis 11—amounting to a purposeful and systematic Soviet strategy to obtain access to Western technology by a moderate foreign policy—should be treated with caution. At least such a motive, if it exists, must not be taken for granted as the exclusive and unique cause underlying the Soviet emphasis on "peaceful coexistence." Rather, the astonishing boom of technology transfer seems to constitute one of the many elements interconnected in various ways with the general change of relations between East and West.

5.2.4 Empirical Evidence Regarding the Consequences and Inner Logic of "Détente"

Whereas in the preceding sections some hypotheses about the "causes" of "détente" (or tension) were examined, in this section some hypotheses regarding the consequences of "détente" will be subject to empirical tests based on the data collected in this study. The most favored hypothesis put forward in this context asserts that political "détente" will promote a liberalization of the political system of Socialist countries and facilitate improved human contacts.

Table 5.15. Relationship Between FRG-USSR Technology Transfers and FRG-USSR Relations (at t+3, t+2, t+1, t, t-1, t-2, t-3)

	FRG behavior directed to USSR		USSR behavior directed to FRG	
	cooperative	conflictive	cooperative	conflictive
FRG SITC-7 exports to USSR				
at t+3	.49*	-.64**	.54**	-.74**
at t+2	.37	-.61**	.56**	-.72**
at t+1	.12	-.63**	.41*	-.65**
at t	.05	-.61**	.41*	-.58**
at t-1	-.10	-.54**	.29	-.52**
at t-2	-.17	-.50*	.31	-.47**
at t-3	-.26	-.56**	.09	-.38

There are two opposing schools of thought as to the effects of "détente" on the human contacts situation. Some authors argue that "détente" has made a certain liberalization in the Socialist countries possible (hypothesis 12), if not within these countries as originally hoped, so at least with respect to human contacts. Other authors have pointed at the increasing dependence of the Socialist countries on the West resulting from increased cooperation and newly established links in many fields, economic and human most of all; therefore, feelings of being destabilized in one or the other respect might lead to efforts "delimitating" the Socialist world from those contacts considered to have destabilizing effects in the long run (hypothesis 14). In the Table 5.16, these two contradictory hypotheses are examined by looking at the volume of emigration from the Socialist countries.

Only in the case of Jewish emigration from the Soviet Union is there a clear relationship between "détente" and liberalization measures. American cooperation favored the Jewish emigration while the Soviet Union apparently used the emigration issue as a means of conflict behavior by limiting the opportunities to leave the country. Similarly, conflicts between the Federal Republic of Germany and the Soviet Union would have a negative effect on the emigration figures. The same is true for the official emigration from the GDR, while conflicts between the GDR and the FRG stimulated illegal emigration in the early sixties before the construction of the Berlin wall. Cooperation with Czechoslovakia also facilitated emigration but the whole problem was solved in the late sixties/ early seventies and thus the frequencies declined. Therefore, de-

Table 5.16. Coefficients of Correlation Between the Number of Persons Leaving East European Countries and Interactions Between the Country of Origin and the Country of Destination (Time-Series 1960–1980)

	behavior of FRG		behavior of country of origin	
	cooperative	conflictive	cooperative	conflictive
Migration USSR - FRG	.01	-.51*	.32	-.57**
Migration CZCH - FRG	.46*	.52*	.33	.31
Migration PLND - FRG	-.20	-.18	-.28	-.38
Migration USSR - ISRL	.69** (1)	.05 (1)	.30	-.45*
Migration total GDR - FRG	-.33*	.37*	-.31*	.05
GDR - FRG with off. permission	-.21	-.46**	-.25	-.25
GDR - FRG without off. permission	-.29	.41**	-.26	.08

[1] In these correlations, the independent variable is US behavior.

creasing emigration figures since cannot be attributed to an increasing level of conflict between the FRG and Czechoslovakia. Neither cooperation with Poland nor with the GDR has an effect on the number of persons emigrating from these countries with official permission. On the contrary, with increasing cooperation between the GDR and the FRG, the number of persons crossing the border with or without permission by GDR authorities declined. Obviously, in this case "delimitation" took the very manifest form of improvements in the border-security installations of the GDR, and it is becoming increasingly difficult to cross the border without permission. Meanwhile the number of persons being allowed to emigrate declines anyway, as in the case of the emigration from Czechoslovakia, although for different reasons.

Whereas in the preceding table the trend toward internal liberalization in the Soviet Union was measured by the number of persons having been granted permission to leave the country, a more direct, although more controversial, indicator is being used in Table 5.17 referring to the number of internal sanctions and relaxation of sanctions as registered by the events data bank published in Taylor 1981.

The results presented in Table 5.17 are of utmost interest: If American cooperation with the Soviet Union increases, both Soviet sanctions *and* steps toward a relaxation of sanctions become more frequent, and they do so simultaneously (at *t*) or immediately following (with one year's time lag) American cooperative activities. This result may seem contradictory—at least if seen in the perspective proposed by hypothesis 12. The findings strongly suggest a more complex interpretation of the processes envisaged by this hypothesis. They clearly indicate that the progress of "détente" (defined here as the growth of the frequency of American cooperative activities vis-à-vis the Soviet Union) leads to increased attention devoted, by the Soviet authorities, to problems of internal discipline and security; this in turn promotes increasing administrative activities with regard to both intensification and relaxation of sanctions. In other words, as "détente" progresses, the issue of domestic discipline becomes more crucial in the Soviet Union, but in contrast to the expectations expressed by hypothesis 12, this does not imply a general trend toward a general slackening and liberalization of domestic politics.

Looking at the balance of sanctions and relaxation of sanctions (last column), the correlation coefficients indicate that the general trend even points at the opposite direction. The correlation coefficients for the relationship between American–Soviet cooperation and the balance of Soviet sanctions minus Soviet relaxation of sanctions are clearly significant. These findings constitute another example of a context where commonly held assumptions are disconfirmed by a sober analysis using social-science research tools.

Similar conclusions have to be drawn with regard to hypothesis 13, which suggests a decrease of block cohesion taking place as a

Table 5.17. Relationship Between the Number of Internal Sanctions Exerted by the Soviet Union and Relaxation of Sanctions, and Major-Power Cooperation and Conflict

	sanctions	relaxation of sanctions	difference (sanctions minus relaxation)
US cooperation with USSR			
at t_o	.60**	.73**	.40*
at t-1	.57**	.62**	.44*
at t-2	-.03	.23	-.13
at t-3	.01	.22	-.09
US conflictive behavior directed at USSR			
at t_o	.22	-.21	.38
at t-1	.24	-.23	.42*
at t-2	-.23	-.45*	-.10
at t-3	-.37	-.18	-.41
USSR cooperation with USA			
at t_o	.35	.33	.29
at t-1	.21	.29	.14
at t-2	-.25	.15	-.39
at t-3	.16	.16	.14
USSR conflictive behavior directed at USA			
at t_o	.13	-.32	.31
at t-1	-.10	-.35	.03
at t-2	-.36	-.54**	-.23
at t-3	-.46*	-.40	-.44**

result of the general relaxation of tension. As was pointed out in Section 5.1.4, this hypothesis rests on the assumption that "détente" implies a process of depolarization. The empirical evidence produced by previous studies (Goldmann 1974) shed some doubts about the pertinence of this assumption; the findings presented in Table 5.18 do not disclaim these doubts. The coefficients presented in this table refer to correlations between American and Soviet behavior (in terms of cooperative and conflictive behavior directed at each other) and the number of interactions with NATO countries in terms of the percentage of all external interactions

Table 5.18. Relationship Between US–USSR Relations and WTO Member Interactions with NATO Countries (at t+3, t+2, t+1, t, t-1, t-2, t-3)

	US behavior directed to USSR		USSR behavior directed to USA	
	cooperative	conflictive	cooperative	conflictive
WTO member interactions (excl. USSR) with NATO countries (in % of total interactions)				
at t+3	-.04	-.44*	-.43*	-.25
at t+2	-.05	-.21	.38	.22
at t+1	.10	-.16	.42*	.15
at t	.28	-.10	.12	-.31
at t-1	.12	-.33	-.08	-.26
at t-2	-.20	-.02	-.26	-.14
at t-3	-.08	-.07	-.12	-.09

by WTO countries except the USSR (that is, by Bulgaria, Czechoslovakia, GDR, Hungary, Poland, Romania); the correlations are calculated with time lags in the latter variable.

Only three out of twenty-eight correlations are significant, but the respective correlation coefficients are not strong, and they seem to be contradictory as far as the direction of the relationship is concerned. In other words, the activities by WTO countries directed to nonblock partners do not depend on the progress of major-power "détente," and "détente" has not accomplished any weakening of WTO solidarity let alone any tendency toward a dissolution of military blocks. Yet, on the other hand, "détente" also did not contribute toward a clearer separation of East and West. In sum, it did not affect the structure of interactions by the smaller WTO member countries. At least and as far as the Eastern part of Europe is concerned, the military alliances seem to constitute a firmly established reality not to be overcome or altered in any sense by the efforts aimed at improved major-power relations.

In the context of hypothesis 17, the question has been raised whether "détente" in Europe will affect the East-West confrontation in the Third World. This question will now be answered by examining the statistical relationships between US-USSR relations, on the one hand, and major-power activities (both cooperative and conflictive), on the other hand. The findings are based on events time-series data and summarized in Tables 5.19–5.22. The approach and the data used are identical with those of hypothesis 5 (see Section 5.2.2), yet in this context the direction of time lags will be reversed.

In Latin America, the global process of "détente" is accompanied and followed by initiatives toward more cooperation by both major powers; American conflictive behavior vis-à-vis the Soviet Union is followed by a growth of conflictive relationships with Latin American countries. Similar results can be found for the Middle East region although no clear trend is emerging. As far as Africa is concerned, a tendency toward polarization cannot be denied. Both cooperative and conflictive relations between the two major powers seem to have an impact on US and USSR behavior in Africa; reactions are quick, in most cases taking place simultaneously (at time *t*), but in a few instances there are also time lags at work. This also applies to Asia; Table 5.22 presents a considerable number of significant correlations.

It is interesting to note that in all regions the cooperative and the conflictive behavior of major powers vis-à-vis Third World countries is equally affected by the "détente" in the "central-balance" context. The conclusion suggests that the process of "détente" therefore works probably as a mechanism promoting Third World engagements by the major powers. This may lead to additional rivalry and hence generate new risks.

A comprehensive survey of the significant correlations is presented in Table 5.23. Compared with the comprehensive summary

Table 5.19. Relationship Between US–USSR Relations (at t_o, t-1, t-2, t-3) and Major-Power Activities in Latin America

	US behavior directed to USSR								USSR behavior directed to USA							
	cooperative				conflictive				cooperative				conflictive			
time lags	t	t-1	t-2	t-3	t	t-1	t-2	t-3	t	t-1	t-2	t-3	t	t-1	t-2	t-3
US behavior directed to Latin America:																
cooperative	.67**	.50*	.32	-.19	-.02	.22	.23	-.17	.20	.19	.17	-.21	-.01	.13	-.10	-.39
conflictive	-.18	.19	-.16	-.33	-.09	.43*	.27	.43*	-.21	-.07	-.06	-.01	.37	.31	.11	.39
USSR behavior directed to Latin America																
cooperative	.49*	.71**	.32	-.11	-.16	.12	.08	.05	-.18	-.00	.20	.09	-.08	-.25	-.20	-.01
conflictive	.21	.00	-.28	-.41	.01	.06	-.06	-.04	-.19	-.21	.40	-.23	.06	.08	.12	.11

Table 5.20. Relationship Between US–USSR Relations (at t_o, t-1, t-2, t-3) and Major-Power Activities in Africa

	US behavior directed to USSR								USSR behavior directed to USA							
	cooperative				conflictive				cooperative				conflictive			
time lags	t	t-1	t-2	t-3	t	t-1	t-2	t-3	t	t-1	t-2	t-3	t	t-1	t-2	t-3
US behavior directed to Africa																
cooperative	.11	-.23	.04	.35	-.03	-.35	-.06	-.08	.27	-.01	.33	-.03	-.06	-.19	.43*	-.33
conflictive	.13	-.16	.17	.44*	.27	-.42*	-.23	-.07	.49*	.13	.08	-.18	-.11	-.27	.01	-.30
USSR behavior directed to Africa																
cooperative	-.19	-.52*	-.44*	-.08	.18	-.16	.03	.25	.24	.03	-.03	-.04	-.49*	.18	.42*	.25
conflictive	-.04	-.28	-.17	-.09	.05	-.26	-.19	-.39	.47*	-.14	.21	-.14	-.05	-.02	-.04	-.09

Table 5.21. Relationship Between US-USSR Relations (at t_o, t-1, t-2, t-3) and Major-Power Activities in the Middle East

	US behavior directed to USSR								USSR behavior directed to USA							
	cooperative				conflictive				cooperative				conflictive			
time lags	t	t-1	t-2	t-3	t	t-1	t-2	t-3	t	t-1	t-2	t-3	t	t-1	t-2	t-3
US behavior directed to the Middle East:																
cooperative	.32	.39	-.07	.29	.15	-.07	-.61*	-.32	.34	.38	-.04	.18	.01	-.03	-.48*	-.39
conflictive	.46*	.01	-.28	-.08	.14	-.11	-.34	-.28	.06	.39	-.09	.09	-.13	.12	-.14	-.22
USSR behavior directed to the Middle East																
cooperative	-.07	-.18	-.42*	-.32	-.22	-.11	-.02	-.13	-.11	.38	.07	.06	-.01	.17	.26	.11
conflictive	-.05	-.32	-.33	-.31	.01	-.16	-.27	-.28	.05	-.03	-.13	.48*	.24	.02	-.38	-.44*

Table 5.22. Relationship Between US–USSR Relations (at t_o, t-1, t-2, t-3) and Major-Power Activities in Asia

	US behavior directed to USSR								USSR behavior directed to USA							
	cooperative				conflictive				cooperative				conflictive			
time lags	t	t-1	t-2	t-3	t	t-1	t-2	t-3	t	t-1	t-2	t-3	t	t-1	t-2	t-3
US behavior directed to Asia:																
cooperative	.01	-.50*	-.55*	-.52*	.28	.24	.08	.09	.25	-.26	-.05	-.08	.62*	.44*	.19	.20
conflictive	-.09	-.50*	-.43*	-.45*	-.09	-.11	-.14	.24	.11	-.30	-.22	-.04	.24	.15	.14	.54*
USSR behavior directed to Asia:																
cooperative	-.34	-.29	-.52*	-.46*	-.08	.26	.13	.29	.02	-.22	-.01	-.01	.62*	.49*	.28	.42
conflictive	-.05	-.32	-.33	-.30	-.07	-.13	-.17	-.01	.05	-.03	-.12	-.48*	.05	.14	.07	.39

Table 5.23. A Summary of Significant Correlations Found for the Impact of US–USSR Relations on the Relations Between Major Powers and Third World Countries*

	US behavior directed to USSR		USSR behavior directed to USA	
	cooperative	conflictive	cooperative	conflictive
US behavior directed to Third World				
cooperative	5	1	0	4
conflictive	5	3	1	1
USSR behavior directed to Third World				
cooperative	7	0	0	4
conflictive	0	0	2	1

*The theoretical maximum number of significant correlations in each case is 16. A comprehensive survey of the significant correlations is presented in Table 5.24.

presentation of the findings regarding hypothesis 5 (see Table 5.9) in this table the number of significant correlations has increased (thirty-four compared to thirty-one). The interpretation of this fact is obvious: It means that the impact of US–USSR behavior on major-power activities in the Third World is at least as important and maybe slightly more important than the consequences Third World confrontations have on the evolution of bilateral "détente."

A most remarkable trait is the number of cooperative reactions made by the Soviet Union in Third World countries and going hand in hand with American cooperation vis-à-vis the Soviet Union (seven significant correlations). The United States does not act accordingly (zero correlations) hence there is no symmetry. Seen in a Western perspective, this feature offers a proof for the Soviet intention to exploit "détente" in extra-European regions. Seen in the perspective expressed by Socialist governments, this behavior constitutes a logical and necessary consequence of "détente" for the benefit of what the Socialist countries perceive as the struggle for national liberation and social progress in the Third World.

Furthermore, as in the empirical investigations made in view of hypothesis 5, and even more articulate here, actions and reactions are more important in the cooperative field than in the conflictive field (twenty-one correlations as compared with thirteen correlations).

In conclusion, the relationship between major-power politics aimed at the Third World and major-power politics aimed at each other is clearly recursive. The process of "détente," in fact, cannot be separated into different geographical processes; the world political system, as an integrated whole, quickly transmits any incentives and challenges into other geographic problem areas.

Similar methods can be applied in view of an empirical examination of hypotheses 18 and 19 and the various corollary hypotheses suggesting specific forms of relationships between "détente" and armaments viz. disarmament. The correlation coefficients presented in Table 5.24 may serve as a basis for doing this; they refer to statistical relationships between American and Soviet behavior (both in the cooperative and conflictive fields) and American and Soviet military expenditure; leads and lags introduced into the analysis allow for a thorough investigation of the possible cause–effect relationships.

According to hypothesis 18, the evolution of "détente" goes hand in hand with an ongoing arms race because the opponents engaging in a policy of "détente" feel a need for a kind of reinsurance by military power. The correlations in Table 5.24 do clearly not support this hypothesis in the case of the United States. The more cooperative the United States behaves, the smaller three years later the US military expenditure ($r = -.50$ at $t+3$, significant at the .05 level). But hypothesis 18 is clearly and significantly confirmed in the case of the Soviet Union: The less conflictive the

Table 5.24. Relationship Between US–USSR Relations and US and USSR Military Expenditure (at t + 3, t + 2, t + 1, t, t -1, t -2, t -3)

	US behavior directed to USSR		USSR behavior directed to USA	
	cooperative	conflictive	cooperative	conflictive
US military expenditure				
at t+3	-.50*	-.37	.42	.10
at t+2	-.34	-.17	.39	.17
at t+1	-.07	-.06	.42	.13
at t	.09	-.09	-.14	-.06
at t-1	.05	-.20	-.33	-.35
at t-2	.13	-.17	-.26	-.43
at t-3	.40	-.10	-.04	-.37
Soviet military expenditure				
at t+3	.45*	-.36	.16	-.57**
at t+2	.52**	-.03	.21	-.52*
at t+1	.55**	-.02	.22	-.49*
at t	.54**	-.09	.27	-.54**
at t-1	.41*	-.13	.17	-.59*
at t-2	.43*	-.02	.10	-.66**
at t-3	.52*	.32	.23	-.39

Soviet Union behaves, the higher the Soviet military expenditure. It has been noted previously that while "détente," in US policy, means more cooperation, on the Soviet side it implies a lessening of the hostile attitude and a diminution of the frequency of conflictive acts directed at the West; as can be seen now, these two differing conceptions of "détente" have awkward consequences for the field of armament and disarmament. The Soviet Union obviously felt compelled to require a kind of reinsurance or simply to take advantage; it may be left to further speculation whether the additional investment in the armed forces in the last resort roots in a basically defensive attitude of Soviet foreign policy, as is sometimes suggested by students of Soviet affairs, or whether it originates from the inherently offensive and expansionist nature of a major power allegedly still driven by ideological fervor to struggle for the "ultimate victory of socialism." Whatever interpretation is correct,—it cannot be denied that the decrease in conflictivity of Soviet behavior is significantly and constantly (at $t+3$, $t+2$, $t+1$) correlated with or followed by accelerated Soviet defense spending.

Having resulted in these findings, the analysis of the data also largely implies the propositions suggested by hypothesis 19. If this hypothesis is correct, "détente" does promote armaments and handicaps disarmament; yet this is said not to be harmful to "détente." On the contrary, according to hypothesis 19, the "reinsurance" of "détente" by armed strength is assumed to be even beneficial or at least not detrimental to the further progress of "détente." In other words, "détente" proceeds irrespective of whether or not there is a growth in arms expenditure. Again this hypothesis is partly disconfirmed and partly confirmed by the data. The US defense spending (at $t-3$, $t-2$, $t-1$) does not affect US and USSR behavior; no significant correlations can be found for any of these relationships. However, there is a decisive impact of Soviet military spending: The more the Soviet Union spends (at $t-3$, $t-2$, and $t-1$), the more cooperatively the United States behaves. And the more the Soviet Union spends in the armaments sector (at $t-2$ and $t-1$), the less conflictive her behavior vis-à-vis the United States becomes. Hence there is a twofold asymmetry: Apart from the different emphasis put by the US and the USSR on cooperation and lessening of conflictivity, the impact of defense spending also clearly differs depending on which of the two major powers is investing resources in armed strength. Whereas US defense expenditure has a negligible impact on the evolution of "détente," Soviet defense expenditure seems to be conducive to a further improvement of East-West relations, or, more precisely: "Détente," on the American side, is making progress *despite* continuing Soviet armaments, and, on the Soviet side, maybe *because* of Soviet armaments.

For these reasons, the conclusion can also be drawn that the corollary hypothesis 19a is not supported by the data. According to this hypothesis, which is justified by seemingly plausible arguments, "détente" is jeopardized if the attempts to halt and to curb the arms race fail. The findings specified in view of hypothesis 19 clearly contradict this assumption.

The corollary hypothesis 18a, on the other hand, expresses the hope that "détente," after some time, leads to progress in the field of disarmament, whereas any setback in "détente," that is, any resurgance of tension and hostility, will trigger ensuing increases in arms spending. As has been pointed out with reference to hypothesis 18, the correlation coefficients presented in Table 5.24 do not offer any conclusive findings valid for either major power: If the United States behaves cooperatively, they are also willing to reduce their defense expenditure while Soviet defense spending continues to grow with undiminished pace. And while the Soviet Union reduces her rate of hostile behavior, her defense spending proceeds fiercely and unbendingly.

According to hypothesis 20, political "détente" is closely connected with cooperation in "nonpolitical" fields, particularly with trade. As has been pointed out in Section 5.1.4, the theoretical literature suggests at least three different—and contradictory—variations of this hypothesis, depending on the direction of the causal relationship supposed to exist between these to variables: Either cooperation promotes "détente" (hypothesis 20a) or "détente" promotes cooperation (hypothesis 20b) or cooperation and "détente" are interlinked in a "dialetical process" (hypothesis 20c). There is, however, no need to rely on philosophical preconceptions only in order to determine which of the three variations is the "true" one, that is, which one corresponds most properly to the historical facts. As the three variations of hypothesis 20 refer to different types of historical sequence (trade prior to "détente" or vice versa), an empirical examination of the hypothesis can be done by simply looking at correlations between time-lagged (and time-led) variables. The results of a correlation analysis based on this idea are presented in Table 5.25.

Looking first at US cooperative behavior directed to the Soviet Union, the conclusion to be drawn from the correlation statistics are quite obvious. If the cooperative behavior in the political field is lagged (that is, if US or USSR values at one or two or three prior years are compared with political cooperative behavior taking place one or two or three years later), no significant correlation occurs. However, correlations are definitively significant if the time lag is introduced to test the historical sequence evolving in the opposite direction, that is, assuming that it is political "détente" that promotes cooperation and not vice versa. The correlation coefficients corroborate hypothesis 20b, which proposes that the more "détente" progresses, the more trade will expand as a consequence.

The results are different, however, with regard to the conflictive behavior. Although the correlations, in principle, point at the same

Table 5.25. Relationship Between US–USSR Relations and US–USSR Trade (at t + 3, t + 2, t + 1, t, t -1, t -2, t -3)

	US behavior directed to USSR		USSR behavior directed to USA	
	cooperative	conflictive	cooperative	conflictive
US exports to USSR				
at t+3	.43*	-.31	-.08	-.49*
at t+2	.48*	-.10	.42*	-.32
at t+1	.28	.15	.25	-.36
at t	.30	.08	.23	-.36
at t-1	.17	.13	.34	-.23
at t-2	.15	.42*	.36	-.18
at t-3	-.01	.51*	.14	-.19
USSR exports to USA				
at t+3	.18	-.30	.10	-.38
at t+2	.29	.07	.47*	-.27
at t+1	.40*	.37	.43*	-.28
at t	.39*	.21	.23	-.38*
at t-1	.23	-.06	.08	-.39*
at t-2	.04	.07	.08	-.29
at t-3	.13	.47*	.46*	-.06

direction as expected according to the previous findings (that is, the less conflictive US behavior, the greater the volume of trade), the respective correlation coefficients are weak and not significant. There are, however, positive and significant correlations if political behavior is lagged: The more (or the less) trade at $t-3$ and $t-2$, the more (or the less) conflictive actions are undertaken by the United States vis-à-vis the Soviet Union. As was pointed out in Chapter 3, US cooperation and US conflictive behavior evolve in an asymmetric way, expressing the willingness to engage in a policy of "détente" mainly by increasing the volume of cooperation rather than decreasing the volume of conflictive behavior. Therefore, it seems justified to interpret the findings reported in Table 5.25 as confirming hypothesis 20b in the field of cooperation. On the other hand, the relationship between activities in the field of trade and ensuing conflictive activities on the part of the United States may be attributed to developments of East–West relations taking place independently from each other. Or, to put it more precisely, the growth of US exports to the USSR did not impede the United States in exhibiting again a higher level of hostility two or three years later.

As far as the Soviet behavior directed at the United States is concerned, the correlations observed generally confirm the findings made with respect to US behavior, taking into account, however, the basic asymmetry existing between American and Soviet behavior: The more cooperative Soviet foreign policy, the greater the growth of trade relations one or two years later. And the less conflictive Soviet behavior directed to the United States, the greater the volume of American exports to the Soviet Union. Similar findings can be observed with regard to Soviet exports; yet, in addition, Soviet exports also correlate significantly with Soviet behavior taking place subsequently. That fact may point at the tendency to use foreign trade as a political instrument to signal a willingness to ease relations even before the change in attitude becomes visible in terms of a lessening of hostility and expansion of cooperation.

A somewhat different picture is offered by the correlations concerning relations between the Federal Republic of Germany (FRG) and the Soviet Union. It reflects the peculiar philosophy developed by West German diplomacy in view of achieving a "change through approximation" ("*Wandel durch Annäherung*"), which is based on two assumptions: First, the FRG diplomacy vis-à-vis the East very much relied on the functionalist presumption supposing a politically beneficial impact of trade promotion. Second, the FRG, more powerful in economic than in political terms, heavily capitalized on this instrument, thus avoiding any particular political move that could cause concern with both her allies and the East. That is why FRG–USSR commercial relations, independent of the direction of the trade flows, so constantly and significantly correlate with diminishing hostility. Both the promotion of intersystems trade and the will to reduce tension by avoiding conflictive activities seem to constitute two pillars of the same long-term policy. This policy is obviously honored by corresponding Soviet moves away from a high level of hostility. (Table 5.26).

Yet in the cooperative field the picture becomes much more varying. As can be seen from the absence of any significant correlations, West German cooperative behavior seems to be completely detached from trade relations. As far as the Soviet Union is concerned, both FRG–USSR and USSR–FRG exports correlate with Soviet cooperative behavior more strongly at time $t+3$ than prior to this time. In other words, in the case of Soviet "Westpolitik," again "peace promotes trade" and not vice versa. Politics dominate economics.

To what extent does the degree of symmetry or asymmetry prevailing in the structure of cooperation between East and West affect the further evolution of East–West relations? If hypothesis 21 is correct, asymmetry in the long run constitutes a hindrance due to the fact that it is raising concern on the part of those who feel to be disadvantaged by the asymmetric structure of cooperation, thus giving incentives to halt the growth of any such contacts. Except for two years (1966 and 1968), the value of American goods sold to the Soviet Union exceeded the corresponding value for USSR–US trade; in other words, the ratio of USSR–US to US–USSR trade, for almost the entire period 1960–1980 was smaller than 1.00. It was particularly low in the seventies. According to the hypothesis, this must have led the USSR to a less friendly behavior vis-à-vis the US. However, as can be seen in Table 5.27, precisely the opposite results can be found: There are practically no significant correlations between prior asymmetry in trade and Soviet behavior, except for the correlation (time lagged at $t-2$), which, however, is negative and thus contrary to theoretical expectations. On the other hand, the two variables correlate constantly in a significant and negative way at t and $t+1$, $t+2$, and $t+3$; the verbalized meaning of this relationship is: The less conflictive the Soviets behave vis-à-vis the United States, the more symmetrical is East–West trade (that is, the less asymmetric at the expense of the Soviet Union). At the same time US behavior directed at the USSR becomes more cooperative. When trying to interpret these findings in a cautious manner, one may perhaps suggest that the symmetry or asymmetry of trade relations evolves according to its own inherent logic and independently of the prior state of political relationship.

Finally, as proposed by hypothesis 22, progress of "détente" is ascribed to the balance existing between the evolution of East–West relations in various fields, and correspondingly crises and setbacks of "détente" are explained by imbalanced evolution. This hypothesis is examined in Table 5.28 below.

The degree of balance or imbalance does not seem to have any predictive power with regard to US–USSR relations, as the cor-

Table 5.26. Relationship Between FRG–USSR Relations and FRG–USSR Trade (at t + 3, t + 2, t + 1, t, t -1, t -2, t -3)

	FRG behavior directed to USSR		USSR behavior directed to FRG	
	cooperative	conflictive	cooperative	conflictive
FRG exports to USSR				
at t+3	.31	-.66**	.65**	-.75**
at t+2	.20	-.63**	.42*	-.68**
at t+1	.15	-.62**	.40*	-.64**
at t	.08	-.61**	.40*	-.60**
at t-1	-.04	-.57**	.31	-.60**
at t-2	-.16	-.51*	.34	-.55**
at t-3	-.20	-.56**	.15	-.50*
USSR exports to FRG				
at t+3	.12	-.61**	.56**	-.66**
at t+2	.00	-.59**	.41*	-.58**
at t+1	.02	-.57**	.30	-.53**
at t	.00	-.59**	.30	-.55**
at t-1	-.04	-.58**	.37	-.53**
at t-2	-.16	-.54**	.22	-.49*
at t-3	-.20	-.54**	.31	-.46*

Table 5.27. Relationship Between the Ratio of USSR-US/US-USSR Trade and US-USSR Relations (at t+3, t+2, t+1, t, t-1, t-2, t-3)

	US behavior directed to USSR		USSR behavior directed to USA	
	cooperative	conflictive	cooperative	conflictive
ratio of Soviet-US/US-Soviet trade				
at t+3	-.54*	.15	-.09	.48**
at t+2	-.54**	-.15	-.08	.33
at t+1	-.24	.14	-.10	.52**
at t	-.40*	.03	-.16	.02
at t-1	-.25	-.15	-.11	.16
at t-2	-.43*	-.21	-.61**	.04
at t-3	-.15	-.13	.17	.32

Table 5.28. Relationship Between Balance/Imbalance of East-West Relations in Various Fields and US-USSR Relations (at t+3, t+2, t+1, t, t-1, t-2, t-3)

	US behavior directed to USSR		USSR behavior directed to USA	
	cooperative	conflictive	cooperative	conflictive
degree of imbalance[1]				
at t+3	.43*	.05	.18	-.22
at t+2	.66**	-.10	-.00	-.44*
at t+1	.50*	-.02	-.21	-.49*
at t	.41*	-.13	.02	-.42*
at t-1	.13	.03	-.03	-.09
at t-2	.44*	.13	.52*	-.15
at t-3	.03	.12	.24	-.14

[1]Degree of imbalance is the measure of dispersion calculated on the basis of the index values of the master dimensions (see Chapter 4). The measure of dispersion refers to the squared differences between all *N*-tuples.

relations calculated for time $t-1$, $t-2$, and $t-3$ are practically always nonsignificant. If, however, the degree of imbalance is time-led, significant correlations can be found—yet they point at different directions: The more cooperative the US behaves vis-à-vis the USSR, the greater the degree of imbalance; and the more conflictive the Soviet Union behaves vis-à-vis the other major power, the more balanced East-West relations tend to become. There is no need to point out that these findings are wholly inconsistent with any theoretical expectation, and they cannot be interpreted in any meaningful way.

This finding represents another indication that may serve as a warning against seemingly plausible theoretical assumptions. The process of East-West relations undoubtedly implies some inherent logic. It has been possible in this section to identify some crucial element of this logic and is underlying causality. At the same time the attempt to test a number of hypotheses by empirical means also clearly demonstrated that a considerable number of theoretical assumptions held and cherished by students of East-West relations cannot be supported if subject to rigorous empirical testing, and some of them also must be outright rejected. Yet the debunking of some untenable assumptions may certainly be as useful for a better understanding of East-West relations as the confirmation of valid hypotheses.

Chapter 6

The Outlook: "Détente"—an Episode?

The materials presented in the foregoing chapters offer, we hope, a sincere, exact, reliable account—maybe even a kind of "photography" by means of modern social-science methods—of the period of East–West relations sometimes called "détente." This photography comprises both subjective and objective elements, that is, perceptions by the political actors as well as the hard facts they produce by their behavior. So far this study, being mainly descriptive by nature, contributes to the history of this period ranging from the sixties up to the beginning of the eighties. In addition, Chapter 5 analyzed the material in view of discovering some elements of the internal logic of East–West relations, in particular causal relationships among various dimensions of East–West relations such as conflict and cooperation in the diplomatic, security, economic, and other fields. Thus it was possible to identify a number of important factors conducive to or impending the further improvement of East–West relations seen as a type of interaction characterized by less conflict and more cooperation.

As has been shown in the descriptive parts of this study, there is a definite turning point to be discerned at the end of the seventies. Most indicators on both the perceptual and the factual level thereafter exhibit values close to or even inferior to the ones observed for the sixties when the Cold War was transformed into what came to be known as the policy of "détente." Does this finding mean that "détente" has come to an end, leaving behind as a temporary, transient episode what twenty years ago was proudly announced as the "age of détente"? In order to answer this question, it is imperative to rely on knowledge confirmed by empirical means. Although the evidence presented in Chapter 5 offers a series of insights useful for this purpose, it does not allow any general and final judgment as expected by that question. Any answer appropriate to questions of this kind requires a general theory about the process and structure of East-West relations. Such a general theory not being available at the present moment (and possibly also not in the future), one is left with the option of engaging in some speculative considerations. It may be permitted, in terms of a concluding remark, to offer some speculative thoughts, supported, however, by empirical evidence at least partly and to the maximum extent possible. Such a general explanatory framework may serve as a proper basis for further considerations regarding the future perspective of East-West relations.

When looking for a general theory of East-West relations, four comprehensive explanatory frameworks may be envisaged: (1) the theory of growth and saturation, (2) the theory of incongruous evolution, (3) the theory of asychronous evolution, and (4) the theory about connections between shifting perception and changing actions.

6.1. THE RISE, SATURATION, AND FALL OF EAST-WEST COOPERATION

The majority of graphs presented in this volume exhibits curves that are comparable and alike in appearance: They always depict an evolution that—at the beginning of the seventies—is characterized by a sudden take-off followed by a period of exponential growth and concluded—so far—by a certain slowing down of this growth process after roughly eight years and ending in a phase of stagnation or even retrogression. The curves are S-shaped and thus resemble the typical scheme of logistic growth that so many aspects of societal evolution exhibit, comprising the three phases of take-off, growth, and stabilization at a higher level. The similarity with processes such as political integration or social change is too obvious and too suggestive to be overlooked, and it must not be neglected. If the assumption expressed by this comparison is correct, the implicit conclusion can be only that the progress achieved in East-West relations in the course of the seventies will hardly continue indefinitely because at some point the process inevitably leads into a period of saturation. Seen in this analytical framework, the "crisis of détente" diagnosed since the late seventies would not constitute a transitory phase to be overcome shortly by unbending progress.

Yet the reference to the S-shaped nature of practically all types of societal evolution may be a little bit too general as to offer a satisfactory explanation and a sound foundation for prospective reflections. All it offers is a somehow modest philosophy of history. The very intriguing question to be asked in this context may lead beyond this general framework. The key problem certainly is why, at a certain moment, a sudden evolutionary leap forward was initiated and for what reason the period of exponential growth took off. And a second important question may refer to the underlying process that ended the period of rapid growth initiating a period of stabilization. Quite probably there is not any single clear-cut answer to these questions. Yet the foregoing analyses provide knowledge to make these processes at least partly transparent. In particular, they point at the absence of any logic providing the evolution of East-West relations with the property of a self-perpetuating process immune against any setbacks.

Additional insights into the rationale and background of the processes mentioned may be obtained by using the other explanatory general framework presented in Sections 6.2–6.4. As a matter of fact, these frameworks aptly complement the first one.

6.2. THE RIDDLE OF INCONGRUOUS EVOLUTION

The second comprehensive explanatory framework refers to the elementary fact that East-West relations are not identical with West-East relations. The interaction structure evolving between East and West, in other words, is by nature incongruous and characterized by various asymmetries. In the course of the foregoing chapters, many asymmetries have been mentioned; in an overall picture of East-West relations, they combine into a bewildering network where any analyst will have difficulties in identifying any coherence.

Two principal asymmetries require attention. First, as repeatedly demonstrated in this study, there is an asymmetry between cooperation and conflict. Although one would expect that "détente," whatever its definition, implies a growth of cooperation and corresponding decrease in conflictivity on both sides, this feature does not turn out to be true. In practice, "détente" means more cooperation by the West and less conflictive behavior by the East. Second, East and West have adopted entirely dissimilar policies in sectors crucially central to the future of East-West relations such as armaments and disarmament. While the West reduced defense spending in conformity with the general evolution of intersystems relations, the East sought a kind of reinsurance against the whims of "détente" by increasing defense expenditure.

Apart from these two principal asymmetries, there are many additional dissimilarities, especially in the context of cooperation in the field of economics, of science and technology. One might argue that precisely the overcoming of such perplexing contrasts constitutes one of the stark achievements of the process of East-West negotiations. One also might suggest that, after all, combining seemingly incompatible positions into one single comprehensive bargain is the very essence of any diplomatic compromise; seen in this perspective, the compromise reached in 1975 and written down in the Final Act would represent a major diplomatic success not in spite of but precisely because of the accomplishment to reconcile incongruous policies, at least as expressed in words. The fact that the Final Act was agreed on may serve as a sufficient proof for the mutually advantageous nature of this compromise—if it had not been mutually advantageous, the thirty-five CSCE states would not have adopted that text. And also the deeds experienced since the last sixties, irrespective of their doubtful compatibility, may be interpreted as a victory of skilled and patient diplomacy. As a matter of fact, the evolution of intersystems relations may be ridden by a myriad contradictions—but it cannot be denied that there was a tangible evolution.

It would certainly be unwise to fail to appreciate the merits of the work done by a number of statesmen and diplomats in both East and West in the past two decades. Yet, it would also be dangerous to have a false idea of the risks inherent to such an incongruous evolution.

A central risk is created by the fact that incongruous behavior also implies incongruous expectations. In order to understand the logic of East–West relations, it is necessary to look not only at the behavioral level but to include also perceptual data, that is, cognitive elements and their normative implications. Expectations from one side that are not met by corresponding behavior by the other side cause disappointment, and disappointment may in turn affect basic attitudes toward intersystems cooperation and conflict. This problem will be dealt with more amply in Section 6.4 since it roots in a context that deserves an analysis based on a distinct theoretical approach.

A more immediate consequence of the incongruous evolution of intersystems relations can be discerned in what has been called the "linkage" problem. As was shown in Chapter 5, a considerable majority of theoretical concerns for intersystems relations aim at discovering the logic of interrelations among different fields of East–West cooperation. Among the central questions are: How does trade affect political cooperation? Will a lessening of the degree of hostility encourage internal liberalization? There are reasons to assume that the statesmen and diplomats responsible for developing the policies of intersystems relations took linkages between different fields for granted or they were at least hoping for the efficacy of such linkages and spill-overs. The assumption is strongly supported by paragraphs in the Final Act explicitly expressing the conviction that specific measures to be taken in various fields will contribute to the strengthening of peace and security.

For a social scientist, it is not surprising to realize that these hopes can hardly be honored in reality. Four decades of discussion about the "functionalist paradigm," proposing hypotheses along just these lines, have exhaustively demonstrated that if there is any spill-over at all, it usually works the other way around: Rather than involving increasingly more fields into the progress of cooperation, rather than creating interdependencies pushing for further cooperation and relaxation of tension, rather than starting from small beginnings gradually and irrevocably enmeshing more and more issues into a growing network of interlocking intersystems relations, spill-overs on the contrary tend to handicap progress in one field by interferences originating in other fields. Progress of East–West relations in fields endowed with their own dynamic momentum is constantly retarded and sometimes also interrupted by problems arising in other fields not as much activated by a momentum of East–West relations. That is what diplomats and newspapers commentators usually have in mind when they complain about the absence of a "political will" to promote more and faster progress in some specific fields of East–West cooperation.

In conclusion, there is little hope that the incongruence inherent to intersystems relations will simply be "healed" by a kind of automatically equalizing process of spill-over among different fields. On the contrary, it constitutes a challenge continuously instigating expectations and responses by means doomed to fail and causing more and more frustration about the growing intricacies of intersystems relations.

Calling for more symmetry in East–West relations would not be helpful either. The incongruence existing in this type of intersystems relations has roots that are deeply imbedded in different ideological orientations of the states involved in this process and in the diversity of their economic and social systems. It is furthermore determined by plain facts of geographic location, inequality in size and wealth and different structures and levels of economic development. Only if these diversities were removed or mitigated would it be meaningful and realistic to recommend an approximte symmetry in East–West relations.

6.3 THE PAINS OF COORDINATING ASYNCHRONOUS PROCESSES

Most approaches to the problem of East–West relations focus on national interests, national policies, and their impact on the course of events. Starting from the assumption that decision-makers are constrained by factors such as limited resources, fading popularity, election campaigns, and pressure groups, they usually end up with the conclusion that, if the decision-makers were really willing to promote East–West cooperation, a large part of those constraints could be overcome. That is the central idea of what may be called the "voluntaristic" approach to international politics.

Yet this approach tends to underestimate the intrinsic logic of the East–West system itself as seen from a systems perspective.

In this system, there are some powerful mechanisms at work, comprising both dynamic and inert elements, which to a very large extent are out of the reach of any attempt to shape and reshape political reality by political decisions. In other words, the East-West system has the nature of a complex system difficult to control. As there are many subsystems within the comprehensive system, the problem arises of coordinating asynchronous processes. More often than not, attempts to solve this problem are doomed to failure.

The subsystems correspond to the dimension of East-West relations identified in Chapter 2 of the present study, mainly, (1) the security subsystem as defined by the balance of defense expenditure and arms deployment, (2) the diplomatic subsystem comprising the structure of cooperative and conflictive interactions (3) the economic subsystem determined by the structure of exchange and cooperation in the commercial, financial, and technological fields, (4) the domestic political and national environment(s) of the states participating in the evolution of East-West relations and (5) the "block" structure subsystem. As these five subsystems evolve in the absence of any coordination and without control of any overarching logic, the processes advance with different rhythm. In the diplomatic subsystem changes can occur within a few months. The observed cycles in diplomatic climate have phase lengths of three or four years. In contrast, major shifts in defense policies require between five years and a decade. Time is running at different speeds in the various subsystems.

Evidently, a system characterized by such a large degree of asynchrony is unpredictable. If, for example, confidence-building measures are agreed on simultaneously with arms-control measures, there will hardly be any mutual benefit from these two measures because the confidence (if any) generated by confidence-building measures will emerge only with considerable time lag and at any rate too late for supporting the efforts undertaken in the field of arms control; when confidence is finally established, maybe the arms-control measures have already failed in the meantime due to lack of confidence.

Systems theory (see Forrester 1970, pp. 109 ff.) has provided some tools for analyzing more thoroughly the problem of asynchrony existing in complex systems. In particular, four difficulties can be identified in this context.

First, complex systems are characterized by counterintuitive behavior. Due to the asynchronous nature of any complex system, it often reacts in a surprisingly unexpected way. The history of East-West relations offers many illustrations for this effect: The expectations held with regard to the domestic liberalization in Socialist countries as a consequence of East-West "détente" did not materialize. Similar "surprises" were experienced in the field of trade when most of the premises and assumptions held by those who promoted East-West trade were simply not confirmed by reality. Trade did not promote peace, as put forward simplistically by many statesmen, but East–West trade relations became an instrument in the conduct of political conflict. Growing tourism did not foster friendship between the peoples of East and West, nor was the promotion of cultural exchange capable of furthering mutual understanding on a broad scale.

Second, a complex system tends to be insensitive to changes in many systems parameters: Although in the diplomatic subsystem the most dramatic shift of political climate occurred by virtually melting away the Cold War, the effects on other subsystems were poor and almost nonexistent. For instance, the radical improvement of the political climate was not able to affect the arms race in neither the global strategic and Eurostrategic field.

Third, complex systems offer resistance to policy changes and prove also insensitive to any attempts to move it. In the East–West context, policies designed to have a specific impact often simply missed the point. Such was the effect of President Nixon's decision to grant the Soviet Union the most-favored-nation status.

Fourth, corrective programs are counteracted by the system. Sometimes efforts to influence the system are doomed to failure not because of a lack of any reaction by the system but by an adjustment process developed by the system neutralizing any efforts. This is illustrated by the counteraction of the armaments subsystem: Although the collective efforts undertaken by the two major powers culminated in the two SALT agreements, the arms race spilled over from the quantitative sphere into the qualitative sphere; in addition and despite of the attempt to control the central strategic balance, the arms race was transformed into what became the Eurostrategic arms race, into a fierce competition regarding arms suppy to Third World countries and into a naval-arms race between the two major powers. The momentum inherent to the armaments subsystem proved to be stronger than any attempt to control the system.

6.4 THOUGHT VERSUS ACTION IN INTERSYSTEMS RELATIONS

Finally, one has to bear in mind that the evolution of East–West relations is preceded by an evolution of expectations regarding East–West relations. In Chapter 2 of this study, attention focused on the perceptual aspects of intersystems relations as reflected in the statements made by the representatives of the states participating in the CSCE negotiations. Since the profiles of expectations differ from country to country and even more so from group to group, the facts resulting from the evolution of East–West relations can by no means satisfy all expectations. Hence the evolution of East–West relations in the long run cannot avoid feelings of disappointment and eventually also frustration increasingly risen at various places.

In addition, as was demonstrated by the description of the

process of East–West relations in terms of different expectations as presented in Chapter 4, the striking truth is that due to shifting perceptions, some governments in 1980 tend to interpret the history of "détente" as a much less promising picture than they did before, for example, in 1975. In other words, irrespective of whether the facts change, a mere shift in the structure of expectations may already be sufficient to project a considerably different meaning into the reality of East–West relations. As can be inferred from what happened in the sixties and seventies, this twofold interrelation between thought and action in intersystems relations leads to a kind of vicious circle that can be summarized in the following diagram:

Graph 6.1. Reality and Expectation in East–West Relations.

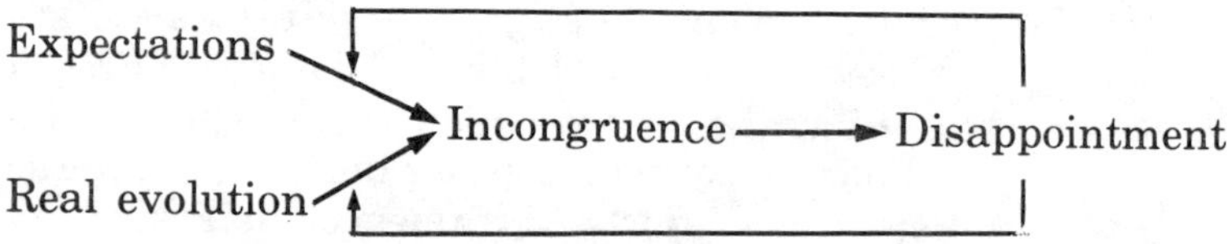
Expectations
Incongruence
Disappointment
Real evolution

If the expectations about "détente" are not matched by corresponding facts in the real evolution, incongruence will result and lead to feelings of disappointment. Disappointment, in turn, will feed back on both the expectations and the real evolution: On the level of expectations, greater emphasis will now be put on those aspects of East–West relations where there was no or little progress so far. Thus the absence of "progresses" is being felt in a much more painful and agonizing manner than it originally used to be. At the same time disappointment and frustration are hardly conducive to reaffirm the willingness to engage in additional and more decisive steps forward; thus, also on the factual level, the evolution of intersystems relations eventually slows down and, in some fields, is even being reversed.

In Western democracies the importance of this mechanism is amplified by the logic of internal political rivalry. Especially in periods prior to elections foreign-policy issues, and among them quite often issues of East–West relations, tend to become subjects of heated debate. Whoever wishes to criticize the government frequently does so by highlighting those aspects of East–West relations that fall short of expectations. This situation breeds a constant tendency to finding new arguments for raising and supporting feelings of disappointment, irrespective of the virtual merits and demerits of East–West relations.

On the other hand, in some countries (for example, in the Federal Republic of Germany), the government rigorously tries and possibly also succeeds in raising support in the electorate by pointing at its design for improved East–West relations and by propagating the benefits of "détente"; however, in such cases, the popularity of the policy of "détente" for better or for worse is linked with the popularity of the incumbents, and it is bound to decline when the popularity of the incumbents begins to whither away. This process puts additional stress on the viability of the policy of "détente."

Whether or not similar processes are at work also in Socialist countries, especially in the Soviet Union, cannot be expounded in this book. Yet it seems reasonable to assume that within the political elite in Socialist countries too, there are discussions about the rationale of the policy of "peaceful coexistence" and about the political strategies and tactics to be adopted in view of this policy. In particular, arguments about whether or not it was worthwhile at all to engage in such a policy do seem to constitute a standard element of internal discussions. To some extent they parallel the debates genuine to Western democracies, and, like these debates, they are hardly an element conducive to a smooth evolution of East-West relations.

From an analytical point of view, one may deplore such unfortunate complications as the result of tragic misunderstanding due to mutual misperceptions or to lacking ability to take due note of each others expectations. Nevertheless, the perceptual element must not be neglected or ignored since it also constitutes an essential part of reality. To regret its existence is no substitute for practical contributions.

Also the question is not on how to influence or manipulate these expectations but how to make the best use of a situation characterized by different and shifting expectations. There are obvious and less obvious, sometimes hidden limits to the future growth of "détente." A creative policy of East-West relations will therefore concentrate all efforts on constructive activities *within* the scope of action defined by these limits in a way conducive to the aims proclaimed in the opening paragraph of the Final Act: "in the interest of the peoples, to improve and intensify their relations and to contribute in Europe to peace, security, justice and cooperation as well as to rapprochement among themselves and with other states of the world." An indispensable precondition for any practical measures is the knowledge of and insight into the intrinsic logic and structure of East-West relations. It is hoped that this study augments this insight.

Bibliography

Abouchar, A. (1979). *Economic Evaluation of Soviet Socialism.* New York: Pergamon Press.

Alker, Hayward R., and Puchala, Donald (1968). "Trends in Economic Partnership in the North Atlantic Area, 1928–1963," in J. David Singer (ed.), *Quantitative International Politics.* New York: Free Press, pp. 287–316.

Allan, Pierre (1979). "L'impact du climat international sur les dépenses militaires soviétiques," *Annuaire suisse de science politique* 19, pp. 15–24.

Allan, Pierre, and Luterbacher, Urs (1981). "Détente Processes in Europe: A Tentative Model," in Daniel Frei (ed.), *Definitions and Measurement of Détente: East and West Perspectives.* Cambridge, Mass.: Oelgeschlager, Gunn & Hain, pp. 173–194.

Alting von Geusau, Frans A. M. (1981). "Economic Cooperation and Political Détente in Europe: Actors, Interactions, and Implications," in Bo Huldt and Atis Lejins (eds.), *East-West Economic Interaction: Possibilities, Problems, Politics, and Prospects.* Stockholm: The Swedish Institute of International Affairs, pp. 79–100.

Andrén, Nils (1980). "Expectations and Disillusionment," in: Nils Andrén and Karl E. Birnbaum (eds.), *Belgrade and Beyond: The CSCE Process in Perspective.* Alphen, pp. 89–98.

Andriole, Stephen J., and Young, Robert A. (1977). "Toward the Development of an Integrated Crisis Warning System," *International Studies Quarterly* 21, pp. 107–150.

Arbatow, Georgij A., and Oltmans, Willem (1981). *Der sowjetische Standpunkt. Über die Westpolitik der USSR.* Munich: Rogner & Bernard.

Arbeitsgruppe "Entspannung" (1977). *Indikatoren der Entspannung in Europa* (Kleine Studien zur Politischen Wissenschaft, No. 118-119). Zürich: Universität Zürich.

Ash, Robert W. (1980). "Power Parity and the Outbreak of War," in Daniel Frei (ed.), *Beiträge zur Kriegsursachenforschung* (Zürcher Beiträge zur Politischen Wissenschaft, No. 187). Zürich, pp. 51-58.

Axelrod, R. (ed.) (1976). *Structure of Decision.* The Cognitive Maps of Political Elites. Princeton, N.J.: Princeton University Press.

Azar, Edward E. (1975). "Ten Issues in Events Research," in Edward E. Azar and Joseph D. Ben-Dak (eds.), *Theory and Practice of Events Research.* New York: Gordon & Breach, pp. 1-17.

——. (1977). Codebook and User's Package for the Conflict and Peace Data Bank (COPDAB). Chapel Hill: University of North Carolina, mimeo.

Azar, Edward E., and Ben-Dak, Joseph D. (eds.) (1975). *Theory and Practice of Events Research. Studies on Inter-Nation Actions and Interactions.* New York: Gordon and Breach.

Azar, Edward E., and Havener, Thomas (1974). "Discontinuities in the Symbolic Environment: A Problem in Scaling Events," New Orleans: International Studies Association, mimeo.

Azar, Edward E.; McLaurin, R.D.; Havener, Thomas; Murphy, Craig; Sloan, Thomas; and Wagner, Charles A. (1977). "A System for Forecasting Strategic Crises: Findings and Speculations About Conflict in the Middle East," *International Interactions* 3, pp. 193-222.

Azar, Edward E., and Sloan, Thomas J. (1975). *Dimensions of Interactions: A Source Book for the Study of the Behavior of 31 Nations from 1948-1973.* Pittsburgh: International Studies Association.

Baumer, Max, and Jacobsen, Hanns-Dieter (1980). "Die Wirtschaftsbeziehungen des RGW mit dem Westen im Spannungsfeld zwischen weltweiten Beschränkungen und europäischen Möglichkeiten," in *DGFK-Jahrbuch 1979/80.* Baden-Baden: Nomos, pp. 557-577.

Bell, Coral (1977). *The Diplomacy of Détente.* London.

Bertsch, Gary K. et al. (1979). "Technology Transfer, Export Controls, and East-West Relations." Paper presented to the 1979 IPSA World Congress.

Bethkenhagen, Jochen; Kupper, Siegfried; and Lambrecht, Horst (1980). "Aussenwirtschaftliche Interessen der DDR und Entspannung," in *Die DDR im Entspannungsprozess.* Köln, pp. 1-17.

Bindschedler, Rudolf (1978). "Die Konferenz von Belgrad—Episode oder Wendepunkt?" *Europäische Rundschau,* no. 3, pp. 15-24.

Bonham, G. Matthew, and Shapiro, Michael J. (1973). "Simulation in the Development of a Theory of Foreign Policy Decision-Making," in P.J. McGowan (ed.), *Sage International Yearbook of Foreign Policy Studies.* Beverly Hills, Calif.: Sage, pp. 55-71.

——. (1976). "Explanation of the Unexpected: The Syrian Intervention in Jordan in 1970", in R. Axelrod (ed.), *Structure of Decision.* Princeton: Princeton University Press, pp. 113-141.

——. (1977). *Thought and Action in Foreign Policy.* Basel: Birkhäuser.

Bonham, G.M.; Shapiro, M.J.; and Nozicka, G.J. (1976). "A Cognitive Process Model of Foreign Policy Decision Making," *Simulation and Games* 7, pp. 123-152.

Borst, G., et al. (1977). *Militärwesen in der Sowjetunion.* Wehrforschung Aktuell 5. München: Bernard & Graefe.

Brainard, Lawrence J. (1981). "Eastern Europe's Uncertaint Future: The Outlook for East-West Trade and Finance," in Bo Huldt and Atis Lejins (eds.), *East-West Economic Interaction: Possibilities, Problems, Politics, and Prospects.* Stockholm: The Swedish Institute of International Affairs, pp. 39-53.

Bredow, Wilfried von (1979). *Die Zukunft der Entspannung.* Köln: Pahl-Rugenstein.

Brock, Lothar (1976). "Möglichkeiten und Grenzen einer konstruktiven Abrüstungspolitik in den intersystemaren Beziehungen," in Gerda Zellentin (ed.), *Annäherung, Abrenzung und friedlicher Wandel in Europa.* Boppard: Boldt, pp. 191-216.

Bundesminister der Verteidigung (1980). *Die nuklearen Mittelstreckenwaffen. Modernisierung und Rüstungskontrolle.* Bonn: Planning Staff of the Federal Ministry of Defense of the FRG.

Burzig, Arno (1977). "Intersystemare ökonomische Beziehungen und Entspannung in Europa," in Annemarie Grosse-Jütte and Rüdiger Jütte (eds.), *Entspannung ohne Frieden.* Frankfurt: S. Fischer, pp. 207-217.

Calvocoressi, Peter (1968). *World Politics since 1945.* London: Longman.

Cherkasov, P.P., and Proektor, D.M. (1978). "The Problem of Deepening the European Détente," in Soviet Committee for European Security and Cooperation (ed.), *European Security and Cooperation.* Moscow: Progress, pp. 306-346.

Cherry, Colin (1967). *Kommunikationsforschung-Eine neue Wissenschaft,* 2nd ed. Hamburg.

Choucri, Nazli, and North, Robert C. (1976). *Nations in Conflict (Code Book).* Ann Arbor: ICPSR.

Corson, Walter H. (1970a). "Conflict and Co-operation in East-West Relations: Measurement and Explication" Ann Arbor: Institute for Social Research, mimeo.

——. (1970b). "Measuring Conflict and Cooperation Intensity Between Nations." Ann Arbor: Institute for Social Research, mimeo.

Czempiel, Ernst-Otto, et al. (1980). "Amerikanisch-sowjetische Beziehungen im weltpolitischen Kontext: Rahmenbedingungen der Entspannungspolitik in Europa," in: *DGFK-Jahrbuch 1979/80.* Baden-Baden: Nomos, pp. 35-64.

Daly, Judith A., and Andriole, Stephen J. (1980). "The Use of Events/Interaction Research by the Intelligence Community," *Policy Science* 12, pp. 215-236.

Deutsch, Karl W., and Eckstein, Alexander (1960/61). "National Industrialization and the Declining Share of the International Sector, 1890-1959," *World Politics,* vol. 13, pp. 267-299.

Deutsch, Karl W., and Isard, Walter (1966). "A Note on a Generalized Concept of Effective Distance," *Behavioral Science* 6, pp. 308-311.

Dobroczynski, Michal (1980). "Abhängigkeiten, Strukturen und Perspektiven einer Politik der Zusammenarbeit in Europa," in Hansjürgen von Kries (ed.), *Friede durch Zusammenarbeit in Europa.* Berlin: Berlin-Verlag, pp. 114-126.

Dobrosielski, Marian (1977). "Aspects of European Security After the Helsinki Conference," *Studies in International Relations,* No. 8, pp. 7-16.

Entspannungsbegriff und Entspannungspolitik in Ost und West (1979). Berlin: Duncker & Humblot.

Etzioni, Amitai (1962). *The Hard Way to Peace.* New York: Knopf.

Feger, Hubert (1976). "Annäherung und Abgrenzung politisch-sozialer Systeme aus sozialpsychologischer Sicht," in Gerda Zellentin (ed.), *Annäherung, Abgrenzung und friedlicher Wandel in Europa.* Boppard: Bolt, pp. 451-490.

Ferraris, Luigi Vittorio (1979). *Report on a Negotiation.* Alphen: Sijthoff & Nordhoff.

Finsterbusch, Kurt (1975). "Trends in International Integration as Indicated by Trends in International Mail Flows," in Edward E. Azar and Joseph D. Ben-Dak (eds.), *Theory and Practice of Events Research.* New York: Gordon & Breach, pp. 128–141.

Forrester, Jay W. (1970). *Urban Dynamics.* Cambridge and London: MIT Press.

Frankel, Joseph (1975). *British Foreign Policy, 1945–1973.* London: Oxford University Press.

Frei, Daniel (1980). *Evolving a Conceptual Framework of Inter-Systems Relations.* New York: UNITAR.

—— (ed.) (1981). *Definitions and Measurement of Détente: East and West Perspectives.* Cambridge, Mass.: Oelgeschlager, Gunn & Hain.

Friedliche Koexistenz in Europa (1977). Berlin: Staatsverlag der DDR.

Füllenbach, Josef, and Schulz, Eberhard (eds.) (1980). *Entspannung am Ende?* München: Oldenbourg.

Galtung, Johan (1975). "East-West Interaction Patterns," in Edward E. Azar and Joseph D. Ben-Dak (eds.), *Theory and Practice of Events Research.* New York: Gordon & Breach, pp. 95–120.

Gamson, William, and Modigliani, André (1971). *Untangling the Cold War: A Strategy for Testing Rival Theories.* Boston: Little, Brown.

Gantman, Vladimir (1977). "Zwischen Helsinki und Belgrad." Paper presented to the HSFK Conference on European Security, Frankfurt.

Garnham, David (1976). "Power Parity and Lethal International Violence, 1969–1973," *Journal of Conflict Resolution* 20, pp. 379–394.

Gastil, Raymond D. (1978). *Freedom in the World: Political Rights and Civil Liberties.* New York: Freedom House.

Gaupp, Peter (1976). *Die Rollentheorie als Analyseinstrument von Aussenpolitik und internationalen Beziehungen* (Kleine Studien zur Politischen Wissenschaft, No. 75–77). Zürich: Universität Zürich.

Goldman, Marshall I. (1980). *The Enigma of Soviet Petroleum: Half-Empty of Half-Full?* London: George Allen and Unwin.

Goldmann, Kjell (1972). "Bipolarization and Tension in International Systems: A Theoretical Discussion," *Cooperation and Conflict* 7, pp. 37–63.

——. (1973). "East-West Tensions in Europe, 1946–1970: A Conceptual Analysis and a Quantitative Description," *World Politics* 26, pp. 106–112.

——. (1974). *Tension and Détente in Bipolar Europe.* Stockholm: Esselte Studium.

——. (1979). *Is My Enemy's Enemy My Friend's Friend?* Lund: Studentlitteratur.

——. (1980). "Cooperation and Tension Among Great Powers: A Research Note," *Cooperation and Conflict* 15, pp. 31–45.

——. (1981). "Change and Stability in Foreign Policy: Détente as a Problem of Stabilization." Stockholm, mimeo.

Goldmann, Kjell, and Lagerkranz, Johan (1977). "Neither Tension nor Détente: East-West Relations in Europe, 1971–1975," *Cooperation and Conflict* 12, pp. 251–264.

Greven, Michael Th. (1976). "Internationale Politik und Gesellschaftsformation," in Gerda Zellentin (ed.), *Annäherung, Abgrenzung und friedlicher Wandel in Europa.* Boppard: Boldt, pp. 217–291.

Guetzkow, Harold, and Ward, Michael Don (eds.) (1981). *Simulated International Processes: Theories and Research in Global Modeling.* Beverly Hills, Calif.: Sage.

Haftendorn, Helga (1975). "Versuch einer Theorie der Entspannung," *Sicherheitspolitik heute* 2, pp. 223–242.

Hart, Thomas G. (1976). *The Cognitive World of Swedish Security Elites.* Stockholm: Esselte Studium.

———. (1979). *The Spread of Extra-European Conflicts to Europe: Concepts and Analysis.* Stockholm: The Swedish Institute of International Affairs (Research Report UI-79-1).

Havener, Thomas, and Peterson, Alan (1975). "Measuring Conflict/Cooperation in International Relation. A Methodological Inquiry," in Edward E. Azar and Joseph D. Ben-Dak (eds.), *Theory and Practice of Events Research.* New York: Gordon & Breach, pp. 57–61.

Hermann, Charles F. (1973). "Indikatoren internationaler politischer Krisen," in Martin Jänicke (ed.), *Herrschaft und Krise.* Opladen: Westdeutscher Verlag, pp. 44–63.

———. (1981). "Some Initial Problems and Possible Solutions in Measuring Détente Processes: Prospective of an American Social Scientist," in: Daniel Frei (ed.), *Definitions and Measurement of Détente: East and West Perspectives.* Cambridge, Mass.: Oelgeschlager, Gunn & Hain, pp. 11–23.

Hermann, Charles F., and Hermann, Margaret G. (1976). "CREON: Comparative Research on the Events of Nations," *Quarterly Report* 1. Columbus: Mershon Center.

Hermann, Margaret G. (1979). "Acceptance and Rejection." Columbus: Mershon Center (draft manuscript, unpublished).

Hinkel, Günter, and Nicolai, Wolfgang (1978). *Entspannung und wirtschaftliche Zusammenarbeit in Europa.* Berlin: Staatsverlag der DDR.

Hoffmann, Stanley (1976). "Paris Dateline. The Case of the Vanishing Foreign Policy," *Foreign Policy* 23, pp. 221–230.

———. (1981). "Voraussetzungen und Ziele der Entspannung in den 80er Jahren," in *Protokoll Nr. 67 des Bergedorfer Gesprächskreises.* Hamburg, pp. 11–19.

Hoggard, Gary D. (1975). "An Analysis of the 'Real' Data," in Edward E. Azar and Joseph D. Ben-Dak (eds.), *Theory and Practice of Events Research.* New York: Gordon & Breach, pp. 19–27.

Hopple, Gerald W. (1980). "Automatic Crisis Warning and Monitoring: Exploring a Staircase Display Option." McLean, Va., mimeo.

Holsti, Ole R. (1966). "External Conflict and International Cohesion: The Sino-Soviet Case," in P.J. Stone et al. (eds.), *The General Inquirer.* Cambridge, Mass.: MIT Press, pp. 343–358.

———. (1969a). *Content Analysis for the Social Sciences and Humanities.* Reading, Mass.: Addison-Wesley.

———. (1969b). "The Belief System and National Images: A Case Study," in J.N. Rosenau (ed.), *International Politics and Foreign Policy.* New York: Free Press, pp. 543–550.

———. (1972). *Crisis, Escalation, War.* Montreal: McGill/Queen University Press.

Holsti, Ole R.; Brody, R.A.; and North, R.C. (1965). "Measuring Affect and Action in International Reaction Models: Empirical Materials from the 1962 Cuban Crisis," *Papers of the Peace Research Society (International) II,* pp. 170–190.

———. (1968). "Perception and Action in the 1914 Crisis," in J.D. Singer (ed.), *Quantitative International Politics: Insights and Evidence.* New York: Free Press, pp. 123–158.

Hopman, Terry (1967). "International Conflict and Cohesion in the Communist System," *International Studies Quarterly* 11, pp. 212–136.

Hutchins, Gerald (1979). "Affect." Columbus: Mershon Center (draft chapter of manuscript).

Iker, H.P. (1974). "A Historical Note and the Use of Word-Frequency Contiguities in Content Analysis," *Computers and the Humanities* 8, pp. 93–98.

——. (1974/75). "SELECT: A Computer Program to Identify Associationally Rich Words for Content Analysis. I. Statistical Results; II. Substantive Results," *Computers and the Humanities* 8, pp. 313–319; 9, pp. 3–12.

Iker, H.P., and Klein, R. (1974). "WORDS: A Computer System for the Analysis of Content," *Behavior Research Methods and Instrumentation* 6, pp. 430–438.

Iker, H.P., and Harway, N.I. (1969). "A Computer System Approach to the Recognition and Analysis of Content," in G. Gerbner et al. (eds.), *Analysis of Communication Content.* New York: John Wiley & Sons.

Inozemtsev, Nikolai N. (ed.) (1980). *Europe Before a Choice: Confrontation or Relaxation of Military Tension.* Moscow.

International Institute for Strategic Studies (1959/60). *The Military Balance.* London.

Institut für Internationale Beziehungen an der Akademie für Staats- und Rechtswissenschaft der DDR (1979). *Konfrontation, Entspannung, Zusammenarbeit.* East Berlin: Staatsverlag der Deutschen Demokratischen Republik.

——. (1980). *Die DDR und die Verwirklichkung der Schlussakte von Helsinki. Dokumente und Materialien.* East Berlin: Staatsverlag der Deutschen Demokratischen Republik.

Jacobsen, Hans-Adolf (1980). "Bedingungsfaktoren realistischer Entspannungspolitik," in *DGFK-Jahrbuch 1979/80.* Baden-Baden: Nomos, pp. 65–90.

Jacobsen, Hanns-Dieter (1976). "Kooperation und Abgrenzung in den wirtschaftlichen Beziehungen zwischen Ost- und Westeuropa," in Gerda Zellentin (ed.), *Annäherung, Abgrenzung und friedlicher Wandel in Europa.* Boppard: Boldt, pp. 417–443.

Jahn, Egbert (1977). "Die Wiedergeburt funktionalistischer Theorie in der Ost-West-Kooperation: Eine Kritik," in Annemarie Grosse-Jütte and Rüdiger Jütte, *Entspannung ohne Frieden.* Frankfurt: S. Fischer, pp. 183–190.

——. (1977a). "Zur Ambivalenz der Entspannungspolitik nach der KSZE," in Dalbrücke Jost et al. (eds.), *Grünbuch zu den Folgewirkungen der KSZE.* Köln: Verlag Wissenschaft und Politik, pp. 57–78.

Jenkins, Robin (1969). "Perception in Crises," in *IPRA Studies in Peace Research*, IInd Conference, vol. 1, Assen, pp. 157–175.

Jodice, David A., and Taylor, Charles L. (1979). "Quantitative Materials for the Study of East-West Relations." Paper for Delivery at the Moscow IPSA Congress.

——. (1981). "Détente and Its Effects: A Measurement of East-West Trade," in Daniel Frei (ed.), Definitions and Measurement of Détente. Cambridge, Mass.: Oelgeschlager, Gunn & Hain, pp. 153–172.

Johnson, Stephen C. (1967). "Hierarchical Clustering Schemes," *Psychometrika* 32, pp. 241–254.

Jütte, Rüdiger (1979). "Europäische Friedensstruktur," in Annemarie Jütte-Grosse and Rüdiger Jütte (eds.), *Entspannung ohne Frieden.* Frankfurt: S. Fischer, pp. 148–172.

Kadushin, Charles (1968). "Reason Analysis," in *International Encyclopaedia of the Social Sciences*, vol. 13. New York: Macmillan, pp. 338–343.

Kaltefleiter, W. (1976). "Entspannung und Eskalation," in *Zeitschrift für Politik* 23, pp. 30–40.

Katzenstein, Peter (1975). "International Interdependence," *International Organization* 29, pp 1021–1034.

Kipp, Jacob W. (1978). "Détente Politics and the US–USSR Military Balance," in Della W. Sheldon (ed.), *Dimension of Détente*. New York: Praeger, pp. 197–216.

Kiss, Laszlo J. (1978). "Western Conceptions of Détente," in *Külpolitika (Foreign Policy)*. A Selection from the 1978 Issues of the Periodical. Budapest: Hungarian Institute of Foreign Affairs, pp. 38–51.

Klein, Peter, et al. (1977). *Friedliche Koexistenz in Europa*. Berlin: Staatsverlag der DDR.

Knight, Albion W. (1980). "The Changing Strategic Balance: Its Effect on European Security," in Alfred Domes (ed.), *Ost–West: Erfahrungen und Perspektiven*. München: Hanns-Seidel-Stiftung, pp. 148–157.

Knirsch, Peter (1980). "Die Möglichkeit der Weiterführung der Ost-West-Wirtschaftsbeziehungen nach der sowjetischen Intervention in Afghanistan," in *DGFK-Jahrbuch 1979/80*. Baden-Baden: Nomos, pp. 667–675.

———. (1981). "Economic and Political Interdependence Between East and West Reconsidered," in Bo Huldt and Atis Lejins (eds.), *East–West Interaction: Possibilities, Problems, Politics, and Prospects*. Stockholm: The Swedish Institute of International Affairs, pp. 55–78.

Kohl, W. L. (1971). *French Nuclear Diplomacy*. Princeton, N.J.: Princeton University Press.

Köhler, Gernot (1975). "Ein Verfahren zur Messung internationaler Spannungen auf der Basis von Ereignisdaten," in *Konfliktforschung* 5, pp. 87–99.

Kolodziej, Edward A. (1974). *French International Policy under de Gaulle and Pompidou.: The Politics of Grandeur,* Ithaca, N.Y.: Cornell University Press.

———. (1979). "Measuring French Arms Transfer: A Problem of Sources and Some Sources of Problems with ACDA Data," *Journal of Conflict Resolution* 23, pp. 195–227.

Koloskov, I. A. (1978). "Prerequisites for a Security System in Europe," in Soviet Committee for European Security and Cooperation (ed.), *European Security and Cooperation*. Moscow: Progress, pp. 27–47. *Konfrontation, Entspannung, Zusammenarbeit* (1979). Berlin: Staatsverlag der DDR.

Kulish, Vasily (1977). "Détente, International Relations, and Military Might," *Co-Existence* 14, pp. 175–195.

Kulski, Wladyslaw W. (1966). *De Gaulle and the World: The Foreign Policy of the Fifth Republic*. Syracuse, N.Y.: Syracuse University Press.

Kusnezow, Wladlen (1975). *Internationale Entspannungspolitik aus sowjetischer Sicht*. Vienna: Europa Verlag.

Lasswell, Harold. D.; Lerner, Daniel; and Pool, Ithiel de Sola (1952). *The Comparative Studies of Symbols*. Stanford, Calif.: Stanford University Press.

Lawrence, E. J., and Sherwin, R. G. (1978). "The Measurement of Weapons-Systems Balances: Building Upon the Perceptions of Experts," in D. C. Daniel (ed.), *International Perceptions of the Superpower Military Balance*. New York: Praeger.

Lebedev, Nikolai I. (1978). *Eine neue Etappe der internationalen Beziehungen*. Berlin: Staatsverlag der DDR.

Lee, William T. (1980). *The Estimation of Soviet Defense Expenditures, 1955–75: An Unconventional Approach*, New York: Praeger Publishers.

Leitenberg, M. (1979). "The Counterpart of Defense Industry Conversion in the United States: The USSR Economy, Defense Industry, and Military Expenditure," *Journal of Peace Research* 26, pp. 262-277.

Leng, Russell J. (1975). "The Future of Events Data Marriages," *International Interactions* 2, pp. 45-62.

Lerner, Daniel; Pool, Ithiel de Sola; and Lasswell, Harold D. (1951). "Comparative Analysis of Political Ideologies: A Preliminary Statement," *Public Opinion Quarterly* 15, pp. 713 ff.

Link, Werner (1980). *Der Ost-West-Konflikt.* Stuttgart: Kohlhammer.

Lomejko, Wladimir B. (1980). "Stabilität, Gleichgewicht und Zusammenarbeit in Europa," in Hansjürgen von Kries (ed.), *Friede durch Zusammenarbeit in Europa.* Berlin: Berlin-Verlag, pp. 92-106.

Luhn, H. P. (1958). "The Automatic Creation of Literature Abstracts," *IBM Journal of Research and Development* 2, pp. 159-165.

———. (1959/68). "Keywood-in-Context for Technical Literature (KWIC Index)." New York: IBM Corporation. Reprinted in C. K. Schultz (ed.), *H. P. Luhn: Pioneer of Information Science.* New York: Spartan Books.

Luterbacher, Urs (1976). "Towards a Convergence of Behavioral and Strategic Conceptions of the Arms Race: The Case of American and Soviet ICBM Build-up," *Papers, Peace Science Society (International),* 26, pp. 1-21.

Luterbacher, Urs; Allan, Pierre; and Imhoff, André (1979). "SIMPEST: A Simulation Model of Political, Economic, and Strategic Interactions Among Major Powers." Paper presented at 1979 IPSA World Congress.

Luttwak, Edward N. (1979). Statement Before the Committee on Foreign Relations, in John Sparkman (ed.), *Perceptions: Relations Between the United States and the Soviet Union.* Washington, D.C.: Committee on Foreign Relations, United States Senate, pp. 340-343.

Lutz, Dieter S. (1980a). "Das militärische Kräfteverhältnis bei den euronuklearen Waffensystem," in *DGFK-Jahrbuch 1979/80.* Baden-Baden: Nomos, pp. 357-399.

———. (1980b). "Das militärische Kräfteverhältnis im Bereich der 'Nuklearkräfte in und für Europa,'" in Gert Krell and Dieter S. Lutz (eds.), *Nuklearrüstung im Ost- und West-Konflikt: Potentiale, Doktrinen, Rüstungssteuerung.* Baden-Baden: Nomos pp. 13-89.

Mateew, W. A. (1981). "Voraussetzungen und Ziele der Entspannung in den 80er Jahren," in *Protokoll Nr. 67 des Bergedorfer Gesprächskreises.* Hamburg, pp. 5-11.

Mazrui, Ali A. (1977). "State of the Globe Report 1977," *Alternatives* 3, pp. 151-320.

McCamant, John I. (1981). "A Critique of Present Measures of Human Rights Development and an Alternative," in Ted P. Nanda et al. (eds.), *Global Human Rights.* Boulder, Colo.: Westview Press, pp. 123-146.

McClelland, Charles A. (1972). "The Beginning, Duration, and Abatement of International Crises," in Charles F. Hermann (ed.), *International Crises: Insights from Behavioral Research.* New York: Free Press, pp. 83-105.

McClelland, Charles A., and Hoggard, Gary D. (1969). "Conflict Patterns in the Interactions Among Nations," in James N. Rosenau (ed.), *International Politics and Foreign Policy: A Reader in Research and Theory.* New York: Free Press, pp. 711-724.

Merritt, R. L. (1966). *Symbols of American Community, 1735-1775.* New Haven, Conn.: Yale University Press.

Milstein, Jeffrey S., and Mitchell, William Charles (1968). "Dynamics of the Vietnam Conflict: A Quantitative Analysis and Predictive Computer Simulation," in *Papers, Peace Science Society (International)* 10, pp. 163–187.

Mitrovic, Tomislav (1977). "La continuité et l'institutionalisation de la Conférence sur la sécurité et la coopération en Europe," *Jugoslavenska Revija za Medunarodno Pravo* 24, pp. 160–177.

Morawiecki, Wojciech (1977). "Die Struktur der Ost-West Beziehungen im europäischen System," in Annemarie Grosse-Jütte and Rüdiger Jütte (eds.), *Entspannung ohne Frieden.* Frankfurt: S. Fischer, pp. 110–130.

Moses, Lincoln E.; Brody, Richard A.; Holsti, Ole R.; Kadane, Joseph B.; and Milstein, Jeffrey S. (1967). "Scaling Data on Inter-Nation Action," *Science* 156, pp. 1054–1059.

Mouritzen, Hans (1981). "Prediction on the Basis of Official Doctrines," *Cooperation and Conflict* 16, pp. 25–38.

Müller, Hans-Gerhard; Neubert, Wolfram; and Pirsch, Hans (1980). *Friedliche Koexistenz, Konfrontationspolitik, bürgerliche Entspannungstheorie* (IPW-Forschungshefte 4). East Berlin: Staatsverlag der DDR.

Nastasescu, Stefan (1980). "The Dialectic of Détente," *Revue Roumaine d'Etudes Internationales* 14, pp. 362–365.

Newcombe, A. G.; Newcombe, N. S.; and Landrons, G. D. (1974). "The Development of an Inter-Nation Tensiometer," *International Interactions* 1, pp. 3–18.

Newcombe, Alan G., and Andrighetti, Robert (1977). "Nations at Risk: A Prediction of Nations Likely to Be in War," *International Interactions* 3, pp. 135–160.

Newcombe, Hanna, and Wert, James (1979). *The Affinities of Nations: Tables of Pearson Correlation Coefficients of U.N. General Assembly Roll-Call Votes* (1946–1973). Dundas, Ontario: Peace Research Institute-Dundas.

Nogee, Joseph L., and Donaldson, Robert H. (1981). *Soviet Foreign Policy Since World War II.* New York/Oxford: Pergamon Press.

North, Robert C.; Holsti, Ole R.; Zaninovich, M. George; and Zinnes, Diana A. (1963). *Content Analysis: A Handbook with Applications for the Study of International Crisis.* Evanston, Ill.: Northwestern University Press.

Nygren, Bertil (1979). *Peaceful Interaction in Ten Great Power Relations* (Research Report UI-79-2). Stockholm: Swedish Institute of International Affairs.

Nygren, Bertil, and Lavery, Donald (1981). Cooperation Between the Soviet Union and Three Western Great Powers, 1950–1975 (Research Report 6). Stockholm: Swedish Institute of International Affairs.

Osgood, Charles E. (1959). "The Representative Model and Relevant Research Methods," in Ithiel de Sola Pool (ed.), *Trends in Content Analysis.* Urbana, Ill.: The University of Illinois Press, p. 33ff.

———. (1962). "Studies on the Generality of Affective Meaning Systems," *American Psychologist* 17, pp. 10–28.

———. (1962a). *An Alternative to War and Surrender.* Chicago: The University of Illinois Press.

———. (1966). *Perspectives in Foreign Policy.* San Francisco: Pacific Press.

———. (1969). "Calculated De-escalation as a Strategy," in Dean G. Pruitt and Richard C. Snyder (eds.), *Theory and Research on the Causes of War.* Englewood Cliffs, N.J.: Prentice-Hall, pp. 213–216.

Osgood, Charles E., and Anderson, Louis (1956). "Certain Relations Between Experienced Contingencies Association Structure, and Contin-

gencies in Encoded Messages," *American Journal of Psychology* 70, pp. 411ff.
Osgood, C. E.; Suci, George J.; and Tannenbaum, Percy M. (1957). *The Measurement of Meaning.* Urbana, Ill.: The University of Illinois Press.
Pastusiak, Longin (1978). "Objective and Subjective Premises of Détente," *Polish Round Table* 8, pp. 53-72.
Phillips, Warren (1968). "Investigations into Alternative Techniques for Developing Empirical Taxonomies: The Results of 2 Plasmodes" (Research Report No. 14). University of Hawaii, Dimensionality of Nations Project.
Pool, Ithiel de Sola (1951). *Symbols of Internationalism.* Stanford, Calif.: Stanford University Press.
———. (1952). *The "Prestige Press": A Survey of Their Editorials.* Stanford, Calif.: Stanford University Press.
———. (1962). *Symbols of Democracy.* Stanford, Calif.: Stanford University Press.
Poser, G. (1977). *Militärmacht Sowjetunion 1977. Daten, Tendenzen, Analyse.* München: Olzog.
Richardson, Lewis F. (1960). *Arms and Insecurity.* Pittsburgh: Boxwood, and Chicago: Quadrangle.
Ropers, Norbert (1977). "Die KSZE und ihre Folgewirkungen," in Jost Delbrück et al. (eds.), *Grünbuch zu den Folgewirkungen der KSZE.* Köln: Verlag Wissenschaft und Politik, pp. 477-509.
———. (1980a). "Transnationale Reisen und Kontakte zwischen Ost und West," in *DGFK-Jahrbuch 1979/80.* Baden-Baden: Nomos, pp. 701-748.
———. (1980b). "Entspannungspolitik in Europa 1979/80," in *DGFK-Jahrbuch 1979/80.* Baden-Baden: Nomos, pp. 835-881.
Rossa, Paul J.; Hopple, Gerald W.; and Wilkenfeld, Jonathan (1980). "Crisis Analysis: Indicators and Models," *International Interactions* 7, pp. 123-163.
Rotfeld, Adam Daniel (1977). "Implementation of the CSCE Final Act and the Development of Détente in Europe" (Studies on International Relations, No. 8). Warsaw: Polish Institute of International Affairs.
Ruloff, Dieter (1975). *Konfliktlösung durch Vermittlung: Computersimulation zwischenstaatlicher Krisen.* Basel: Birkhäuser.
Rummel, Rudolph J. (1972). *The Dimensions of Nations.* Beverly Hills, Calif.: Sage.
———. (1976). *The Dimensionality of Nations Project (Codebook).* Ann Arbor, Mich.: ICPR.
Russett, Bruce M. (1970). "Indicators for America's Linkages with the Changing World Environment," *The Annals* 388 (March), pp. 82-96.
Samoschkin, Juri, and Gantman, Wladimir (1980). "Die marxistische Konzeption der Ideologie, Ethik und Aussenpolitik in den frühen achtziger Jahren," *Wissenschaft und Frieden,* No. 4, pp. 4-13.
Scarritt, James R. (1981). "Definitions, Dimensions, Data, and Designs," in Ved P. Nanda et al. (eds.), *Global Human Rights.* Boulder, Colo.: Westview Press, pp. 115-122.
Scoble, Harry M., and Laurie S. Wiseberg (1981). "Problems of Comparative Research on Human Rights," in Ved P. Nanda et al. (eds.), *Global Human Rights.* Boulder, Colo.: Westview Press, pp. 147-171.
Schissler, Jakob (1980). *Symbolische Sicherheitspolitik. Die Bedeutung der KSZE-Schlussakte für die Sicherheitspolitik der Bundesrepublik Deutschland.* München: Minerva.
Schneider, William (1980). "Factors Affecting East-West Economic Rela-

tions," in Alfred Domes (ed.), *Ost-West Erfahrungen und Perspektiven.* München: Seidel-Stiftung, pp. 205-223.

Schössler, Dietmar (1977). "Détente im Meinungsbild von sicherheitspolitischen Experten der Bundesrepublik Deutschland" (mimeo). Mannheim: University of Mannheim.

Schwarz, Günter, and Lutz, Dieter S. (1980). *Sicherheit und Zusammenarbeit. Eine Bibliographie zu MBFR, SALT, KSZE.* Baden-Baden: Nomos.

Schwarz, Hans-Peter (1979). "Die Entspannungspolitik der westlichen Staaten," in *Entspannungsbegriff und Entspannungspolitik in Ost und West.* Berlin: Dunker & Humblot, pp. 45-60.

——. (1979a). "Supermacht und Juniorpartner. Ansätze amerikanischer und westdeutscher Ostpolitik," in H.-P. Schwarz and Boris Meissner (eds.), *Entspannungspolitik in Ost und West.* Köln: Heymanns, pp. 147-191.

——. (1979b). "Die Alternative zum Kalten Krieg? Bilanz der bisherigen Entspannung," in H.-P. Schwarz and Boris Meissner (eds.), *Entspannungspolitik in Ost und West.* Köln: Heymanns, pp. 275-303.

Shuell, T. J. (1969). "Clustering and Organization in Free Recall," *Psychological Bulletin* 72, pp. 353-374.

Simes, Dimitri K. (1980). "The Death of Détente?" *International Security* 5, pp. 1-25.

Singer, J. David, and Small, Melvin (1974a). *The Wages of War, 1816-1965 (Codebook).* Ann Arbor, Mich.: ICPSR.

——. (1974b). "Foreign Policy Indicators: Predictors of War in History and in the State of the World Message," *Policy Sciences* 5, pp. 271-296.

SIPRI (1968/69-1981). *SIPRI Yearbook: World Armaments and Disarmament.* Stockholm: Stockholm International Peace Research Institute (various publishers).

Sloan, Thomas J. (1975). "The Development of Cooperation and Conflict Interaction Scales," in Edward E. Azar and Joseph D. Ben-Dak (eds.), *Theory and Practice of Events Research.* New York: Gordon & Breach, pp. 29-39.

——. (1978). "The Association between Domestic and International Conflict Hypothesis Revisited," *International Interactions* 4, pp. 3-32.

Snyder, Richard D.; Hermann, Charles F.; and Lasswell, Harold D. (1976). "A Global Monitoring System: Appraising the Effects of Government on Human Dignity," *International Studies Quarterly* 20, pp. 221-260.

Sonnenfeldt, Helmut (1977/78). "Russia, America and Détente," *Foreign Affairs* 56, pp. 274-294.

Spröte, Wolfgang (1980). "Die Rolle der ökonomischen Zusammenarbeit im Entspannungsprozess," in Hansjürgen von Kries (ed.), *Friede durch Zusammenarbeit in Europa.* Berlin: Berlin-Verlag, pp. 230-237.

Stankovsky, Jan (1980). "Handels-und Kreditbeziehungen zwischen Ost und West," *DGFK-Jahrbuch 1979/80.* Baden-Baden: Nomos, pp. 527-555.

——. (1981). Industrial East-West Cooperation: "Motivations, Developments, and Prospects," in Bo Huldt and Atis Lejins (eds.), East-*West Economic Interaction: Possibilities, Problems, Politics, and Prospects.* Stockholm: The Swedish Institute of International Affairs, pp. 9-27.

Stehr, Uwe (1980). *Wirtschaft und Politik in den Sowjetischen Westbeziehungen.* Frankfurt: Campus.

Stone, P. J.; Dunphy, D. C.; Smith, M. S.; and Ogilvie, D. M. (1966). *The General Inquirer: A Computer Approach to Content Analysis in the Behavioral Sciences.* Cambridge, Mass.: MIT Press.

Stone, P.J., and Mochmann, E. (1976). "Erweiterung des Instrumentariums der Sozialforschung durch inhaltsanalytische Techniken," in M.R. Lepsius (ed.), *Zwischenbilanz der Soziologie. Verhandlungen des 17. Deutschen Soziologentages.* Stuttgart; Enke, pp. 163–174.

Stratmann, K.-Peter (1981). *Kritische Anmerkungen zu Darstellungen des "Euro-strategischen" Kräfteverhältnisses von NATO und Warschauer Pakt* (Arbeitspapier 2284). Ebenhausen: Stiftung Wissenschaft und Politik, FRG.

Sullivan, Michael P. (1976). *International Relations—Theories and Evidence.* Englewood Cliffs, N.J.: Prentice-Hall.

Sütö, Otto (1978). "Détente in Europe," *Külpolitika (Foreign Policy). A Selection from the 1978 Issues of the Periodical.* Budapest: Hungarian Institute of Foreign Affairs, pp. 3–16.

Taylor, Charles L. (1981). *The World Handbook of Political and Social Indicators,* 3rd ed. Vol. I: *Aggregate Data;* Vol. II (together with David A. Jodice): *Political Events Data.* Berlin: International Institute for Comparative Social Research (Reports 80–127 and 81–124).

Teunissen, Paul J. (1980). "Strukturen und Perspektiven der Sicherheit und Zusammenarbeit in Europa," in Hansjürgen von Kries (ed.), *Friede durch Zusammenarbeit in Europa.* Berlin: Berlin-Verlag, pp. 13–49.

Thalheim, Karl C. (1980). "Wirtschaftliche Beziehungen im Wandel," in Alfred Domes (ed.), *Ost West: Erfahrungen und Perspektiven.* München: Hanns-Seidel-Stiftung, pp. 183–204.

Thompson, William R., and Modelski, George (1977). "Global Conflict Intensity and Great Power Summitry Behavior," *Journal of Conflict Resolution* 21, pp. 339–376.

Timberlake, Charles E. (1978). *Détente. A Documentary Record.* New York: Praeger.

Urban, G.R. (1976). *Détente.* New York: Universe Books.

US Arms Control and Disarmament Agency (1975; 1976; 1977). *World Military Expenditures and Arms Trade,* 1963–1973; 1965–1975; 1966–1975. Washington, D.C.

Vahl, Winfried (1979). "Von der Vision zum Pragmatismus: Französische Entspannungspolitik von de Gaulle bis Giscard d'Estaing," in H.P. Schwarz and Boris Meissner (eds.), *Entspannungspolitik in Ost und West.* Köln: Carl Heymans, pp. 227–243.

Väyrynen, Raimo (1977). "Abrüstung und Entspannung: Divergierende oder konvergierende Phänomene?" in Annemarie Grosse-Jütte and Rüdiger Jütte (eds.), *Entspannung ohne Frieden.* Frankfurt: S. Fischer, pp. 218–241.

——. (1977a). "Zur Dynamik des Unfriedens in Europa," in Annemarie Grosse-Jütte and Rüdiger Jütte (eds.), *Entspannung ohne Frieden.* Frankfurt: S. Fischer, pp. 60–67.

Wallace, Michael D. (1979). "Early Warning Indicators from the 'Correlates of War Project'," in David J. Singer and Michael D. Wallace (eds.), *To Augur Well. Early Warning Indicators in World Politics.* Beverly Hills, Calif.: Sage, pp. 17–36.

Walter, F. (1977). "Zum Problem der Belastung der Sowjetwirtschaft durch die Militäraufwendungen," *Wehrforschung Aktuell* 7 (München: Bernard & Graefe), pp. 90–111.

Weede, Erich (1981). "Methods, Problems and Some Results in Evaluating Détente-Related Policies," in Daniel Frei (ed.), *Definitions and Measurement of Détente: East and West Perspectives.* Cambridge, Mass.: Oelgeschlager, Gunn & Hain, pp. 141–151.

Weltman, John (1979). "Détente and the Decline of Geography," *Jerusalem Journal of International Relations* 4, pp. 75-94.
Wettig, Gerhard (1981). *Die Sowjetischen Sicherheitsvoestellungen und die Möglichkeiten eines Ost-West-Einvernehmens.* Baden-Baden: Nomos.
Weymann, A. (1973). "Bedeutungsfeldanalyse," *Kölner Zeitschrift für Soziologie und Sozialpsychologie* 25, pp. 761-776.
White Book (1979). *Weissbuch 1979-Zur Sicherheit der Bundesrepublik Deutschland und zur Entwicklung der Bundeswehr.* Edited by the Federal Minister of Defense on behalf of the Federal Government of the FRG. Bonn: Federal Government of the FRG.
Wiberg, Hakan (1979). "Détente in Europe?" *Current Research on Peace and Violence* 2, pp. 104-113.
Wilkenfeld, Jonathan; Hopple, Gerald W.; and Rossa, Paul J. (1979). "Sociopolitical Indicators of Conflict and Cooperation," in David J. Singer and Michael D. Wallace (eds.), *To Augur Well. Early Warning Indicators in World Politics.* Beverly Hills, Calif.: Sage, pp. 104-151.
——. (1980). "Crisis Analysis: Indicators and Models," *International Interactions* 7, pp. 123-163.
Willms, Bernard (1976). "Zur Dialektik von Kooperation und Abgrenzung im Entspannungsprozess zwischen Ost und West," in Gerda Zellentin (ed.), *Annäherung, Abgrenzung und friedlicher Wandel in Europa.* Boppard: Boldt, pp. 45-78.
Wojnar, Marian (1981). "Patterns of East-West Trade and Cooperation," in Bo Huldt and Atis Lejins (eds.), *East-West Economic Interaction: Possibilities, Problems, Politics, and Prospects.* Stockholm: The Swedish Institute of International Affairs, pp. 29-37.
Wright, Quincy (1942). *A Study of War.* Chicago: The University of Chicago Press.
Wrightson, M.T. (1976). "The Documentary Coding Method," in R. Axelrod (ed.), *Structure of Decision.* Princeton, N.J.: Prince for University Press, pp. 291-332.
Zaleski, Eugene, and Wienert, Helgard (1980). *Technology Transfer between East and West.* Paris: OECD.
Zinnes, Dina A. (1968). "The Expression and Perception of Hostility in Prewar Crisis: 1914," in J.D. Singer (ed.), *Quantitative International Politics: Insights and Evidence.* New York: Free Press, pp. 85-119.

About the Authors

Daniel Frei is professor of Political Science at the University of Zurich and director of the Political Science Research Institute, University of Zurich. He was educated at Zurich University, the London School of Economics and Political Science, the University of Michigan, and the Geneva Graduate Institute of International Studies. He is the author of several publications (most of them in German) on theory of international relations, security problems, and neutrality. He is also the editor of *Definitions and Measurement of Détente: East and West Perspectives* (1981).

Dieter Ruloff is lecturer of Political Science at the University of Zurich and research associate at the Political Science Research Institute, University of Zurich. He received his M.A. in Political Science and History from the University of Constance (Federal Republic of Germany), and his Ph.D. in Political Science from the University of Zurich. His work includes publications on computer simulation in the field of International Relations and methodological questions of both Political Science and History.

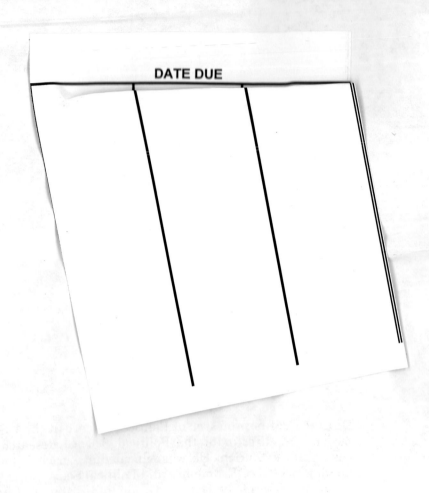